EU security governance

MANCHESTER
1824

Manchester University Press

EU security governance

Emil Kirchner and
James Sperling

Manchester University Press

Published by Manchester University Press
Altrincham Street, Manchester M1 7JA, UK
www.manchesteruniversitypress.co.uk

British Library Cataloguing-in-Publication Data is available

Library of Congress Cataloging-in-Publication Data is available

ISBN 978 0 7190 7469 1 paperback

First published 2007

This paperback edition published 2014

Printed by Lightning Source

Dedication

To Jo and Joy

Contents

Illustrations

Figures

Tables

Preface

Important changes have taken place in the European state system over the past fifty years and those changes were accelerated by the collapse of the post-war bipolar world. These changes initiated the enquiry into our understanding of security and the nature of security threats, the target of those threats, and the instruments best matched to meeting them. Moreover, the European Union (EU) has emerged as an important security actor *qua* actor, not only in the non-traditional areas of security, but increasingly as an entity with force projection capabilities. Why has the EU emerged as a security actor and why have its member states turned to the EU to resolve the security dilemmas that they face? The intersection of the military and non-military elements of the contemporary security agenda and the role of the European Union as a central provider of European security constitute the empirical focus of *EU security governance*. We link the challenges of governing Europe's security to the changing nature of the state, the evolutionary expansion of the security agenda, and the insufficiency of the traditional forms and concepts of security cooperation. *EU security governance* redresses conceptual gaps in the study of security governance, particularly as it pertains to the EU.

EU security governance investigates how the concept of security relates to or deals with different categories of threat, explores the relationship between forms of coordination among states, international institutions, and the EU in the provision of European security and the execution of security governance, and investigates whether the EU has been effective in realising its stated security objectives and those of its member states. Three interrelated questions are posed: Has the EU's growing role as a security actor been driven by a fundamental change in the security agenda? This particular question raises the subsidiary question of whether this change in the security agenda has transformed pre-existing threats to national security into a problem of collective action. How have the functional and operational milieu goals of security governance affected the way in which security is sought and the type of authority structures relied upon to achieve those goals? We argue that EU institutional mechanisms continue to rest uneasily with the member states' retention of sovereign prerogatives. Has the emergence of the EU as a security actor complemented the role of the state as a security provider, progressively displaced the state in critical areas, or simply remained a forum for intergovernmental bargaining? Unsurprisingly, perhaps, the EU's role as a security actor vis-à-vis its member states is functionally dependent.

EU security governance is divided into six chapters: a conceptual introduction to the problem of European security governance; four substantive chapters that investigate the security policies of assurance, protection, prevention and compellence; and a conclusion that identifies the limitations and promise of the EU as a security actor and suggests the division of labour between the state, the EU, and other institutions of European security in the twenty-first century.

The introduction focuses on three major issues: the changing nature of the European state, the changing nature and broadening of the security agenda, and the problem of security governance in the European political space. There are four functional challenges facing the EU as a security actor: the resolution of interstate conflicts, the management of intrastate conflicts, state-building endeavours, and building the institutions of civil society. The central organising principle is the classification of these security challenges according to four categories of policy response: prevention, assurance, protection and compellence. The empirical section is designed to demonstrate that policy instruments should be carefully matched to the nature of the security threat, that an over reliance on one instrument of policy – either 'soft' or 'hard' power in Joseph Nye's nomenclature – is likely to produce suboptimal, if not counterproductive, security outcomes.

Chapter 2 examines policies of prevention, particularly the pre-emption of conflict within Europe and its neighbourhood. The starting point is the express European preference outlined in the European Security Strategy for policies of pre-emptive engagement to redress the sources of violent conflict and instability. We examine governance efforts designed to prevent conflict, to create the basis for anticipating sources of conflict, and to provide conflict resolution mechanisms that employ 'civilian' rather than traditional forms of statecraft, notably military force. The EU has undertaken efforts to externalise the norms and rules of statecraft that operate within it. This process began with the conditionality attached to the aid programmes designed for developing countries in the 1980s and for Central and Eastern European countries in the in the early 1990s to facilitate the transition to the market and democracy. The latter process was deepened with the enlargement process that has extended the EU to the borders of the former Soviet Union. These efforts to extend the norms and practices of the EU system of governance have been most recently codified in the European Neighbourhood Policy. Each of these policies has been designed to prevent the outbreak of armed conflict (inter or intrastate) by pre-empting conflict via the building of democratic institutions domestically and the extension of a nascent civil society externally. We trace these developments since 1990 towards understanding how the changing nature of the state and the role of the EU have altered calculations of interest and threat as well as the critical importance of matching an appropriate set of policy instruments to specific categories of security policy challenge.

Chapter 3 examines policies of assurance, particularly the problem of peace-building in south-eastern Europe. Here we investigate the EU's peace-building or sustaining role where there has been a violent interstate or intrastate conflict, especially the origins and performance of the Stability Pact for south-eastern Europe as well as the Stabilisation and Association Programme for the western Balkans. Attending the conflicts in south-eastern Europe was the collapse of civil order or the renting of the social fabric in Macedonia, Bosnia and Kosovo. Policies of assurance designed for the region include police and judicial training, the building of civic institutions and civil societies, and the contribution to the restoration of order and state legitimacy. More generally, these policies seek the transfer of transfer EU norms and practices towards extending into the whole of Europe the EU system of security governance. The empirical analysis leaves little doubt that the task of institution building, the projection of EU norms along its periphery, and the employment of 'civilian' policy instruments are central to the long-term security of the continent.

Chapter 4 examines policies of protection which capture the challenge of internal security. The challenge of internal security is not merely a reaction to 11 September 2001 or 11 March 2004; this particular task was identified as a central security task in the Treaty of Amsterdam (1997). The evolution of the long-standing democratic and capitalist EU member states into post-Westphalian entities has also transformed internal security into a regional collective action problem entailing the necessary erosion of sovereign prerogatives within and between borders. The task of creating the treaty-mandated area of freedom, security and justice frames EU policies designed to meet the threats posed by terrorism, transnational crime and migration. Open borders within the EU have complicated efforts to control the flow of political and economic refugees. The rise of radical Islamic terrorism, compounded by the sizeable Muslim diaspora resident in Europe, in conjunction with indigenous separatist movements, have made cross-border cooperation in this issue area more pressing. The support of terrorism through criminal activities and the corrosive effect of criminalised economies on democratising states have transformed policing issues into security issues, particularly the use of chemical, biological or radiological weapons, with regional rather than national ramifications. The policies of protection highlight the erasure of the boundary between inside and outside that has typically framed the analysis of security policy.

Chapter 5 investigates policies of compellence, particularly the EU effort to implement a common security and defence policy, to develop a power projection capability, to undertake autonomous peace-making, peace-keeping, and peace-enforcement missions. Changes in the approach to defence are best exemplified by the progress towards realising a European Security and Defence Policy after 1998, particularly the enhancement of European defence capabilities permitting credible force projection, the creation of a framework for EU–NATO (NATO: North Atlantic Treaty Organisation) defence cooperation, and the consolidation of the EU defence industrial base. Intervention in conflicts once they occur has been the focus of much empirical work on the problem of European security governance, particularly the difficulty the EU or EU member states have experienced in effectively intervening after the outbreak of intrastate or interstate conflict. The role of the EU has ranged from the permissive (the premature recognition of Croatia), to the ineffective (the inability to intervene militarily in the first Balkan conflict and the poor performance in Kosovo), to the constructive (the interventions in Macedonia and the Congo). We investigate the barriers to and progress towards a European force projection capability, the limits of cooperation in the projection of force, and the continuing importance of NATO as a military security actor in Europe. Attention is devoted to the EU's Amber Force deployment to the former Yugoslav Republic of Macedonia; the deployment of EU member state forces to Bosnia (IFOR/SFOR) (IFOR: Police Implementation Force; SFOR: Stability Force) and Kosovo (KFOR) (Police Implementation Force, Kosovo); the peace-keeping mission to the Congo; the deployment and eventual command of allied peace-keeping forces in Afghanistan (ISAF); and the failure to develop a common policy with respect to the 2003 American-led war in Iraq.

The conclusion summarises the present role of the EU as a security actor, the sources of that emerging role, and the likely evolution given the pressures for enlargement and the apparent failure to combine the three EU pillars into a single framework, even though each pillar is tasked with security responsibilities. The conclusion also addresses the important question of institutional cooperation and coordination in discharging successfully the task of security governance. The empirical analysis strongly supports four conclusions: first, the EU will become an increasingly important security actor at the expense of its member states; second, the EU system of security governance is increasingly viewed by its member states as the essential forum for providing order and security in all of its dimensions; third, the role of non-governance or the absence of governance is an important factor accounting for the EU's growing role as a security actor, even at the expense of state prerogatives; and finally, traditional security arrangements like NATO are increasingly incapable of meeting the challenges posed by the full spectrum of threats to the security and stability of post-Westphalian states.

Each chapter follows a common rubric. It allows the book to be read horizontally (aspects common to each category of security governance) or vertically (examining each functional security category in form). We first explore and expand upon the content and form of each security challenge, identify the issue areas addressed, and provide a justification for our case selection. The second task is to explain how the EU emerged as a security actor, particularly the rationale for an EU rather than national response. The identification of the collective action problem facing the EU member states and the EU account for different rationales that plausibly explain security cooperation: a simple functionalist logic that the EU is the only actor that can efficiently achieve a particular class of security objectives; the emergence of post-Westphalianism in Europe necessitates deep security cooperation; and the emergence of a collective European identity makes the collective response to security threats a function of those threats being defined as collective rather than individual.

The third section of each chapter examines the goals, principles, and rules governing or informing the statecraft of the individual member states and the ability to deepen security cooperation. The first step towards that goal is the identification of EU security goals. The completion of this task will serve two objectives: it clarifies what the EU security agenda is in a specific issue area; it establishes a yardstick for measuring the EU's effectiveness as a security actor. The principles and rules governing joint action in each specific area or category of security governance will be drawn from the three post-Cold War treaties – Maastricht, Amsterdam and Nice – Commission or Council of Ministers framework decisions, regulations, joint actions, and recommendations with respect to specific issues, European Council presidency reports, and the European Security Strategy.

We then turn to the precise institutional arrangements for meeting the variety of security challenges facing the EU states. We examine the institutional innovations and refinements undertaken to meet collectively defined security challenges, the choice of whether the EU member states settle for merely coordinating national policies or adopting the more ambitious goal of common EU policies or a single EU policy. These institutional innovations help clarify where the EU acts as a mere clearing house for national preferences, where the EU provides a convenient forum for creating EU 'coalitions of the willing', where the EU acts as a security actor that is at least partially independent of its member states, or where the EU serves as an adjunct to or equal partner with the other multilateral security institutions, particularly NATO.

The chapter then proceeds to assess the EU's performance as a security actor. Such an assessment is necessarily tentative and subject to the metric used for that purpose. Our metric of choice does not demand that the EU take on the attributes, prerogatives, or instruments of a state, but measures the value added by the EU in the provision for European security and stability. Value-added can be assessed by matching EU goals with outcomes, no matter how modest or ambitious, or by determining whether the member states could have achieved the same level of performance in the absence of the EU. Five questions are asked and answered: Did the EU succeed where states had previously failed or underperformed? Has the EU functioned as anything other than an internal coalition of member states? Do the treaties, framework documents, and presidency conclusions constitute evidence of an emerging collective security identity that translates into the transfer or pooling of sovereignty to the EU? To what extent has the EU been empowered to act as if it were a 'sovereign' state? What barriers remain to common policies as well as to a single policy parallel to European monetary union?

Each chapter concludes with the answering of a single question: Has the long-recognised capabilities-expectations gap in the field of security given rise to a more unsettling and unbridgeable capabilities-expectations paradox? The more that the EU is able to do, the more that will be expected of it and the greater the potential for disappointment or disillusionment. We investigate how and why the EU persists as a forum for security cooperation. We focus on three possible explanations: first, existing security pathologies are not resolved or new security pathologies emerge that require a collective response; second, the 'idea' of Europe sustains cooperation in a specific field even if specific security or more general milieu goals are put in place; third, institutional inertia – rather than instrumental necessity – allows the EU to persist as a security actor. The reclamation of state prerogatives in the area of security also requires attention. Four possible explanations exist: first, states may reclaim security prerogatives owing to failure at the EU level; second, security pathologies are resolved and the need for collective effort ends with it; third, the institutional network facilitating cooperation is too weak to hold states together, particularly when national interests diverge; and fourth, other institutions may be viewed as better equipped to address a specific security challenge (e.g., NATO as the forum for collective defence).

Acknowledgements

Many people have helped us in the preparation of this book. We are particularly indebted to Han Dorussen, Magnus Ekengren, Marek Hanusch, Hanna Ojanen, Kostas Infantis, Heiko Walkenhorst, Hugh Ward and Mark Webber for their comments and suggested improvements. We owe special thanks to the external reader for the sound advice on improving the final manuscript. We are also very grateful for the valuable research assistance of Max Paiano and the sterling editorial assistance of Katja Mirwaldt and Susan Sydenham. Financial support was provided by the Network on Global Governance (GARNET), which is financed by the European Commission's 6th Framework Programme. We would like to thank our commissioning editor for his advice, assistance and patience, in what has been a long and demanding process.

Finally, we would like to thank our families for their encouragement and support.

Abbreviations

AA	Association Agreement
AAR	Air-to-Air Refuelling
ACP	African, Caribbean and Pacific
AENEAS	Financial and Technical Assistance to Third Countries in the Areas of Migration and Asylum
AFSOUTH	Allied Forces Southern Europe
ALA	Asia, Latin America
AMM	Aceh Monitoring Mission
APA	Association Partnership Agreements
ASEAN	Association of South-East Asian Nations
ASEM	Asia-Europe Meetings
Althea	(Operational name for EUFOR in Bosnia)
AU	African Union
AWF	analysis working file
BICHAT	Task Force on Biological and Chemical Agents
BOMCA	Border Management in Central Asia Programme
C³I	Command, Control, Communications, and Intelligence
CA	Cooperation Agreement
CARDS	Community Assistance for Reconstruction, Development and Stabilisation
CBRN	chemical, biological, radiological or nuclear
CCC	Commission Crisis Centre
CEE	Central and Eastern Europe
CEMAC	Central African Economic and Monetary Community
CEPOL	European Police College
CFSP	Common Foreign and Security Policy
CIDA	Canadian International Development Agency
CIVCOM	Committee for Civilian Aspects of Crisis Management
CIWIN	Critical Infrastructure Warning Information Network
COMESA	Common Market of Eastern and Southern Africa
COMEUFOR	EUFOR Commander

COPPS	Co-ordinating Office for Palestinian Police Support
CPP	Conflict Prevention Partnership
CPR	Conflict Prevention and Resolution
CREST	Center for Research and Education on Strategy and Technology
CSP	Country Strategy Papers
CTR	Cooperative Threat Reduction
DCI	Defence Capabilities Initiative
DG	Directorate General
DPPI	Disaster Prevention and Preparedness Initiative
DRC	Democratic Republic of Congo
EADS	European Aeronautic Defence and Space Company
EAR	European Agency for Reconstruction
EBRD	European Bank for Reconstruction and Development
EC	European Community
ECAP	European Capabilities Action Plan
ECDC	European Centre for Disease Control
ECHO	European Community Humanitarian Office
ECMM/ EUMM	EU Monitoring Mission
ECOWAS	Economic Community of West African States
ECSC	European Coal and Steel Community
EDA	European Defence Agency
EDC	European Defence Community
EDF	European Development Fund
EEC	European Economic Community
EGF	European Gendarmerie Force
EIB	European Investment Bank
EIDHR	European Initiative for Democracy and Human Rights
EJN	European Judicial Network
ELPN	European Police Learning Network
ENISA	European Network and Information Security Agency
ENP	European Neighbourhood Policy
ENPI	European Neighbourhood and Partnership Instrument
EPA	Economic Partnership Agreement
EPC	European Policy Centre
ERRF	European Rapid Reaction Force
ESDP	European Security and Defence Policy
ESS	European Security Strategy
ETA	Euskadi Ta Askatasuna (Basque Homeland and Freedom)

EUBAM	European Union Border Assistance Mission
EU	European Union
EUFOR	European Union Force
EUJUST LEX	EU Integrated Rule of Law Mission for Iraq
EUJUST THEMIS	EU Rule of Law Mission to Georgia
EUMC	European Union Military Committee
EUMS	European Union Military Staff
EUPAT	EU Police Advisory Team
EUPM (BiH)	European Union Police Mission (in Bosnia and Herzegovina)
EUPOL PROXIMA	European Union Police Mission in the Former Yugoslav Republic of Macedonia
EUPT Kosovo	EU Planning Team Kosovo
EUROJUST	European Union Judicial Cooperation Unit
EUROPOL	European Police Office
EUSEC DR Congo	EU Security Sector Reform Mission in the Democratic Republic of the Congo
EUSR	European Union Special Representative
FATF	Financial Action Task Force
FIU	financial intelligence unit
FIU.NET	financial intelligence unit network
FFI	Friend or Foe Identification
FLEGT	Forests Law Enforcement, Governance and Trade
FLNC	National Front for the Liberation of Corsica
FRONTEX	European Agency for the Management of Operational Cooperation at the External Borders of the Member States of the European Union
FTA	Free Trade Agreement
GCC	Gulf Cooperation Council
GDP	Gross Domestic Product
GFAP	General Framework Agreement for Peace
GNI	Gross National Income
GNP	Gross National Product
GPS	Global Positioning System
GRECO	Groups of States against Corruption
HEU	Highly Enriched Uranium
HHG	Helsinki Headline Goal
HLWG	High-Level Working Group on Asylum and Migration
HQ	Headquarters
IAEA	International Atomic Energy Agency
ICG	International Crisis Group

ICTY	International Criminal Tribunal for the former Yugoslavia
IDP	Internally Displaced Person
IFOR	Implementation Force
IISS	International Institute for Strategic Studies
Interreg	Community interregional cooperation initiative
IPA	Instrument for Pre-Accession
IPTF	International Police Task Force
IRA	Irish Republican Army
IRFFI	International Reconstruction Fund Facility for Iraq
ISAF	International Security Assistance Force
ISG	Infrastructure Steering Group
ISPA	Instrument for Structural Policies for Pre-accession
ITDB	Illicit Trafficking Database
JHA	Justice and Home Affairs
JIT	joint investigation team
KFOR	Kosovo Force
LDC	Least Developed Countries
LEU	Low Enriched Uranium
MAPE	Multi-Advisory Police Element
MARRI	Migration, Asylum, Refugees Regional Initiative
MEDA	EC Assistance Programme for Mediterranean Countries
MIP	Mission Implementation Plan
MONUC	Mission in the Democratic Republic of the Congo
NALAS	Network of Associations of Local Authorities
NATO	North Atlantic Treaty Organisation
NBC	Nuclear, Biological and Chemical
NGO	Non-Governmental Organisation
OAU	Organisation of African Unity
OBNOVA	Aid for the former Republics of Yugoslavia
OCCAR	Joint Organisation for Armaments Cooperation
ODA	Official Development Assistance
OHR	Office of the High Representative
OLAF	European Anti-Fraud Office
OSCE	Organisation for Security and Co-operation in Europe
PCA	Partnership and Cooperation Agreement
PCTF	Police Chiefs' Task Force
PD	Political Dialogue
PHARE	Poland and Hungary Action for Restructuring of the Economy

PIO	Peace Implementation Council
PR	Political Rights
PSA	Partnership Agreement
PSC	Political and Security Committee
PU	Plutonium
QMV	qualified majority vote
R&D	research and development
R&T	research and technology
RACVIAC	Regional Arms Control Verification and Implementation Assistance Centre
RAS–BICHAT	Rapid Alert System–Task Force on Biological and Chemical Agents
RRM	Rapid Reaction Mechanism
RSP	Regional Strategy Papers
SAA	Stabilisation and Association Agreement
SAARC	South Asian Association for Regional Cooperation
SACU	Southern African Customs Union
SADC	South African Development Community
SAP	Stabilisation and Association Process
SAPARD	Special Accession Programme for Agriculture and Rural Development
SAR	Stability and Association Report
SBS	State Border Service
SECI	South East European Cooperative Initiative
SEE	south-eastern Europe
SEECP	South East European Cooperation Process
SEEPAG	SEE Public Prosecutors Advisory Group
SEESAC	South Eastern and Eastern Europe Clearinghouse for the Control of Small Arms and Light Weapons
SFOR	Stabilisation Force
SG/HR	Secretary General of the Council of Ministers and High Representative of CFSP
SHAPE	Supreme Headquarters Allied Powers Europe
SIPA	State Investigation and Protection Agency
SIPRI	Stockholm International Peace Research Institute
SIS	Schengen Information System
SitCen	Joint Situation Centre
SME	small and medium sized enterprises
SP	Stability Pact
SPAI	Stability Pact Anti-Corruption Initiative
SPOC	Stability Pact Initiative against Organised Crime
STM	SAP Tracking System

TACIS	Technical Assistance to the Commonwealth of Independent States
TAFKO	European Commission Task Force for Kosovo
TAI	Turkish pre-accession instrument
TEC	Treaty establishing the European Community
TEU	Treaty on European Union
UAV	Unmanned Aerial Vehicles
UK	United Kingdom
UN(O)	United Nations (Organisation)
UNDP	United Nations Development Programme
UNHCR	United Nations High Commissioner for Refugees
UNMIK	United Nations Interim Administration Mission in Kosovo
UNPROFOR	United Nations Protection Force
UNSC	United Nations Security Council
US(A)	United States (of America)
USAID	United States Agency for International Development
WB	World Bank
WEAG	Western European Armaments Group
WEAO	Western European Armaments Organisation
WEU	Western European Union
WMD	weapons of mass destruction

1

Introduction: the EU and the governance of European security

In its earliest manifestation, the European project was explicitly a security project. The European Coal and Steel Community, in addition to providing an institutionalised mechanism for consolidating and rationalising the European coal and steel industries after the war, provided France and the other European states a security guarantee against a rearmed Germany. The failed European Defence Community (EDC) also had two purposes: it served the positive goal of creating a European armed force that could conceivably complement and perhaps substitute for American forces stationed in Europe; it served the negative goal of enabling German rearmament while denying Germany anything other than indirect control of its own armed forces. The failure of the EDC became the signal lesson for those interested in pushing forward the integration of Western Europe; it became the conventional wisdom that the Treaty of Rome should expand cooperation and integration in the European economy and leave foreign and security policy unmolested.

So long as the bipolar conflict between the United States and Soviet Union played out principally in Europe, the definition of security and the object of defence policy were self-evidently defined as maintaining the political and military balance between the west and east. The end of the Cold War, the dissolution of the Soviet Union, and the task of constructing stable democratic polities with competitive market economies from the Elbe to the Urals along an east–west axis and from the Baltic Sea to Asia Minor along a north–south axis transformed the understanding of security and the role of the European Union (EU) as a security actor. Moreover, the dissolution of Yugoslavia and internecine conflicts that emerged in Croatia, Bosnia–Herzegovina, Serbia and Kosovo resurrected the Balkans as the tinder-box that could engulf a prosperous and stable Europe in a conflagration. Europeans, particularly the major member states of the EU, recognised the importance and imperative of transforming the EU into a capable military actor that could either supplement or replace NATO when European interests were threatened by the outbreak of interstate or civil war.

The changes in the geopolitical environment facing the EU and its member states occasioned the broadening of the security agenda to include issues as diverse as transnational organised crime, the acquisition of force projection capabilities, the provision of technical and financial assistance to regions undergoing political and economic transformations, and the preparation for pandemics of natural causes or human agency. These issues emerged on the security agenda of the European states in particular owing to a second major development in the international system; viz., the rise of the post-Westphalian state and vulnerabilities to exogenous shocks attending it. The post-Westphalian character of the EU member states has drained those states of de facto sovereignty while leaving jurisdictional sovereignty intact. The structural mechanisms transmitting endogenous and exogenous shocks throughout the EU and the inability of the individual states to mitigate the shocks unilaterally has created the impulse to elevate the EU as the actor responsible for coordinating if not assuming the security responsibilities once the uncontested preserve of states.

The content of security in the contemporary European system requires a system of governance capable of fulfilling the policy tasks of assurance, prevention, protection, and compellence. These four tasks have been delegated in different measure to the EU; in many cases the states have retained their responsibility for those security policies even where a collective response is acknowledged as technically superior (i.e., more efficient) to national responses. Yet the imperative of solidarity and collective action remains hostage to the residual attachment to sovereign prerogatives. This tension between solidarity and sovereignty holds the key to understanding the limits and promise of the EU as a security actor and the EU's role in the governing of European security.

The changing nature of the European state: towards post-Westphalianism

The evolution of the European state towards a post-Westphalian identity is perhaps the most fundamental change that has taken place in the modern European state system. The Westphalian state that has defined the European state system since 1648 has slowly given way to a post-Westphalian state where sovereignty is both compromised and qualified (Caporaso, 2000); where stated security goals have increasingly become preoccupied with matters of protecting existing levels of economic welfare as well as the social fabric from external disruptions. This change has been compounded by the failed Westphalian states along Europe's perimeter extending into Central Asia and the Middle East and the persistence of sovereign free territory attending that failure. When these two developments are considered together – the emergence of the post-Westphalian state within Europe and the disintegration of Westphalian states along Europe's southern periphery into central Asia – the potential for increased threats to societal and state security rises with a corresponding diminution of the state's ability to defend against them.

The contemporary international system consists of heterogeneous actors producing interactions fundamentally different than those occurring between states with a uniform homogeneous Westphalian character. Consequently, there are three general and distinct patterns of interaction reflecting the divergent characteristics of states in the late twentieth and early twenty-first centuries: interactions between post-Westphalian states, between Westphalian states, and between Westphalian and post-Westphalian states.[1] These two categories of state face different kinds of vulnerabilities and act according to different security calculi: Westphalian states face traditional concerns about territorial integrity, but retain the ability to control it; post-Westphalian states face the traditional concern with territorial integrity compounded by an inability to protect borders and a rising preoccupation with the threats posed to societies by transnational, non-state actors. Post-Westphalian states are incapable, owing to internal norms and substantive policy concerns, to act as effective gate-keepers between internal and external transactions. This transition to the post-Westphalian state, largely completed for the established members of the EU and proceeding rapidly for the most recent member states, has required deepened cooperation and collaboration to meet the welfare and security obligations underwriting the social contract. The loss of sovereignty attending post-Westphalianism has created an alternative form of statecraft (civilian power) and has produced an emergent civil order in the geopolitical space defined by the EU. The emergence of a rule and norm based civil order, the perforated sovereignty of the state, and the expansion of the security agenda has introduced the problem of security governance without government, internally or externally.

The sovereignty norm of the Westphalian state forms a significant barrier to security cooperation – even in the Atlantic area. The key characteristic of the Westphalian state is its 'territoriality', described by John H. Herz (1957) as a 'hard shell' protecting states and societies from the external environment. Territoriality is increasingly irrelevant, not only in Europe but in Eurasia and beyond. States no longer enjoy the luxury of a 'wall of defensibility' that leaves them relatively immune to external penetration. As Wolfram Hanrieder noted, even though Herz later changed his mind about the demise of the territorial state, 'his argument on the changed meaning and importance of territoriality was clearly valid' (Hanrieder, 1978: 1280–1). This change not only forces us to modify our conception of power – shifting attention from the military-strategic to the economic and political requirements of security – but to change our understanding of threat. As the boundaries between the state and the external environment have become increasingly blurred, it leaves open the possibility that the new security threats may operate along channels dissimilar to the traditional threats posed to the territorial state.

The 'interconnectedness' of the post-Westphalian state system, most visible in Western Europe, was facilitated and reinforced by the success of the post-war institutions of American design as well as by European economic and political integration.[2] Geography, technological innovation, the convergence around the norms of political and economic openness, and the rising 'dynamic density' – defined by John Ruggie (1986: 148) as the 'quantity, velocity, and diversity of transactions' – of the Atlantic political space have progressively stripped away the prerogatives of sovereignty and eliminated the autonomy once afforded powerful states by exclusive territorial jurisdiction. These elements of the contemporary European state system appear to have linked the states of Europe together irrevocably.

The porousness of national boundaries in the contemporary European state system has made it less likely that 'domestic' political, economic or even environmental disturbances will be contained within a single state. Moreover, those disturbances are easily diffused throughout Europe without regard to internationally recognised frontiers or EU membership; neither provides protection from external shocks, political or otherwise. The postulated ease with which domestic disturbances are transmitted across national boundaries *and* the difficulty of defending against those disturbances underline the strength and vulnerability of the contemporary state system: the openness of these states and societies along an ever expanding spectrum of interaction provides greater levels of collective welfare than would otherwise be possible, yet the very transmission belts facilitating that welfare also serve as diffusion mechanisms hindering the ability of the state to inoculate itself against disturbances within the subsystem.

Stephen Krasner (1999) has challenged the argument that the state has undergone a fundamental change in character, referring famously to sovereignty as organised hypocrisy. Krasner does a service in his decon-struction of sovereignty into its constituent elements, yet his argument that post-Westphalianism is a premature description of states is only possible owing to his extreme characterisation of the sovereignty problem.

First, he rejects post-Westphalianism because 'violations of the principles of territoriality and autonomy have been an enduring characteristic of the international system before and after the peace of Westphalia' (Krasner, 1995/1996: 123); second, he asserts that states have never been able 'to regulate perfectly transborder flows'; and finally, he excludes from consideration the evolution of the wealthiest and some of the most powerful states in the international system – the members of the EU. Both the evolution of those states and the emergence of the EU as an actor possessing sovereign prerogatives are dismissed as 'neutral mutation(s)' without apparent consequence for the international system (Krasner, 2001: 283–4).[3] These arguments cannot withstand even superficial scrutiny: first, the violation of the principles of territoriality and autonomy is distinct from the voluntary acceptance of mutual governance and the loss of autonomy attending it; second, the question is not whether states have been able to control transborder flows, but the qualitatively different nature and volume of those flows and the subsequent impact those flows have on the government's ability to govern; and third, dismissing the EU member states and the EU itself as neutral mutants represents a suppression of an inconvenient counterfactual.

If the post-Westphalian hypothesis is accepted, it violates a central assumption held by most system level theories of international politics; viz., the homogeneity of the state as actor. The rejection of this assumption means that there are two 'kinds' of states in the international system, an assumption Robert Powell (1991) argued prevents a system-level of theory of international politics. Positing the existence of two kinds of states in the international system with different preference structures does lack theoretical elegance, but the existence of states that deviate significantly from the Westphalian ideal-type requires a conceptual explication. Introducing the post-Westphalian state conforms better to the empirical world. It identifies the structural conditions necessary for the emergence of a European security community; it explains the rationale for the delegation of state responsibility for security to the EU. By relaxing the homogeneity assumption in this way, it is possible to explain why the EU member states have embraced an alternative form of multilateral security governance.

The most compelling reason for accepting the distinction between Westphalian and post-Westphalian states can be traced to the spectrum of threats faced by these states, which are directly connected to the perforated sovereignty of post-Westphalian states. The spectrum of threats and instruments available for redressing those threats is largely a function of state attributes. The preoccupations of Westphalian states are traditional security concerns of territorial integrity, autonomy and independence, retaining the role of gate-keeper between internal and external flows of goods, capital, people and ideas, and avoiding external interference in domestic constitutional arrangements. Post-Westphalian states are not disinterested in maintaining territorial integrity, but have largely abandoned the gate-keeper role owing to the preoccupation with maximising economic and social welfare. The openness of the post-Westphalian state and the dependence of internal welfare on external cooperation have devalued the core foreign policy preferences of the Westphalian state; viz., autonomy and independence (Baumann *et al.*, 2001: 38–42).

Sovereignty has been devolved to regional or supranational or international institutions. These states recognise the prerogatives of non-governmental actors in traditional areas controlled by the state and have furthermore accepted the seizing of sovereign prerogatives by individual economic agents. Perforated sovereignty has left states incapable of meeting their private security requirements, let alone threats that have the character of a regional collective bad. It is this very characteristic of the contemporary European state system, particularly the pressure towards norm convergence within Europe conjoined by the openness of both European states and societies, which provides the mechanism whereby external disequilibria are projected into the EU. This development has altered the conception of security threats away from the narrow concern with national defence to a broader understanding and concern with security. There has been a reorientation towards broad and collective milieu goals; those milieu goals, in turn, have replaced or modified the particularistic, national goals associated with traditional statecraft.[4] These structural changes in the nature of the European state and state system mitigate the conceit that there has not been a qualitative change in the interrelationships between European states and societies that requires a re-examination of the nature and sources of security threats in the new century.

The transition to the post-Westphalian state – and the changes in the security threats and security dilemmas these states face – have also transformed the nature of the collective action problem in the security domain. Post-Westphalian states must rely upon institutions – ranging from specific legal understandings to comprehensive regimes to quasi-governmental institutions where sovereignty is pooled – to facilitate the derivation of a security calculus that effectively integrates the traditional and new security agenda. Moreover, post-Westphalian states face a more ambiguous threat environment. First, states now play a relatively minor role as protagonists in the present security system; non-state actors are the agents of threat and beyond the reach of or immune to diplomacy and coercion, conventionally understood. Moreover, the emergence of non-state actors as the principal agents of threat is complemented by the rise of private, transnational actors supplying security independently of the state or acting as subcontractors for it. Secondly, threats against the state are indirect rather than direct. Non-state actors generally target societal infrastructure or the foundations of the social contract rather than the state. These actors are able to exploit the internal and external vulnerabilities of the post-Westphalian state: first, these governments are incapable of effectively controlling their territory owing to the state's (in)voluntary loss of de facto sovereignty and the inability of some other entity to redress that sovereignty gap; and second, these states are incapable of removing the havens protecting those actors, particularly sovereign free territory in failed and failing states. For all the above reasons, it makes empirical sense to relax the homogeneity assumption.

The contemporary security agenda: threat and response

The long-lived distinctions between the 'high' and 'low' politics of international affairs and between domestic and foreign policy have been increasingly rendered obsolete by the changed context of state action and changing nature of the European state (Hoffmann, 1998: 110–16). The contemporary threats posed to European stability are generally aimed 'above' and 'below' the state. Many of the new security challenges target the functioning of society or threaten societal integrity. Other security challenges target the governance structure of the European state system or the milieu goals of its member states, particularly a continent dedicated to democracy and the market. In both cases, the state itself is largely bypassed as a target of threat. As problematically, the state is not the likely source of threat in the new security environment; the majority of probable threats to European security are likely to be perpetrated by non-state actors in the service of objectives not readily recognisable by international relations scholars. Nonetheless, only the state can discharge the important functional role of responding to these disparate security threats. In that sense the state remains alive and well, yet its ability to discharge its security function has been severely compromised.

Nonetheless, the line between foreign and domestic policy for these states has become so blurred that the distinction has lost much of its conceptual force. The emergence of new arenas and sources of conflict –

weak state structures, ethnic conflict, environmental threats – and new technologies that render state boundaries increasingly porous – cyberspace and the globalisation of commerce and capital – have broadened the systemic requirements of security (see Buzan *et al.*, 1998; Sperling and Kirchner, 1998). The contemporary security agenda raises two important questions: Why have new categories of security threats risen to prominence in the post-Cold War period? What are the putative threats to the systemic or milieu goals of the EU member states? Put differently, can the security threats posed to Europe be treated as the relatively simple problem of identifying state-to-state threats along its periphery that unequivocally represent a state-centric security calculus where the state is both the subject and object of analysis?

The European threat complex advises against restricting our understanding of security policy to a set of choices limited to dyads of states. Threats can no longer be simply disaggregated into the capabilities and intentions of states; primacy can no longer be attributed to the state as either agent or object (see Snyder, 1991: 126–7). A definition of security restricted to the traditional concern with territorial integrity or the protection of ill-defined but well understood 'national interests' would exclude threats to the social fabric of domestic or international societies or threats emanating from states with imperfect control over their territory, weakened legitimacy, or persistent interethnic conflicts within or overlapping state boundaries. Moreover, the growing irrelevance of territoriality and the continuing importance of jurisdictional sovereignty have left states vulnerable to these new categories of threat: national responses are no longer adequate, yet the division of political space into states jealously guarding their sovereign prerogatives inhibits collective responses to these diffused threats. The residual persistence of the Westphalian sovereignty norm in post-Westphalian states places a continuing barrier to cooperative outcomes in the security domain, broadly or narrowly conceived.

Four readily identifiable mechanisms diffuse threats throughout the system irrespective of territorial boundaries: the growing dynamic density of the European political space; flawed or underdeveloped civil societies or democratic political institutions in regions adjacent to the EU, particularly in south-eastern Europe and the wider Mediterranean basin; the ubiquitousness of cyberspace; and simple geographical propinquity. Geographic propinquity and the absence of effective interstate barriers to migration mean that domestic disturbances anywhere in the Eurasian political space – whether ethnic strife or environmental degradation or the criminalisation of national economies or state structures – could be externalised and initiate destabilising migratory flows. Cyberspace, in turn, has erased national boundaries and signified the potential irrelevance of geographic space. Transactions across cyberspace – for good or ill – elude effective state control. Cyberspace provides the perfect sanctuary for non-state and societal actors targeting a specific state or aspect of society.

Europe's dynamic density provides the most pervasive and nettlesome mechanisms of diffusion, particularly as transactions between the EU and the regions abutting it rise in number and quality. The EU member states have experienced the progressive erosion of national boundaries and the steady loss of state control over the decisions of individuals, most markedly within the sphere of the economy. The very transmission belts of economic prosperity – largely unrestricted capital markets, high levels of trade, and the absence of exchange controls – also facilitate the criminalisation of national economies, initiate the erosion of the authority and legitimacy of weak states in transition, and generate exogenous shocks to national economies that states can no longer effectively control, especially as Eurasian and Mediterranean states become increasingly integrated into the European political and economic system. Moreover, the states along the perimeter of affluent Europe are plagued by weak civil societies, ineffective or corrupted judiciaries and other democratic structures, and economies that are either criminalised or escape effective national jurisdiction. These states are not only hostage to their interdependence with the rest of Europe, but that interdependence has the potential to transform domestic disequilibria outside the EU into potential security threats for the affluent within it.[5]

National authorities in the EU can no longer unilaterally fulfil their primary security responsibilities of maintaining territorial integrity and ensuring economic growth. Not only do security threats now trespass into areas once considered to be strictly domestic, but the transformation of the European state has made it increasingly difficult to achieve its security goals owing to the vulnerabilities of the post-Westphalian state to external shocks. The mitigation of those vulnerabilities evades a national solution; it warrants joint rather than unilateral policies that conflict with notions of national independence, identity, and purpose. Moreover, security threats have acquired a system-wide significance that demands an alternative conceptualisation of the security dilemmas facing states and the institutional responses to them.

Within Europe, the Cold War dilemma creating military insecurity in a bipolar world has been replaced by the post-Cold War dilemma of ensuring political and economic stability along its borders. The nations of Western Europe fear the negative consequences of political and economic insecurity in southern and eastern Europe and well beyond. Consequently, any measures taken by those nations along Europe's eastern periphery to enhance their national security – including enhanced military capabilities – are viewed as positive contributions to the stability and security of Europe rather than as a threat to either. This alternative civilian security dilemma, derived from the contest over the allocation of scarce national resources between policies that generate domestic plenty and those that generate external stability, also provides an incentive for the EU member states to cooperate with their eastern neighbours even at the risk of being exploited: security free-riding by these nations poses a lesser threat than does the re-emergence of authoritarian regimes or economic collapse that could disrupt the anticipated reconciliation and reintegration of historical Europe.

Europeans have been largely relieved of the security dilemma identified by Robert Jervis and the attending policy paradox. The European state is no longer compelled to guard against any disadvantageous change in the military status quo or pursue an advantageous change in its position along the regional military–strategic hierarchy. The policies redressing the civilian security dilemma, which are preoccupied with fostering states that are domestically secure, economically prosperous and politically legitimate, could produce a disadvantageous change in the regional hierarchy of states. Nonetheless, the preoccupation with destabilising changes in the regional hierarchy of power has lost much of its practical if not theoretical purchase: just as the United States underwrote a disadvantageous change in the hierarchy of the North Atlantic states via the European Reconstruction Program and the toleration of trade discrimination by the Europeans and Japanese alike, the United States created a more stable 'West' but at the cost of diminishing its relative power. In parallel fashion, the EU states have made a similar calculation with respect to its eastern and southern neighbours, even though the EU is driving a much harder set of bargains with its clients than did America.

While an emphasis on the non-military elements of security invites the rejoining of the contentious debate on their status as threats *qua* threats (Baldwin, 1997: 5–26), there is a growing consensus that the content of security is changing and that security threats since the end of the Cold War have become more complex and far reaching (Cottey and Averre, 2002). Instead of facing the existential threat of a nuclear exchange, the EU member states now face myriad threats that are of smaller magnitude, harder to anticipate, and even more difficult to counter. This phenomenon was tragically manifest with the terrorist attacks on New York, Madrid and London between September 2001 and July 2005. Those attacks, in particular, demonstrated that networked terrorism is not sourced from a specific region and cannot be reliably reduced to an identifiable set of individual actors with a fixed abode.

The European Security Strategy (ESS), adopted by the Thessoloniki European Council in December 2003, singled out terrorism, the prolifer-ation of weapons of mass destruction, regional conflicts, state failure and organised crime as the five key threats facing the EU. However, the changing nature of the security environment was recognised as early as 1991 when the North Atlantic Council noted that the 'Alliance security interests can be affected by other risks of a wider nature, including proliferation of weapons of mass destruction, disruption of the flow of vital resources and actions of terrorism and sabotage' (North Atlantic Council, 1991: para. 12). NATO restated these risks as the priority con-cerns of the Alliance in its 1999 Strategic Concept, although 'acts of terrorism' posed the greatest risk to member state security (North Atlantic Council, 1999: para. 24). These adjustments to the hierarchy of threat have weakened the distinctions between different kinds of security – national and regional, military and economic, internal and external – but also point to the difficulty of differentiating between those threats. It is no longer possible to address the problem of terrorism separately from the issues of money laundering, organised crime, cybervandalism, or drug trafficking. Mass population movements fleeing civil war, for example, raise the prospect of spreading infectious diseases and over-taxing public health systems to the detriment of the host nation's society and economy. Likewise, migration driven by economic destitution or environmental instability arising from climatic change threatens equally disruptive consequences for the affluent states of Europe. These kinds of threats to the Europe's economic and social integrity make it an increasingly unlikely proposition that steps can be taken to mitigate one to the exclusion of the others (Hall and Fox, 2001/2002: 8). Arguably, the EU enlargement and stabilisation policies anticipated this develop-ment; the New York, Madrid and London terrorist bombings should also demonstrate to those sceptical of the proposition that the content and sources of threat have undergone a fundamental transformation since the end of the Cold War.

The expansion of the security agenda requires the development of criteria that distinguish analytically a security threat from other potential sources of disorder in the international system or its component parts. Barry Buzan *et al.* (1998) offered an early definition of security that incorporates the various elements of the new security agenda, but none-theless stayed attached to the traditional meaning generally ascribed to security by international relations scholars. They argue that 'security is about survival. It is when an issue is presented as posing an existential threat to a designated referent object'.[6] Thus, the concept of security relates, not only to the preservation of state boundaries, but also to the protection of societies and individuals within states (Buzan *et al.*, 1998). Accordingly, security exists where states and societies are capable of maintaining their independent identity and functional integrity. More fundamentally, they argue that the definition of what does and does not constitute a security threat is determined by the process of 'securitisation', which in turn describes how specific groups or state elites take particular issues 'out of the sphere of every day politics' by redefining them as secur-ity problems (Buzan *et al.*, 1998; cf. Krause, 1998). This approach to understanding how political problems or challenges are transformed into security threats allows that the security agenda of states are plastic and contingent on the preferences and perceptions of elites. It should be clear that elites do have a large role in shaping what constitutes a threat as well as the best means for meeting it. It should be just as clear that threats do exist independently of elite preferences or perceptions and force them-selves onto the agenda. The process of securitisation is best understood as the interaction of 'real' events that threaten an enduring set of state interests with the political process of recognising the event as a security threat, the development of the policies deemed appropriate to meet that threat, and the allocation of resources to achieve the goal of threat pacification. Yet, this definition of security is too restrictive given the novel nature of the threats posed to the European system of governance and the prominence of non-state actors as the primary agents of threat.

The analytical solution to the problem of defining the elements of the contemporary security agenda could take any number of forms. A first approach would be a general dismissal of the 'new' security agenda as the response of those seeking to provide an alternative rationale for the continuation of NATO as a security organisation as well as those who would favour an expansive remit for international institutions in the false hope of mitigating international anarchy. A second category of response would assume the position that these threats have persisted throughout the modern period and it is only the absence of great power conflict that has pushed these issues to the surface. Put somewhat differently, it is only now that the Cold War has ended that sufficient attention and intellectual resources can be paid to these long-standing threats to societal, state and systemic stability. A third category of response – and the one favoured here – suggests that the European transition to post-Westphalianism has made these states easily penetrated by malevolent non-state and state actors.

The perforated sovereignty of the post-Westphalian state has intensified the problem of collective action, particularly as it pertains to security. The security requirements of the EU are beyond the reach of any individual state; EU milieu security goals can only be attained by interventions outside of Europe – establishing the conditions of an international civil society within Europe does not afford the luxury of splendid isolation but instead requires the externalisation of EU norms and rules. The emergence of post-Westphalianism requires institutions – ranging from single-issue specific legal understandings to regimes managing an issue area to quasi-governmental institutions that pool sovereignty – that facilitate cooperation across most areas of security, ranging from the security calculus attending traditional security agenda to that attending the new security agenda.

It is clear that security threats are no longer limited to the existential questions of national survival or territorial integrity. There are at least two ways for developing a typology of threats. The first is to focus on the change in both the agents of security provision (state and non-state actors) and in the target of security threats (state and society). These distinctions provide the basis for typology of security threats that locates the primary threats to post-Westphalian states as being posed by transnational non-state actors that are directed towards societal rather than state structures (see Figure 1.1) (Kirchner and Sperling, 2002).

As is clear from Figure 1.1, the contemporary threats posed to European stability are generally aimed 'above' and 'below' the state.

The difficulty of managing these security threats derives from two conditions: the inability of European governments to control territory owing to the state's involuntary loss of de facto sovereignty; and the problem of non-governance outside the EU, either owing to the corrosive competition endemic to Westphalian anarchy or to revisionist, dysfunctional states. Consequently, the EU member states, collectively and

Agent of threat	Target of threat	
	State	*Society*
State	Traditional war	Societal security
Non-state	Asymmetric war	Human security

Figure 1.1 Threat typology

individually, must abandon a positive definition of security, where security is defined as expanding the zones of unconditional viability, and adopt instead a largely negative definition of security, where security is defined as seeking to minimise the zones of conditional viability that are particularly marked along the eastern and southern perimeter.[7]

While this first approach details the target and agent of threat, it does not lend itself to the development of a comprehensive understanding of the EU as a security actor or the way in which these threats are being collectively addressed. A second approach to the problem of disentangling and understanding the current threat environment is to focus on how those threats are manifested. In this case, security challenges are defined by the arena of conflict (state or society) and the instruments of conflict resolution (coercive or persuasive). These two variables produce a typology presenting four categories of security challenge that have either confronted the EU or continue to do so: interstate and intrastate conflict, state-building, and the construction of the institutions of a civil democratic society (see Figure 1.2). These four policy challenges overlap. In some cases they require the simultaneous application of the coercive and persuasive instruments of statecraft; in many cases the distinction between intra- and interstate conflicts is unhelpful; and in still others, the policy challenges and tasks are sequential.

While each of these different typologies provides a window on the changing nature of security threats, neither provides an analytically satisfying typology of security policy. Towards that end, we opt for a functional categorisation of security policy which, in turn, identifies the tasks of security governance. Such an approach allows us to combine the functional and instrumental requirements for meeting the security challenges facing Europe today. Security governance performs two functions – institution-building and conflict resolution – and employs two sets of instruments – the persuasive (economic, political and diplomatic) and the coercive (military intervention). Taken together, four categories of security governance suggest themselves: assurance, prevention, protection, and compellence (see Figure 1.3).

		Instruments	
		Coercive	*Persuasive*
State		Interstate conflict	State-building
Arena of conflict			
Society		Intrastate conflict	Institutions of civil society

Figure 1.2 Governance challenges

Instruments

		Persuasive	Coercive
	Institution-building	Prevention	Protection
Functions			
	Conflict resolution	Assurance	Compellence

Figure 1.3 Governance policies

Policies of assurance identify efforts aimed at post-conflict reconstruction and attending confidence-building measures. Policies of prevention capture efforts to prevent conflict by building or sustaining domestic, regional or international institutions that contribute to the mitigation of anarchy and the creation of order. Policies of compellence capture the tasks of conflict resolution in states outside the EU via military intervention, particularly peace-making and enforcement. And policies of protection describe those efforts to fulfil the traditional function of protecting society from external threats. These four tasks of security governance are often pursued concurrently; it is also clear that economic and military instruments can be used towards the achieving not dissimilar goals. We make two assumptions: first, that there is an elective affinity between the category of instrument employed to meet a specific governance challenge; and second, that there is a normative preference in the EU for the employment of civilian instruments of statecraft and a disinclination to rely upon military force.

Security governance

The final question we address is the critical one. Why security governance? The fundamental problem of international politics – and security provision in particular – is the supply of order and the regulation of conflict without the resort to war. Anarchy – and the benefits afforded the state by it – precludes the emergence of global or even regional government to manage its liabilities. The regulation of international politics, particularly the management of disorder, can be best thought of as a problem of governance as well as non-governance.[8] There are alternative conceptualisations of security arrangements, but they are mutually exclusive (collective defence or concert) and are defective for the purpose of understanding the problem of security today owing to their inherent limitations, the most important of which is a preoccupation with the military aspect of security. The traditional security arrangements like collective defence alliances or concerts are oriented outward towards an identifiable state adversary and system stability; collective security and security communities are oriented towards a specific in-group that inevitably casts non-members as either unimportant or as a galvanising other.

A final implication of the post-Westphalian character of the European state is the obsolescence of traditional alliances as a guide for understanding the requirements of security. Alliance theory has provided the framework for understanding not only the evolution of the post-war European security order, but the evolution of the European state system since 1648.[9] Alliances, as either formal or informal institutions, have been rightly regarded as mechanisms for regulating disequilibria in the international system. The contemporary debate on alliances has been framed by the question of whether states balance power, interests or threats.[10] The traditional concern of the theory of alliances – the determination of which states will align with other states and the reasons for doing so – is not particularly relevant to our understanding of contemporary European security. Not only have the source of threat and the security objectives of the state changed in fundamental ways, but the vocabulary security analysts have relied on is less relevant to the task of clarifying the appropriate statecraft for a changed external environment. It makes little sense to calculate whether European states, in seeking EU membership, are engaged in balancing or bandwagoning against a putative or recognised adversary. The new security agenda has rendered this particular debate somewhat beside the point: the state is neither the sole actor nor the primary target of the threats posed to European security and stability. Consequently, the nomenclature of alliances fails to capture the dilemmas state face since there is no specific antagonist posing an unvarying threat.

This nomenclature depends too heavily upon a conceptual understanding of statecraft that is hemmed in by a misleading reliance upon the state as security antagonist, upon an ability to calculate a balance of power, threat or interest, and upon behaviour that can be reduced to the pursuit of a narrow set of national goals. Alliance theory also suffers from two conceptual disabilities: it remains overly state-centric and cannot account for non-Westphalian modes of behaviour. States are no longer the sole actor, either as agent or as target of threat, in the international system, particularly in Europe. Alliance theory has little to offer in explaining the institutional choices made in Europe today; there are no power disequilibria in the current European state system.

The problems posed by chain gangs and buck-passing do remain relevant in the current European system, despite the evolution towards a security community within the EU (Christensen and Snyder, 1990). While the European state system cannot be considered multipolar in any meaningful sense unless the United States is removed as a European actor, the period of bipolarity has clearly passed and the European system is more fluid today than at any time since the 1930s. Consequently, the behaviour associated with buck-passing and chain gangs will continue to vex those crafting solutions to the challenges posed by the new security agenda, even though these two behaviours are conventionally held to be mutually exclusive.[11] Buck-passing may be treated as a reformulation of the free-rider problem that plagues the provision (elimination) of impure collective or club goods (bads). In the contemporary European system, buck-passing takes two forms. First, the individual European states have made an effort to 'pass the buck' for the political and financial costs of redressing the structural disabilities of the states in transition to international and regional financial institutions, particularly the EU. Second, the consequence of this buck-passing, as in all cases of free-riding, is the sub-optimal provision of an impure collective good, in this case the amelioration of the underlying causes of the post-Cold War security threats to Europe.

Less tractable is the problem posed by chain gangs.[12] The parallels between Christensen and Snyder's formulation of chain gangs and the contemporary European state system are inexact, but highly suggestive. If geographic propinquity, the ubiquitousness of cyberspace, high levels of interaction density, and the fragility of civil and political institutions along Europe's periphery do function as mechanisms of diffusion, then it follows that the security of the European states are 'integrally inter-twined'. Consequently, the states of prosperous Europe – the full members of NATO and the EU in particular – cannot allow those states along its periphery to function as 'petri dishes' fostering the new security threats, since the collapse of political authority or a national economy could be transformed into a system-wide threat.

The obsolescence of alliance theory, with the possible exception of buck-passing and chain gangs (which are in any case independent of the theory of alliances), calls for an alternative method for understanding why the EU has become a security actor and, as such, how it goes about identifying and meeting threats. Empirically, there is little room to doubt that national governments have subcontracted many of their security tasks to the EU, particularly those tasks which fall outside the traditional concern with territorial defence. Consequently, the formulation and execution of security policy cannot be disciplined or translated into the traditional rubric of sovereign jurisdiction or assessments of the capa-bilities and intentions of identifiable adversaries with a state identity.

Only by relying on an alternative concept – governance – can we capture the challenges and instruments of attaining within group security as well as security from 'out' groups. Thus, the regulation of international politics can best be thought of as a problem of governance.

Security governance has received increasing attention since 1989 (Rosenau, 1992, 1997; Young 1999; Keohane, 2001; Webber, 2002; Webber *et al.*, 2004). Its rising conceptual salience is derived in large measure by the challenges presented by the 'new' security agenda. Security governance has been expansively defined as 'the coordinated management and regulation of issues by multiple and separate authorities, the interventions of both public and private actors . . . formal and informal arrangements, in turn structured by discourse and norms, and purposefully directed toward particular policy outcomes' (Webber *et al.*, 2004: 4). This definition of security governance is elastic enough to accommodate analytical frameworks treating: institutions as mechanisms employed by states to further their own goals (Koremenos *et al.*, 2001: 761–99); states as the primary actors in international relations where some states are more equal than others (Waltz, 1978; Gilpin, 1981); power relationships determined not only by underlying material factors, but norms and identities (Checkel, 1998; Hopf, 1998; Barnett and Duvall, 2005); and states as constrained by institutions with respect to proscribed and prescribed behaviour (Martin and Simmons, 1998; March and Olsen, 1998). This broad conceptual definition of security governance permits an investigation of the role institutions play in the security domain, particularly the division of labour between the state and institution, the proscribed and prescribed instruments and purposes of state action, and the consolidation of a collective definition of interest and threat.

Security governance has been employed in four general ways: as a general theory (Webber, 2000), as a theory networks (Krahmann, 2003), as a system of international and transnational regimes (Young, 1999), and as a heuristic device for recasting the problem of security management in order to accommodate the different patterns of interstate interaction, the rising number of non-state security actors, the expansion of the security agenda, and conflict regulation or resolution (Sperling, 2003 and 2007). We treat security governance as a heuristic device, acknowledging that security governance remains largely pre-theoretical. Security governance possesses the virtue of conceptual accommodation: it allows for hierarchical and heterarchical patterns of interaction as well as the disparate substantive bundling and normative content of security institutions. Security governance possesses the additional virtue of neither precluding nor necessitating the privileging of the state or non-state actors in the security domain; it leaves open the question of whether states are able to provide security across multiple levels and dimensions unilaterally or whether states are compelled to work within multilateral or supranational institutional frameworks.

The study of security governance in geographical Europe has generally focused on two distinct features: first, the institutional characteristics of governance, with particular attention directed to the geographical boundary of those governance structures; and second, a marked tendency to emphasise the military aspects of security and consequently the role of NATO. Less attention has been given to identifying and establishing the relative importance of common interests, shared and divergent cultural identities, and the norms and rules giving rise to and 'binding' the European governance structure.[13] The broadening of the contemporary security agenda is a central rationale for adopting the concept of governance rather than the more established frameworks and concepts in the security field. Moreover, the emergent role of the EU as a security actor – and a corresponding erosion of state prerogatives in this policy domain – requires a more plastic framework allowing the simultaneous consideration of EU and member state interests as well as the embrace of the enlarged security agenda, both in terms of instruments and goals.

Robert O. Keohane and Robert Jervis have addressed the requirements of one particular form of security governance, the security community (Keohane, 2001; Jervis, 2002). Jervis argues that the evolution of a European security community was contingent upon five necessary and sufficient conditions. The first requires national elites generally to eschew wars of conquest and war as an instrument of statecraft, at least with one another; the second that the costs of waging such a war outweigh any conceivable benefits, material or other. The third condition requires national elites to accept that the best path to national prosperity is peaceful economic intercourse rather than conquest or empire. The fourth calls for the existence of domestic democratic governance in order that the domestic practice of compromise, negotiation and rule of law are projected externally and characterise relations between states. The final condition stipulates that states be satisfied with the territorial status quo, a condition that mitigates the security dilemma (Adler and Barnett, 1998; Jervis, 2002; Keohane, 2001). It is our position that the EU, in discharging the four policies meeting the challenges of security governance – assurance, prevention, protection and compellence – is seeking to fulfil these conditions in the candidate states for accession to the EU, particularly those in south eastern Europe and into Asia Minor as well as states that are unlikely candidates for accession in eastern Europe and the littoral states of the Mediterranean basin stretching from Lebanon to Morocco.

While the role of the individual EU member states remains critical and many states exercise considerable freedom of action outside the EU on security matters (particularly France and the United Kingdom), the EU nonetheless remains the aspiration and focus of efforts to meet jointly the tasks of security governance that cannot be met alone or only met poorly by any individual state.[14] Moreover, the EU serves as an autonomous security actor *as well as* a clearing station for member state efforts to cope with the array of security challenges. Thus, a more relevant set of questions about the future role of the EU in governing European security would include: What are the implications of enlargement and the potentially imperfect socialisation of states along Europe's periphery for the EU security system? Will the process of enlargement or the persistence of failed or failing states along its peripheries debase the existing EU security community? What are the potential consequences of the EU's failure to meet its self-defined security challenges? These questions are central because they touch upon two more fundamental ones: can the EU function as an effective security actor independent of the member states and as a complement to, if not substitute for NATO? Can the process of post-Westphalianism in Europe be reversed and with what consequence for the European security order?

Conclusion

Important changes have taken place in the European state system since the 1950s and those changes were accelerated by the collapse of the post-war bipolar world. These changes require an alternative understanding of the nature of security threats, the target of those threats, and the instruments best matched to meeting them. Since 1999, NATO's role has been challenged by the European determination to develop an autonomous military capability, including force projection, as well as diminished by the enduring divisiveness that the administration of President George W. Bush introduced into European–American relations after 2002. NATO can no longer be treated as Europe's self-evident security institution of first choice, particularly when the security issues of prevention, protection or assurance are in play. NATO may remain indispensable as the guarantor of military stability in European geostrategic space, but the EU has emerged by design as the key economic institution for governing and maintaining order in the European geoeconomic space, and by default as a traditional security institution encroaching upon the pre-existing and unchallenged prerogatives enjoyed by NATO.

Why has the EU emerged as a security actor? The first and most important reason has been the transformation of the European state. The international state system is no longer homogeneous in Waltz's sense. Rather, there are at least two categories of states – the Westphalian and post-Westphalian – that produce interstate interactions that are qualitatively different. Second, there has been an increase in the nature and kind of key actors in international politics, particularly the European Union, which has filled the gaps left by the involuntary loss of sovereignty attending transformation of state as well as the purposeful pooling of sovereignty to achieve regional collective goods or private goods common to a specific set of states. Third, the EU and its member states have recognised that the significant gap between Europe's influence and capabilities has left them dependent upon an increasingly undependable American partner. As in the case of monetary unification, the emergence of the EU as a security actor reflects a dissatisfaction with and vulnerability to American policies which are inconsistent with European sensibilities or interests. The EU claimed a regional role as the sherpa leading the former Warsaw Pact states towards their transitions to democracy and the market economy after 1990; as the decade progressed, the security ambitions of the EU expanded as the Balkans disintegrated and in response to American pressures for the individual EU states to acquire force projection capabilities. When the European Council approved the ESS in December 2003, the EU formally proclaimed a global role for itself that would in time yield global influence commensurate with its aggregate military, economic and diplomatic resources. The precise role that the EU would play vis-à-vis the United States remained ambiguous: Britain, Poland and Italy, for example, expected the EU to support the United States outside Europe, while France and Schröder's Germany anticipated that an EU with a global profile would distance Europe from American policies inimical to European interests. The EU has emerged as military actor, albeit a severely circumscribed one, capable of intervening in intrastate conflicts within and outside Europe; it also functions as a mature civilian power extending its methods and norms of governance along its southern and eastern European perimeter and as an integral part of the institutional fabric of the transatlantic security order. Finally, the changing nature of the contemporary security agenda has altered Europe's collective understanding of security and the instrumental requirements for meeting the security challenges facing the EU and its member states, and has expanded the arenas of conflict relevant to Europe's security.

The four security governance tasks of assurance, prevention, protection, and compellence reveal the limitations and possibilities of transferring sovereign prerogatives from the member states to the EU. The continuing reticence of the member states to relinquish sovereignty, even where it is clearly recognised that the persistence of sovereignty is the barrier to achieving higher levels of security, frustrates the execution of those governance tasks by the EU. At the same time, the imperative of solidarity creates the rationale for greater security cooperation, the abnegation of state sovereignty, and the pooling of sovereign prerogatives in the EU. The EU and its member states have struck different balances between sovereignty and solidarity in meeting each of these governance tasks: the tasks of protection and compellence have posed the greatest resistance to sovereign pooling – publics expect national governments to remain responsible for public health, to protect the underlying social contract manifested in judicial procedure and penal law, and the commitment of blood and treasure; and the tasks of assurance and prevention – particularly the enlargement process, the Stability Pact for South Eastern Europe and the European Neighbourhood Policy – have been largely delegated to the Union. It is the post-Westphalian condition of the European state that requires the subordination of sovereign prerogatives to the imperative of solidarity, yet the electorate's continuing expectation that national governments remain responsible for governing – that they remain sovereign – demarcates the limitations and promise of the EU as a security actor in the twenty-first century.

Notes

1 We identify Westphalian states as being functional or dysfunctional rather than creating a third category of pre-Westphalian. The hesitancy to create that third category stems from the historical circumstance that the dominant pre-Westphalian form of European political organisation was feudalism, as well as from the questionable usefulness of that categorisation since Westphalian states can be categorised as either functional (exert sovereign control over territory) or dysfunctional (exert partial sovereign control over territory).

2 On the transition to a post-Westphalian state in Europe, see March and Olsen (1998: 944–7).

3 For dissenting views on these two points, see also Osiander (2001: 283–4); more generally, see Caporaso (1996), Falk (2002) and Cooper (2003: 26–37).

4 A similar argument is often made with respect to Germany. A prominent example is Bulmer *et al.* (2000). For an overview of this literature, see Sperling (2004).

5 The literature on diffusion is highly suggestive with respect to how the mechanisms of transmission can spread rapidly within a regional system

populated by post-Westphalian states. On diffusion, see Most and Starr (1980: 932–46), Siverson and Starr (1990) and Goertz (1994).

6 Notably, Buzan *et al.*'s definition of a referent object excludes milieu goals and collapses state and societal security into an undifferentiated category. See Buzan *et al.* (1998: 21).

7 The concepts of conditional and unconditional viability were developed by Kenneth Boulding (1962). Conditional viability exists where a state is dominated by other actors; unconditional viability exists where a state is dominant. The importance of milieu goals and the agents of contagion in post-Cold War Europe suggest that the European states will seek to reduce the zones of conditional viability along the European periphery in an effort to sustain and extend order.

8 We would like to thank Haruhiro Fukui for suggesting that the presence of non-governance creates the permissive context generating these new categories of threat.

9 For the period 1648–1945, see Langer (1950), Taylor (1954), Holsti (1991) and Schweller (1998). For the post-war period, see Wolfers (1959), Osgood (1962), Liska (1962) and Walt (1987).

10 These three approaches are represented by, respectively, Waltz (1978), Walt (1987) and Schweller (1998).

11 In their formulation, each category of behaviour emerges in restrictive conditions: buck-passing only occurs with multipolarity and a perceived defensive advantage; chain-gangs only occur in multipolarity when there is a perceived offensive advantage. In the new security environment, the offensive–defensive balance has lost much of its relevance. See Christensen and Snyder (1990: 144–7).

12 The liability of chain gangs manifests itself when there is a 'high degree of security interdependence within an alliance . . . each state feels that its own security is integrally intertwined with the security of its alliance partners. As a result, any state that marches to war inexorably drags its alliance partners with it. No state can restrain a reckless ally by threatening to sit out the conflict, since the demise of a reckless ally would decisively cripple its own security' (Christensen and Snyder, 1990: 140).

13 Important exceptions are Risse (1995) and Hampton (1998/99).

14 Security governance also has the advantage of providing an analytical framework that reconciles the coexistence of disparate state interests *and* the consolidation of the EU's role as a full spectrum security actor. Security governance can explain member state reliance upon the EU to execute the four policies of prevention, assurance, protection and compellence, but also account for the three critical aspects of the British, French, German and Italian orientations towards the external environment that constitute significant barriers to security cooperation and the emergence of the EU as a unitary actor: idiosyncratic security concerns; disparate interaction patterns; and the balance between traditional and civilian instruments of statecraft. While Britain, France, Germany and Italy have a largely

overlapping set of common security concerns and a preoccupation with regional stability, these states also have security concerns that are non-intersecting (e.g., France is particularly preoccupied with conventional war, Islamic extremism, and organized crime; Britain and Germany view environmental degradation as a serious security threat). As important, these states have differentiated geopolitical orientations (Africa constitutes a specific region of threat for Britain and France, Italy and France have a direct security interest in the stability of the littoral states of the Mediterranean, and Germany is most preoccupied with central and eastern Europe). A second important divergence is found in the interaction patterns favoured by the major European states: the UK and France rely on the full range of interaction patterns, ranging from unilateralism to multilateralism, Italy favours bilateralism (with the US) and multilateralism, while Germany remains careful to work within multilateral frameworks. Even though all four states exhibit a preference for institutionalised multilateralism, the British favour action within NATO while the others favour cooperation within the EU. A third factor complicating common action is the balance each country strikes between a reliance and preference for the traditional and civilian forms of statecraft. Britain and France are most wedded to the traditional instruments of diplomacy, particularly military interventions and nuclear deterrence, while Germany and Italy (albeit less so) are equally wedded to the civilian instruments. The British and French are willing to resort to military action up to full-scale war, while the Italians and Germans are only willing to countenance peace-keeping or peace-enforcement operations. None of the other categories of security multilateralism – concerts, collective defence or security arrangements, security communities – provides the analytically flexibility necessary to account for the emergence of the EU as a security actor and the continuing pull of sovereign prerogatives. See Sperling (2007).

2

Policies of prevention: preempting disorder along the periphery

Introduction

It is difficult to perceive present-day Europe from the standpoint of the nation state model because the characteristics of the nation state after the Treaty of Westphalia are generally defined by the three elements of domain, nation and sovereignty. In the EU, those elements are not always under the control of a single government. There are some cases where the EU executes policies over national interests because of the integration not only of economic areas, but also of legislative processes creating law and order and political systems as its foundation. This dispersed power structure is found also in the field of security where, due to the porous borders of the European Union, as required by the participation in the internal market and the Schengen agreement, EU member states have progressively evolved towards post-Westphalianism as they effectively surrender control of their internal borders in exchange for free movement provisions.[1] Owing to the post-Westphalian nature of the states in the EU in comparison to the states neighbouring the EU, member states recognised the need for joint action, the need to act as a collective. The European Security Strategy (ESS) acknowledges and illuminates the Westphalian/post-Westphalian dichotomy as 'Neighbours who are engaged in violent conflict, weak states where organised crime flourishes, dysfunctional societies' or other security concerns on the EU's 'borders all pose problems for Europe'. Subsequently, such predicaments necessitated and facilitated the evolution of the EU as a security actor.

The rise of the EU as a security actor is connected with the fact that the threat spectrum has broadened. New categories of threat have emerged in the post-Cold War period, marked by such phenomena as intrastate conflicts, terrorist attacks[2] and the proliferation of weapons of mass destruction (WMD). Security is no longer limited to the task of territorial defence and the use of military force to do so. Owing to the inability to effectively control national borders, to deter terrorist attacks or to respond effectively to environmental or health threats, the overlap between internal and external security policy is growing. Thus, enlargement of the EU, association agreements, the Schengen Convention, the volume and diversity of travel/migration reflect in part the interdependence of the EU's external environment and the realisation of its milieu goals. In turn, these milieu issues have made conflict prevention a critical aspect of security governance in Europe today. They have also highlighted that what the EU was already doing in the field of conflict prevention came to be considered as important for security.

Besides the EU, a host of other actors, ranging from non-governmental organisations (NGOs) to financial or technical agencies to NATO and the Organisation for Security and Co-operation in Europe (OSCE), are involved in conflict prevention. These actors combine to 'entrench particular forms of behaviour among their participants by prescribing rules of entry, norms of interaction and constraints on behaviour' (Keohane, 1988: 384). Conflict prevention has become, at least as a strategy, an important element of EU Common Foreign and Security Policy (CFSP), and is particularly enshrined in the objectives of the 2003 ESS, which stresses early preventive action to defuse a potential crisis. Among the general reasons why conflict prevention occupies a prominent place in the CFSP are its own particular history, inadequate military capabilities, strength of economic power, and dependence on external markets and raw materials. The EU takes pride in its own experience as having successfully transformed enmity into amity and as having mostly relied on voluntary, peaceful and economic means to achieve peace, stability and prosperity. There is therefore a temptation on the part of the EU to export its model to other parts of the world, analogous to the Kantian strife for 'universal peace', in the hope that this will create a bandwagon effect (Hill, 2001: 325) and contribute to a safer and more stable world. Of course, what can also be noted is the eagerness of other regions to import its model. Given the economic and financial assets of the EU and its member states more generally, and the deliberate choice to concentrate on economic rather than military matters, the EU has a more elaborate set of economic instruments at its disposal to mitigate the underlying causes of civil and interstate conflict. Furthermore, the EU frames its conflict prevention efforts within a specific normative framework (Maull, 2005: 779). EU values are based on the attractiveness of the European way of life. European values and resources are expended via a number of aid, trade, democratisation and association programmes. These are complemented, in specific instances, with economic sanctions, rule of law or police missions, and other crisis management measures. Emphasis on conflict prevention has further been strengthened through the successful post-Cold War enlargement strategies the EU has undertaken, with regard to some Mediterranean and Central and East European countries. EU enlargement has helped to create a widening area of freedom, democracy and stability, stretching from southern Europe to central and eastern Europe, with the eventual inclusion of the Balkan countries and (possibly) Turkey. Besides these general reasons, there is also a specific reason that is simply that it is 'better' (in economic and political terms) to prevent conflict rather than to manage it. More generally, the EU has integrated conflict prevention strategies, including the rebuilding of post-conflict societies, as a core element of the CFSP. The prevention of conflicts in its own neighbourhood, particularly the Balkans, has led the EU to undertake peace-keeping operations and, on some occasions, even peace-enforcement, e.g., Macedonia in 2001 and the Democratic Republic of the Congo in 2003.[3]

How then does the EU engage in conflict prevention, i.e., what are the key characteristics of the EU's 'actorness' in this field? The extent and type of EU response is in part related to the nature of the task at hand, or what is meant by conflict prevention. Leonard and Gowan (2004: 8) define preventive engagement as an action with the aim 'to stop crises by marshalling resources to shape the behaviour of problem countries'. In another way preventive engagement implies the need to be able to act before the unstable countries deteriorate, when signs of proliferation are detected, and before humanitarian emergencies arise. For our purposes, conflict prevention policies have two dimensions: first, those policies prevent the occurrence of a major conflict or, once started, stop it from spreading; second, the policy instruments consist of financial and technical assistance, economic cooperation in the form of trade or association agreements, the promise of EU membership, nation-building efforts, and support of internal democratisation. It should be noted that there is often a fluid continuum between conflict prevention activities, the management of actual crises, and the reconstruction and development of post-conflict societies. While the management of violent intracommunal or interstate conflicts is an important aspect of conflict prevention, we concentrate on civilian crisis management – the operation forte of the EU.

Conflict prevention may emerge from different sources and can engage a wide array of instruments. General prevention aims at tackling the alleged root causes of potentially violent conflicts such as economic inequality and deficient democracy, as well as exclusive state and nation-building strategies. By contrast, special prevention employs specific measures aimed at a specific conflict at a specific stage (Zellner, 2002: 18–19). The conflict over the nature and purpose of the Iranian nuclear power programme is a case of special prevention. Economic, financial/

technical, and political efforts can be particularly effective when dealing with security threats such as organised crime, narcotics trafficking, environmental problems (including nuclear safety), migratory pressures, and low-level ethnic conflicts. Indirectly, they may also help to contain the proliferation of weapons of mass destruction (WMD) and the activities of international terrorist organisations. When compared with crisis management situations, conflict prevention measures appear generally mundane, less dramatic and often medium to long-term oriented. Moreover, it is not always easy to separate conflict prevention measures from other EU actions. In other words, there is a question as to whether prevention measures are classified as such to deal with the problems cited or whether conflict prevention is a by-product of something else that the EU does.

This chapter explores the responsibilities assumed by the EU and the resources it possesses to implement conflict prevention measures. Two important questions are addressed: In which aspects of conflict prevention does the EU excel? Where does it fall short? In other words, we undertake the task of assessing the EU's 'coping capacity'. A broad spectrum of conflict prevention policies and instruments are considered, including aid, humanitarian assistance, trade, democratisation measures, association agreements and political dialogue. Given that the EU performs an increasing role in its neighbourhood through the development of sustainable, effective and efficient statehood activities (Maull, 2005) and assigns importance to developing a prosperous and peaceful periphery, special attention is devoted to the European Neighbourhood Policy (ENP). One of the points of analysis will be whether the ENP contains an inclusive strategy that allows the EU to perform effectively. As the ENP is an integral component of the security strategy articulated in the ESS, a review of some of the key characteristics of this strategy will also be made. The findings will be drawn from primarily textual analysis and qualitative assessment of key documents and the behaviour and rhetoric of the EU.

The chapter proceeds in a stepwise fashion. Firstly, the internal rationale for the EU as a security actor is explored, together with an examination of the goals, principles, norms and rules in the field of conflict prevention. The second task entails the presentation of the various treaty provisions, mode of decision-making, and financial arrangements that demarcate EU competencies in the policy area of conflict prevention. Thirdly, we detail the specific action and programmes undertaken by the EU as well as the resources expended in the field of conflict prevention the previous decade. The chapter concludes with an assessment of the EU's effectiveness as a security actor in the field of conflict prevention. This will be followed with a summary of the findings.

Rationale, goals, principles and rules in the governing of conflict prevention

Rationale

The need for EU action in the field of conflict prevention is tied up with the rationale of the EU as a security actor. The adoption of an EU collective security agenda can be attributed to such factors as the evolution of the EU as a political actor, the emergence of an EU identity and the inability of single countries to tackle today's complex security problems on their own, both in the immediate neighbourhood and further afield. The latter three factors appear particularly relevant as rationales for EU action and will be briefly described. In order to secure itself against the unexpected consequences that EU policies and actions would generate, the EU matured into a security actor. Consequently, as a result of adopting policies aimed at the free movement of labour capital, goods and services as well as a borderless political organisation within a defined territory, the EU automatically relocated its focus from the purely economic to a security agenda which required joint action, in order to accommodate an internally unrestricted area from external security threats and concerns. Expressions of this can be found in the strategic importance which the Feira European Council of June 2000 attributed to the Mediterranean region, namely, that a 'prosperous, democratic stable and secure region, with an open perspective towards Europe, is in the best interest of the EU and Europe as a whole'.[4] Additionally, the EU's economic[5] and financial strength animated a sense of obligation to respond to conflicts in its neighbourhood and to sharing 'responsibility for global security' (Solana, 2003a: 1). Hence, the evolution of the EU as a political actor offers a rationale for the establishment of the EU as a security actor.

A further rationale for the emergence of the EU as a security actor that engages in collective action can be traced back to the weak existence of an EU identity which clearly delimits the EU from other security actors. As such, in its discourse concerning security, the EU often refers to itself against others, for example, 'beyond the EU's borders, enlargement will change the shape of the EU's political and economic relations with other parts of the world' (ESS: 3). Hence, the EU clearly demarcates its territorial existence from other geographical spaces and areas by stating that the 'EU's political and economic relations' will be altered, thereby implying that an EU identity exists to a certain extent. Additionally, the EU considers itself a collective of 'European countries . . . committed to dealing peacefully with disputes and to cooperating through common institutions' (Solana, 2003a: 1). Subsequently, the EU clearly conceives of itself as an organism in which the peaceful resolution of disputes and cooperation with others via institutions delimits and differentiates the EU from other organisms, organisations and states. Hence, in the ESS, the constant use of the word 'we' peppers the strategy during the presentation of 'policy implications for Europe' (Solana, 2003a). In order for a 'we' to exist, a counter-balancing and 'other' group must exist. Consequently, Solana (2003a: 13) asserts that 'the point of Common Foreign and Security Policy (CFSP) and European Security and Defence Policy (ESDP) is that we are stronger when we act together', perfectly illustrating that the EU evolved into a collective unit in which a clearly delineated and discernible 'we' exists in comparison to other actors which affect and represent the Union's 'partners' and 'neighbours'.

While the aforementioned are rationales for the emergence of the EU as a security actor as well as rationale for joint action, another explanation centres upon the EU existing as the only actor that can achieve a particular security goal. Essentially, the EU recognises that 'no single country is able to tackle today's complex problems on its own' and as such engages in collective action (Solana, 2003a: 1). Due to each member state's strength, position in the international order, and military capabilities as well as the collective clout and reputation of the EU, the Union emerges as an actor capable of achieving a security goal that individual states and other international and regional organisations could not attain. Consequently, in order to combat security threats emanating from unstable neighbouring states, terrorism, organised crime, failing states and the proliferation of WMD (ESS; Solana, 2003a), the EU enrolled in certain collective security initiatives. As such, the Union freely and specifically recognises that 'problems are rarely solved on a single country basis, or without regional support' (Solana, 2003a: 13). Subsequently, a rationale for the emergence of the EU as a security actor centres upon its role as the only actor capable of achieving a collective security goal.

Hence, the security problems identified in the ENP and the ESS emerge as primarily collective goods in which the member states of the EU must cooperate as a collective. Essentially, the ENP is a primarily pure collective good in that the funding of the policy, the overall ambit, and the basis for the policy – for example, existing Association Agreements (AA) and Partnership and Cooperation Agreements (PCA) – require and subside in Community[6] initiatives and frameworks. In other words, individual member states and national governments work within the framework of existing EU agreements in order to accomplish such objectives. Individual member states could never offer or even suggest such an entrance into the single market without the cooperation and coordination of the other member states. Similar characteristics can be attributed to the ESS which proffers a framework in which the EU and its member states formulate the collective's foreign and security policies. However, at the same time, the ESS also acts as an impure collective good in that the opaqueness and the imprecise nature of the strategy allow member states to incorporate and behave in a manner according to their own national needs.[7] In other words, due to the fact that the ESS does not contain or incorporate any particular policies into the strategy that requires joint action but rather exists to identify the security threats facing the EU today which may require joint action as well as the EU's 'strategic objectives', the ESS permits member states to advance initiatives which promote the national security objectives of individual member states, such as the UK in relations with the US. Consequently, the ESS emerges as both a pure and impure collective good.

Goals and principles

Although the EU has pursued conflict prevention objectives over several decades, developments since the 1990s are particularly noteworthy. Among these is the Commission's Communication on conflict prevention in 1996, which introduced the concept of structural stability for development policy.[8] Further steps on conflict prevention measures were taken at the Feira European Council of 2000, which emphasised the development of capacity to deploy member states' resources in the fields of police, rule of law, civil protection and public administration. The Communication of the Commission (April 2001) identified a number of factors that aggravate conflict, or can be seen as 'root causes' of violent conflict, such as poverty, economic stagnation, uneven distribution of resources, weak social structures, undemocratic governance, systematic discrimination, oppression of the rights of minorities, destabilising effects of refugee flows, ethnic antagonisms, religious and cultural intolerance, social injustice and the proliferation of WMD and small arms. The recommendations for specific actions advanced in this document were further developed at the Göteborg European Council of 2001, which adopted a Programme for the Prevention of Conflicts and called for the identification of priority areas and regions at the outset of each EU Presidency. The ESS of December 2003 argues for an integrated approach to conflict prevention and crisis management, as well as to other security threats (terrorism, WMD, regional conflicts, state failure and organised crime) and calls for a mixture of both civilian and military instruments. In line with the objectives of the ESS, a new framework for conflict prevention, more geared to the European region, was adopted with the ENP in 2004. Finally, the so-called European Consensus on Development (2005) by the Council, the EP and the Commission, develops comprehensive plans for countries where there is a significant danger of conflict.

For the purpose of this chapter three main policy areas will be examined through which EU conflict prevention measures are pursued: regional integration policy, development and cooperation policy and related issues, and special policy initiatives for specific purposes, mostly of crisis management kind. Although there is some overlap between these three areas, there are a number of reasons for this breakdown that go beyond a mere analytical justification. As stated by the Commission, 'regional integration remains key to overall conflict prevention in potentially unstable regions'.[9] It involves EU enlargement strategies, the ENP, and support for regional integration efforts through, for example, association and trade agreements in various parts of the globe. With regard to EU development policy, there is, according to Commissioner Benita Ferrero-Waldner (2005) 'an emerging consensus that development and security are interlinked'. Development policy and other cooperation programmes are identified by the Commission as providing 'the most powerful instruments at the Community's disposal for treating the root cause of conflict'.[10] Although a number of crosscutting issues, such as drugs, small arms, natural resources, environmental degradation, population flow and human trafficking appear both in regional policy and in development and cooperation policy, they will be primarily dealt with in the latter policy sector. Special policy initiatives, the third policy category, include humanitarian and emergency assistance, crisis management situations (with the emphasis on civilian rather than military tools) and issue-specific instances, like the EU attempt to seek a solution to the Iran dispute over the development of nuclear energy/weapons. While being fully prepared to engage in all these policy instances, either with direct measures, or through the insistence of reform conditions, the Commission also highlights the need for cooperation with international partners and the need for coordination of responses to pre-crisis situations. An examination of the three different policy components will help to determine the areas where the EU either does well or fails in the pursuit of conflict prevention. Details of the respective three policy sectors will be provided in the following.

Mobilisation through regional organisations

Within Europe   Two considerations have guided EU policy towards its European neighbours. Firstly, the decision to grant membership to European states has helped to create a widening area of freedom, democracy and stability in Europe. The by-products of this have been reduced border disputes and nationalist tensions, the integration of minorities into the civil structure of societies, a boost to economic development, and a consolidation of the overall reform process in the accession countries. Secondly, there are limits to the EU capacity to absorb new members, coupled with relatively weak social, economic and political development of would-be member states from the European periphery. Yet, in order to protect the porous borders of the EU and to safeguard the gains of the internal market, the EU needs to engage its neighbours with sufficient incentives for cooperation shy of actual membership. The substitute for membership has been the EU's ENP that seeks to develop a zone of prosperity and a friendly neighbourhood – a 'ring of friends' – with whom the EU enjoys close, peaceful and cooperative relations.[11] As inducement for cooperation, the EU offers neighbouring states 'preferential trading relationships', access to the Internal Market programme, cooperation in cross-border security measures,[12] and new sources of financing. Furthermore, the EU supports the establishment of a Euro-Med free trade area by 2010, and seeks to facilitate the Middle East peace process.[13] EU pledges of economic and financial assistance are linked (principle of conditionality) to the neighbouring states' demonstrations of 'shared values and effective implementation of political, economic and institutional reforms, including aligning legislation with the *acquis*'.[14] The EU retains the right to freeze assistance or slow down the ENP implementation phase. Overall, the ENP contains provisions on 'democracy, pluralism, respect for human rights, civil liberties, the rule of law and core labour standards'.[15] However, the ENP also manifests a certain amount of tension between its regional or multilateral aims, for example, with regard to the Euro-Mediterranean Free Trade Area and its bi-lateral emphasis (a point which will be covered more fully in the assessment section below).

Outside Europe   In line with its own experience of regional integration, the EU seeks to supports common regional structures elsewhere such as the Association for Southeast Asian Nations (ASEAN), the Gulf Cooperation Council (GCC) and the Andean Community.[16] With some of these regional entities, Association Agreements (AA) and Economic Partnership Agreements (EPA) exist and regular meetings at either the level of summits, foreign ministers or senior EU officials take place. The EU interjects the inter-regional links with programmes designed to alleviate regional specific problems. For example, in the Asian region the EU supports the rebuilding of Afghanistan, assists the establishment of democratic governments in Cambodia and East Timor, mediates in Aceh, and seeks a solution to the Korean Peninsula problem. In the case of

Africa, particularly the Great Lakes region, EU support is given to regional organisations with a clear conflict prevention mandate, such as the Economic Community of West African States (ECOWAS) and the African Union (AU). Similarly, the EU has supported Mercosur's consolidation of democracy and the rule of law, as well as confidence-building measures in the field of defence. Links with the GCC were established in part to safeguard oil supplies and in part to assist the 'EU's policy in the Arab–Israeli conflict and to help bridge tensions between the EU and such other key actors in the region as Libya, Iraq and Iran' (Alecu de Flers and Regelsberger, 2005: 329). Most of the established links contain a combination of political, economic and cultural measures. Since 9/11 the dialogue has been extended to include the fight against international terrorism. This is particularly noticeable in the Asia–Europe Meetings (ASEM) and in links with the South Asian Association for Regional Cooperation (SAARC). In relations between the EU and regional groupings in Central and Latin America the dialogue has been extended to the fight against traffic in drugs and crime (H. Smith, 1998: 161). While inter-regional cooperation has enabled the EU to contribute towards greater stability, and the creation of zones of democracy, in many areas of the world, (M. Smith, 2005: 173) it is less suited to conduct crisis management operations in concrete situations (Alecu de Flers and Regelsberger, 2005: 338). Before turning to the more specific cases of crisis management operations, a brief examination of EU development and cooperation policy will be made.

Development policy goals

Since 1996,[17] the Commission has stressed the need for an integrated approach on its development and cooperation policy which puts the emphasis on sustainable economic development, democracy, the rule of law and respect for human rights, viable political structures and healthy environment and social conditions, with the capacity to manage change without resort to conflict. The link between economic development and conflict prevention is reinforced in the so-called EU Consensus document on development.[18] Besides making conflict prevention and resolution an important ingredient of EU development, the EU also introduces motives into its development policy that are closer to home, such as controlling migration, refugee and human trafficking flows into the EU. Beneficiary countries of EU economic and financial assistance are asked to ratify and implement a certain number of international conventions on sustainable development and good governance.[19]

For more than thirty years the EU has been linked by special economic treaties with, by now, over seventy developing countries, known collectively as the African, Caribbean and Pacific (ACP) states. This link, fostered through a number of successive conventions under the name of Lomé and Cotonou, represents the most important economic cooperation agreement between industrialised and developing countries in the world. Its aim is 'to promote and expedite the economic, cultural and social development of the ACP states, and to consolidate and diversify their relations in a spirit of solidarity and mutual interest'. This aim is to be pursued notably by: privileged commercial relations, for example, free access for ACP products to the EU market; commodity export compensation for falls in export earnings by the ACP countries via the systems of Stabex, Sysmin and Flex; and financial aid. Subsequent conventions have sought to strengthen the political dialogue and reinforce commitments to human rights and democracy.

Most of the identified aims of EU development policy are pursued in long-term programmes, which are complemented by sectoral programmes and emergency assistance. Sectoral programmes involve crosscutting issues, such as drugs, mines, natural resources and immigration. For example, with regard to drugs, the Feira European Council introduced an action plan for 2000–2004, with the aim to impede the two main drug routes into the EU via the Balkans and Latin America. Subsequently, a comprehensive Action Programme to combat drug trafficking was adopted with twenty-nine Caribbean countries and entities. In an effort to alleviate the illegal trade of diamonds, the EU joined the Kimberley Process. This international trade regime, which began in 2000, aims at eliminating 'conflict diamonds' from the legitimate diamond trade. Similar aims are stipulated in the EU Action Plan for Forests Law Enforcement, Governance and Trade (FLEGT), which, through a licensing scheme, seeks to ensure that only legal timber enters the EU. Programmes dealing with the management of and access to natural resources involving water management and environmental cooperation programmes are also covered. The main objective of the EU's policy in the area of anti-personnel landmines is to assist countries that suffer from the presence of landmines and unexploded ordnances and to restore the conditions necessary for the security of their populations and their economic and social development.[20] Furthermore, the EU seeks to foster links between migration and development, which is the aim of the AENEAS Programme. Among its aims are: promoting well-managed labour migration; fighting illegal migration and facilitating the re-admission of irregular immigrants; protecting migrants against exploitation and exclusion; and promoting asylum and international protection.[21] Another goal of the EU has been to strengthen the control of its arms exports, with the aim of avoiding

Table 2.1 Types of policies, instruments, monitoring tools and financial means of EU conflict prevention

Main policy	Main instruments	Main complement. tools	Main monitoring tools	Main funding means	Countries involved
EU membership	Euro agreements, acquis–Neg. APA[a]	Political dialogue (PD)	Annual reports	PHARE EBRD, EIB SAPARD ISPA	2004 new EU members Bulgaria and Romania
				TAI[b]	Turkey
	SAP[c] SAA	PD	SAR[d]	CARDS	Six western Balkans
ENP	Existing PCA/AA[e], plus Action Plans	PD Internal market access	CSP and RSP[f] Commission mid-term reports	TACIS MEDA ENPI from 2007	16 neighbouring countries
Development and cooperation	PSA[g] – Lomé/ Cotonou	PD Trade privileges	CSP	EDF	79 African, Caribbean and Pacific countries
	AA • ASEAN	PD	RSP	ALA	7 SE Asian nations
	• Chile/ Mexico	Free trade agreement	CSP	ALA	Chile and Mexico
	CA[h] • Mercosur	Free trade area PD	RSP	ALA	Argentina, Brazil, Paraguay, Uruguay
	• Andean Community	PD	RSP	ALA	Five Andean countries
	• Central America	PD	RSP	ALA	Six CA countries
	EPA[i] • Gulf Coop. Council	Trade PD	SPMME[j]		Seven Gulf countries

Notes:

a APA = Association Partnership Agreements.

b From 2007 the new instrument for pre-accession (IPA) will replace the 2000–2006 pre-accession instruments (PHARE), Instrument for Structural Policies for Pre-accession (ISPA), Special Accession Programme for Agriculture and Rural Development (SAPARD), the Turkish pre-accession instrument (TAI), and the Community Assistance for Reconstruction, Development and Stabilisation (CARDS).

c The SAP, SAA and CARDS entries are instruments of EU Assurance Policy, and are only mentioned for the purpose of comparison here. They are treated more fully in Chapter 3.

d SAR = Stability and Association Report.

e PCA = Partner and Cooperation Agreements; AA = Association Agreements.

f CSP = Country Strategy Papers; RSP = Regional Strategy Papers.

g PSA = Partnership Agreements.

h CA = Cooperation Agreements.

i EPA = Economic Partnership Agreements.

j SPMME = Strategic Partnership for the Mediterranean and the Middle East.

EU-manufactured weaponry being used against civilian populations or to aggravate existing tensions or conflicts in developing countries, and to limit the uncontrolled proliferation of small arms and light weapons.[22] The ESS acknowledges the relationship between international diseases, such as AIDS, tuberculosis and malaria, and some of the key threats such as regional stability and state failure. As part of its new policy framework entitled 'A Coherent European Policy Framework for external action to confront HIV/Aids, Malaria and Tuberculosis', introduced in 2004, the EU links with and contributes to the Global Fund to Combat AIDS, Tuberculosis and Malaria. The main incentive structures and instruments used in the pursuit of conflict prevention in both regional integration efforts and development policy are highlighted in Table 2.1. Humanitarian assistance, though related to aid assistance, and sometimes used in a complementary fashion, can be seen primarily as an emergency fund, and will be treated in the following section on specific policy initiatives.

Specific policy initiatives/crisis management

The ESS calls for 'early, rapid and, when necessary robust intervention' and is willing to support 'preventive engagement that could avoid more serious problems in the future'.[23] Besides recognising the importance of political, diplomatic and economic pressures, it also advocates greater use of coercive rather than persuasive means to encourage better governance. In line with this ESS emphasis, this section will briefly examine EU crisis management goals, as they relate to civilian policy measures, such as those advanced in the Civilian Headline Goal for 2008,[24] emergency humanitarian assistance, and mediation exercises in conflict situations.

EU Civilian Crisis Management measures have been developed in four priority areas: police rule, rule of law, civilian administration and civil protection. To carry out some of these tasks, France, Italy, the Netherlands, Portugal and Spain have committed themselves in 2004 to the European Gendarmerie Force (EGF). The force will be about 3,000 strong, with a rapid version element of approximately 800 gendarmes, and will have an initial reaction capability of thirty days. The EGF is first and foremost put at the service of the European Union, then at the disposal of international organisations (UNO, NATO, OSCE), or *ad hoc* coalitions. It is meant as an integrated police tool, comprising police duties as a whole, and gathering information on all relating missions, such as maintaining public order, public safety, detective police, and intelligence research and work. As a transition tool for crisis handling, the EGF will be fit to carry out all its missions, under military command, in the wake of a power device in a high intensity conflict, or under civilian authority for the establishment of a democratic regime.[25]

Furthermore, a European Agency for the Management of Operational Cooperation at the External Borders (FRONTEX) of the member states of the European Union was established through Council Regulation (EC) 2007/2004/ (26.10.2004, *OJ L* 349/25.11.2004). Among the aims of FRONTEX are to coordinate operational cooperation between member states in the field of management of external borders, to assist member states in the training of national border guards, and to carry out risk analyses. It liaises closely with other Community and EU partners responsible for the security of the external borders, such as the European Police Force, European Police College and the European Anti-Fraud Office (EUROPOL, CEPOL and OLAF), in order to promote overall coherency.[26]

The EU also undertakes various mediation exercises in situations of conflict. In some instances the EU acts collectively and autonomously, for example, the offer to act as 'third-party mechanism' in any future negotiation and talks between the Israel and the Palestinian Authority.[27] A second form is when individual member states act on behalf of the EU in crisis management situations, such as the EU-3 in Iran. Mediation efforts undertaken by the High Representative of CFSP, Javier Solana, such as in Macedonia in 2001 and in the Ukraine in 2004, represent yet another example. Finally, the EU often links with UN, OSCE or NATO efforts to resolve potential conflict or actual conflict situations. Some of these exercises are complemented by EU humanitarian assistance, in the shape of the European Community Humanitarian Aid Office (ECHO) Programme, or exploratory or assistance missions (rule of law, police missions, etc.), assisted by the crisis management facilities known as the Rapid Reaction Mechanism (RRM), and the European Initiative for Democracy and Human Rights (EIDHR). These mechanisms will be further described below.

When comparing the EU conflict prevention goals in the three areas under consideration, the most specific or purposive aims and principles are provided by the ENP and to a considerable extent by the development and cooperation policy. This is evident in the extent to which conditionality factors are stipulated, such as targets and policy reform requirements. Specific policy instances or crisis management goals do not manifest this degree of specificity, which is perhaps not surprising given the nature of the tasks involved. However, even here the five security threats identified in the ESS provide important guiding principles. Implementing these goals requires comprehensive and effective institutional and financial facilities.

Institutional and financial arrangements for conflict prevention

How are the conflict prevention goals translated into action and successful outcomes, especially in those areas of particular concern to the EU: peace and stability in the European geographic region, the elimination of root causes of violent conflict, and the successful handling of crisis management situations? Of importance in this regard is the method of decision-making to be adopted, that is, Community or CFSP, the selection of instruments, such as Association Agreements, and the amount of finance allocated. The Community method involves the Council of Ministers, the European Commission, the European Parliament and the Court of Justice, and allows for qualified majority decision-making in the Council of Ministers. It prevails in such areas as trade, economic incentives, humanitarian emergencies, rehabilitation and institution building, and is mostly based on decisions taken by qualified majority. By contrast, the key instruments of CFSP, as derived both from the Treaty on European Union (TEU) and the Amsterdam Treaty consist of general guidelines, common strategies,[28] joint actions and common positions. With regard to conflict prevention measures, Article 11 of the TEU is particularly revealing, in seeking to preserve peace and strengthen international security, to promote international cooperation, and to develop democracy and the rule of law, including human rights. Overlap can be noticed in some instruments, such as the ESS, which incorporates and pervades all three pillars. The security issues contained in the ESS centre upon traditional territorial security concerns such as proliferation and territorial conflicts (CFSP), terrorism and organised crimes (Justice and Home Affairs: JHA), and the maintenance and promotion of international law (Community pillars). CFSP decisions are taken either by the General Affairs Council or the European Council and are mostly subject to unanimity rule. (For further clarifications of the different competencies and financial arrangements assigned to the European Community and to CFSP, see Table 2.2). There is a symbiotic relationship between the political initiatives taken by the EU under CFSP/ESDP and the assistance delivered by the Community, with the first involving declarations, démarches, joint actions and sanctions, and the second economic cooperation and trade policy instruments, humanitarian aid, social and environmental policies, and diplomatic instruments in support of long-term strategies of the Union. The latter may take the form of bilateral EU agreements, or mixed agreements involving the Community and its member states, with the range of agreements reflecting differing degrees of political, trade and cooperation assistance. In general, the greater the level of political cooperation foreseen, the more detailed the political conditionalities and the more explicit the sanctions.

Country and Regional Strategy Papers are among the main tools used by the Commission to assess risk factors of violent conflict. These papers seek to explore issues such as the control of the security forces and the ethnic composition of the government for ethnically divided countries. Together with the Conflict Prevention Guidelines, these papers provide information on how to integrate a conflict perspective and design new programmes for conflict prevention. The Commission is supported by Conflict Prevention Partnership (CPP) headed by the International Crisis Group (ICG), and liaises with NGOs working in conflict prevention, such as International Alert and the European Policy Centre (EPC).

In budgetary terms, there are three possible categories of conflict prevention or crisis management operations:

1   Operations under a Community instrument, which are financed under the appropriate budget line. Examples include humanitarian aid, reconstruction, de-mining, consolidation of democracy, and institution building.
2   CFSP operations not having military or defence implications that are financed under the CFSP budget line (Article 28). These involve Joint Actions and include issues such as non-proliferation, disarmament, security monitoring, security support for peace processes and stabilisation efforts, projects to combat terrorism, political facilitation and tasks undertaken by Special Representatives of the EU as well as related preparatory fact-finding missions.

Table 2.2 Financing of crisis management operations

	Type of action		
Crisis management operations[a]	*Civilian operations*: e.g. as humanitarian aid, food aid, securing the livelihoods and safety of refugees, civilian emergency assistance rehabilitation, reconstruction, infrastructure development, demining, economic aid, consolidation of democracy and the rule of law, institution building, human rights	*Civilian Petersberg tasks, which are not covered by Community Competence*:[b] e.g. non-proliferation, disarmament, security monitoring, certain executive police missions, including assignments to substitute for local police, and fact-finding missions preceding and envisaged operation related thereto	*Military operations*: military Petersberg tasks i.e. peace-keeping tasks and tasks of combat forces in crisis management, including peace-making
Legal base	*1st pillar: Treaty establishing the European Community (TEC)* See relevant Regulations such as Regulation no. 1257/96 (ECHO); Regulation no. 2666/2000 (CARDS); Regulation no. 1080/2000 (UNMIK and OHR), Regulation no. 381/2001 creating the RRM, in particular its annex enlisting 'Geographical' Regulations/Decisions and 'Sectoral' Regulations and Decisions (food aid, reconstruction, NGOs, etc.)	*2nd pillar: Title V (CFSP) of the Treaty on European Union (TEU)* Specific joint action adopted under Article 14 TEU coupled with corresponding financing decision of the Commission	*2nd pillar: Title V (ESPD within CFSP) of the TEU* Specific joint action adopted under Article 14 TEU
Decision-making procedure	Depending on relevant Regulation, if based on Article 179 (ex-Article 130w) TEC qualified majority; if based on Article 308 (ex-Article 235) TEC unanimity; implementation usually conferred on the Commission in accordance with so-called 'comitology' procedures as set up by Decision 1999/468/EC	Depending on Joint Action, generally unanimity following Article 23 (1) TEU, unless taken on basis of a common strategy, then qualified majority following Article 23 (2) first indent TEU	Joint Action and implementing decision always adopted by unanimity following Article 23 (1) and (2)

continued over the page . . .

Table 2.2 continued . . .

	Type of action		
Applicable budget	Budget of the European Communities.	Budget of European Communities, or, exceptionally, operational expenditure may be charged to member states	Outside Budget of EC: operational and administrative[c] expenditure, which is **not** attributable to the European Institutions is charged to the member states

Source: European Commission (2001) 'Communication from the Commission to the Council and the EP: Financing of Civilian Crisis Management Operations', Brussels, 28 November 2001, COM(2001) 647 final.

Notes:
a P.M.: Title VI TEU (JAI) not applicable as only related to police, rule of law etc. action inside Union, no external crisis management, even if executed by member state police forces.
b According to Articles 3 and 47 TEU the financing of civilian crisis management operations through the Community and through CFSP financing are complementary, but they are not substituting each other nor are they interchangeable.
c Administrative expenditure stemming from military operations but attributable to European Institutions to be charged to the Council's section of the budget. (The Commission is not involved in military operations.)

3 ESDP operations having military or defence implications, which fall outside the Community budget. Member states finance such operations based on GNP scale unless the member state abstained during the initial vote authorising Community action.

The Europe-Aid Cooperation Office, established by the Commission in 2001, has the task to implement the external aid instruments of the European Commission that are funded by the European Community budget and the European Development Fund. While it does not deal with pre-accession programmes, such as Poland and Hungary Action for Restructuring the Economy (PHARE), humanitarian activities, CFSP or the RRM, it manages two of the main funding mechanisms of the ENP, to be treated in the following section, which will detail institutional provisions relating to the three identified areas of EU conflict prevention concern.

Institutional and financial arrangements for the ENP
In terms of institutional innovations and refinements, the ENP primarily subsists and functions as an extension of the existing institutional components of the Association Agreements (AA) and Partnership and

Cooperation Agreements PCA) which form the foundation of the ENP. Hence, in the ENP, '[p]rogress in meeting agreed priorities will be monitored in the bodies established by the PCAs or AA', and all Neighbourhood Policy Action Plans shall be 'approved by the respective Cooperation or Association Council'.[29] The Action Plans will regulate the relations between the EU and each neighbour, creating the basis for EU economic aid and cooperation, and provide an indication of the way conflict prevention aims are mainstreamed.[30] They include legally binding commitments on human rights. The Country Reports give a factual analysis of political economic and institutional reforms in the country concerned, with a particular focus on areas that would form the basis of any future Action Plans. They are meant to assess potential conflict situations according to established potential indicators. Essentially, when a state signs an AA or a PCA the Union creates two institutions in order to implement the AA or the PCA.[31] Hence, as regards AAs, the Union mandates the creation of an Association Council (Ministerial) and Association Committee (Senior Official level). In reference to PCAs, the Union creates a Ministerial Cooperation Council and a Senior Official level Cooperation Committee. However, due to the fact that both the councils and committees existed prior to the adoption of the ENP and the Action Plans, this does not mark an institutional innovation but, rather, an institutional refinement. While it may appear that the ENP therefore proffers no institutional innovations, it actually includes one in the form of the European Neighbourhood Policy Instrument (ENPI). Essentially, the ENPI 'will complement assistance provided under the existing financial instruments or their successors (EC Assistance Programme for Mediterranean Countries: MEDA; Technical Assistance to the Commonwealth of Independent States: TACIS; European Initiative for Democracy and Human Rights: EIDHR), and will focus specifically on cross-border cooperation and related activities'.[32] Once Action Plans are approved, each country presents three-monthly reports on their implementation. These are examined by sub-committees for each country, with the participation of the European Parliament. The Commission prepares mid-term reports on any progress achieved and sets the basis for adapting and reviewing the Action Plan.

While the ENP incorporates and involves all three pillars that define the structure of the EU, different pillars receive divergent levels of concentration. The Community pillar, which involves the incorporation of democratic ideals, receives the primary focus despite the increasing saliency of security concerns emanating from border control or lack thereof (e.g., the problem surrounding Transdniestria which involves Moldova and the Ukraine) (Gonzales, 2004).

The two financial instruments of ENP are TACIS and MEDA. Since 1991, TACIS provides grant-financed technical assistance to twelve countries of Eastern Europe and Central Asia.[33] TACIS supports institutional legal and administrative reform, economic and social development, infrastructure development, environmental protection, and nuclear safety. Since 1995, MEDA offers technical and financial support measures to six Mediterranean countries and the Palestinian Authority in the West Bank and the Gaza Strip. From 2007, TACIS and MEDA will be unified in the newly established ENPI. This will allow greater concentration of financial efforts under the ENP and follows a similar pattern of concentration as witnessed with the CARDS programme for the western Balkan. Having examined the institutional and financial instruments of the ENP, attention will now turn to development and cooperation policy.

Institutional and financial arrangements in development and cooperation policy

Development and cooperation policy is a shared competence between the European Community (Articles 177 to 181) and the member states. The principles of Article 11 of the Cotonou Partnership Agreement and the political dialogue of its article 8 offer scope for addressing conflict prevention in ACP countries. Since the mid-1990s, the European Community has included more or less systematically a so-called democracy and human rights clause in its bilateral trade cooperation agreements with third countries and in association agreements such as the Cotonou convention (Hänggi and Tanner, 2005: 29). Under these provisions it has suspended trade and aid relations with, for example, Lesotho in 1994, Niger and Sierra Leone in 1996, and Cameroon in 1997 (Youngs, 2001). In the preparation and assessment of the Community's development policy, the Country and Regional Strategy Papers represent important instruments. They include a checklist for potential conflict situations, which, in countries found to have a high conflict potential, leads to the adoption of conflict prevention measures.[34] Increasingly, in the EU's insistence on performance indicators, conditionality is evolving towards the concept of a 'contract' based on negotiated mutual commitments formulated in terms of results.[35] Political dialogue is another monitoring measure, which seeks to ensure that the preventive dimension is upheld and that the fight against corruption, illegal migration and the trafficking of human beings is being addressed.[36]

The EDF is the main instrument for Community aid, going as it does to the ACP countries, but it does not come under the general Community budget, as it is funded by member states, covered by unique financial rules, and managed by a specific committee.

Institutional and financial arrangements for specific crisis management tasks

With regard to reacting quickly to nascent conflicts or crisis management situations, a number of civilian instruments have been introduced, stretching from a policy planning and early warning unit to the RRM, political dialogue, special representatives, and sanctions. The policy planning and early warning unit is assigned to the High Representative of the CFSP. A committee for civilian aspects of crisis management has been created in order to improve relations between the military and the civilian components, including instruments from the first pillar.[37] A further task of coordination is performed by the European Anti-terrorism Coordinator.

The RRM was established in 2001[38] to provide rapid financing for crisis management. This aid takes the form of grants, encompasses all of the activities not covered by the ECHO and is designed to enhance the EU's civilian capacity to intervene quickly and effectively in crisis situations in third countries. The RRM has flexibility in types of assistance: assessment of possible Community response to a crisis; preventive action during emergency crises; acute crisis management; post-conflict reconciliation; and post-crisis reconstruction (Hänggi and Tanner, 2005: 35). Another crisis management facility is the EIDHR,[39] which supports human rights, democratisation and conflict prevention activities (to be carried out primarily in partnership with NGOs and international organisations). The EIDHR budget was €125 million in 2004. In addition to the RRM and the EIDHR, some EU specialised sectoral instruments provide emergency support to politically unstable environments, which can be complemented by exceptional financial assistance. The latter are subject to an accelerated decision-making procedure, based on article 179 of the European Community for developing countries (Article 181a EC for non-developing countries). European Community humanitarian assistance, mostly carried out by ECHO, is delivered solely on the basis of need, and cannot be subsumed to the political logic of crisis management. Nonetheless, it is an important element of the overall package of assistance delivered by the Community in a crisis management situation.[40] The legal basis for humanitarian aid is Council Regulation (EC) no. 1257/96; and Chapter 6 of the Cotnonou agreement.

Political dialogue and the use of Special Representatives are further important instruments in conflict prevention tasks, especially when advanced under CFSP. Political dialogue is build into the framework of Community and mixed agreements with third countries, such as Article 96 of the Cotonou Agreement. In the case of the CFSP, it is based on Article 18 and 26 of the TEU, and its objectives are: mediation,

Table 2.3 Possible crisis actions and related EC instruments

Regulation / Action	ECHO	Food security	Uprooted people	Rehabilitation	NGO co-financing	EIDHR	Mine action	Civil protection	MEDA	TACIS	CARDS	ALA	EDF	RRM
Eligible regions	All	All	Asia, Latin America	All except SE Europe	All developing	All	All	All	Mediterranean	E Europe Central Asia	SE Europe	Asia, Latin America	Africa, Pacific Caribbean	All
Humanitarian aid	✓	✓	✓					✓					✓	(✓)
Food aid	✓	✓	✓										✓	✓
Food security		✓											✓	✓
Securing the livelihoods and safety of refugees/ refugee return	✓		✓	✓	(✓)	(✓)		✓	✓			✓	✓	✓
Civilian emergency assistance			✓	✓				✓				✓	✓	✓
Mine action	✓			(✓)			✓	✓			✓	✓	✓	✓
Rehabilitation			✓								✓	✓	✓	✓
Reconstruction				✓							✓	✓	✓	✓
Infrastructure development									✓	(✓)	✓		✓	✓
Economic development									✓	✓	✓	✓	✓	✓
Budgetary support									✓		✓	✓		
Consolidation of democracy					✓	✓			✓	✓	✓	✓	✓	✓
Rule of law					✓	✓			✓	✓	✓	✓	✓	✓
Institutional, legal and regulatory framework					(✓)	(✓)			✓	✓	✓	✓	✓	✓
Human rights					✓	✓			✓	✓	✓	✓	✓	✓
Elections						✓							✓	✓
Conflict prevention						✓					✓	✓	✓	✓
Customs/border management					✓				✓	✓	✓	✓	✓	✓

Source: http: //europa.eu.int/comm/external_relations/cfsp/doc/cm03.pdf.

arbitration, confidence building, and rallying support for EU positions. CFSP political dialogue is exercised through declarations, démarches, diplomatic contacts by the Presidency, the High Representative of CFSP, Members of the Commission and EU Special Representatives.[41] The EU is able to draw upon the diplomatic resources of member states, as well as the network of 130 European Commission Delegations. It will also be able to draw on the planned EU External Action Service that is intended to reinforce as well as to coordinate the EU external representation. (For more details on possible crisis actions and related EC instruments, some of which were covered under the above sections of ENP and EU development policy, see Table 2.3).

The use of sanctions is deemed yet another instrument in crisis management situations, albeit being of a coercive rather than persuasive nature. Sanctions will generally be imposed after conflicts have broken out or human rights breaches have taken place with the aim of denying a 'target' (i.e., country, party, entity) the means to prolong or escalate the violence. These typically include arms and other war materials, export earnings, foreign capital, other imported goods and technology, or travel facilities. Other types of sanctions such as visa ban or the reduction of diplomatic representation are generally meant to give a strong political signal. The EU applies the following forms of sanctions:

1 suspension of specific sectoral agreements between the Community and third countries (these are usually not formally linked to wider political commitments);
2 interruption of economic and financial relations between the Community and third countries following an UN Security Council resolution;
3 autonomous EU measures of the same kind;
4 other restrictions, coordinated by member states through a CFSP Common Position, and implemented through national measures adopted by member states, for example, flight bans, or restrictions on admission of third country nationals.[42] Common Positions are adopted by unanimity under Article 15 of the TEU. (Further details on CFSP budget and decision-making procedures are also provided in Table 2.6).

Performance

Having examined EU motives, goals and institutional provisions of conflict prevention, it is now time to turn to the aspect of performance and impact. There are some difficulties in establishing a one-to-one comparison between EU conflict prevention action and actual achievements, as there are many intervening factors, such as the conflict prevention activities of other actors (states, international organisations, NGOs, etc.). In the absence of accurate assessment measures, performance indicators will be used in a general sense. This will involve examining the actual implementation of EU programmes, comparing its financial record with that of other actors, assessing the self-appraisal of the EU of its activities, and reviewing secondary sources on the subject. These aims will be pursued in a two-step approach. The first step, to be undertaken in this section, is to attempt a factual or quantitative assessment of the record of accomplishment. The second step will involve a more critical or qualitatively oriented assessment, which will be made in next section. In line with the general policy areas outlined in the section on goals and institutional provisions for conflict prevention, the emphasis will be on the ENP, EU development and cooperation policy, and specific policy initiatives or crisis management situations.

Performance in ENP

By April 2007, twelve of the sixteen ENP countries had final versions of the respective Action Plans. The exceptions were Algeria, Belarus, Libya and Syria. The year 2006 also marked the tenth anniversary of the Barcelona Process, and the establishment of the Euro-Mediterranean Parliamentary Assembly and the Euro-Mediterranean Foundation for the Dialogue of Cultures. A review of the ENP implementation by individual countries and their respective financial contributions is provided in Table 2.4.

Table 2.4 ENP performance

	Political instrument	Financial instrument	Implementation
Algeria	Cooperation Agreement (1979) AA (2005)	1995–1999 MEDA I €164m[a] 2000–2004 MEDA II €232.8m	MEDA evaluation report 2003
Armenia	PCA (1999)[c]	1991–2005 TACIS[b] €88.9m	ENP country report (02/03/2005)
Azerbaijan	PCA (1999)[c]	1991–2005 TACIS €140.2m	ENP country report (02/03/2005)
Belarus	PCA (signed March 1995, not yet in force) Action Programme 2003	1991–2005 TACIS €75.6m	TACIS evaluation report 2006
Egypt	Cooperation Agreement (1976)[c]	1995–1999 MEDA I €686m 2000–2004 MEDA II €353.5m	ENP country report (02/03/2005)

Georgia	PCA (1999)[c]	1991–2005 TACIS €125.96m	ENP country report (02/03/2005)
Israel	AA (2000)[c]	No MEDA direct , payments but involvement in regional programmes and cooperation agreements	ENP country report (12/05/2004)
Jordan	AA (2002)[c]	1995–1999 MEDA I €254m 2000–2004 MEDA II €204.4m	ENP country report (12/05/2004)
Lebanon	AA (2002)[c]	1995–1999 MEDA I €182m 2000–2004 MEDA II €73.7m	Country report (02/03/2005)
Libya	EuroMed: observer status		
Moldova	PCA (1999)[c]	1991–2005 TACIS €154.6m	ENP country report (12/05/2004)
Morocco	AA (2000)[c]	1995–1999 MEDA I €660m 2000–2004 MEDA II €677.1m	ENP country report (12/05/2004)
Syria	Cooperation Agreement (1977) AA (signed 2004, ratification pending)	1995–1999 MEDA I €101m 2000–2004 MEDA II €135.7m	EU–Syria Cooperation annual report 2005
Tunisia	AA (1998)[c]	1995–1999 MEDA I €428m 2000–2004 MEDA II €328.6m	ENP country report (12/05/2004)
Ukraine	PCA (1999)[c]	1991–2005 TACIS €1009m	ENP country report (12/05/2004)
Palestinian Authority	Interim association Agreement (1997)[c]	1995–1999 MEDA I €111m 2000–2004 MEDA II €350.3m	ENP country report (12/05/2004)

Sources:
Europe Aid Cooperation Office, http: //ec.europa.eu/comm/europeaid/projects/med/financial/1995-2004.pdf.
Europe Aid Cooperation Office, http: //ec.europa.eu/comm/europeaid/projects/tacis/financial_en.htm.

Notes:
a MEDA payments have been broken down into MEDA I (1995/1999) and MEDA II (2000/2004). All figures refer to commitments.
b All TACIS data refers to funds committed 1991–2005.
c Countries for which an Action Plan has been adopted and to undergo implementation.

Overall ENP financial commitments for 2000–2006 were €8.49 billion; approximately €1.21 billion per year, with the share of TACIS being €3.14 billion, and that of MEDA representing €5.35 billion.[43] In addition, the EU is the biggest donor to the Palestinian Authority.[44] In the case of MEDA, some funding also goes into regional projects, such as the Israel–Jordan–Palestine regional water management project.

As Table 2.5 indicates, some MEDA recipients receive a greater per capita share of the funds than others. This is particularly the case with the Palestinian Authority and Jordan. Equally, some countries are better in calling up or absorbing the allocated commitments into actual payments, with Jordan doing particularly well (118 per cent rate) and Syria (29 per cent) having the worst conversion record.[45] A more consistent picture emerges with regard to TACIS per capita payments.

Table 2.5 Per capita payments and absorption rates

	Population[a] (m)	Payments[b] (m€)	Payments (€/capita/year)	Absorption capacity (%)[c]
MEDA				
Algeria	32.4	74.7	0.46	32
Egypt	68.7	360.1	1.04	102
Israel	6.8			
Jordan	5.4	241.8	8.9	118
Lebanon	3.4	103.4	6.08	140
Libya	5.7			
Morocco	30.6	443.2	2.89	65
Syria	17.8	39	0.43	29
Tunisia	10	320.7	6.41	98
Palestinian Authority	3.3	327.2	19.83	93
TACIS				
Armenia	3	8.8	0.58	33
Azerbaijan	8.3	20.2	0.48	41
Belarus	9.8	0	0	0
Georgia	4.5	11	0.48	28
Moldova	4.2	8	0.38	18
Ukraine	48	45.5	0.18	19

Sources:
a World Bank, except Libya from www.cia.gov.
b MEDA: EuropeAid Cooperation Office, MEDA financial statistics, http: //ec.europa.eu/comm/europeaid/projects/med/financial/1995-2004.pdf. TACIS: EuropeAid Cooperation Office evaluation report 2006 'Evaluation of Council Regulation 99/2000 (TACIS) and its implementation – ref. 728', vol. 5, p. 101, http: //ec.europa.eu/comm/europeaid/evaluation/document_index/2006/728_docs.htm.
c The formula is: money paid/money allocated × 100.

TACIS and MEDA activities are complemented by other EU funding projects. For example, the EIDHR has sponsored human rights training for military personnel (in the Ukraine) or awareness raising activities aimed at the military and civilians. The Border Management in Central Asia Programme (BOMCA), which is supported by the RRM and TACIS, also contributes to the OSCE Police Assistance Programme in Kyrgyzstan. Furthermore, the EU and its member states contribute to the G8 Global Partnership programme aimed at disarmament, non-proliferation, counter-terrorism and nuclear safety. This programme also runs under the label of Cooperative Threat Reduction (CTR)[46] and has assisted Russia and eligible states of the former Soviet Union. So far the European Commission has contributed €1 billion (mostly through TACIS) and the EU member states have contributed €4.06 billion of the $6.8 billion pledged by the G8 (Lindstrom, 2005: 113). (For a fuller treatment of the CTR see Chapter 4). Moreover, the EU includes non-proliferation clauses in international agreements, and with countries such as Syria, Albania and Tajikistan (Lindstrom, 2005: 75).

There is a debate as to whether financial and technical assistance is sufficient to bring about economic and political reforms in EU neighbouring states in the absence of EU accession prospects (Missiroli, 2004). However, when combined with the Internal Market access and the interaction through political dialogue and other programmes,[47] there seems to be some room for optimism, which to some extent is borne out in the adoption and implementation of Action Plans with these countries. In addition, even without the prospects of EU accession, the magnetic power of Europe remains strong. In Georgia in 2003 and Ukraine in 2004, it could be argued that democratic breakthrough happened because local activists appealed to EU norms and standards, and because they received strong support from the EU and its member states.

Performance in development policy

The problems of translating financial assistance, trade privileges and political dialogue exercises into compliance with human rights, democracy, the rule of law and good governance provisions on the part of developing countries are even more difficult than those encountered under the ENP.[48] Nonetheless, for many observers, aid, trade access and political dialogue for developing countries is perceived to be beneficial (Ferrero-Waldner, 2005; Krasner and Pascual, 2005; for a counter view see Chauvet and Collier, 2004). Moreover, it is not only the amount of aid granted, but also the associated mechanisms, such as the stabilisation features of primary products (Stabex, Sysmin and Flex) within the Cotonou Partnership Agreement, or the link to human rights clauses and to the drug and small arms trade which need to be taken into consideration when assessing the impact of EU development and cooperation policy. A brief elaboration of these points is attempted below.

The EU is the world's largest aid donor, comprising half of the world's official development assistance. The Commission's €6.9 billion in 2004 alone represent approximately 11 per cent of the world total; one-fifth of the Official Development Assistance (ODA) is delivered by the EU and its member states.[49] A large part of EU aid is taken up by the EDF budget for the ACP countries, which amounted to €13.5 billion for the period 2000–2005. The EU seeks to increase its ODA commitment, to reach a collective 0.56 per cent ODA/GNI (Gross National Income) by 2010, which will result in an additional annual €20 billion ODA by 2010.[50] The EU allocates at least 50 per cent of the agreed increase in ODA resources to Africa.[51] Funding goes mostly to civil society actors and NGOs in order to promote the social underpinnings of democracy (Youngs, 2004: 533). With the report in November 2004 on 'advancing coordination harmonisation and alignment', the EU has also made efforts to improve the quality and effectiveness of ODA, by streamlining development assistance at the EU level and calling for a division of labour and complementarity at country level in the context of joint, multi-annual programming based on the partner country's poverty reduction strategies.[52] Although being more indirectly than directly related to development policy, EU humanitarian assistance amounts to €500 million annually, with about one-third going to projects run by the UN humanitarian agencies (Lindstrom, 2005: 88).

The EU scheme of generalised tariff preferences from 2002 to 2005 lists both general arrangements and a number of special incentive arrangements. Under the general arrangements, so-called non-sensitive products imported into the Union from beneficiary developing countries are exempt from customs duties; goods from the textile and clothing sector receive a 20 per cent reduction; and sensitive goods receive a 3.5 per cent reduction The special incentive arrangements relate to the protection of labour rights and the environment, least-developed countries, and the combating of drug production and trafficking. Noteworthy is the 'Everything But Arms' initiative, adopted by Regulation 416/2001, which extends duty-free access without any quantitative restrictions to products originating in the least developed countries, with the exception of arms and ammunition. With regard to the link with drugs, specific arrangements entailing the complete suspension of customs duties applicable to industrial and agricultural products are established for the Andean Pact countries, Central America and Pakistan. These arrangements aim to promote political, economic and social stability in these countries threatened by drug production and trafficking.[53]

The EU strongly endorsed the millennium development goals adopted by the UN in September 2002. It has also supported multilateral efforts to constrain the use and instruments of force through arms control and disarmament initiatives and has provided financial and technical assistance for projects to combat the accumulation and spread of small arms (e.g., in Cambodia, South Africa, Mozambique and Georgia/South Ossetia). It also collaborates with UN High Commission for Refugees (UNHCR) through the Financial and Technical Assistance to Third Countries in the Areas of Migration and Asylum (AENEAS) Programme (2004–2008) for financial and technical assistance to third countries in the area of migration and asylum, including the issue of human trafficking and the High-Level Working Group on Asylum and Migration (HLWG).

European Community cooperation assistance when linked with political incentives can be an important lever of change in third countries to defuse crises, resolve disputes, or safeguard human rights and democratic processes. This is particularly evident in the Cotonou Agreement of 2000 which succeeded Lomé and calls for political dialogue between the parties expressly 'to promote peace and to prevent, manage and resolve violent conflict' (Articles 8 [5] and 11). It was a reaction to the high incidence of political, military and humanitarian crises in ACP countries, and had frustrated much of the development effort made under previously Lomé Convention (Martenczuk, 2000: 466). Moreover, in a number of instances the EU has imposed sanctions (Haiti 2002, after election irregularities), withheld aid from the EDF (Fiji 2000, after the suspension of constitutional rule; and Ivory Coast, regarding human rights violations and violence during elections) and introduced so-called 'smart sanctions' against the Mugabe regime of Zimbabwe.[54]

Democracy and human rights assistance are important ingredients of EU development aid budgets. As noted by Youngs (2003), efforts have been made to invest developmental approaches with genuine political impact and to ensure mutually enhancing linkages between democracy projects and mainstream good governance initiatives. Shortcomings remain, however, both in the conceptualisation of the link between democracy-building and local level social development, and in the more overtly political dimensions of European strategies (Youngs, 2003). It is to these political aspects and crisis management tasks that we will turn next.

Performance in specific policy initiatives
(mostly crisis management situations)

Since 2001, the EU has begun to play a more prominent role in crisis management and the issue of the non-proliferation of WMD. This has meant an increase of so-called 'mediation' efforts to prevent violent conflicts or to arrange ceasefire agreements. In this connection, the use of sanctions as a tool of conflict prevention and crisis management has also become more important. Furthermore, the Community has established competencies and expertise in training, assistance of local management personnel, and local capacity building. This includes police missions, fact-finding missions, and civilian monitoring missions, with the financial backing of the EHDR and the RRM. In the case of the RRM, the main emergency instrument, support has been given to:

- mediation efforts and monitoring of implementation of peace or ceasefire agreements: Liberia, Ivory Coast, Sudan, Indonesia/Aceh, Sri Lanka;
- confidence-building measures: Macedonia, Sri Lanka, Horn of Africa;
- civil society development: Bolivia, Indonesia, Afghanistan;
- emergency electoral support: Georgia, Kyrgyzstan, Ukraine, Chechnya;
- high level policy advice: Afghanistan, Macedonia, Iraq, Lebanon;
- demobilisation and reintegration of combatants: Democratic Republic of Congo, Indonesia/Aceh;
- reform programmes in border management and police in Central Asia, and between the Ukrainian and Moldavian border;
- post-tsunami reconstruction support: Sri Lanka, Maldives, Indonesia.

Moreover, the EU, through ESDP, has undertaken a number of police missions, rule of law missions, monitoring missions and border assistance missions. The specific cases are European Police Mission (EUPM) Bosnia (January 2003); European Union Police Mission in the Former Yugoslav Republic of Macedonia (EUPOL Proxima) (December 2003); EU Rule of Law Mission (EUJUST); Arthemis in Georgia (July 2004); EUPOL Kinshasa (January 2005); EUJUST LEX–EU Integrated Rule of Law Mission for Iraq (March 2005; ESDP monitoring mission in Aceh (September 2005); and the EU Policy Mission in the Palestinian territories (EUPOL–COPPS) (COPPS: Co-ordinating Office for Palestinian Police Support) to monitor the Rafah border control (January 2006). These are not military missions, but rather to assist in local capacity building and involve police reform, judicial reform and integrated border management in post-conflict settings, and in defence reform, such as the restructuring of armed forces. A fuller picture of these civilian oriented missions is provided in Chapter 3.

The EU also established in 2004 a €250 million fund, called the 'Peace Facility', to support African peace-keeping and conflict prevention operations.[55] This Facility helps to support the OAU Mechanism for

Table 2.6 Common foreign and security policy budget (in euros)

Heading	Appropriations 2007		Appropriations 2006		Outturn 2005	
	Commitments	Payments	Commitments	Payments	Commitments	Payments
Monitoring and verification of conflicts and peace processes	21,000,000	16,800,000	17,135,000	9,281,240	12,283,287.75	11,935,063.02
Non-proliferation and disarmament	25,500,000	20,800,000	13,000,000	17,000,000	5,029,000.–	9,143,064.81
Conflict resolution and other stabilisation measures	15,900,000	10,000,000	13,635,000	5,781,240	10,283,287.75	8,010,154.94
Emergency measures	23,900,000	15,000,000	3,000,000	1,000,000	0.–	0.–
Preparatory and follow-up measures	3,200,000	2,600,000	400,000	400,000	212,416.–	270,031.77
EU Special Representatives	14,000,000	11,200,000	7,500,000	7,000,000	9,368,000.–	7,075,158.87
Police missions	55,700,000	44,000,000	47,730,000	20,237,520	35,997,163.50	28,039,948.31
Chapter 19 03 – Total	159,200,000	120,400,000	102,400,000	60,700,000	73,173,155	64,473,421.72

Source: (Preliminary draft budget 2007) http: //europa.eu.int/eur-lex/lex/budget/data/AP2007_VOL4/EN/nmc-titleN188CA/nmc-chapterN19003/index.html.

Conflict Prevention Management and Resolution, the ECOWAS conflict prevention mechanism, the Lusaka Peace Process in the Democratic Republic of Congo, and the Burundi Peace Negotiations. However, as Table 2.6 shows, only a relatively small CSFP budget is available.

In addition to these missions and measures, the EU has imposed a number of sanctions such as the financial sanctions against former Yugoslavia in 1998–2000, Burma/Myanmar[56] and Zimbabwe in 2001. It has also suspended the TACIS programme in Russia in response to events in Chechnya.[57] Whilst doubts can be raised about the usefulness of sanctions, questions may also be posed about the timing of sanctions. EU sanctions have generally been introduced after conflicts have broken out or human rights breaches have taken place with the aim of denying a 'target' (i.e., country, party, entity) the means to prolong or escalate the violence. There is good reason, however, to look at how sanctions could be used preventively to deny a potential belligerent the means to start a conflict. Many export control regimes (targeting atomic energy, missiles, chemical production, small arms etc.) are in effect a form of preventive sanction. Similarly, measures to impede the proliferation of WMD are often linked with sanctions, as will be shown in the case of Iran.

Non-proliferation: the case of Iran   According to the ESS, one of the primary threats to the EU emanates from the proliferation of WMD. Although the EU has made non-proliferation an important element of its various agreements with so-called third countries, the non-proliferation issue surrounding Iran has been seen as a test case of the 'preventive philosophy' advocated in the ESS. In order to ensure the non-proliferation of WMD in Iran in direct relation to the threat identified in the ESS, the United Kingdom (UK), France and Germany (or the EU-3) engaged in negotiations over the cessation of uranium enrichment activities on behalf of the entire EU. [58] In order to secure the acquiescence of the Iranian delegation to such demands, the EU-3 offered Iran 'a vast trade, technology and political cooperation agreement' (Bulletin Quotidien Europe, 2005b). However, Iran continually refused to exchange its ability to enrich uranium for 'civilian' purposes such as nuclear power plants for such an agreement, instead declaring that the 'definitive European position, namely the demand for the definitive suspension of our enrichment activities, is nothing but a dream' (Bulletin Quotidien Europe, 2005c). Consequently, the economic and political incentives offered by the EU emerged as uninfluential in dampening the Iranian resolve. Indeed, such a conclusion became evident in August 2005 when Iran 'rejected a package of aid measures, including an offer of nuclear fuel in exchange for a promise to abandon plans for uranium enrichment' and subsequently 'restarted its Isfahan plant that converts uranium to gas, which is the last step in processing the radioactive ore before it can undergo enrichment' (USA Today, 2005). Essentially, the EU's traditional security strategy of offering economic and political incentives to obtain its security objectives failed. Indeed, previously in the negotiations, the EU obtained Iranian suspension[59] only to find that Iran started the process once talks derailed. Following the election in June 2005 of President Mahmout Ahmadinejad, negotiations have further protracted, to the point that in January 2006, Britain, France and Germany together with other states sent the Iran dossier before the Security Council, with the objective of issuing sanctions against Iran. Ahmadinejad further raised the stakes when he announced in April 2006 that Iran had joined the group of those countries that have nuclear technology, though technology was to be used only for civilian purposes. Further attempts by the US, Russia, China, France, Britain and Germany in June 2006 to persuade Iran to join the talks and reach a compromise[60] were rebuffed by Iran. This resulted in the permanent UNSC members and Germany referring Iran back to the UNSC and the subsequent passing by the UNSC on 31 July of a resolution calling for Iran to suspend uranium enrichment by 31 August. With Iran failing to comply, economic and diplomatic sanctions were subsequently introduced. Hence, despite the efforts and the support of the institutions and member states, the EU and its chosen policy instruments appear to be incapable of dissolving the burgeoning proliferation threat inherent in Iran. In part this was because 'the US and Iran never fully recognised the EU-3 as credible arbiters' (Harnisch and Linden, 2005: 54). Nonetheless, as Harnisch and Linden suggest, the EU-3 provided strong internal policy coherence, strengthened the role of the IAEA as a nuclear watchdog, and acted as 'a diplomatic buffer between diverging forces of the United States and Iran, thereby giving a broadly recognised meditation mission a fair chance to resolve the conflict diplomatically' (Harnisch and Linden, 2005: 53).

Assessment

In order to ascertain the effectiveness of the EU as a security actor, an assessment of the EU's performance as a security actor will be made. This will concentrate on ENP and ESS implementation, that is, coherence and uniformity of application, and on the relevance of the EU's multilateral strategy. Analysing the EU as a security actor according to the ENP and ESS, one should be able to observe whether the EU as an international institution is 'effective to the extent that its operations can be shown to impel actors to behave differently than they would have behaved in the absence of the institution' (Rosenau, 1995: 27). Assessing the ENP will shed light on the EU's conflict prevention record in an area of self-held high priority. It will also enable an assessment on how far EU efforts to 'promote a ring of well governed neighbouring countries' have progressed. As the ENP is an important element of the ESS, a review of this strategy will provide a broader perspective on the EU's capacity for action in conflict prevention. While the ESS guides us to an assessment of the various instruments used in conflict prevention, it also encourages a review of the EU's participation in and commitment to multilateral efforts in the pursuance of conflict prevention. The latter will represent the third component of the assessment exercise.

Assessment of ENP

Two aspects appear of relevance when assessing the ENP: firstly, whether the EU has been able to induce or achieve cooperation with its neighbours in the absence of membership promises, and if so, what degree of cooperation has been reached; secondly, whether the ENP has treated both regions similarly, both in the application of economic and political conditions and with regard to bilateral or multilateral criteria. This issue arises as originally the ENP was intended for the east European countries only, then the Mediterranean ones were added, which resulted in the quarrel as to whether the two entities can be put together at all, and whether there should be one policy for all, given the membership prospective of the east European countries which the Mediterranean ones do not have.

The rhetoric and expectations between the eastern and the southern regions of the ENP differ drastically. Whereas the Mediterranean countries primarily view their relations with the EU as an economic partnership – a view which seems to be shared by the EU – the eastern European nations primarily view their relations with the EU in terms of an economic and political partnership that will, at least in the views of the Ukraine and Georgia, ultimately culminate in membership. In contrast, the Mediterranean nations are less interested in EU membership[61] and focus primarily on economic concerns. Secondly, due to the fact that the foundation of the ENP partners' relations with the EU are the AAs and the PCAs that the partners signed with the EU, differences exist in their relations from the beginning. Essentially, in terms of contractual relations, 'Association Agreements [a]re more substantial than the Partnerships and Cooperation Agreements' (Cameron and Rhein, 2005). The AAs signed with the Mediterranean nations concentrate on economic and trade relations between the Mediterranean and the EU with norms such as democracy and respect for human rights occupying a secondary position.[62] Traditionally, in other words, the EU has supported the status quo in the South – whereas in eastern Europe, it has supported transition. The PCAs negotiated and signed by the eastern European countries detail and primarily concern the establishment of democracy, respect for human rights; the rule of law with economic and trade relations taking a more secondary role.[63] Consequently, in their relations with the EU, the Mediterranean countries expect the primary focus to concern economic initiatives and for the EU to remain more 'hands off' as regards democratic and human rights provisions (Tanner, 2004). In part, this reflects disagreements between, for example, Algeria and the EU as to the exact definition of human rights and democracy (Aliboni, 2004: 10). Therefore, Mediterranean countries, like Algeria, are lukewarm towards the ENP and view the ENP as a mere 'declaratory acceptance' of those values aimed at political and economic reforms rather than as an affirmation of democratic commitment (Tanner, 2004: 140–1; Gomez and Christou, 2004: 194). This perception is condoned by the EU and partly linked to EU economic interests.[64] While there is reluctance on the part of ENP to fund trade unions, there is also deference to Arab sensitivities regarding a supposed incompatibility between Islamic and democratic norms (Youngs, 2003: 135). Situations like this are not conducive to instil into the southern partner-states a sense of 'ownership' of the political reforms. Simply put, multi-party elections in Lebanon, Tunisia and Egypt mean little if freedom of speech, press and association are not implemented. The ENP has so far not created the necessary conditions for southern partners to activate sufficient political reforms (Aliboni, 2004: 7).

The lacking reforms can also be illustrated in the slow process of some ENP members to safeguard political rights, promote civil liberties and reduce levels of corruption. As can be seen from Table 2.7, no significant variation have taken place between 2000 and 2005, with some slight improvements in the case of Algeria, Egypt and Georgia and, to a limited extent, with regard to Azerbaijan. The most significant improvement in democratic indicators was observed in Ukraine, especially in the period 2004–2005, which can possibly be linked to the pro-European 'orange revolution'. Some countries even recorded a slight worsening of democratic and corruption indicators (Lebanon, Morocco, Armenia, Belarus and Moldova). Overall, Syria, Libya and Belarus recorded the worst democratic performance, being constantly not 'free' since the early 1990s. In the corruption index, Azerbaijan (arguably the country with the most economic potential, due to significant unexploited oil and gas reserves, and thus the largest flux of capital, both domestic and foreign) was the worst performer, being placed at the bottom of the CPI table not only relatively to ENP countries, but also in relation to world performance.

Table 2.7 ENP democratic indicators, 2000–2005

Year	Indicator	MEDA									
		Algeria	Egypt	Israel	Jordan	Lebanon	Libya	Morocco	Syria	Tunisia	Palestine
2000	PR	6	6	1	4	6	7	5	7	6	NA
	CL	5	5	3	4	5	7	4	7	5	NA
	FR	NF	NF	F	PF	NF	NF	PF	NF	NF	NA
	CPI	NA	3.1	6.6	4.6	NA	NA	4.7	NA	5.2	NA
			63	22	39			37		32	
2001	PR	6	6	1	5	6	7	5	7	6	NA
	CL	5	6	3	5	5	7	5	7	5	NA
	FR	NF	NF	F	PF	NF	NF	PF	NF	NF	NA
	CPI	NA	3.6	7.6	4.9	NA	NA	NA	NA	5.3	NA
			54	16	37					31	
2002	PR	6	6	1	6	6	7	5	7	6	NA
	CL	5	6	3	5	5	7	5	7	5	NA
	FR	NF	NF	F	PF	NF	NF	PF	NF	NF	NA
	CPI	NA	3.4	7.3	4.5	NA	NA	3.7	NA	4.8	NA
			62	18	40			52		36	
2003	PR	6	6	1	5	6	7	5	7	6	NA
	CL	5	6	3	5	5	7	5	7	5	NA
	FR	NF	NF	F	PF	NF	NF	PF	NF	NF	NA
	CPI	2.6	3.3	7	4.6	3	2.1	3.3	3.4	4.9	3
		88	70	21	43	78	118	70	66	39	78
2004	PR	6	6	1	5	6	7	5	7	6	NA
	CL	5	5	3	4	5	7	4	7	5	NA
	FR	NF	NF	F	PF	NF	NF	PF	NF	NF	NA
	CPI	2.6	3.3	7	4.6	3	2.1	3.3	3.4	4.9	3
		97	70	26	37	97	108	77	71	39	108
2005	PR	6	6	1	5	5	7	5	7	6	NA
	CL	5	5	2	4	4	7	4	7	5	NA
	FR	NF	NF	F	PF	PF	NF	PF	NF	NF	NA
	CPI	2.8	3.4	6.3	5.7	3.1	2.5	3.2	3.4	4.9	2.6
		97	70	28	37	83	117	78	70	43	107

		TACIS					
		Armenia	Azerbaijan	Belarus	Georgia	Moldova	Ukraine
2000	PR	4	6	6	4	2	4
	CL	4	5	6	4	4	4
	FR	PF	PF	NF	PF	PF	PF
	CPI	2.5	1.5	4.1	NA	2.6	1.5
		76	87	43		74	87
2001	PR	4	6	6	4	2	4
	CL	4	5	6	4	4	4
	FR	PF	PF	NF	PF	PF	PF
	CPI	NA	2	NA	NA	3.1	2.1
			84			63	83
2002	PR	4	6	6	4	3	4
	CL	4	5	6	4	4	4
	FR	PF	PF	NF	PF	PF	PF
	CPI	NA	2	4.8	2.4	2.1	2.4
			95	36	85	93	85
2003	PR	4	6	6	4	3	4
	CL	4	5	6	4	4	4
	FR	PF	NF	NF	PF	PF	PF
	CPI	3	1.8	4.2	1.8	2.4	2.3
		78	124	53	124	100	106
2004	PR	5	6	7	3	3	4
	CL	4	5	6	4	4	3
	FR	PF	NF	NF	PF	PF	PF
	CPI	3	1.8	4.2	1.8	2.4	2.3
		82	140	74	133	114	122
2005	PR	5	6	7	3	3	3
	CL	4	5	6	3	4	2
	FR	PF	NF	NF	PF	PF	PF
	CPI	2.9	2.2	2.6	2.3	2.9	2.6
		88	137	107	130	88	107

Note: PR and CL stand for Political Rights and Civil Liberties, respectively; 1 represents the most free and 7 the least free rating. FR is the overall Freedom Rating, where F stands for Free, PF stands for Partially Free and NF stands for Not Free (from www. freedomhouse.org). CPI Score (Corruption Perception Index) relates to perceptions of the degree of corruption as seen by business people and country analysts and ranges between 10 (highly clean) and 0 (highly corrupt). The top figure refers to the score, the bottom figure refers to the overall ranking (from www.transparency.org/).

Besides the democratic and political objectives of the ENP, there are also more direct security objectives inherent in the ENP. One such objective concerns the Moldovan breakaway region of Transdniestria. Basically, Transdniestria emerges as the 'black hole of transborder organised crime, including drug smuggling, human trafficking and arms smuggling' and the region houses a 'Soviet-era dump of 40,000 tons of ammunition' (Fuller, 2004: 1). In addition to the influence of the former Soviet Union as represented by the arms dump, Russia maintains a small force in Transdniestria. Essentially, the EU remains a secondary actor in Transdniestria as it allows other states and organisations to attempt to reach a peaceful settlement to the Moldovan problem (Fuller, 2004: 1). Consequently, in the years directly preceding the claim for independence by Transdniestria, the EU supported the multilateral attempts of Russia, Ukraine and Moldova under the guidance and within the framework of the OSCE to mediate settlement discussions (Fuller, 2004: 1). In the EU/Moldova Action Plan for the ENP, the EU continues to adhere to its previous stance that the Transdniestrian conflict should be resolved and negotiated within the confines of the OSCE mediation process. This policy has not changed, despite the fact that in response to the combined request by the Moldovan and Ukrainian governments the EU agreed to send a monitoring mission in 2005 to the Ukrainian/Transdniestrian border. Hence, while border control remains an important objective and a primary component in securing peace and stability in the neighbour-hood as ascribed to in the ENP, the primary concern should be not in attempting to keep the ammunitions in Transdniestria but in resolving the Transdniestria issue in a peaceful and fair manner to ensure stability and peace within Moldova and the region as a whole. Largely, the EU fails in this endeavour and instead focuses on the easiest solution available to it at this point in time, namely to engage in a monitoring mission to the Transdniestrian border. There has been a similar reluctance on the part of the EU to intervene in the border conflicts in Georgia and Armenia–Azerbaijan (MacFarlane, 2004). No doubt the EU has to strike a balance between a more 'hands-on' approach in these situations and Russian sensitivities about 'encroachment into spheres of interest'. The latter is also a factor in how the EU can achieve greater leverage over political reforms in Belarus. There is also a question on whether EU–Russian relations either support or impede ENP reform efforts generally. The Medium-Term Strategy for Developing Relations of 1999 between the Russian Federation and the EU outlines an ambitious approach to the EU up to 2010 premised on 'strategic partnership', enhanced political dialogue, 'an effective system of collective security in Europe', and 'a pan-European economic and legal infrastructure'.[65]

In comparing the relations between the EU and each region, one observes that contradictions in EU relations with each region exist. While the ENP emerges as the development of 'bilateral relations between the EU and individual countries, in an attempt to influence their internal and external policies', the policy includes certain multilateral and regional instruments that differentiate the eastern European nations from the Mediterranean nations (K. Smith, 2005: 762). Essentially, the EU's relations with the Mediterranean presuppose a regional dimension and regional policies. As such, in the communication 'Wider Europe', the Commission (ESS: 8) states that 'in the Mediterranean, an explicit regional dimension encouraging the development of intra-regional initiatives and cooperation in a broad range of sectors is included' whereas 'encouragement for regional political cooperation and/or economic integration has not so far formed a strong component of EU policy towards [eastern Europe]'. Consequently, in its relations with the Mediterranean nations, the EU continually discusses the establishment of an 'Arab Maghreb Union', the development of 'south–south' trade, regional group meetings, the Agadir Agreement and the Euro-Mediterranean Parliamentary Assembly.[66] In stark contrast, the EU neither addresses nor attempts to construct such a similar regional relationship among the Eastern European countries but, rather, engages in bilateral relations with the individual countries. Therefore, whereas the EU adopted a Common Strategy towards the entire Mediterranean region, as regards the eastern European nations the EU only concluded Common Strategies on individual east European countries. In any case, the ENP does not set up regular meetings of all neighbours at any level.

Problems over the coherence and effectiveness of the ENP might easily be exacerbated once the EU starts to address acute or simmering conflict flash points such as the unstable internal situations in Algeria and Morocco, as well as the Middle East conflict generally. A solution to these problems is not facilitated by such factors as the second Intifada, the invasion of Iraq, the election of Hammas as the governing body of the Palestinian Authority and the renewed hostilities between Israel and Palestinians in the Gaza Strip and of intense fighting between Israel and Hezbollah in Lebanon in mid-2006. Some of these problems are being addressed in a wider framework, such as the international quartet to which the EU belongs, together with the US, UN and Russia, and which has sponsored the 'road map' for overcoming the Middle East conflict. These issues raise wider questions about the EU's effectiveness as a security actor generally and about the role of the ESS specifically.

Assessment of the European Security Strategy

While the ESS emerges as a timely document designed to facilitate European communication and action in the field of security, as revealed by the implementation of the strategy itself, the ESS only provides a framework in which to develop European strategy. Indeed, 'The Strategy itself is not an immediately operational document in the sense that it is not a detailed plan of action: it lays down the overall objectives of EU external action and the principal ways of achieving these' (Biscop, 2004: 37). In other words, the ESS provides a framework for areas in which to engage in common action but fails to provide an operational structure or policy prescription. Subsequently, European operational decisions and security policies 'have to then be elaborated in specific policy plans, across the pillars, with regard to states, regions and global issues as well as with regard to the development by the EU itself of the instruments and capabilities that the implementation' of the ESS necessitates (Biscop, 2004: 37). Essentially, in order to accomplish any task or operation within the ESS, the EU, its member states and its institutions must coalesce and opine a commonly adhered to strategy according to 'specific' policy plans in each area of activity. While such a task alone is an odious and difficult assignment, engagement in the ESS emerges as even more difficult when taking into consideration the notorious reluctance, 'grand' statements aside, of member states to adopt a common stance in their relations with major global players in preference to pursuing distinct national strategies (Ideas Factory Europe, 2004: 7; Quille, 2004: 434). The ESS remains subject to the principle and voting rule of unanimity in the Council of Ministers. While this preserves the intergovernmental character and with it the potential for conflict among the member states due to differing national interests, it may deter from the clear set of principles of the EU as a collective actor and thus may result in *ad hoc* measures. The inclusion of military means to avert security threats remains contested and the use of force is considered as an instrument of last resort, in principle to be applied only with a Security Council mandate (Biscop, 2005). However, the basic function of the ESS might still be to show unity and to open a dialogue with the US.

Assessment of the EU's development policy and
emphasis on multilateralism

According to the ESS, a primary component of European security resides in the principle of 'effective multilateralism' (Solana, 2003a). The EU believes in seeking multilateral solutions to global problems. It therefore attaches great importance to effective multilateralism, with a strong UN at its heart. Consequently, the principle and notion of multilateralism defines the EU's willingness and belief in participating with other international organisations and entities in order to achieve its security objectives. As a result, the EU often engages in many programmes with the UN and utilises UN resolutions to validate its actions and behaviour in the international security environment. Subsequently, the EU acts in response to mandates and UN-sanctioned military engagements in conformity with the notion of multilateralism. However, while the ESS states that effective multilateralism buttresses the EU's strategy, in order to effectively implement provisions of the strategy, which call upon the EU to emerge as a more active and involved actor with deployable military capabilities, certain tensions may arise. Essentially, the UN expressed its concerns that 'the EU's system of rapidly deploying troops to hotspots, particularly in Africa, could make it more difficult for the EU's countries to contribute to UN operations' (Cronin, 2005: 6; Graham, 2004; Ojanen, 2006; Ortega, 2005). In other words, certain elements of the ESS may conflict with one another thereby creating a situation in which Europe cannot effectively act or meet its responsibilities as identified in the ESS. Consequently, if, in order to achieve its objectives in one area of the ESS, the EU must neglect its responsibilities in another area, the ESS cannot emerge as a coherent and unitary document of an effective security actor. However, multilateralism requires not only broad international support and legitimacy, but also the capacity to generate initiatives, and political leadership to set the agenda, define deadlines, mobilise resources and promote effective implementation. A key qualification in this context is the ability to form and sustain broad-based coalitions (Maull, 786).

Yet, in all these considerations about leadership and multilateral cooperative efforts, the question remains as to what is being achieved on the ground. This is particularly pertinent with regard to development and cooperation issues and their associated endeavours to diminish the root causes of violent conflicts. As Table 2.8 demonstrates, ACP countries have changed very little over 2000 to 2005 in terms of the Freedom House indicators on democracy. However, overall the Caribbean countries are doing better than the African ones in their democratic performance. African countries also had an unenviable record with regard to the Corruption Perception Index. According to this Index for 2005, where 10 represent a highly clean situation and 0 a highly corrupt one, 5 African countries scored 5 or more; 9 countries scored between 3 and 4.9; and 29 scored 2.9 or less.[67] A country-specific breakdown of the CPI scores and Freedom House indicators is provided in Appendix 2.1.

Table 2.8 ACP democratic indicators, 2000–2005

	Africa (48) (%)				Caribbean and Pacific (29) (%)			
	NF No. %	PF No. %	F No. %	NA	NF No. %	PF No. %	F No. %	NA No. %
2005	14 (29)	23 (48)	11 (23)	2 (7)	6 (21)	19 (65)	2 (7)	
2004	14 (29)	23 (48)	11 (23)	2 (7)	7 (24)	18 (62)	2 (7)	
2003	15 (31)	22 (46)	11 (23)	2 (7)	8 (27)	17 (59)	2 (7)	
2002	15 (31)	22 (46)	11 (23)	2 (7)	7 (24)	18 (62)	2 (7)	
2001	15 (31)	24 (50)	9 (19)	2 (7)	7 (24)	18 (62)	2 (7)	
2000	16 (33)	23 (48)	9 (19)	2 (7)	6 (21)	19 (65)	2 (7)	

Note: See Table 2.7.

The lack of real progress in economic development is further illustrated in the World Bank findings that '40 of the 63 countries in the World Bank's unenviable category of least-developed countries (LDCs) in 2000 were ACP member states' (World Bank, 2000). In other words, over half of the membership of the ACP group was among the world's poorest countries the year Lomé expired in 2000 (Babarinde and Faber, 2004: 46–7). What makes the situation difficult is that many ACP countries, especially African ones, continue to suffer from armed conflicts. Global economic shocks and the success or failure of multi-lateral trade negotiations are additional factors that impede development.

Conclusion

This chapter set out to explore a number of themes. Firstly, to what extent is the EU functioning as a collective actor in the field of conflict prevention? Secondly, is the EU acting coherently and effectively across a number of policy areas and instruments in conflict prevention? In other words, in what aspects of conflict prevention does the EU excel, and where not? Part of this examination was to establish the extent to which the EU relies on multilateral partnership in the pursuit of conflict prevention. Thirdly, what measures have been taken to cope with coordination problems both internally to the EU and between the EU and other international organisations in the area of conflict prevention? What observations then can be drawn from these investigations, particularly in the chosen areas of the ENP, EU development and cooperation policy, and crisis management situations?

EU collective behaviour can be observed in conflict prevention tasks, though it is more strongly evident in development and cooperation policy, or the ENP, than with regard to crisis management tasks. There is sufficient agreement among EU member states that collective action in development and cooperation policy is needed to contribute to international peace and stability, that EU values and experience can act as a model for emulation in developing countries, that joint efforts between member states and Community programmes are necessary, and that the Commission should play a lead role in streamlining the activities in this sector. As a consequence, there are both long-standing and well entrenched collective behavioural characteristics (i.e., the Community method) guiding this policy area. Similarly, in order to combat security threats emanating from unstable neighbouring states, terrorism, organised crime, failing states, and the proliferation of WMD (ESS; Solana, 2003a), the EU enrolled in certain collective security initiatives, such as the ENP. As pointed out by Biscop (2005: 3) the neighbourhood can be seen as the area in which the EU deems it has specific responsibility for peace and security, and therefore aspires to a directly leading role, as opposed to its general contribution to global stability through the UN as outlined under the objective of 'effective multilateralism'. The need to protect EU freedom of goods and services and with it the existence of porous borders has made the EU abandon strict adherence to the Westphalian dictum of territorial defence in favour of milieu security goals. It has also resulted in the EU responding to international conflicts more pro-actively, comprehensively (civilian and military means) and multilaterally. Through the ESS, the EU tries to establish a philosophy of crisis management, based on two components. Firstly, it broadly defines potential threats to the Union and its citizens. Secondly, the EU's implicit vision dictates that such threats are a matter of common interest and mutual solidarity. While *ad hoc* measures can be useful in the application of the ESS, more clearly formulated policies, organisational structures, available resources and rules of interaction are needed to make the ESS an effective instrument of conflict prevention or crisis management. This will no doubt be a long and arduous process (Boin and Rhinard, 2005: 15).

Important as this lack of policy effectiveness might be, it is only one area in which to assess the coherence and effectiveness of EU conflict prevention. But it raises the question as to what emphasis to put on civilian measures generally and, even here, whether technical assistance, trade and association agreements are deemed more effective than the rule of law or police missions. Through a range of financial and technical assistance, economic cooperation in the form of trade or association agreements, or enlargement provisions and nation building and democratisation efforts, the EU has helped to shape the behaviour of problem countries (Hill and Smith, 2005: 402). But different tasks require different instruments or measures, which cannot be easily assessed in terms of outcomes. The involvement of several international actors, the complexity of what works in the short rather than the long term, and whether priority is to be given to democratic development rather than peace often impede accurate assessment. For example, support for democracy may not always bode well for the sustainability of peace (Youngs, 2004). Equally, insistence on human rights might be good long-term goals, but might worsen relations between EU and the governments concerned in the short term (Hill, 2001: 318).

A more straightforward picture emerges when consideration is given to the way the EU has conducted its ENP. Besides having streamlined a formerly *ad hoc* approach, the ENP has contributed to 'shared values' and effective implementation of political, economic and institutional reforms in neighbouring states. The 'institutional mechanisms created in the ENP agreements have locked the EU and these neighbouring states into a tight relationship' which resulted in the 'EU becoming more deeply engaged in them' and in the development of 'positions on a range of questions, relating to domestic developments in the eastern neighbours' which would not have occurred without the establishment of such agreements (Lynch, 2003: 45). The reform progress in Georgia and the Ukraine is part of this impact. Yet obstacles remain, of which a main one is how to use the ENP as a policy tool in which to 'include' rather than to 'exclude' its neighbours, as some neighbours have membership aspirations. Essentially, the EU neglects to apply the ENP in a consistent and corresponding fashion to every partner in the ENP but, rather, distinguishes between partners based on region (the Mediterranean area) as against bilateral relations (eastern Europe) or on specific (drug trafficking, terrorism, oil and migration[68] issues) instead of on democratic ones. Moreover, as illustrated by the Transdniestria problem, the scale and quality of EU crisis management in the ENP countries will have to be upgraded (Aliboni, 2004). Thus, despite bringing prosperity and stability to its neighbours, the ENP is essentially a 'stop-gap measure and does not yet convey a long-term thinking about how further integration should proceed. The EU needs to set clearer benchmarks, clearer priorities and clearer incentives' (K. Smith, 2005).

These drawbacks, which also beset the ESS, are exacerbated by coordination problems, both within the EU and between the EU and other international actors. Despite Article 3 of the EU Treaty calling on the Union to 'ensure . . . the consistency of its external activities as a whole in the context of its external relations, security, economic and development policies', many obstacles stand in the way of internal EU coordination such as hesitation regarding how much authority to delegate to the EU level or undue references to the subsidiarity principle. These obstacles and hesitations limit EU action with regard to resource pooling, coordination, monitoring, information (intelligence) sharing, regulation, mobilisation and funding. While there is a relatively high degree of coordination between member states and Community programmes in the area of development and cooperation, it also suffers from a lack of overall coordination in EU external relations which cuts across the different pillars.[69] Some efforts have been made to promote coordination such as the Committee for Civilian Aspects of Crisis Management (CIVCOM), which was created in order to improve relations between the military and the civilian components, including instruments from the first pillar, and the link between Counter-Terrorism Group and the EU Situation Centre, which was set up to facilitate and assess intelligence gathering and sharing. But these efforts are tenuous and remain more an expectation than a practice.

Lack of internal coordination also affects the level of coordination or cooperation the EU can achieve with other international actors. The EU has strong links with the Council of Europe, the OSCE's Conflict Prevention Centre, the UN Trust Fund on Prevention Action, and the Conflict Prevention and Resolution (CPR) network, in which the United States Agency for International Development (USAID), Canadian International Development Agency (CIDA), the World Bank and certain member states are particularly active. All these links help to exchange information on the progress of conflict prevention activities and contribute to the spread of common values and the acceptance of some shared obligations. But, besides inter-locking benefits among international organisations, there can also be inter-blocking ones (Hill, 2001: 325–6). For example, as suggested by Everts (2004: 685), there is a danger that Europeans and Americans will pursue competing democratisation strategies in the Middle East if no effective coordination between the two sides is introduced. As he points out, US aid to the Middle East is to a great extent influenced by considerations in the Global War on Terror drive. The EU, on the other hand, is placing its aid emphasis on alleviating poverty, responding to crises, and contributing to regional stability.

Certainly, military means are essential to topple undemocratic regimes, but building a democratic polity requires time and normative values such as pluralism, dialogue and consensus, and social inclusion. Early warning, nipping in the bud the kind of activity which conflict prevention requires is crucial. It is in this respect that the EU makes an important contribution, especially with regard to civilian measures. But even in crisis management engagements, improvements have taken place to foster joined-up policymaking and to ensure that decisions are followed up in the field of counter-proliferation and counter-terrorism.

Appendix 2.1 ACP democratic indicators by individual countries, 2000–2005

	2000				2001				2002				2003				2004				2005			
	PR	CL	FT	CPI	PR	CL	FT	CPI	PR	CL	FT	CPI	PR	CL	FT	CPI	PR	CL	FT	CPI	PR	CL	FT	CPI
Angola	6	6	NF	1.7 (85)	6	6	NF		6	5	NF	1.7 (98)	6	5	NF	1.8 (124)	6	6	NF	2.0 (133)	6	5	NF	2.0 (151)
Benin	2	2	F		3	2	F		3	2	F		2	2	F		2	2	F	3.2 (77)	2	2	F	2.9 (88)
Botswana	2	2	F	6.0 (26)	2	2	F	6.0 (26)	2	2	F	6.4 (24)	2	2	F	5.7 (30)	2	2	F	6.0 (31)	2	2	F	5.9 (32)
Burkina Faso	4	4	PF	3.0 (65)	4	4	PF		4	4	PF		4	4	PF		5	4	PF		5	3	PF	3.4 (70)
Burundi	6	6	NF		6	6	NF		6	5	NF		5	5	PF		5	5	PF		3	5	PF	2.3 (130)
Cameroon	7	6	NF	2.0 (84)	6	6	NF	2.0 (84)	6	6	NF	2.2 (89)	6	6	NF	1.8 (124)	6	6	NF	2.1 (129)	6	6	NF	2.2 (137)
Cape Verde	1	2	F		1	2	F		1	2	F		1	1	F		1	1	F		1	1	F	
Cent. African Republic	3	4	PF		5	5	PF		5	5	PF		7	5	PF		6	5	PF		5	4	PF	
Chad	6	5	NF		6	5	NF		6	5	NF		6	5	NF		6	5	NF	1.7 (142)	6	5	NF	1.7 (158)
Comoros	6	4	PF		6	4	PF		5	4	PF		5	4	PF		4	4	PF		4	4	PF	
Congo (Brazzaville)	6	4	PF		5	4	PF		6	4	PF		5	4	PF	2.2 (113)	5	4	PF	2.3 (114)	5	5	PF	2.3 (130)
Congo (Kinshasa)	7	6	NF		6	6	NF		6	6	NF		6	6	NF	2.2 (113)	6	6	NF	2.0 (133)	6	6	NF	2.1 (144)

Country																								
Djibouti	4	5	PF		4	5	PF		4	5	PF		5	5	PF		5	5	PF		5	5	PF	1.9 (152)
Equatorial Guinea	7	7	NF		6	6	NF		7	6	NF		7	6	NF		7	6	NF		7	6	NF	2.6 (107)
Eritrea	7	5	NF		7	6	NF		7	6	NF		7	6	NF		7	6	NF	2.6 (102)	7	6	NF	2.2 (137)
Ethiopia	5	5	PF	3.2 (60)	5	5	PF		5	5	PF	3.5 (59)	5	5	PF	2.5 (92)	5	5	PF	2.3 (114)	5	5	PF	2.9 (88)
Gabon	5	4	PF		5	4	PF		5	4	PF		5	4	PF		5	4	PF	3.3 (74)	6	4	PF	2.7 (103)
Gambia	7	5	NF		5	5	PF		4	4	PF		4	4	PF	2.5 (92)	4	4	PF	2.8 (90)	5	4	PF	3.5 (65)
Ghana	2	3	F	3.5 (52)	2	3	F	3.4 (59)	3	3	F	3.9 (50)	2	2	F	3.3 (70)	2	2	F	3.6 (64)	1	2	F	
Guinea	6	5	NF		6	5	NF		6	5	NF		6	5	NF		6	5	NF	2.6 (102)	6	5	NF	
Guinea Bissau	4	5	PF		4	5	PF		4	5	PF		6	4	PF		4	4	PF		3	4	PF	
Ivory Coast	6	5	PF	2.7 (71)	5	4	PF	2.4 (77)	6	6	NF	2.7 (71)	6	5	NF	2.1 (118)	6	6	NF		6	6	NF	1.9 (152)
Kenya	6	4	NF	2.1 (82)	6	4	NF	2 (84)	4	4	PF	1.9 (96)	3	3	PF	1.9 (122)	3	3	PF	2.1 (129)	3	3	PF	2.1 (144)
Lesotho	4	4	PF		4	4	PF		2	3	F		2	3	F		2	3	F		2	3	F	3.4 (70)
Liberia	5	6	PF		6	5	PF		6	6	NF		6	6	NF		5	4	PF		4	4	PF	2.2 (137)
Madagascar	2	4	PF		2	4	PF		3	4	PF	1.7 (98)	3	3	PF	2.6 (88)	3	3	PF	3.1 (82)	3	3	PF	2.8 (97)

continued over the page …

Appendix 2.1 continued ...

	2000				2001				2002				2003				2004				2005			
	PR	CL	FT	CPI	PR	CL	FT	CPI	PR	CL	FT	CPI	PR	CL	FT	CPI	PR	CL	FT	CPI	PR	CL	FT	CPI
Malawi	3	3	PF	4.1 (43)	4	3	PF	3.2 (61)	4	4	PF	2.9 (68)	3	4	PF	2.8 (83)	4	4	PF	2.8 (90)	4	4	PF	2.8 (97)
Mali	2	3	F		2	3	F		2	3	F		2	2	F	3.0 (78)	2	2	F	3.2 (77)	2	2	F	2.9 (88)
Mauritania	6	5	NF		5	5	PF		5	5	PF		6	5	NF		6	5	NF		6	4	PF	
Mauritius	1	2	F	4.7 (37)	1	2	F	4.5 (40)	1	2	F	4.5 (40)	1	2	F	4.4 (48)	1	1	F	4.1 (54)	1	2	F	4.2 (51)
Mozambique	3	4	PF		3	4	PF		3	4	PF		3	4	PF	2.7 (86)	3	4	PF	2.8 (90)	3	4	PF	2.8 (97)
Namibia	2	3	F	2.2 (81)	2	3	F	5.4 (30)	2	3	F	5.7 (28)	2	3	F	4.7 (41)	2	3	F	4.1 (54)	2	2	F	4.3 (47)
Niger	4	4	PF		4	4	PF		4	4	PF		4	4	PF		3	3	PF	2.2 (122)	3	3	PF	2.4 (126)
Nigeria	4	4	PF	1.2 (90)	4	5	PF	1.0 (90)	4	5	PF	1.6 (101)	4	4	PF	1.4 (132)	4	4	PF	1.6 (144)	4	4	PF	1.9 (152)
Rwanda	7	6	NF		7	6	NF		7	5	NF		6	5	NF		6	5	NF		6	5	NF	
Sao Tome & Principe	1	2	F		1	2	F		1	2	F		2	2	F		2	2	F		2	2	F	
Senegal	3	4	PF	3.5 (52)	3	4	PF	2.9 (65)	2	3	F	3.1 (66)	2	3	F	3.2 (76)	2	3	F	3.0 (85)	2	3	F	3.2 (78)

Country	PR	CL	FR	CPI	PR	CL	FR	CPI	PR	CL	FR	CPI	PR	CL	FR	CPI	PR	CL	FR	CPI	PR	CL	FR	CPI
Seychelles	3	3	PF		3	3	PF		3	3	PF		3	3	PF		3	3	PF	4.4 (48)	3	3	PF	4.0 (55)
Sierra Leone	4	5	PF		4	4	PF		4	4	PF		4	3	PF	2.2 (113)	4	3	PF	2.3 (114)	4	3	PF	2.4 (126)
Somalia	6	7	NF		6	7	NF		6	7	NF		6	7	NF		6	7	NF		6	7	NF	2.1 (144)
South Africa	1	2	F	5.0 (34)	1	2	F	4.8 (38)	1	2	F	4.8 (36)	1	2	F	4.4 (48)	1	2	F	4.6 (44)	1	2	F	4.5 (46)
Sudan	7	7	NF		7	7	NF		7	7	NF		7	7	NF	2.3 (106)	7	7	NF	2.2 (122)	7	7	NF	2.1 (144)
Swaziland	6	5	NF		6	5	NF		6	5	NF		7	5	NF		7	5	NF		7	5	NF	2.7 (103)
Tanzania	4	4	PF	2.5 (76)	4	4	PF	2.2 (82)	4	3	PF	2.7 (71)	4	3	PF	2.5 (92)	4	3	PF	2.8 (90)	4	3	PF	2.9 (88)
Togo	5	5	NF		6	5	NF		6	5	PF		6	5	PF		6	5	PF		6	5	NF	
Uganda	6	5	PF	2.3 (80)	6	5	PF	1.9 (88)	6	4	PF	2.1 (93)	5	4	PF	2.2 (113)	5	4	PF	2.6 (102)	5	4	PF	2.5 (117)
Zambia	5	4	PF	3.4 (57)	5	4	PF	2.6 (75)	4	4	PF	2.6 (77)	4	4	PF	2.5 (92)	4	4	PF	2.6 (102)	4	4	PF	2.6 (107)
Zimbabwe	6	5	PF	3.0 (65)	6	6	NF	2.9 (65)	6	6	NF	2.7 (71)	6	6	NF		7	6	NF	2.3 (114)	7	6	NF	2.6 (107)

Note: PR and CL stand for Political Rights and Civil Liberties, respectively; 1 represents the most free and 7 the least free rating. FR is the overall Freedom Rating, where F stands for Free, PF stands for Partially Free and NF stands for Not Free (from www.freedomhouse.org). CPI Score (Corruption Perception Index) relates to perceptions of the degree of corruption as seen by business people and country analysts and ranges between 10 (highly clean) and 0 (highly corrupt). The top figure refers to the score, the bottom figure refers to the overall ranking. (from www.transparency.org/). The Republic of Congo and the Democratic Republic of Congo are listed as 'the Republic of the Congo' up to 2003.

Notes

1　For a fuller description of the EU as post-Westphalian actor see Caporaso (1996) and Pentland (2000).

2　While terrorist activities were a phenomenon in several west European States, the scale and scope of terrorist attacks took on a new significance after the terrorist attacks in New York/Washington, Madrid and London between 2001 and 2005.

3　These and other military missions demonstrate that the EU cannot be considered as a mere 'civilian power' (Hill, 2001: 317). These military missions and the consequences for the EU as a military actor are fully addressed in Chapter 5.

4　European Council (2000) '. . . Santa Maria da Feira European Council . . .': Annex V Common Strategy of the European Union on the Mediterranean region.

5　The EU produces a quarter of the world's Gross National Product (GNP).

6　Throughout this text, a distinction will be made between the so-called Community method and the EU generally. Unlike the term EU, which covers all three pillars, the Community method is associated solely with Pillar I competences and is characterised by a strong agenda-setting role for the Commission, the right of the European Parliament to amend proposals, decision-making by qualified majority vote (QMV) in the Council and the introduction of oversight by the European Court of Justice. For further details see Wallace and Wallace (1997).

7　This assumes that the ESS really exists for the member states or that they feel it is crucial in their daily lives. But this might be too optimistic an assumption for some. We are grateful to Hanna Ojanen for pointing this out to us.

8　For further details, see European Commission (1996) 'The EU and the issue of conflicts in Africa . . .'.

9　European Commission (2002) 'One year on . . .': 5.

10　European Commission (2001) '. . . conflict prevention . . .': 4.

11　European Commission (2003) '. . . wider Europe-neighbourhood . . .': 4.

12　Since the 2003 Ministerial Conference, an ESDP dialogue with the Mediterranean partners has been introduced in order to share information and explore the possibility of cooperation in the area of conflict prevention and crisis management.

13　See for example, European Commission/EuropeAid Cooperation Office DG (2004) '. . . partnership with the Mediterranean . . .'.

14　European Commission (2003) '. . . wider Europe-neighbourhood . . .': 10.

15　European Commission (2003) '. . . wider Europe-neighbourhood . . .': 7.

16　The EU supports also the Common Market of Eastern and Southern Africa (COMESA), the South African Development Community (SADC), the Central African Economic and Monetary Community (CEMAC), the Southern African Customs Union (SACU), the South Asian Association for Regional Cooperation (SAARC), and the Cariforum and Pacific Islands Forum.

17 See, for example, European Commission (1996) 'The EU and the issue of conflicts in Africa . . .'; and European Council and Commission (2000) 'The European Community's development policy . . .'.

18 See Council of the European Union (2005) '. . . The European consensus': Annex 1.

19 Council of the European Union (2005) 'Press release 2650th Council meeting'.

20 The EC Mine Action Strategy 2005–2007 (European Commission/External Relations DG (2007) 'The European Roadmap . . .') calls for a 'zero victim target' to fight anti-personal landmines worldwide. See also Council Regulations (EC) 1724/2001 and 1725/2001 on action against anti-personnel mines.

21 European Commission (2006) 'Commission simplifies external cooperation programmes': 3.

22 Council of the European Union (2005) '. . . The European consensus': 13.

23 See the ESS: 11.

24 The Headline Goals for 2008 were adopted by European Council on 13 December 2004 (16062/04) and have as their objectives: conflict prevention, peace-keeping and tasks of combat forces in crisis management, including peacemaking and post-conflict stabilisation. A Capabilities Requirements List was established in 2005. Civilian capabilities would be available within 30 days of the decision to deploy.

25 www.defense.gouv.fr/sites/defense/english_contents/news/eurogendfor_the_european_gendarmerie_force (accessed 11 August 2006).

26 http://europa.eu.int/agencies/community_agencies/frontex/index_en.htm (accessed 11 August 2006).

27 European Council (2001) 'Laeken European Council . . .'.

28 It should be noted that the initial Treaty provisions regarding common strategies were found somewhat problematic to implement.

29 European Commission (2004) '. . . European neighbourhood policy – strategy paper . . .'.

30 The Action Plans cover political dialogue and reform; trade and measures preparing partners for gradually obtaining a stake in the EU's internal market, justice and home affairs, energy, transport, information society, environment and research and innovation; and social policy and people-to-people contacts (European Commission, 2004 '. . . European neighbourhood policy – strategy paper . . .').

31 European Commission (2003) 'Communication on wider Europe-neighbourhood, 2003'.

32 European Commission (2004) '. . . European neighbourhood policy – strategy paper . . .'.

33 Armenia, Azerbaijan, Belarus, Georgia, Kazakhstan, Kyrgyzstan, Moldova, Russia, Tajikistan, Turkmenistan, Ukraine, Uzbekistan. Mongolia was also covered by the TACIS programme from 1991 to 2003, but is now administered by the Asia, Latin America (ALA) programme.

34 European Commission (2001) '. . . conflict prevention': 11.

35 European Council (2005) '. . . the European consensus . . .': 32.
36 *Ibid.*: 7.
37 European Union Summaries of Legislation (2002) '. . . the Common Foreign and Security Policy . . .'.
38 RRM was set up by Council Regulation (EC) 381/2001 OJ L 57, 27.2.2001. The RRM operates through a separate budget line in the regular budget. Its budget was €30 million in 2005.
39 See Council Regulations (EC) 975/1999 and 976/1999.
40 European Commission (2003) '. . . conflict prevention . . .': 10.
41 The EU has Special Representatives in Afghanistan, Africa the Great Lakes region, the Middle East, Bosnia and Herzegovina, Central Asia, Macedonia, Moldova, South Caucasus, Sudan, Kosovo, and to the Stability Pact for South Eastern Europe, http: //ue.eu.int/cms3_fo/showPage.asp?id=263& lang=EN (accessed 11 August 2006).
42 See also Articles 62 to 64 EC Regulation (EC) no. 539/2001.
43 http://ec.europa.eu/comm/external_relations/ceeca/tacis/index.htm (accessed 11 August 2006).
44 http://ec.europa.eu/comm/external_relations/mepp/index.htm (accessed 12 August 2006).
45 However, it is important to point out that some countries' performance increased significantly from MEDA I to MEDA II (e.g., Egypt) because commitments were lowered and payments increased (hence the improvements may only be partly attributable to the country's actual performance).
46 The CTR was initiated by the American Congress in the early 1990s under the so-called Nunn–Lugar initiative.
47 For example, the Technical Assistance and Information Exchange comports twinning arrangements for Experience exchange at the level of national, regional and local EU member states' administrations, but also encourages participation in Community programmes and agencies.
48 For a critical review of the effectiveness of EU political conditionality, see Zanger (2000) and K. Smith (1998).
49 European Commission (2005) 'Highlights . . .'.
50 See Council of the European Union (2005) 'Press release 2660th Council meeting . . .'.
51 *Ibid.*
52 *Ibid.*
53 European Union Summaries of Legislation (2002) 'SCADPlus: The Common Foreign and Security Policy: Introduction'.
54 For further details see Babarinde and Faber (2004).
55 European Commission (2004) 'Securing peace and stability for Africa'.
56 In April 2005, the Council issued restrictive measures against Burma concerning State-owned enterprises, as well as of persons associated with the Burmese/Myanmar regime and the members of their families for one year (Council of the European Union, 2005, 'Press release 2655th Council meeting . . .').

57 European Council (1999) '. . . Helsinki European Council . . .'.
58 The Council, Commission and the European Parliament backed the dialogue with Iran. It thus represents the unified nature of the EU on the issue of non-proliferation (Bulletin Quotidien Europe, 2005a).
59 Iran had signed the Paris Agreement in November 2004 on the suspension of uranium enrichment, but had seen this as only a temporary suspension, and breached the agreement in late 2005.
60 Javier Solana was instructed to deliver a package of proposals which he did during a visit to Tehran on 6 June 2006.
61 In fact, Morocco emerges as the only Mediterranean country in the ENP to apply for EU membership. However, the EU subsequently rejected its application with a 'definite, permanent no' (K. Smith, 2005: 769). Whether that decision could be revoked, if Turkey as a predominately Muslim country is admitted, remains to be seen.
62 See Gomez and Christou, 2004; Hänggi and Tanner, 2005: 71–2; European Commission (2005) '. . . country report Egypt', Commission (2005) '. . . country report Lebanon'.
63 Commission (2005) '. . . country report Armenia', Commission (2005) '. . . country report Azerbaijan, Commission (2005) '. . . country report Georgia'.
64 On the issue of the EU's desire for market access to the Mediterranean region see Gomez and Christou, 2004: 192–3, on the link with EU's energy import dependence see Tanner, 2004: 142, and on EU concerns about migration flows from North Africa see Tovias and Ugur, 2004: 405.
65 See http://europa.eu.int/comm/external_relations/russia/russian_medium_term_strategy/ (accessed 12 August 2006).
66 European Council (2000) 'Common strategy . . . on the Mediterranean . . .'.
67 For further details of the CPI see http://www.transparency.org.
68 For example, the European Council of December 2005 called for a comprehensive approach on migration from the Mediterranean and African countries Council of the European Union (2006) 'Brussels European Council 15/16 December 2005. . .', especially Annex I, 15 and 16 December 2005, doc. 15914/05.
69 For a more elaborate assessment of the problems of coherence and consistency see Nuttall (2005).

3

Policies of assurance: peace-building in south-eastern Europe

Introduction

As the number of major conflicts, mostly of an intrastate nature, have increased in the post-Cold War period (Wallensteen and Sollenberg, 2001), efforts to re-build states and nations through outside intervention have become regular features in countries such as Afghanistan, the Congo and Iraq, to name but a few. This chapter examines the European Union's peace-building role and assurance policies in the region of the western Balkans,[1] where intrastate strife occurred between 1991 and 2001. These upheavals have not only severely affected the social, economic and political fabric in places like Bosnia and Herzegovina (hereafter Bosnia), Kosovo and Macedonia,[2] they have also had repercussions on neighbouring and EU member states. How the EU has responded to these events, the priorities and instruments it has allocated for this purpose, and the lessons it has drawn from its engagement are important indicators of the EU's role as a security provider. Essentially, EU assurance policies are non-coercive instruments applied in the building of civic institutions, civil societies and the creation of conditions for the promotion of democratic societies playing by EU rules. They include EU enlargement strategies and the associated success of consolidating democracy in Spain, Portugal and Greece and the members that were formerly under Soviet tutelage.

While this chapter will primarily consider EU civilian efforts in re-establishing peace, stability and prosperity in the aftermath of the Bosnian, Macedonian and especially the Kosovo conflicts, Chapter 5 will relate to aspects of EU peace enforcement and crisis management activities in the western Balkans. By exploring the EU's record in assurance policies, inferences can be drawn from why the EU tends to be more successful in post-conflict tasks than in crisis management situations. The form of engagement can be related to whether the EU musters collective engagement, i.e., carries out autonomous EU action rather than a loose coordination of EU member states activities. While the response to the prolonged and intense nature of the ethnic strife in the Balkans has involved measures by both member states and by the EU, there has been a recognition that joint action, whether for civilian or military objectives, is preferable. This realisation surfaced particularly strongly around the time of the Kosovo conflict. The statement by the European Council concerning Kosovo on 23–24 March 1999 declared that 'Europe cannot tolerate a humanitarian catastrophe in its midst. It cannot be permitted that, in the middle of Europe, the predominant population of Kosovo is collectively deprived of its rights and subjected to grave human rights abuses. We, the countries of the EU, are under a moral obligation to ensure that indiscriminate behaviour or violence . . . are not repeated . . . we are responsible for securing peace and cooperation in the region. This is the way to guarantee our fundamental European values, i.e., respect for human rights and the rights of minorities, international law, democratic institutions and the inviolability of borders'.[3]

Three important aspects emerge from this statement. Firstly, a recognition that EU fundamental values are tied up with the peace and stability in its surrounding region. Secondly, a realisation that peace and stability in neighbouring countries is best ensured through the externalisation of core norms and rules. Thirdly, an affirmation that conflicts, such as in the former Yugoslavia, have acquired a European system-wide significance and should be considered collective milieu goals.[4] It gives credence to the notion that domestic disturbances, such as ethnic strife or criminalisation of national economies or state structures are not easily contained within a single state and are easily diffused throughout the European system.

This diffusion factor affects the self-reliance of states as security providers and necessitates that they undertake joint policies and common institutions. Such a development requires a rethinking of the collective action problem, i.e., from where states seek alliances in the defence of national territory threatened by inter-state conflict, to one where the emphasis is on multilateral cooperation and an institutional mechanism in favour of collective (regional) milieu goals. In other words, we are witnessing a change in the way security policy is viewed: a change in which new threats and intra-state conflicts, like ethnic strife, have gained prominence over traditional inter-state warfare, where concerns with national territorial security have given way to milieu goals for a wider geographic region, where the stress has been directed towards economic and political instruments rather than military ones, and where emphasis has shifted to persuasive rather than coercive policy measures.

These traits can be noted in the EU security agenda for the western Balkans, in which two concerns prevail. Firstly, the EU considers it of vital importance to restore peace and stability to the western Balkans and to prevent the conflicts in the region from spreading to neighbouring areas, including the EU. Secondly, the EU is determined to bring these countries closer within its fold through an enlargement strategy, as set out under the Stability Pact for south-eastern Europe (SP) and the Stability and Association Process (SAP). Enlargement, in this respect can thus be seen as a conflict prevention tool.

Before the EU introduced a genuine regional approach entailing the prospect of enlargement, its policy approaches to the western Balkans were mostly directed at symptoms and crises and were reactive rather than pro-active in nature. With the SP and the SAP the attempt is being made, in a comprehensive approach of preventive diplomacy, to address the political and economic structural deficits in the countries of the region. Importantly, the stated aims are to be pursued primarily through economic and political instruments, though the necessity for peace-keeping activities is recognised, and the use of persuasive (insisting on norms, setting conditions, and establishing confidence building measures) rather than coercive methods. Through the dissemination of norms and rules to the western Balkans, the EU is seeking to create a community of interest and values, which in turn will sustain cooperation and diffuse reciprocity among the countries involved. If successful, this would facilitate the extension of the EU system of security governance and create an expanding zone of stability in Europe. It is the task of this chapter to explore the extent to which core EU values and principles are transferred into EU peace-building activities and the extent to which institution building and civilian tasks are pursued with persuasive instruments. Part of the exercise will be to establish how the EU has approached the western Balkans over time and what adjustments it has made to its policies. To a limited extent attention will also be paid to EU efforts in post-conflict situations outside the western Balkans.[5] Evidence will be drawn primarily from official documents of the EU.

Goals, principles and norms of EU assurance policy

While the establishment of peace, stability and prosperity for south-eastern European (SEE) countries remained central goals of EU engagement over a fifteen-year period, the priorities and the approach taken to solve the problems have changed. In part, this is a reflection of changing circumstances and, in part, of a learning and adjustment process. The initial EU priorities towards the former Yugoslavia (1991–1995) were to stop hostilities, provide humanitarian assistance throughout the entire region (this was coordinated by United Nations High Commissioner for Refugees (UNHCR), contribute to the reconstruction of economies and infrastructure in the region, and promote regional development. As a complementary measure, the EU installed in 1991/92 the EC Monitoring Mission (ECMM), later re-named as EUMM. After the Dayton Agreement, which terminated the armed conflict in Bosnia, the EU launched the Royaumont Process in December 1996, aimed at promoting regional projects in the field of civil society, culture, human rights and the implementation of the Dayton Peace Agreement. Known as the Process for Stability and Good Neighbourliness in south eastern Europe, it involved EU member states and the institutions of the European Commission and the European Parliament, SEE countries, regional neighbouring countries, the US, Russia, as well as most of the major regional intergovernmental organisations such as the OSCE and the Council of Europe. Its aims have since been modified and the process has been made responsible for inter-parliamentary relations under the SP. The EU complemented the Royaumont Process with a so-called Regional Approach in 1997, with the aim of creating an area of political stability and economic prosperity by promoting and sustaining democracy and the rule of law, respect for human and minority rights and re-launching economic activity. This approach combined the principles of regionalism and conditionality. The former aimed at the strengthening of relations between the western Balkan countries and their neighbours. Under the latter, the degree of compliance with the prevailing conditions would allow the Balkan countries access to trade concessions, financial and economic assistance through the OBNOVA (aid for the former republics of Yugoslavia)[6] and PHARE programmes, and the eventual establishment of contractual relations (trade and cooperation agreements).

However, the so-called Regional Approach was anything but a comprehensive strategy towards the region, acting instead on a country-by-country basis and putting them in different categories in terms of relations with the EU. In one such initiative the EU took over the direct administration of the divided city of Mostar in Herzegovina. This approach was not conducive to the stability of the region and it also introduced friction and competition between the individual Balkan countries, which were competing for closer ties with the EU. They were not encouraged to co-operate among themselves, but to direct their efforts out of the region, towards Western Europe.

Partly during, but mostly after, the Kosovo conflict the EU began to change its focus and introduced two comprehensive new measures. One was the EU initiative in the establishment of the Stability Pact (SP) in

June 1999, which was put under the auspices of the OSCE.[7] This pact
heightened the emphasis for the countries of SEE to demonstrate regional
cooperation, good neighbourly relations and a functioning economic
and security framework. The other was the introduction in 2000 of the
SAP for the western Balkans,[8] which emphasised regional cooperation,
democratisation, capacity building and trade liberalisation, both with
the EU and intra-regionally. It also stipulated full cooperation with the
International Criminal Tribunal for the former Yugoslavia (ICTY) in The
Hague, sought guarantees for the rights of refugees to return to their
homeland and a full commitment to the fight against corruption and
organised crime. The main aim of the SAP is the formation of Stability
and Association Agreements (SAA) with the countries of that region.
SAAs entail the establishment of formal association with the Union over
a transitional period, during which the country concerned gradually
adopts its laws to the core standards and rules of the internal market.
Already the SP had recognised that for EU peace-building activities to be
effective, especially in terms of creating incentives for reforms in the
Balkan countries, the prospect of EU membership had to be included. This
recognition is made more explicit through the introduction of the SAA.

The activities of the SP and the SAP were both complemented and
strengthened through EU peace-keeping and police training missions. This
has given the EU the opportunity to combine effectively economic and
military resources and to contribute to the establishment of civil–military
relations in the Balkan countries. (EU peace-keeping will be examined in
Chapter 5). In 2003, the EU introduced police training missions in Bosnia
(EUPM) and in Macedonia (EUPOL PROXIMA). EUPM comprises
around 500 police officers and 300 international and local civilian staff,
and seeks to establish local law enforcement capabilities in Bosnia and
to contribute to stability in the region through monitoring, mentoring
and inspection activities. It succeeded the UN's International Police Task
Force (UNIPTF). PROXIMA was to assist Macedonia *inter alia* in the
consolidating of law and order, the promotion of integrated border
management, and the enhancement of cooperation with neighbouring
states in the area of policing. In the following, the institutional and
financial aspects of EU policies and missions are further examined.

Institutional arrangements for meeting challenges of security governance

Having considered the main aims of the SP and the SAP, it is apt now
to deal with the institutional setting, to examine the legal basis of these
two key policy initiatives and to explore the roles played by member

states and by EU institutions in the implementation of these policies. Attention will first turn to the way in which the SAP and the pact were established.

The Stability Pact for South Eastern Europe

The SP was created in June 1999 in response to the Kosovo crisis and its main aim is 'lasting peace, prosperity and stability for South Eastern Europe'.[9] The EU commits itself to bringing south-eastern Europe 'closer to the perspective of full integration'[10] with the EU by giving it 'firm European anchorage'.[11] The pact has eleven objectives: conflict prevention through multilateral and bilateral agreements; creating mature democratic political processes; creating peaceful and good-neighbourly relations in the region; protection of minorities; creating vibrant market economies; promoting economic cooperation; promoting contacts among citizens; combating (organised) crime, corruption and terrorism; preventing forced population displacement and migration generated by poverty; ensuring the safe return of all refugees; and creating the conditions, for countries of south-eastern Europe, for full integration into political, economic and security structures of their choice. It is the first attempt at addressing the political and economical structural deficits in the countries of the region through a comprehensive approach of preventive diplomacy, and thus to move beyond crisis management. An innovative aspect is that it fully draws in the countries of SEE as partners, indeed as *owners* of the stabilisation (Hombach, 1999). The pact is committed to all the principles and norms enshrined in the UN Charter, the Helsinki Final Act, the Charter of Paris, the 1993 Copenhagen Document and other OSCE documents and, as applicable, to the full implementation of relevant UN Security Council Resolutions, the relevant conventions of the Council of Europe, the General Framework Agreement for Peace in Bosnia, and the Treaty on European Union and the Amsterdam Treaty. In short, it is intended as a comprehensive, long-term conflict prevention instrument.

The pact supports regional projects that are implemented through a South Eastern European Regional Table. All partners of the pact are entitled to participate in the Regional Table, which acts 'as a clearing house for all questions of principle relating to the substance and implementation of the Stability Pact as well as a steering body in the Stability Pact process'.[12] It is further subdivided into three working tables on: Democratisation and Human Rights; Economic Reconstruction, Development and Cooperation; and Security. A fuller description of these three working tables is provided in Appendix 3.1. The working tables develop plans for their respective areas. Their objective is to discuss issues in a multilateral framework, to identify projects conducive to their respective ends and to provide momentum to areas that are lagging behind.

The pact coordinates the work of over sixty participating international organisations and governments (Busek, 2004). The Special Co-ordinator of the pact and his team of around thirty members fulfil an important coordination role. The EU appoints the Special Co-ordinator, after consulting the OSCE. Erhard Busek, who holds this post, succeeded Bodo Hombach in January 2002. He chairs the Regional Table, streamlines the participants' strategies and coordinates their initiatives. He cooperates with the governments and relevant institutions of the countries and the international organisations concerned. He also provides periodic progress reports to the OSCE.

The European Commission and World Bank coordinate the economic assistance measures and chair a High Level Steering Group. Here, the finance ministers of the G8 and the country holding the EU presidency collaborate with the international organisations and the Special Co-ordinator. The Steering Group ensures strategic direction in the reconstruction, stabilisation, reform and development processes. It also supervises and streamlines the resources available in order to ensure consistency. It is here, as well as in its chairing of the working table on Economic Reconstruction, that the Commission seeks to ensure the 'complementarity' of its actions, including the Community Assistance for Reconstruction, Development and Stabilisation (CARDS) programme,[13] with national governments and the international community.[14] In terms of funding, the Commission co-chairs and is guided by the High Level Steering Group for South East Europe which provides overall guidance on donor coordination. Second, the Commission maintains a Joint Office with the World Bank to help coordinate and develop support to the region.[15] Due to its role, at least on the budgetary side, with the European Union Force (EUFOR) in Bosnia, which is a 7,000 strong peace-keeping force, and the EUPM in Bosnia and the EUPOL PROXIMA in Macedonia, the Commission is also linked with these operations, and is connected with the EU Special Representative in Bosnia and Macedonia; respectively Christian Schwarz-Schilling and Erwan Fouere. There is also close interaction between the SP and the SAP. Further details on the link between the SP and the SAP, as well as on the respective structural features of each organisation are provided in the diagram of Appendix 3.2.

The Stabilisation and Association Process

The SAP was established in 2000 and seeks to promote stability (including reconciliation and the return of refugees) and democracy within the region, whilst also facilitating closer associations with the EU. The SAP strategy towards the western Balkans is designed to underpin the Dayton/ Paris and Erdut[16] agreements of 1995 by bringing stability and prosperity to the region. The SAP's aims are specifically outlined in its two main funding components for technical assistance, namely the CARDS and the European Agency for Reconstruction (EAR).[17] CARDS has four major objectives: reconstruction, democratic stabilisation, reconciliation and the return of refugees; institutional and legislative development, including harmonisation with EU norms and approaches, to underpin democracy and the rule of law, human rights, civil society and the media, and the operation of a free market economy; sustainable economic and social development, including structural reform; promotion of closer relations and regional cooperation among SAP countries and between them, the EU and their new members of central Europe.[18] The EAR aims at supporting good governance, institution building and the rule of law; the development of a market economy; to invest further in critical infrastructure and environmental actions; and to promote the social development and the strengthening of civil society.

A key element of the SAP, for countries that have made sufficient progress in terms of political and economic reform and administrative capacity, is a formal contractual relationship with the EU in the form of SAA.[19] The intention of the SAA is to help each country to progress at its own pace towards greater European integration. It includes aid, trade preferences, political dialogue and technical advice. Associated countries are instructed (entailing a binding commitment) to adapt their laws to the core standards and rules of the Single Market.

The SAP reflects the liberal democratic values held by the EU, as proclaimed, for example, in the Treaty on European Union, the Amsterdam Treaty and the Nice Treaty. These norms centre primarily on democracy, multi-culturalism and human rights, and are essential building blocks to a more stable and secure order, both within and between states in this part of Europe.

The SAP is based upon the European Council's 1996 initiative on the 'Process of Stability and Good Neighbourliness in South-Eastern Europe', and was more explicitly expressed in the *Common Position* of 9 November 1998 defined by the Council on the basis of *Article J.2* of the Treaty on European Union (98/633/CFSP). While the Council originally introduced the idea of a comprehensive policy towards the states in the western Balkans, the Commission ultimately introduced the SAP. Essentially, the Commission proposed to enhance this approach (the Process of Stability . . .) 'into a Stabilisation and Association process'.[20] The European Council affirmed that the SAP was the 'centrepiece' of its policy towards the western Balkans at the Lisbon Extraordinary European Council in March 2000. The Stability and Association Council[21] reviews progress of SAA developments. Compliance is assured through the annual country reports, which – if they show sufficient positive results – enable the country in question to proceed to a feasibility study. The successful conclusion of feasibility studies results in the opening of negotiations for a SAA.

The European Council, in the Helsinki Presidency Conclusions of December 1999, gave the initial push behind the CARDS programme. Essentially, the Council stated that, in order to improve the efficiency and effectiveness of EU assistance in the western Balkans, a 'single regulatory framework for financial assistance' was required. It was officially introduced in December 2000 through Council Regulation (EC) 2666/2000[22] and was based on Article 308 of the Treaty on the European Union (TEU).[23]

The EAR was introduced at the European Council in the Cologne Presidency Conclusions of 4 June 1999, and was formally established through Council Regulations (EC) 2454/1999 and Regulation (EC) 2667/2000. The former Regulation states in Article 14 that:

> The reconstruction of refugee programmes will initially target Kosovo, and when conditions are right may also target other parts of the FRY [Federal Republic of Yugoslavia] . . . Any decision to extend the Agency's activities to parts of the FRY other than Kosovo shall be taken by the Council acting by qualified majority on a proposal from the Commission.

To extend the EAR's purview to Macedonia, the Council adopted Council Regulation (EC) 2415/2001 which amended Regulation (EC) 2667/2000 to include the management of EC assistance to Macedonia as a responsibility of the EAR. The EAR is accountable to the Council and the European Parliament and is overseen by a Governing Board composed of representatives from the 27 EU member states and two representatives from the Commission. The Governing Board adopts decisions by a two-thirds majority and it works for and reports to the European Commission. The Commission adopts the annual EAR report and submits it to the European Parliament and the Council. The EAR has four Operational Centres: Belgrade, Prestina, Podgorica and Skopje. Its headquarters are in Thessaloniki. The EAR has regular bilateral meetings with other donors via UNMIK and supports the UNMIK strategy for reconstruction. It also cooperates with European Invest Bank (EIB), the European Bank for Reconstruction and Development (EBRD), the World Bank (WB), the OSCE and the United Nations Development Programme (UNDP) in Serbia, USAID, and many NGOs.

Burden-sharing arrangements: borne collectively
or 'where they fall'

With regard to the CARDS programme, according to Regulation (EC) no. 2666/2000: 'The Community shall provide assistance . . . in accordance with the Council Financial Regulation of 21 December 1977 applicable to the general budget of the European Communities'.

The EAR's budget is provided for in the Community budget (Articles 2(3), 6(3) and 7(3) of Regulation 2667/2000) and by member state contributions in the form of donations. In addition, under Article 7(3) 'the Commission shall assess the draft budget of the Agency having regard to the priorities it has established and the overall financial guidelines for Community assistance for the reconstruction of the Federal Republic of Yugoslavia'. It also asks the Commission to include the indicative annual contribution to the EAR budget in the preliminary draft general budget of the European Union.

The projects under the umbrella of the SP are funded through a combination of long-term debt, grant finance, budgetary funds of recipient countries, bilateral concessional funds and private sector involvement. Donors include the European Commission and the EU's member states as well as non-EU states, international organisations like the UN, OSCE, UNCHR and international financial institutions. Grants and loans are pledged at the so-called regional funding conferences. The first Regional Funding Conference was held in Brussels in March 2000, the second in Bucharest in October 2001.

The two police missions EUPM and EUPOL PROXIMA were established by EU Joint Actions respectively. The aim of both was to support the police reform process in Bosnia and Macedonia respectively and to develop and consolidate local capacity and regional cooperation in the fight against major and organised crime. EUPM was the first mission initiated under the ESDP, and followed on from the UNIPTF's mission. When established in January 2003, it was envisaged to cover a three-year period. A follow-on mission was agreed for the period January 2006 to the end of 2007. As of January 2006, EUPM numbered 198 international staff members – 170 seconded police officers and 28 civilians, as well as some 200 Bosnian nationals.[24] EUPOL PROXIMA was launched in December 2003 and completed in December 2005. PROXIMA was replaced for another six months by the EU Police Advisory Team (EUPAT). EUPM and EUPOL PROXIMA received around €15 million start-up finance each out of the general EU budget. In each case member states paid for salaries and travel expenses of the police officers and other staff to the operation of the missions and to and from the region.

Competencies and management aspects

Within the EU, training and technical assistance, the mainstay of assurance policies, are covered under Pillar I regulations. In contrast to intergovernmental proceedings, which characterise the hard core of CFSP and ESDP actions and involve peace-keeping and police mission exercises, Pillar I activities provide a central role for the European Commission and involve the European Parliament, as well as the Court of Justice. Decisions can be taken by qualified majority vote and finance is assured through the Community budget. The Commission has an extensive role in the implementation of the SAP, especially as it relates to administering CARDS and EAR. Both CARDS and the EAR are administered by the EuropeAid Office, which the Commission established in 2001 to manage *inter alia* all regional financial programmes. The Office is a department of the Commission and is subject to the normal operating procedures of the Institution. It is to concentrate on management of Pillar I matters and is thus excluded from the management of CFSP projects, which are handled by the Relex Counsellor's unit. It does not deal with humanitarian activities but does treat related issues such as development, good governance and capacity-building of civil society through, for example, the Democracy and Human Rights Unit (EIDHR) and the NGO Co-financing Unit. The EIDHR[25] funds projects without clearance from recipient country governments. Moreover, there is also a possibility for the European Commission to complement its activities with the Rapid Reaction Mechanism (RRM). This mechanism was founded in 2001 and aims at providing rapid civilian stabilisation of crises, for example, mediation or police training, while plans for long-term assistance and reconstruction are underway. With a budget of €30 million (2005), it provides support to the political strategy of the Commission faced with a crisis in a third country.[26] Like ECHO, the RRM is eligible to apply for funds from the emergency aid reserve (an additional source that is distinct from its normal budget line).

The European Commission also fulfils a critical role in the preparing and monitoring of SAAs. In the case of Kosovo, it administers the SAP's Tracking System (STM). The Commission's role in the Stability Pact and the SAP is complemented by its responsibilities generally in the field of EU enlargement rounds; many of the EU policies towards the western Balkans have been moved from the Directorate General of External Relations to the Commission's Directorate General of Enlargement in November 2004.

Through its key role in the management of the CARDS, EAR and EIHDR programmes, the Commission is able to control most of the carrots and sticks in the SAP. This differs from the so-called 'mixed agreements' covering, for example, police missions, peace-keeping operations, the role of Special Representatives,[27] or the administration of the city of Mostar,[28] which are a combination of EC representation and representation of member states or 'administrative agreements' that refer to both CFSP and EC competencies' (Smith, 2004: 225). Administrative costs of CFSP are covered by the EU budget immediately; in contrast, operative costs of CFSP are decided by a unanimous vote in the Council (Rummel and Wiedemann, 1998: 56).

With regard to the police missions EUPM and EUPOL PROXIMA, the police heads of these missions report to the Secretary General and High Representative of CFSP (SG/HR) via the EU Special Representatives in the host countries.[29]

EU performance as a security actor

What evidence is there to suggest that the proposed methods are working as expected? Or to put that differently, to what extent are the principles, norms and rules of the SP and the SAP fulfilled? How do EU assurance policy goals relate to performance? We will start with examining the financial allocations made by the EU in order to get an understanding of the sectors the EU and/or the Commission has chosen to support. A second task will be to explore whether the financial allocations have translated into relevant initiatives, networks or concrete results. The evidence gathering will rely on self-assessment of the EU (e.g., Council presidency reports, Commission monitoring and reporting, and reports for the Office of the Special Representative of the Stability Pact) on stipulated goals. However, it should be noted that there are some complications when comparing SP and SAP expenditure. This is because of the overlap in financial accounting between the two instruments and the fact that the SP caters for more countries than the SAP, i.e., Bulgaria, Romania and Moldova.

Tables 3.1 and 3.2 provide summaries of the funding provided by the SP and by the CARDS programme of the SAP. Table 3.1 indicates the shares of the respective donors by grants and loans. The annual budget has been fairly similar in size, averaging around €6.5 billion. In contrast, CARDS is entirely financed by the EC budget and based on grants. Table 3.2 lists the CARDS shares obtained by the recipient countries.

A number of things can be noted with regard to the figures supplied in Table 3.1. Firstly, the EU and its member states are the major contributors to the budget.[30] Secondly, loans are beginning to replace grants as the main source of funding.

In contrast to the Stability Pact, the CARDS Budget is smaller, comprising €4.65 billion for the period 2000–2006.[31] Before CARDS,[32] the European Community's assistance programmes to the western Balkans totalled €5.5 billion. Table 3.2 provides a country breakdown of CARDS allocations for the years 2002–2005/6, which shows that the lion's share of contribution has gone to Serbia/Montenegro, representing a larger sum than that of the other four countries combined.

For what purposes are SP and SAP funds being allocated? Different western Balkan countries have experienced and are experiencing different problems and therefore have required different types of assistance. For example, donor support for reconstruction and reform in Bosnia peaked in the years after the Dayton Agreement of 1995 and already much had

Table 3.1 Stability Pact allocations: total assistance to south-east Europe by donor, 2001–2005 (in million euros)

Donor	Total grants	Total loans	Final total
EU member states + EC budget	12,728.56	943.80	13,672.36
Non-EU countries	3,228.08	225.49	3,453.57
International financial institutions	91.40	15,772.51	15,863.91
Total	16,048.04	16,941.80	32,989.84

Source: Office for South East Europe (European Commission/World Bank), 'Financial Flows to South East Europe', *Continued High Assistance Flows to South East Europe* [Online], 9 June 2005. Available in pdf format from www.seerecon.org/region/documents/financial-flows-see.htm.

Table 3.2 CARDS Programme country allocations by countries for 2002–2005/06

	2002	2003	2004	2005/06	Total
Albania	44.9	46.5	63.5	89.0	243.9
Bosnia	71.9	63.0	72.0	100.0	306.9
Croatia[a]	59.0	62.0	81.0		202.0
Macedonia	41.5	43.5	55.5	85.0	225.5
Serbia and Montenegro[b]	359.6	331.3	312.4	540.0	1543.3
Total	576.9	546.3	584.4	814.0	2521.6

Notes:
a CARDS payments stopped in 2004 and were superseded by a pre-accession funding.
b Includes the province of Kosovo, which is currently under UN administration.
Source: *Financial Statistics*: http://ec.europa.eu/enlargement/financial_assistance/cards/statistics2003-2004_en.htm, and http://ec.europa.eu/enlargement/financial_assistance/cards/statistics2000-2006_en.htm#2.

been achieved by 1999, and reconstruction needs were on a downward trend. In Albania and Macedonia on the other hand, the Kosovo crisis caused immediate and dramatic budget support needs and humanitarian needs. As Table 3.3 reveals, the largest amount of SP assistance by 2005 was still being directed towards the development of infrastructure (e.g., roads, railways, electric power, and water) that is crucial for economic growth in the region. Ranking second was support for private and financial sector development, to encourage the expansion of output and trade as well as the development of sound banking facilities on which small and medium-sized enterprises (SMEs) depend. Funds have also been allocated for efforts to restructure and downsize military forces and the military-related sector. But there was also recognition that economic development, social inclusion and regional stability in SEE hinge on the strengthening of institutions, governance and a lowering in the level of corruption. This shift is recognised in the significant increase for the sector of government and institution building between 2002 and 2005.

A different or more balanced distributive picture emerges when the CARDS programmes by sector are examined, at least as far as four of the western Balkan countries are concerned. This is provided in Table 3.4.

Table 3.3 Stability Pact donor assistance to south-east Europe by sector, 2002–2005 (million euros)

Sector	2002	2003	2004	Estimates 2005	Total
Private and financial sector development	1,726.0	1,448.0	1,161.0	1,425.0	5,760.0
Economic infrastructure	2,278.0	2,063.0	2,085.0	2,834.0	9,260.0
Agriculture and rural development	314.0	450.0	394.0	349.0	1,507.0
Social	716.0	1,076.0	430.0	926.0	3,148.0
Government and institution building	924.0	1,087.0	1,243.0	1,308.0	4,562.0
Unspecified sector support	596.0	215.0	481.0	404.0	1,696.0
Sector support total	6,554.0	6,339.0	5,794.0	7,246.0	25,933.0
Undesignated budget support	175.0	222.0	189.0	7.0	593.0
Total allocation	13,283.0	12,900.0	11,777.0	14,499.0	52,459.0

Source: Office for South East Europe (European Commission/World Bank), 'Table: Assistance to South East Europe by Sector', *Donor Commitments to South East Europe: Past and Prospects* [Online], 9 June 2005: 11. Available from: www.seerecon.org/region/documents/financial-flows-see.htm.

If allocations for Serbia and Montenegro and Kosovo are excluded, then we can observe that the CARDS' focus has gradually shifted from infrastructure rehabilitation and democratic stabilisation (including aid to refugees) to institution building and justice and home affairs. With the new focus CARDS seeks to (1) integrate border management issues in order to help tackle cross-border crime, to facilitate trade across borders and to stabilise the border regions themselves; (2) increase the effectiveness of public institutions to allow them to implement their administration duties more effectively with regard to the SAP and SAAs; (3) improve the functioning of Interpol and the networks of judiciary throughout the region; (4) facilitate a move towards the compatibility of visa and entry policies with the EU *acquis*; and (5) integrate the region's transport, energy and environmental infrastructure into the wider European networks.[33]

As Table 3.5 shows, different priorities emerge with regard to CARDS allocation for Serbia and Montenegro as well as Kosovo, where a large proportion is still assigned to the rebuilding of infrastructure and to economic projects. It is for this reason that the EAR was established with its own budget line.

Table 3.4 CARDS assistance by sector and year for Albania, Bosnia and Herzegovina, Croatia[a] and the former Yugoslav Republic of Macedonia, 2002–2005/06 (million euros)

Sector	2002	2003	2004	2005–06	Total
Justice and Home Affairs	54.5	62.5	111.35	69	297.35
Administrative Capacity Building	42.5	40.8	42.6	75	200.9
Economic and Social Development	55.8	48.4	67.35	88	259.55
Environment, Natural Resources	13.5	14.8	17.2	3	48.5
Democratic Stabilisation	45	41.5	30.5	11	128
Other	6	7	6.5	28	47.5
Total allocation	217.3	215	275.5	274	981.8

Note:
a CARDS payments stopped for Croatia in 2004 and were superseded by a pre-accession funding.
Source: Financial Statistics: http: //ec.europa.eu/enlargement/financial_assistnce/cards/ statistics2003–2004 en.htm, and http: //ec.europa.eu/enlargement/financial_assistance/ cards/statistics2000–2006 en.htm cards 2005.

Table 3.5 CARDS assistance by sector and year for Serbia and Montenegro and Kosovo, 2002–2005 (million euros)

Sector	2002	2003	2004	2005	Total
Serbia and Montenegro					
Governance and institution building	37.7	62.5	74.0	58	232.2
Economic and social stabilisation	142.0	149.0	126.0	94.8	511.8
Democratic stabilisation	10.0	25.5	23.5	17.7	76.7
Other	15.0	18.0	13.5	6	52.5
Kosovo					
Governance and institution building	24.2	12.0	15.0	19.6	70.8
Economic and social stabilisation	101.0	46.28	54.9	26.9	229.08
Democratic stabilisation	9.8	5.0	4.0	6	24.8
Other	19.9	13.0	1.5	1.5	35.9
Total allocation	359.6	331.28	312.4	230.5	1233.78

Source: http://ec.europa.eu/enlargement/financial assistance/cards/statistics2000-2006_en.htm cards 2005.

Table 3.6 CARDS regional programme, 2002–2004 (million euros)

Sector	2002	2003	Total
Integrated border management	1.0	1.0	2.0
Institution building	19.9	21.8	41.7
Democratic stabilisation	7.6	5.0	12.6
Regional infrastructure	14.0	3.7	17.7
Reserve	1.0	0.0	1.0
Total allocation	43.5	31.5	75.0

Note: An additional amount of €105.15 million from the regional funds has been allocated to the country programmes for integrated border management for the period 2002–2004.
Source: European Commission (Enlargement), CARDS: Financial Statistics [Online], 2005. Available from: http://europa.eu.int/comm/enlargement/cards/financial_en.htm.

Some 10 per cent of the available CARDS budget is being directed to support regional cooperation. A breakdown of the regional programme is provided in Table 3.6. The European Commission's Multiple Indicative Programme 2002–2004 also recommended that the Interreg programme be fully associated with the development of the national integrated border management strategies.

Indeed, many of the challenges facing the western Balkan countries are not only common to all but also have cross-border dimensions. Refugee return, infrastructure and economic development and the fight against organised crime are examples of areas where the countries need to cooperate closely to achieve results. As Table 3.7 illustrates, a number of initiatives have been undertaken through the funding of the SP and the

Table 3.7 Regional networks

Regional initiatives	Regional centres and forums	Regional groups, commissions, etc.	Regional task forces	Region-wide treaties
SEE Cooperation Process (SEECP)	Regional Arms Control Verification and Implementation Assistance Centre (RACVIAC)	Groups of States against Corruption (GRECO)	Anti-corruption Task Force	29 bilateral free trade agreements
Adriatic and Ionian Initiative			Task Force on Parliamentary Cooperation	Energy Community Treaty
Disaster Prevention and Preparedness Initiative (DPPI)		SEE Clearing House for the Control of Small Arms and Light Weapons (SEESAC)	Media Task Force	
	Regional Centre of MARRI Regional Forum on asylum, migration and displacement		Task Force on Education	
Initiative against Organised Crime – SPOC		Sava River Basin Commission	Gender Task Force	
The Stability Pact Anti-Corruption Initiative (SPAI)	Regional Centre for Combating Transborder Crime	The Network of Associations of Local Authorities in SEE (NALAS)	The SP Task Force on Trafficking in Human Beings	
Initiative on Social Cohesion	SEE Cooperative Initiative Regional Centre for Combating Transborder Crime (SECI Regional Centre)		Task Force on Good Governance	
			Infrastructure Steering Group (ISG)	
			The SEE Public Prosecutors Advisory Group (SEEPAG)	

SAP. To reinforce these initiatives, the governments of the western Balkan countries have established the South East European Cooperation Process (SEECP),[34] and the European Commission has introduced a Regional Strategy Paper 2002–2006, and a Multiple Indicative Programme 2002–2004[35] on border management issues. These mechanisms are beginning to bind the countries in a framework of agreed and mutually supportive commitments and to ensure the smooth integration with the networks of the EU. They help to diagnose current policy conditions; set standards for reform; provide country specific recommendations; and monitor progress on reforms. All stress the promotion of good governance, reliable public administration, the rule of law, and an active civil society. Already, they begin to show positive results. Several countries have made agreements concerning refugee return, border crossings, visa regimes and the fight against terrorism, organised crime and human trafficking. The establishment of Euroregions in the SEE can be seen as a further sign of greater intra-regional cooperation. These involve the south Adriatic, Nis/Skopje/Sofia (EuroBalkans Euroregion) and Ohrid/Prespa and the Glijane/Kumanovo/Presevo microregion.[36]

This success can be further demonstrated with a few specific examples. For example, through the initiatives of the SP and the SAP, the regional governments have established 29 bilateral free trade agreements (FTAs), which will stimulate intra-regional trade, boost the economy, attract foreign direct investment, and make the western Balkan countries conform more to the principles of the four Internal Market freedoms. Attempts are now underway to translate these FTAs into a single Free Trade Agreement for the SEE area. Another accomplishment is the establishment of the Energy Community SEE, which is seen as similar to the European Coal and Steel Community in that it could serve as a powerful catalyst of greater economic and political integration (Busek, 2004).

With regard to the return of refugees and their re-integration, a direct link can be made with the CARDS programme and the EAR whose remit has been to assist countries in these efforts (e.g., housing construction and re-integration). As can be seen from Table 3.8, the number of refugees and Internally Displaced Persons (IDPs) has gone down in all western Balkan countries between 1999 and 2005, receding to a trickle in the case of Albania; less than one-tenth in the case of Croatia and Macedonia, and one-quarter in the case of Bosnia and Serbia and Montenegro. As Table 3.8 also illustrates, slightly more than half of all the refugees and IDPs relate to Serbia and Montenegro, followed by nearly 40 per cent for Bosnia. At the end of 2003 over 90 per cent of all property claims in Bosnia arising from the war in the 1990s had been resolved.[37] In Kosovo inadequate security continues to be a major obstacle to returns. The difficult economic situation and other social reasons are additional factors discouraging displaced people from returning. At the end of 2003, the number of displaced persons in Serbia and Montenegro with origins in Kosovo was 225,000, a slight decrease compared to 2002.[38] In the case of Macedonia, the Emergency Assistance Programme (launched following the country's conflict of 2001 and completed by mid-2003) has helped to return 90 per cent of IDPs to their pre-conflict residencies, and a total of 1,165 houses were repaired or reconstructed.[39] However, progress to deal with the remaining 900,000 refugees or internally displaced persons in the western Balkans was hampered by the slowness of the responsible governments to adhere to the access to rights and citizenship approach.[40]

As part of the political dialogue stipulated in the SAP, the western Balkan countries have attempted to find agreements on the fight against organised crime and drug and people trafficking. The continuing prevalence of organised crime and corruption in the region delays political reform, holds back economic development, and puts into question the rule of law. To elevate efforts in the fight against drug trafficking, an Action Plan on Drugs covering the EU and the countries of the western Balkans, and Romania, Bulgaria and Turkey was adopted by the Council in June 2003 and is being implemented. The EU has also introduced visa bans against individuals supporting war criminals and crime figures linked with extremist political groups. Furthermore, Europol has a mandate to negotiate cooperation agreements with all countries in the western Balkans, which will be a useful contribution in the fight against organised crime.

Most countries have adopted anti-corruption strategies and set up bodies to monitor their implementation. However, their work often suffers from unclear or unrealistic objectives and insufficient resources and consequently the strategies are not implemented vigorously enough. The results of anti-corruption measures have so far been limited and corruption is still widespread throughout the region. As Table 3.9 indicates, Albania, Macedonia and Serbia and Montenegro remain amongst the worst offenders on corruption of the 159 countries surveyed worldwide in 2005. In the case of Albania, Bosnia and Croatia performance on eliminating corruption actually deteriorated between 2003 and 2005. On the plus side, Macedonia and Serbia and Montenegro have improved their record over the same period. Slovenia is by far the best performer on both democratic indicators and corruption indexes; outscoring also Bulgaria and Romania, two states that are entering the EU in January 2007. Efforts must therefore intensify to come to grips with these problems. A positive development was that

Serbia and Montenegro joined the Groups of States against Corruption (GRECO) in October 2003. All western Balkan countries are now participating in this inter-governmental anti-corruption cooperation.[41]

Another major problem affecting the western Balkan countries and one of the main reasons for EU intervention has been the existence of weak institutions. As the European Commission notes, civil society is still underdeveloped in the western Balkan countries, although the situation is gradually improving. For example, in 2004 Bosnia was able to establish a state-level High Judicial and Prosecutorial Council, a Ministry of Defence, and a new defence structure based on a civilian, state-led control. Under this arrangement, defence ministries of both Republika Srpska and the Federation ceased to exist and the army was reduced to consist of only professional soldiers. This was a significant leap forward as ten years prior to this unified structure the separate armies had fought each other for four years. Similar successful efforts have been made to unify the city of Mostar. Moreover, Bosnia formed a State Border Service (SBS) in 2000 and a State Investigation and Protection Agency (SIPA) in 2002, which became operational in July 2004; both are under civilian control. The SBS helps to fight cross border crime in Bosnia[42] and works closely with the European Police Mission (EUPM) in Bosnia. SIPA deals with fraud and money laundering[43] and collaborates with the International Criminal Tribunal for the former Yugoslavia (ICTY).

Generally, however, NGOs and other independent bodies need to improve their advocacy skills and their financial viability, relying as they do largely on external donor funding.[44] Further efforts are needed to reform and strengthen the education system, public administration, and the judicial system, as well as to promote a free, independent, and professional media. Institutions guaranteeing respect for human rights need to be supported, adequate funding must be provided and their decisions must be respected and implemented.

It is in the context of improving civil society in the western Balkans that EU efforts to establish closer links with the western Balkan countries come more sharply into focus. In preparing western Balkan countries for membership the EU has sought measures involving institutional and legislative development, including harmonisation with EU norms and approaches, to underpin democracy and the rule of law, human rights, civil society and the media, and sustainable economic and social development. Some of these efforts are not only sponsored by CARDS, but also involve the EIDHR and RRM. For example, the EIDHR has sponsored independent media training aimed at strengthening cross-ethnic civil society organisations in Bosnia and Macedonia.

Table 3.8 Refugees and internally displaced persons (IDPs) in the western Balkans, 1999–2005

Country	Catagory	1999	2000	2001	2002	2003	2004	2005	Total
Albania	1 Refugees	3,930	524	292	20	26	51	56	4,899
	2 IDPs	–	–	–	–	–	–	–	–
	3 Total	3,930	524	292	20	26	51	56	**4,899**
Bosnia and Herzegovina	1 Refugees	97,428	56,867	51,410	69,727	36,529	24,662	11,841	348,464
	2 IDPs	852,930	577,599	518,425	438,266	367,491	327,188	187,911	3,269,810
	3 Total	950,358	634,466	569,835	507,993	404,020	351,850	199,752	**3,618,274**
Croatia	1 Refugees	38,952	41,451	33,742	25,679	14,253	11,203	8,188	173,468
	2 IDPs	76,004	49,628	34,134	23,402	16,969	12,566	7,540	220,243
	3 Total	114,956	91,079	67,876	49,081	31,222	23,769	15,728	**393,711**
FYR Macedonia	1 Refugees	21,200	9,050	94,375	13,583	2,394	1,730	1,274	143,606
	2 IDPs	–	–	74,524	16,371	6,764	–	–	97,659
	3 Total	21,200	9,050	168,899	29,954	9,158	1,730	1,274	**241,265**
Serbia and Montenegro	1. Refugees	1,308,401	609,125	425,920	368,644	300,842	284,826	154,092	3,451,850
	2 IDPs	293,836	267,500	266,131	261,826	259,329	257,610	248,873	1,855,105
	3 Total	1,602,237	876,625	692,051	630,470	560,171	542,436	402,965	**5,306,955**
Total		2,692,681	1,611,744	1,498,953	1,217,518	1,004,597	919,836	619,775	9,565,104

Sources: 1999–2003 data was compiled from the 2003 UNCHR Statistical Yearbook available at www.unhcr.org/cgi-bin/texis/vtx/statistics/opendoc.pdf. 2004 data was compiled from the 2004 UNCHR Statistical Yearbook available at www.unhcr.org/cgi-bin/texis/vtx/events/opendoc.pdf?tbl=STATISTICS&id=42b283744. 2005 data was compiled from the provisional 2005 UNCHR Statistical Yearbook available at www.unhcr.org/cgi-bin/texis/vtx/events/opendoc.pdf?tbl=STATISTICS&id=4486ceb12.

Table 3.9 South-eastern Europe democratic indicators, 2000–2005

	2000				2001				2002				2003				2004				2005			
	PR	CL	FR	CPI	PR	CL	FR	CPI	PR	CL	FR	CPI	PR	CL	FR	CPI	PR	CL	FR	CPI	PR	CL	FR	CPI
Albania	4	5	PF		3	4	PF		3	3	PF		3	3	PF	2.5 / 92	3	3	PF	2.5 / 108	3	3	PF	2.4 / 126
Bosnia Herzegovina	5	4	PF		5	4	PF		4	4	PF		4	4	PF	3.3 / 70	4	3	PF	3.1 / 82	4	3	PF	2.9 / 88
Macedonia	4	3	PF		4	4	PF		3	3	PF		3	3	PF	2.3 / 106	3	3	PF	2.7 / 97	3	3	PF	2.7 / 103
Serbia and Montenegro	4	4	PF		3	3	PF		3	2	F		3	2	F	2.3 / 106	3	2	F	2.7 / 97	3	2	F	2.8 / 97
Croatia	2	3	F	3.7 / 51	2	2	F	3.9 / 47	2	2	F	3.8 / 51	2	2	F	3.7 / 59	2	2	F	3.5 / 67	2	2	F	3.4 / 70
Slovenia	1	2	F	5.5 / 28	1	1	F	5.2 / 34	1	1	F	6.0 / 27	1	1	F	5.9 / 29	1	1	F	6.0 / 31	1	1	F	6.1 / 31
Bulgaria	2	3	F	3.5 / 52	1	3	F	3.9 / 47	1	2	F	4.0 / 45	1	2	F	3.9 / 54	1	2	F	4.1 / 54	1	2	F	4.0 / 55
Romania	2	2	F	2.9 / 68	2	2	F	2.8 / 69	2	2	F	2.6 / 77	3	2	F	2.8 / 83	3	2	F	2.9 / 87	2	2	F	3.0 / 85

Note: PR and CL stand for Political Rights and Civil Liberties, respectively; 1 represents the most free and 7 the least free rating. FR is the overall Freedom Rating, where F stands for Free, PF stands for Partially Free and NF stands for Not Free (from www.freedomhouse.org). Serbia and Montenegro is listed as Yugoslavia for the period 2000–2002. CPI Score (Corruption Perception Index) relates to perceptions of the degree of corruption as seen by business people and country analysts and ranges between 10 (highly clean) and 0 (highly corrupt). The top figure refers to the score, the bottom figure refers to the overall ranking (from www.transparency.org/). More than two-thirds of the 159 nations surveyed in Transparency International's 2005 Corruption Perceptions Index (CPI) scored less than 5 out of a clean score of 10, indicating serious levels of corruption in a majority of the countries surveyed'. The highest CPI score for 2005 was recorded by Iceland (9.9). Other major industrialised countries: UK (8.6, rank 11), Germany (8.2, rank 16), USA (7.6, rank 17), France (7.5, rank 18), Italy (5.0, rank 40), China (3.2, rank 78). Bangladesh and Chad are the worst performers (1.7, rank 158).

Source: Transparency International, *Transparency International Corruption Perceptions Index 2004* [Online], 20 October 2004. Available at: www.transparency. org/cpi/2004/cpi2004.en.html.

To facilitate these efforts, the EU has introduced a number of conditions together with a political dialogue in the SAP. The political dialogue has increased between the EU and the countries of the region and has been further reinforced within the framework of the EU–western Balkans Forum. The first meetings of the Forum were held with the Ministers responsible for Justice and Home Affairs issues in November 2003 and with the Foreign Ministers in December 2003. The latter focused on issues of common concern in the field of CFSP, to review progress of the countries of the region in their road to Europe, and to exchange views on major developments in the EU. Annual meetings of foreign ministers and ministers responsible for Justice and Home Affairs will be held as appropriate. The countries of the western Balkans are regularly invited to align themselves with EU *démarches*, Declarations and Common Positions on CFSP issues. In this context, the Commission regrets that Albania, Bosnia and Macedonia have signed bilateral immunity agreements with the United States, which run contrary to the 'EU guiding principles concerning the arrangements between a state party to the Rome Statute of the International Criminal Court (ICC) and the United States regarding the conditions of surrender of persons to the court' (adopted by the Council on 30 September 2002).[45]

It is the process of 'conditionality', particularly as expressed in the fulfilment of SAAs, which deserves particular attention. Failure to comply with levels of conditionality may result in the delay, suspension or cancellation of the planned or committed assistance without the possibility of reallocating the funds to another sector. In its practical application the SAP involves a series of steps, ranging from the establishment of a Consultative Taskforce, the Feasibility Study on a SAA,[46] to the beginning, conclusion and finally ratification of an Agreement. Countries that have sufficiently reformed their political, economic and administrative systems enter a formal contractual (bilateral) relationship with the EU, a tailor-made SAA. To complement the latter part of the steps, European Partnerships have been introduced. These Partnerships are part of the Thessaloniki Agenda, agreed in June 2003, and were formally adopted on 14 June 2004 through Regulation (EC) 533/2004. Their aim is to establish short- and medium-term priorities for the western Balkan countries, except Croatia, and to help countries of the region to prepare for closer European integration. Other complementary measures have been introduced in agriculture/rural development and environment/transport infrastructure, and through the establishment of a system of 'twinning' in which civil servants from EU member state administrations are seconded to work in government ministries. These SAAs offer local leadership the opportunity to attach fragile domestic institutions and a weak concept of statehood to a large-scale, stable and comprehensive project. As will be seen from Table 3.10, so far Albania, Croatia and Macedonia have signed SAAs. Bosnia and Serbia and Montenegro have started SAA negotiations in December 2005. However, it is likely that, after the independence referendum in Montenegro in June 2006 which sanctioned secession from Serbia, this newly formed country will be allowed to continue SAA talks on its own. In the case of Kosovo, a Stabilisation Tracking Mechanism was started in 2003.[47]

Table 3.10 SAP south-eastern Europe: summary table

	Political instrument	Financial instrument	Monitoring instruments
Albania	SAA signed June 2005 Ratification concluded Jan. 2006	CARDS 2000–2006 €315.5m[a]	Stabilisation and Association Report (SAR) 2004
Bosnia and Herzegovina	SAA negotiations started November 2005	CARDS 2000–2006 €502.8m	SAR 2004
Bulgaria	Accession Treaty April 2005	PHARE, ISPA, SAPARD 1992–2005 Over €2.8 billion[b]	Accession Report 2005
Croatia	SAA signed December 2004 Membership neg. started Oct. 2005	CARDS 2000–2004 €278.8m	SAR 2003
Kosovo	Stabilisation Tracking Mechanism started 2003		SAR 2003
Macedonia	SAA signed 2001 Since Dec. 2005 officially a candidate country	CARDS 2000–2006 €298.2.5m	SAR 2004
Serbia and Montenegro	SAA negotiations November 2005; started suspended in May 2006	CARDS 2000–2006 €2559.8m[c]	SAR 2004
Romania	Accession Treaty April 2005	PHARE, ISPA, SAPARD 2005 €952m[d]	Accession Report 2005

Sources:
a for Albania, Bosnia and Herzegovina, Croatia, Macedonia (Former Yugoslav Republic of) and Serbia and Montenegro: EU, DG Enlargement, Financial Statistics, http://ec.europa.eu/comm/enlargement/cards/financial_en.htm.
b Enlargement DG, http://ec.europa.eu/comm/enlargement/bulgaria/eu_relations.htm.
c Includes the province of Kosovo, currently under UN administration.
d DG Enlargement, http://ec.europa.eu/comm/enlargement/romania/eu_relations.htm.

With the signing of the SAAs, both Croatia and Macedonia have subsequently applied for EU membership. Croatia presented its application for accession to the European Union on 20 February 2003. In April 2003, the Council requested the Commission to submit its Opinion on the application and a series of questions was transmitted to the Croatian authorities in July, to which the Croatian government responded in October. In the spring of 2004 the Commission adopted a positive Opinion, and in June 2004 the European Council gave Croatia the status of accession country and indicated that negotiations could be opened in early 2005, which indeed happened in turn. However, negotiations were temporarily suspended because of the delayed surrender of General Gotovina, the last main remaining Croatian person indicted for war crimes (PIWC) to the ICTY. Macedonia submitted its application for membership on 22 March 2004 and is since December 2005 officially a candidate country.

The issue of cooperation on alleged PIWC raises a wider question, which is how to ensure that conditions are not only stipulated but are complied with and that the desired values norms and principles are not only transmitted but actually absorbed by the states in question. This aspect will be considered further in the section on assessment below. In the western Balkans, the slowness of the responsible governments to adhere to the access to rights and citizenship approach hampered progress.[48]

Assessment of EU assurance policies

This section will seek to address two issues. Firstly, with regard to assurance policies, can we witness the emergence or development at the European level of distinct structures of governance? What contribution have EU institutions made toward the execution of joint actions or institutional innovations in this field? Secondly, to what extent can we observe that governance structures, as well as norms, principles and rules have been successfully transferred from the EU to the western Balkans? To start with, brief consideration will be given to the question of whether EU member states could have achieved as much if they had acted on their own.

Characteristics of EU governance in the field of assurance policies

EU assurance policy is not so much a question of succeeding where states have failed, but one where the collective effort has been able to achieve more than those of individual states. The commitment to a comprehensive programme, like the SAP, would have been difficult, if not impossible by individual member states. This effect can be noticed in the case of CARDS. With the merging in 2000 of OBNOVA, ECHO and PHARE, CARDS became the principal channel for financial assistance to the Western Balkan region, based on a quick disbursing mechanism. The introduction of CARDS allowed the EU not only to enhance its autonomous action capacity for the western Balkans, but also to consolidate the role of the European Commission as an independent authority in the SAP. Similarly, compliance (the practice of setting common objectives/standards; exchange of 'best practice') would have been more difficult if only a few states had insisted on it rather than the group of EU member states. Furthermore, only the EU can offer membership, not individual states; the prospect of membership of the Union is the 'golden carrot' that can most effectively galvanise the necessary internal political and economic transformations among the peripheral states (Dannreuther, 2004: 204).

The EU's approach to tackling the problems of the western Balkans is multi-dimensional. It ranges from strict conditionality regarding cooperation with the ICTY, to visa bans against individuals supporting war criminals and crime figures linked with extremist political groups, to peace-keeping and police operations in Bosnia and Macedonia, to many CARDS programmes in the area of rule of law and border security. The multiplicity of projects and activities are complemented by the activities of EUROPOL, EU sponsored activities within the SP, and bilateral measures by individual member states. The range of EU activities impinge on the demarcation between Pillars I and II (and to some extent III) and raise problems of coordination within the EU. The European Commission's trump card is in Pillar I where it is able to manage, mostly independently, financial and technical assistance programmes, economic issues and enlargement proceedings. In contrast, Pillar II is the arena of member states' governments and gives the High Representative of CFSP, who is also Secretary General of the Council of Ministers (SG/HR), a special role. However, there are important overlaps between the two pillars. For example, the legal and financial preparations for the EU Police Missions in Bosnia and Macedonia, ostensibly ESDP operations, were handled by the Commission. The start-up costs for these operations were also provided through the Community budget. On the other hand, the role of the SG/HR has been straying into Pillar I activities. For example, the Lisbon European Council invited the SG/HR 'to ensure the coherence of EU policies towards the western Balkans, to strengthen the impact of its contribution and to enhance coordination with the SP and other efforts of the International Community'.[49] The SG/HR's position was further strengthened with his successful brokering roles in the Ohrid

Agreement[50] in Macedonia in 2001, and in the Belgrade agreement of 2002 that founded the Union of Serbia and Montenegro.

Four European Union Special Representatives (EUSR) assigned to Bosnia, Kosovo, Macedonia and the SP assist the SG/HR in his dealings with the western Balkans. The EUSR to Bosnia, currently Christian Schwarz-Schilling, combines this post with his role as the High Representative of the Dayton Agreement's Mission Implementation Plan (MIP). In this respect, the Council adopted Joint Action 2004/570/CFSP in July 2004 on the European Union military operation in Bosnia which designates a specific role to the EUSR. Accordingly, the EUSR is to contribute to the reinforcement of internal EU coordination and coherence in Bosnia, e.g., through chairing a coordination group composed of all EU actors present in the field with a view to coordinating the implementation aspects of the EU's action, and through providing guidance to them on relations with the Bosnian authorities. The EU actors with whom the EUSR is to confer include the Council presidency, the Commission, EUPM–Bosnia, EUFOR, the Political and Security Committee, Europol and CARDS. However, the role of the EUSR should not in any way prejudice the MIP as set out in the General Framework Agreement for Peace in Bosnia (GFAP) of 1995 and subsequent Peace Implementation Council conclusions and declarations. The perceived extensive powers of the former EUSR to Bosnia, Lord Ashdown, especially in his capacity as HR of the MIP, resulted in complaints by the Council of Europe, alleging that some of his decisions had violated human rights principles (Knaus and Cox, 2004: 65). Whilst lacking the extensive powers of the combined role of the EUSR to Bosnia, the other EUSRs perform similar important roles in liaising between the authorities on the ground and EU institutions. Moreover, while all EUSRs work closely with the SG/HR, they are accountable to the Commission for all expenditure and administrative detail.

The presence of multiple actors and the deployment of various instruments in EU assurance policies in the western Balkans are a consequence of the nature of the task the EU saw itself confronted with, especially in 1999, and reflect the characteristics of EU governance generally, the absence of hierarchical structures and different but overlapping competences between EU institutions and member states. The initial failures and the depth of the problem faced in the Kosovo crisis made the EU realise that a more concentrated and multi-actor oriented approach was necessary. The SAP (rationalising aid and trade measures) and the CARDS (consolidating various aid instruments) introductions were efforts of greater concentration together with the promise of eventual membership. The involvement of multiple actors in the task of EU assurance policies in the western Balkans enables the EU to draw on the combined strengths of Community instruments (e.g., financial and technical assistance), the ESDP capabilities (e.g. EUFOR, EUPM and EUPOL PROXIMA) and member state bilateral assistance (e.g., their role in the SP). However, the involvement of multiple actors and instruments also creates problems of coordination for the European Commission and the Secretariat of the Council of Ministers. This not only involves problems of internal coordination (within the Commission and between the Commission and the Council Secretariat), or between EU institutions and member states, but also in the field. The latter is particularly tricky in places like Bosnia where effective coordination is required between the Delegation of the Commission, the EUSR, the heads of EUFOR and EUPM, and the Special Co-ordinator of the SP. Similar complexities arise in the case of Kosovo. Given the nature of the task, and given the prevailing structural and jurisdictional characteristics, it is likely that these coordination problems will continue and probably even grow. To deal with war-torn societies requires civilian and economic instruments as well as military capabilities to achieve the required economic and political reforms and to establish peace, stability and order. To what extent the EU has been successful in this effort in the western Balkans will be assessed next.

The transfer of EU values and norms

The Berlin European Council of March 1999 had sought to guarantee fundamental values, i.e., respect for human rights and the rights of minorities, international law, democratic institutions and the inviolability of borders to the western Balkan countries. To what extent have these core values been transferred and successfully incorporated into the state and social fabric of the western Balkans? Has the EU goal of addressing the political and economic structural deficits in the countries of the region through a comprehensive approach of crisis prevention and management been accomplished? And finally, to what extent has the aim of drawing in the countries of SEE as partners, indeed as *owners* of the stabilisation, been achieved?

The transfer of values and norms, the occurrence of preventive diplomacy, or the beginning of 'ownership' cannot happen without incentive structures of economic, financial and technical benefits. For the western Balkan countries, EU and member states funded programmes are essential not only for improving the physical, social and economic environment,[51] but also for establishing new institutions and improving the functioning of existing ones. The former ranges from the clearing of mines, the reconstruction of destroyed homes and electricity supply, to health care and environmental projects. The latter involves local government structures, judicial institutions and non-governmental organisations. It is through these programmes, the establishment of competition standards and access to EU markets[52] that the economies of the western Balkans can be promoted, foreign investment attracted, and physical infrastructure improved. Most importantly, EU democracy programmes help to ensure that civil society can be promoted in these countries and the return and re-integration of refugees can be secured. Thus, the impact of assistance is not limited to the sector directly concerned. Programmes to create competent institutions and judicial systems have a positive impact on economic development and reform and vice versa. As stated in the CARDS Regional Strategy Paper 2002–2006, SAP emerges as 'a strategy for poverty alleviation by aiming to stabilise the region's economies and make their development towards sustainable recovery', thereby enabling the targeting of resources on poverty reduction and reinvestment in not only economic but social spheres. Income levels in the western Balkans generally lag well behind those of the EU members from central and eastern Europe.[53]

However, while the work of CARDS and the EAR is, in many ways, long-term in nature, it also needs to address short-term concerns in order for the western Balkan countries to meet the conditions stipulated for membership in the SAP and SAA. Interaction within the region has improved greatly since the outset of the SP and the SAP in 1999/2000, with contacts between countries at all levels of government and society now routine.[54] Stability within and between the countries of the region has been enhanced by democratically elected governments. Clearly, it would be wrong to attribute the success of these improvements in stability and security to the work of the EU alone. The donors of the SP and the role of international organisations, such as the OSCE, NATO, the Council of Europe and the UN, to name but a few, have had a share in this success. However, the depth and scope of EU financial and technical assistance, and the offer of membership coupled with conditionality principles puts the EU in a stronger position to assist in stabilising the post-conflict situations in the western Balkans than other international actors, or for that matter, single states. But given the enormity of the task in restructuring and rebuilding war-torn states, it is not surprising that problems remain. Some are also country-specific in character. For example, there was a resumption of violence in March 2004 in Kosovo, which caused 19 deaths, the destruction of 730 homes and 29 religious buildings as well as the displacement of over 4,000 people (Lehne, 2004: 116). All the countries of the western Balkans still have difficulties with the functioning of state institutions and viable democracies, respect for human rights and structural economic reforms. Among the most pressing problems are the following. First, racism and xenophobia are still clearly prevalent in the region with the result that minorities continue to feel excluded from the political process. Second, these minority groups often believe that armed conflict and secession are more effective means of satisfying their political demands than democratic debate and the ballot box. Third, political stability in the region cannot be guaranteed while the number of refugees and displaced persons – the most obvious by-product of mistreatment of minorities – is still high in Bosnia and Serbia. Roma are the most vulnerable group with no ID and no passport. Fourth, corruption and organised crime continue to plague the western Balkans. The region remains a potential breeding ground and route for transnational terrorism, as well as a major conduit for refugee flows and trafficking in arms and drugs. Fifth, ICTY cooperation with the western Balkan countries, especially the Republika Srpska, Serbia and Montenegro, remains difficult, as a number of indicted PIWCs remain at large. Sixth, both the SAP and the SP avoid addressing the political solution of Kosovo, which is a potential source of unrest for the entire region.[55] However, the EU decided in April 2006 to establish an EU planning team regarding a future EU crisis management operation in the field of rule of law and possible other areas in Kosovo.[56] Regular discussions on the development in Kosovo also take place within the Contact Group consisting of France, Germany, Italy, Russia, the UK and the US.

Other EU peace-building efforts

Judging from the data presented above, EU efforts to conduct an effective assurance policy in the western Balkans have at least been partially successful. In so doing the EU has undergone a learning process, with the usual trials and tribulations such a process entails. Whether the more positive experience or success of this process can be passed on to post-conflict situations outside the western Balkans is a challenge the EU is facing. There are some early indications that the EU is extending its western Balkan experience. As Table 3.11 shows, the EU is relying primarily on three types of post-conflict engagement: rule of law missions; police missions and border missions; all of which are conducted under the ESDP auspices, and are supplemented by the Commission's contribution to civilian crisis management, which is focused on local capacity-building. The first rule of law mission was employed in Georgia in 2004, and a second followed in Iraq. Besides the rule of law mission in Georgia, the EU has assisted in the establishment of a Georgian–Ossetian police force.[57] In addition, through RRM funding, the EU allocated €4.5 million to Georgia in 2004 to undertake confidence building measures for conflict-affected groups, parliamentary and electoral reforms, and reform of the justice and prison system (Saferworld International Alert, 2005). EUJUST LEX for Iraq aims at the training of some 770 judges, investing magistrates, senior police and penitentiary officers in Iraq. The EU has also worked with other international actors in mobilising contributions to reconstruction and in coordinating international efforts to support Iraq. It hosted the first donors' conference in Madrid in October 2003, which pledged €1.2 billion (combining both member state and European Community budgetary contributions).[58] As part of this financial commitment, the EU has provided electoral support (€31.5 million in 2005) from the Community's Assistance Programme for Iraq 2005 (Posch, 2005: 98). The EU has also promoted the establishment of the International Reconstruction Facility for Iraq (IRFFI) and contributed financially to the programmes run by the IRFFI.

EU police missions have been undertaken in the Democratic Republic of Congo (EUPOL Kinshasa) in 2005 and in the Palestinian Territories (EUPOL–COPPS) in 2006. EUPOL Kinshasa was an extension of its 2003 enforcement or peace-keeping operation Artemis, and is part of the EU cooperation within the United Nations Organisation Mission in the Democratic Republic of Congo (MONUC). The EU has also introduced an advisory and assistance mission for DRC security reform (EUSEC–RD Congo), involving EU military personnel. In addition, in 2003 the EU adopted a series of initiatives related to civilian crisis management in the DRC: a programme totalling €205 million (Tardy, 2005: 57). EUPOL–COPPS, which seeks to contribute to the establishment of sustainable and effective policing arrangement in the Palestinian Territory, is embedded in EU efforts to contribute towards a peaceful resolution of the Middle East conflict, and is connected with the European Neighbourhood Policy, as well as the EU border mission to the Palestinian Territory.

EU Border missions have been introduced at the Gaza–Egypt border (EU BAM Rafah) and at the Moldovan–Ukraine border, involving the troubled region of Transdniestria. Following the agreement between Israel and the Palestinian Authority, the EU agreed to undertake a Third Party role proposed in the Agreement and mounted a monitoring mission at the Rafah Crossing Point between the Gaza–Egyptian border in November 2005. Due to tensions surrounding the kidnapping of Israeli soldiers, Israel temporally closed the Rafah Crossing Point in June 2006. The EU border assistance mission to Moldova and Ukraine is intended to help prevent smuggling, trafficking and customs fraud in the Transdniestra region, by providing training to Moldovan and Ukrainin border and customs services. It has a two-year mandate, which can be extended. The mission includes 69 experts seconded from EU member states, as well as some 50 local support staff. Its wider aims are to seek a solution to the Transdniestria conflict.

The EU, together with five contributing countries from ASEAN as well as with Norway and Switzerland, is conducting a monitoring mission in Aceh (Indonesia). This monitoring mission is designed to monitor the implementation of various aspects of the peace accord between the Indonesian Government and the Free Aceh Movement, which was brokered under the auspices of the Crisis Management Initiative, a non-governmental organisation chaired by former Finnish President Martti Ahtisaari. The EU provided support to the peace process negotiations

Table 3.11 EU civilian missions (excluding the western Balkans)

Country/ territory	Nature of mission	Duration of mission	Objective of mission	Budget of mission and source
Georgia (EUJUST THEMIS)	Rule of law	July 2004–July 2005	support for reform of Georgian criminal judicial system	
Congo-DRC (EUPOL KINSHASA)	Police mission	April 2005	Train and support of Congolese police	4.3 million euro budget; from the EDF, CFSP and M/S
Iraq (EUJUST LEX)	Rule of law	July 2005–July 2006	Training of judges, magistrates, senior police and penitentiary officers	10 million EU budget for the common cost; M/S contrib. for training courses and trainers
Indonesia Aceh Monitoring Mission (AMM)	Monitoring mission	Sept. 2005–Sept. 2006	Monitor peace agreement b/w the Indonesian Govt. and the Free Aceh Movement	9 million euro budget; from CFSP budget, EU M/S and other participating countries
Gaza-Egypt border (EU BAM Rafah)	Border assistance mission	Nov. 2005–Nov. 2006	To provide a third party presence at the Rafah Crossing Point	11.5 million euro (incl. M/S contrib. of 3.8 mill euro)
Moldova-Ukraine border (EUBAM)	Border assistance mission	Dec. 2005–Dec. 2007	Training of Moldov. and Ukrainian border and customs services	Budget 8 million euro
Palestinian Territories (EUPOL-COPPS[a])	Police mission	Jan. 2006–Dec. 2009	To support the PA in establishing police services	EU budget covers common cost (6.1 million euro for 2006); M/S finance projects

Note:
a COPPS stands for Co-ordinating Office for Palestinian Police support.

Sources: The information was extracted from European Union Factsheets in http://europa. eu.int/comm/external_relations; EU Council Secretariat Background, and http://ue.eu.int/ Newsroom.

through the RRM. The monitoring team, from the involved countries and the EU, consists of around 250 monitors. Moreover, while not yet having mounted an official mission in the rebuilding of Afghanistan, the EU has been a major contributor to Afghanistan since the fall the Taliban in 2001; assisting with €200 million annually. These (civilian) efforts can be seen as complementing the (military) peace-keeping activities of the International Security Assistance Force (ISAF).

To monitor progress of the missions and initiatives launched (outside the western Balkans) and to take corrective actions, the EU has designated Special Representatives to post-conflict environments in the South Caucasus, the Middle East, the African Great Lakes region, Afghanistan, Central Asia, Sudan and Moldova. It also uses Country Strategy Paper to assess specific country situations.

As the brief review of the above mentioned missions and initiatives indicates, the EU has not only extended its assurance policies to its geographic periphery (Moldova, South Caucasus and Middle East) but also further afield to places in Africa and Asia. These efforts, and in many ways successful undertakings, also complement its prevention policy in the shape of the European Neighbourhood Policy, the development and cooperation policy, and crisis management measures, which are listed in more details in Chapter 2 of this book. Together they provide evidence of the growing engagement of the EU in security and defence matters, its strength as a collective actor, and its development of a common identity.

Conclusion

As the challenges in post-war Iraq and Afghanistan show, one of the most important missions in conflict-ridden societies is the stabilisation of local situations. While peace-keeping operations and police missions are important elements in the rebuilding of states and nations, civilian efforts are essential for stabilising war-torn states and societies.[59] Equally important is that civilian efforts are not only transferred or imposed by external actors, but are also absorbed by the local population. Only if post-conflict states are drawn in as partners, indeed as *owners* of the stabilisation,[60] will democratic values be secured and sustained.

For peace-building efforts to be successful, appropriate motives or incentive structures, together with a comprehensive policy approach and workable enforcement mechanisms, have to prevail. It was the task of this chapter to explore why and how the EU became committed to its assurance policies in the western Balkans, and why and how the western Balkan countries have complied with these policies.

EU commitment to a more robust, comprehensive and committed assurance policy towards the western Balkans derived mainly from a combination of earlier EU failures to deal with the conflicts in the western Balkans (Edwards, 1997) and from the length and intensity of these conflicts. In particular the Kosovo conflict of 1999 can be seen as a watershed in this respect. These factors made EU member states realise that the security of the EU and that of the western Balkans was inextricably linked and that instability in the western Balkans would negatively affect the stability of the EU (e.g., through uncontrolled migration or illegal trafficking). As stated by the Lisbon European Council in March 2000, 'peace, prosperity and stability of South East Europe are a strategic priority for the European Union'.[61]

However, the magnitude of the task (transforming conflict ridden states and societies into stable and viable units) made the EU also realise that a credible incentive structure was necessary. Falling back on its own success of integration (overcoming internal animosities) and seeing it as a successful strategy for a number of central and east European countries, the EU was prepared to offer its strongest and most effective tool in external relations, namely, the prospects of EU membership. This was done in conjunction with a process of stabilisation for the countries in question. The result was the establishment of two key instruments in the shape of the SP and the SAP. Their aims were to strengthen civil society and state building, promote democracy, enhance regional stability, and bring the Balkan countries closer to the EU. The regional cooperation model, promoted in the two instruments, is essentially an extension of the EU's own philosophy that deeper cooperation with neighbouring countries is a route to national as well as regional stability and growth and that such cooperation serves the mutual interests of all countries concerned.[62] Economic and political means, as well as persuasive (norm setting) rather than coercive methods therefore became the central elements of the SP and the SAP, though the necessity for peace-keeping activities was recognised. What is the evidence of success?

The evidence from the data on the SP, the SAP and the police missions suggests that EU policies of conditionality directly or indirectly benefit progress in peace efforts, in institution-building and in strengthening civil society. Their success can be noted in at least three ways:

- the establishment of rules of good governance, minority protection and freedom of the media in these countries;
- the strengthening of the capacity of governing institutions in these countries;

- the creation of a web of agreements and sectoral strategies that are beginning to bind the Western Balkan countries in a framework of agreed and mutually supportive commitments.

Together with the established regional centres and programmes, these achievements will help to ensure sustainable growth in the region, promote regional confidence building measures, and to ensure the smooth integration with networks of the EU.[63] That is not to neglect the important work that remains to be done with regard to creating peaceful and viable states.[64] On the contrary, the challenge remains how to combine simultaneously stabilisation, transition and integration in the western Balkans and how to secure ownership of the reform process by the governments in question, i.e., governments need to take over the operational, political and also financial responsibility of the regional centres and reform programmes rather than relying on external guidance. More specifically, further initiatives are required to build the capacity of local police forces, reinforce the penal and judiciary systems, encourage civilian oversight of the security sector, and develop civilian awareness and expertise in regard to security issues.[65] Similarly, the EU needs to relax visa requirements, particularly for young people.[66] Yet, in all these efforts the EU has to tread carefully between insisting on reforms while avoid provoking resentment and/or promoting by default extreme nationalist parties, like the extreme Radical Party of Serbia.

While, hitherto, EU policy towards the western Balkans had been mostly reactive and directed at symptoms and crises, the emphasis has shifted to a more pro-active engagement of preventive diplomacy since 2000. Underlying this shift is the awareness by the EU that the stability of the western Balkan region is intrinsically linked with its own. The adoption of the SP and the SAP has allowed the EU to move beyond crisis management procedures (peace-making and peace-keeping) and to instil more permanent seeds of stability and prosperity. This has enabled the EU to disseminate norms and rules to the western Balkans, and to contribute to the establishment of a community of interests and values in this particular region. It has also given the EU an opportunity to extend its system of security governance and to create an expanding zone of stability in Europe. Although operating a complex governance framework, the EU, especially through its two hubs the Commission and the Council Secretariat, has become an important forum for information, discussion, policy-making and coordination in matters of assurance policies. It allows the EU to engage in problem solving and capacity building, two important characteristics associated with the governance. Problem-solving exercises help to formalise interactions among the actors of policy networks specialising in the creation of authoritative European rules. Capacity building is linked with an increase in institutionalisation (an increase in rules, conventions and norms).

Clearly the EU initially failed to react quickly and uniformly to crisis situations in the western Balkans but, as the level of violence has receded,[67] a more coherent policy towards peace-building has emerged in the post-conflict period for this region. Whereas in the first half of the 1990s there seemed to be a general trend to ethnocratic rule which ended in terrible wars, now, for the present phase of transition, the rule of law and respect for human and minority rights have become prerequisites in the SAP. The various elements of the rule of law have become increasingly binding and represent essential indicators for progress towards European integration. All this points to the enormous strides that have been made in the western Balkan's region to build strong, fully functioning states, which are capable of delivering on the needs of their citizens, of ensuring effective regional cooperation and of developing more advanced relations with the EU. The EU will continue improving its assurance policies and procedures on the basis of lessons learned both from its own operations as well as through exchanges with other organisations. While it is too early to judge how far the experience of EU assurance policies can be extended to other parts of Europe or the rest of the world, there are signs that such efforts are underway and, in some cases, already bear initial success.

Appendix 3.1 Working tables of the Stability Pact for SEE

---

1 *Working Table I on Democratisation and Human Rights*: its areas are democratisation and human rights; minorities; free and independent media; civil society building; rule of law and law enforcement; institution building; efficient administration and good governance; border related questions; refugee issues.

2 *Working Table II on Economic Reconstruction, Development and Cooperation*: economic reconstruction, development and cooperation; promotion of free trade; border-crossing transport; energy supply and savings; deregulation and transparency; infrastructure; promotion of private sector business; environmental issues; sustainable reintegration of refugees.

3 *Working Table III on Security*: justice and home affairs; combating (organised) crime, corruption and terrorism; transboundary environmental hazards; transparency and confidence-building; implementation of the Dayton/Paris Article IV Arms Control Agreement and progress of the negotiations of Article V; cooperation on defence/military issues; regional security; conflict prevention. It has two sub-tables: Security and Defence, and Justice and Home Affairs.

Appendix 3.2 Main international structures in south-eastern Europe

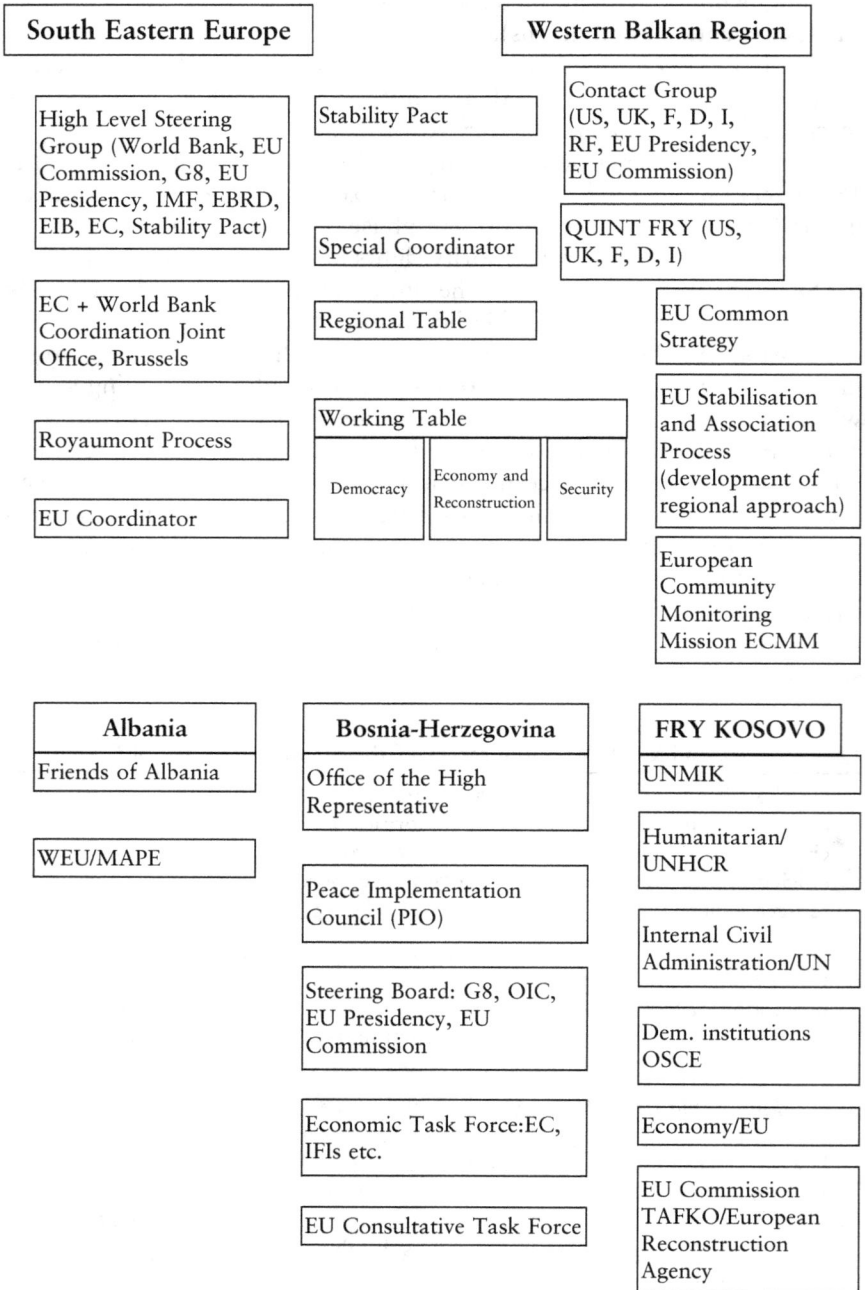

South Eastern Europe		Western Balkan Region

High Level Steering Group (World Bank, EU Commission, G8, EU Presidency, IMF, EBRD, EIB, EC, Stability Pact)	Stability Pact	Contact Group (US, UK, F, D, I, RF, EU Presidency, EU Commission)
	Special Coordinator	QUINT FRY (US, UK, F, D, I)
EC + World Bank Coordination Joint Office, Brussels	Regional Table	EU Common Strategy
Royaumont Process	Working Table	EU Stabilisation and Association Process (development of regional approach)
EU Coordinator	Democracy / Economy and Reconstruction / Security	
		European Community Monitoring Mission ECMM

Albania	Bosnia-Herzegovina	FRY KOSOVO
Friends of Albania	Office of the High Representative	UNMIK
		Humanitarian/ UNHCR
WEU/MAPE	Peace Implementation Council (PIO)	Internal Civil Administration/UN
	Steering Board: G8, OIC, EU Presidency, EU Commission	Dem. institutions OSCE
	Economic Task Force:EC, IFIs etc.	Economy/EU
	EU Consultative Task Force	EU Commission TAFKO/European Reconstruction Agency

Notes

1 It should be noted that reference to the western Balkans and south-eastern Europe will be used interchangeably. Furthermore, although this chapter will consider south-eastern Europe (SEE) in a regional context, it acknowledges the different historical, cultural, political and economic differences between the countries involved in this region. The western Balkans consist of: Albania, Bosnia, Croatia, Macedonia, Serbia and Montenegro. Although the positive outcome of the June 2006 referendum has given Montenegro independence from Serbia, most of the statistical data presented in this chapter reflect the status prior to that event and therefore lists the two as one entity. In addition, although Kosovo has the status of a UN protectorate, this chapter respects the *de jure* link of Kosovo with Serbia and therefore lists aid and trade flows as either part or linked with Serbia.

2 Although the official reference is the Former Republic of Macedonia, the shortened form of Macedonia will be used in this chapter, except where for historical or official (treaty signatures) reasons references to the full name are required.

3 European Council (1999) '. . . Berlin European Council . . .'.

4 For further details on milieu goals see Wolfers (1963).

5 For a more comprehensive review of these efforts see Albrecht *et al.* (2004).

6 It was designed to assist the countries of the former Yugoslavia in reconstruction and rehabilitation, to promote reconciliation between the various parties, and to prevent the resurgence of hostilities. The European Commission also used OBNOVA to in the reconstruction programme of Kosovo.

7 The SEE signatories were Albania, Bosnia, Bulgaria, Croatia, Hungary, Romania, Slovenia, the former Republic of Macedonia and Turkey. The Federal Republic of Yugoslavia joined in 2000, which also included Kosovo. Kosovo is administered by the international community through the United Nations International Mission in Kosovo (UNMIK), which is representing Kosovo within the Stability Pact framework. Moldova became a beneficiary in 2001 and is participating in many of the Stability Pact's activities, task forces and initiatives, albeit often with an extended timeline and tailored arrangements (Special Co-ordinator of the Stability Pact, 2004, 'Newsletter, 4 May 2004': 3).

8 These comprise: Albania, Bosnia and Herzegovina, Croatia, Serbia, Montenegro and the Former Yugoslav Republic of Macedonia. Kosovo benefits from all the elements of the SAP, with the exception of the possibility of contractual relations with the EU. See European Commission (2004) 'The Stabilisation and Association Process . . .': 8.

9 Special Co-ordinator of the Stability Pact for South Eastern Europe (1999) '. . . Cologne Document . . .': para. 3.

10 *Ibid.*, para. 20.

11 *Ibid.*, para. 18.

12 *Ibid.*, Annex, para. 8.

13 A management committee composed of the representatives of the member states and chaired by the representative of the Commission assists the Commission.

14 See European Commission/External Relations DG (2001) '. . . CARDS Assistance Programme . . .'.

15 *Ibid.*: 19.

16 The Erdut agreement between the Serbian and Croatian Governments regarding the of regions of eastern Slavonia, Baranja and western Sirmium was signed in Erdut, on 12 November 1995.

17 Countries covered by CARDS are: Albania, Bosnia and Herzegovina, Croatia, the Federal Republic of Yugoslavia and the Former Yugoslav Republic of Macedonia. The EAR covers Serbia, Montenegro, Kosovo, and the Former Yugoslav Republic of Macedonia. The operational headquarters of the EAR are in Thessaloniki.

18 See European Commission/External Relations DG (2001) '. . . CARDS Assistance Programme . . .'.

19 SAAs involve the Council of Ministers (by way of a Council decision) the EP (by way of the assent procedure) and all member states (by way of ratification). See Pippan (2004: 234).

20 See European Commission (1999) '. . . the EU & south-eastern Europe . . .'.

21 The Stability and Association Council consists of the members of the Council, members of the European Commission and members of the governments of the respective treaty partners.

22 This Regulation repealed Regulation (EC) no. 1628/96 and amended Regulations (EEC) no. 3906/89 and (EEC) no. 1360/90 and Decisions 97/256/EC and 1999/311/EC.

23 Article 308 is known as the 'residual powers clause' and has been used to empower the creation of various agencies and initiatives that were neither originally envisioned by nor incorporated into the Treaties. Accordingly, rather than use Article 308 as a 'codification of implied powers doctrine in its instrumental sense', it has been employed in a creative and radical fashion. As such, Article 308 empowers the Council and the Union to broaden the scope of EU legislation and its legal framework in ways not suggested by the Treaties. For further details see J. H. H. Weiler (1991) pp. 2445–6.

24 EU Operations (2006) 'Factsheet, EU police mission in Bosnia and Herzegovina'.

25 The EIDHR was established in 1994 in an effort to combine all headings that previously dealt specifically with various democratisation and human rights issues. It has an annual budget of around €100 million. It operates according to calls for macro and micro project proposals, but also sponsors some micro projects and grants without a call for proposals. See Europe Aid Cooperation Office (2006) '. . . EIDHR . . .': 4–5.

26 See European Commission/External Relations DG (2005) 'Conflict prevention & civilian crisis management . . .'.

27 The mandate of the Special Representative, who reports to the CFSP High Representative, Javier Solana, but is accountable to the Commission for expenditure, is to promote overall EU political coordination but without prejudice to Community competence.

28 Mostar was one of the first Joint Actions carried out under the Second Pillar of the TEU (Council of the European Union, 1995 '. . . Ombudsman for Mostar . . .').

29 For further details see Merlinger and Ostrauskaite (2005).

30 This is still the case for the years 2003 and 2004, because the European Investment Bank (one of the contributing international financial institutions) is an instrument of the EU.

31 See European Commission/External Relations DG (2001) 'CARDS Assistance Programme . . .'.

32 Until 2000, the EU had used various assistance programmes for the western Balkans. In the main these included PHARE, with a focus on developmental issues, e.g., institution building; ECHO which provided humanitarian aid in the form of emergency supplies, technical assistance and related support; and OBNOVA which was designed to meet the demands of a region emerging from conflict, emphasising reconstruction and rehabilitation, as well as fostering reconciliation between the various parties and preventing resurgence of hostilities.

33 See European Commission (2004) '. . . the stabilisation and association process . . .': 9; and European Commission/External Relations DG (2001) 'CARDS Assistance Programme . . .'.

34 The SEECP is chaired by a country on a rotating basis and includes Romania and Bulgaria. The SEECP plays a crucial role in securing effective regional ownership of the reform process and in bringing about regional cooperation. It works closely with the SAP and the SP. See European Commission (2004) '. . . the stabilisation and association process . . .': 24.

35 This programme advocated a comprehensive approach to border management in which neighbouring countries cooperate on trans-national issues, i.e., inter-agency cooperation between customs and border control services with the objective of developing a commonly agreed and operational Integrated Border Management Strategy for the western Balkan countries.

36 See Special Co-ordinator of the Stability Pact (2004) 'Newsletter, 4 May 2004': 6.

37 Office of the High Representative and EU Special Representative (2004) 'Implementation of the property laws . . .'.

38 *Ibid.*: 15.

39 European Agency for Reconstruction (2004) 'Annual report . . .'.

40 See Special Co-ordinator of the Stability Pact (2004) 'Newsletter, 4 May 2004': 9.

41 See European Commission/External Relations DG (2005) '. . . the stabilisation and association process . . .': 15.

42 For example, whereas in 2000 the state border service had arrested only 23 people, by 2005 the figure had risen to 507. See European Police Mission in Bosnia and Herzegovina (2006) 'Securing the borders . . .'.

43 Already between July 2004 and April 2005, SIPA had frozen €555,000 in 67 fraudulent accounts. See European Police Mission in Bosnia and Herzegovina (2006) 'Fighting Major and Organised Crime . . .'.

44 See European Commission (2004) '. . . the stabilisation and association process . . .': 14.

45 *Ibid.*: 8.

46 For example, in the case of Bosnia the Feasibility Study had stipulated 16 reform measures which Bosnia was asked to fulfil before SAA proceedings could start.

47 Kosovo has no international legal status, thus no SAA can be negotiated. The STM is the mirror process of the SAA.

48 See Special Co-ordinator of the Stability Pact (2004) 'Newsletter, 4 May 2004': 9.

49 European Council (2000) '. . . Lisbon European Council . . .'.

50 The Ohrid Agreement in August 2001 between Macedonia's main political parties, including ethnic Albanians, was aimed at ending the violent conflict between Macedonian security forces and Albanian extremists in the country. Besides the role of Javier Solana as a broker, the actual 'dialogue facilitators' were James Pardew for the United States and François Léotard for the EU. NATO also played a key role in calming the situation in the field.

51 According to the World Bank Poverty Assessments, all of the countries of South Eastern Europe are characterised by low incomes and a high incidence of poverty -especially in relation to the poorest countries of the EU (Ireland, Portugal, the Baltics and central and eastern Europe). Quoted by the Office for South East Europe (2006) 'How much money . . .'.

52 The EU introduced exceptional trade measures for the western Balkans in September 2000, and 95 per cent of products from south-east Europe now enjoy duty-free and unlimited access to the single market. See European Commission/External Relations DG (2001) 'CARDS Assistance Programme . . .'.

53 The average per capita GDP for the western Balkans was €2,400, ranging from about €700 in Kosovo to €5,400 in Croatia. If Croatia is excluded, per capita GDP of the remaining countries average €1,700. This compares with an average of €6,000 for the EU members from central and eastern Europe. See European Commission (2004) '. . . the stabilisation and association process . . .': 16.

54 See Stability Pact for South Eastern Europe (2005) 'Newsletter, 17–18 May 2005 . . .'.

55 The United Nations settlement plan of February 2007 called for separate statehood of Kosovo but did not specifically refer to independence (Macdonald and Wagstyl, 2007).

56 Among the brief is the establishment of an International Civilian Office (ICO) and an EU mission in the rule of law area, comprising around 1,500 international police, judges, prosecutors and customs officials.

57 European Commission (2003) '. . . Tacis National Indicative Programme . . .': 19.

58 The European Community contribution consisted of €200 million for 2003–2004 for reconstruction and €100 million for humanitarian needs. It has since then deployed €320 million with a view to restoring key public services, boosting employment and reducing poverty, as well as strengthening governance, civil society and human rights. The Commission has also adopted a new assistance programme for Iraq in 2005 with a budget of €200 million to cover similar policy aims as outlined for the 2003–2004 budget items. Source: European Union Factsheet (2005): 'EU Support for Iraq'.

59 Carl Bildt (2005) makes a similar point when he notes that: 'hard power can certainly bring down regimes, as Iraq demonstrated, but in order to build new regimes, soft power is largely required'. For a more elaborate treatment of the need to create effective civil society structures and state institutions see Paris (2005).

60 This was the view of Bodo Hombach (1999), the first EU Special Representative to the Stability Pact. For an elaboration of the partnership and ownership principles see Reinhardt Rummel (2004: 3).

61 European Council (2000) '. . . Lisbon European Council . . .'.

62 This is explicitly noted in European Commission/External Relations DG (2001) 'CARDS Assistance Programme . . .'.

63 See European Commission (1999) '. . . the EU & south-eastern Europe . . .': 22.

64 Uncertainties prevail over the status of Kosovo, the fragile democratic transition in Serbia, the new democracy in Montenegro, and the cohesion of Bosnia.

65 For further details on needed reforms see Bianchini *et al.* (2006).

66 EU interior ministers regularly cite threat of organised crime as a reason for not making the visa process easier and quicker. For further details see T. Judah (2006).

67 According to Stefan Lehne (2004: 115), 2002 and 2003 were the first years since 1991 free from violence in the Balkans. This progress in security was reflected in the reduction of international troops deployed in the western Balkans from 65,000 in summer 2000 to 29,000 in May 2004.

4

Policies of protection: meeting the challenge of internal security

Territorial security and domestic tranquillity are the core responsibilities of the Westphalian state. Those tasks have constituted its historical *raison d'être*; domestic legitimacy has long been contingent upon successfully discharging both. The Westphalian sovereignty principle had long justified in theory and praxis the conceptual differentiation between the tasks of external and internal security. Europe's evolution towards post-Westphalianism, in conjunction with the rise of malevolent sovereign-free actors operating outside and targeting Europe, no longer warrants or suffers the conceptual disassociation of internal and external security requirements. European states, particularly the member states of the European Union (EU), have experienced a progressive loss of sovereign control over national territory, a development aggravated by the EU's enlargement and association processes, the signing of trade and cooperation treaties drawing the states of the former Soviet Union into the EU's economic and social orbit, the rising diversity and volume of interactions between the EU and the states along its periphery, and the implementation of the Schengen *acquis* within most of the EU. The growing de facto irrelevance of political-territorial boundaries within Europe makes it increasingly difficult to control the flow of people, goods and ideas. Thus, the very success of the European project has sharply limited the effective exercise of sovereign prerogatives and eroded the sovereignty principle; it has also occasioned the growing vulnerability of society to a broad spectrum of threats.

The threat spectrum has broadened in two senses: first, there has been a simple increase in the kinds of threats originating within and outside the EU; second, governments, attentive elites and the governed have fundamentally changed their perception of threat as well as their collective understanding of the social and political requirements for meeting those threats. The progressive 'securitisation' of societal vulnerabilities has been matched by a relative 'desecuritisation' of the state's traditional security role; viz., the defence of national territory from external attack.[1]

Changes in technology, the consolidation and spread of transnational criminal organisations, and Muslim terrorism have accelerated this securitisation process. The fear of Muslim terrorism, in particular, has been sharpened owing to the largely non-negotiable political and religious agenda, if not millennial nihilism, that extremist Muslims embrace.[2] A more general sense of insecurity derives from the vulnerability of open societies to external disorder, particularly since failed or failing states afford terrorists and transnational criminal organisations safe havens from which to penetrate the soft underbelly of European societies.

This chapter investigates the EU's emerging role as a provider of internal security policies, what we call the policies of protection. The EU has targeted two general threats to internal security, organised crime and terrorism. Both organised crime and terrorism present a security threat when the activities of transnational criminal organisations or terrorist groups perpetrate illicit acts weakening the political, social or economic integrity of a state. The EU members recognise that these two threats to internal security require joint action. Yet, there has been a limited willingness to surrender sovereign policing or judicial prerogatives even when confronted with the spectre of terrorists acquiring chemical, biological, radiological or nuclear (CBRN) materials or devices. The internal security threat complex, the still limited surrender of *de jure* jurisdiction by the member states, and the persistent reticence to adopt supranational solutions or to transform the EU into a major security actor in this policy domain raise a number of questions: why do the content and form of threats to internal security resist a more robust collective response? Under what circumstances have the member states qualified or abandoned national prerogatives in the areas of judicial process or criminal law and enforcement? What barriers remain to the progressive abnegation of sovereign prerogatives in fighting organised crime and terrorism? Can the EU add value in coordinating or defining member state internal security policies?

The rationale, principles and goals in the area of internal security

Since 1997, the EU has played an influential role in coordinating its member states' internal security policies and in setting a common agenda. The rationale for collective or coordinated action to combat organised crime and terrorism is highly developed. An elaborate set of policy principles now define the balance between member-state and EU preroga- tives. Successive action plans and framework decisions identify EU-wide policy objectives. In addition to the problem of terrorism and organised crime, the EU has sought to increase its competency in allied areas of internal security: border control, money laundering, computer and information network security, and health security. Moreover, the EU has strengthened existing coordinating mechanisms at the supranational level, created new institutional avenues for member state cooperation, and carved out special competencies that necessarily impinge upon the sovereign prerogatives of its members.

Rationale for the EU as security actor

The Maastricht Treaty (1992) lent constitutional status to Justice and Home Affairs (JHA) as Pillar III of the EU. The member states accepted the need for a partial abnegation of sovereign prerogatives in internal security affairs that had been uncontestedly national, particularly with respect to penal law and judicial process. The Treaty of Amsterdam (1997) committed member states to construct a European area of 'freedom, security and justice' and to accept an expanded EU role in realising it. While JHA has been the primary nexus of EU and member state efforts, there has been a gradual elision of external and internal security policies, particularly the nascent linkage of Pillar III with Pillar II (CFSP and ESDP).[3]

The Treaty of Amsterdam and four subsequent framework documents – the Vienna Action Plan (1998), the Tampere Milestones (1999), the European Security Strategy (ESS) (2003) and The Hague Programme (2004) – set the policy agenda in the area of internal security. These documents defined the EU's role as the facilitator of joint action, demarcated its role as an autonomous security actor, and legitimised its partial displacement of the state. The Vienna Action Plan, adopted by the JHA Committee in December 1998, was the first step towards conformity with the Amsterdam Treaty provisions.[4] The Tampere Milestones (1999–2004), adopted at the October 1999 Tampere Council Summit, marked a second major step towards deepening police and judicial cooperation. It enumerated the EU's objectives in the area of internal security, particularly with respect to border control and organised crime.[5] The ESS, presented at the December 2003 Thessoloniki Summit, explicitly linked the EU's internal security to the political and social stability of the states along Europe's periphery;[6] it moved terrorism to the top of the policy agenda and identified it as the key challenge to a widening and deepening Union. The five-year Hague Programme (2004–2009) continued and enlarged upon the Tampere Milestones, but gave prominence to terrorism as an internal security threat – a policy objective that accelerated the process of the cross-pillarisation, particularly between Pillars II and III.[7]

The EU strategy against organised crime is found in two documents, the 1997 Action Plan against Organised Crime and the 2000 Millennium Strategy.[8] Those documents contain the rationales for an enhanced EU role in fighting organised crime, develop policy principles guiding joint policy initiatives, and detail specific policy objectives. Parallel documents in the area of terrorism – the 2002 Council Framework Decision on Combating Terrorism, the 2004 Declaration on Combating Terrorism, and 2005 Counter-Terrorism Strategy – serve a similar function.[9] Finally, a raft of miscellaneous framework decisions develop general policy guidelines and specific policy objectives for the broad spectrum of internal security threats, particularly money laundering, border control, computer and information network security, and health security, including the threat posed by weaponised nuclear, radioliogical, biological and chemical materials or agents.

The 2000 New Millennium Strategy presents a compelling two-part rationale for joint EU action in the area of organised crime. First, transnational criminal organisations are indifferent to national borders, either in their activities or base of operation. The ability of transnational criminal organisations 'to take advantage of the free movement of money, goods, personnel and services across the European Union requires joint action to limit effectively the reach of organised crime into European societies'.[10] Second, as criminal organisations increasingly penetrate societies outside EU territory, the effective control of the EU external border becomes an essential component of the fight against organised crime. Criminal acts closely associated with organised crime – money laundering, trafficking in human beings or drugs, and economic crime – were designated as security threats, because the target of activity was 'the social and business structure of European society'.[11]

The 11 September 2001 terrorist attacks in New York and Washington, DC, provided a third rationale for joint action and pushed terrorism to the top of the global policy agenda. The ESS focused on the linkages between organised crime, terrorism, and the proliferation of weapons of mass destruction as well as the critical nexus between terrorism and the laundering of illicit proceeds from transnational crime to finance terrorism. This interconnectedness of two policy domains that had been segregated in practise underscored that 'the internal and external aspects of security are indissolubly linked'.[12] This interdependence of internal and external security policies had ramifications not only for policies directed against terrorism and organised crime, but for EU policies on border control and external relations more generally.

The emergence of terrorism, the growing reach of organised crime, and the safe havens afforded terrorist and criminal organisations outside the

EU were explicitly conjoined to state failure, malevolent sovereign-free actors operating along Europe's periphery, and the EU's growing structural vulnerability. The escalating vulnerability of European societies impelled EU member states to qualify their penal and judicial sovereignty if they were to defend against those threats on a pan-European basis. The Hague Programme, like the ESS, emphasised that transborder terrorism and organised crime made obsolete uncoordinated national policing efforts. The Hague Programme also shifted attention to the protection of critical infrastructures and public safety in the event of a CBRN event.[13] This complex of diffuse and differentiated transnational threats provided a compelling logic for adopting common policies, enhancing coordination between police and judicial authorities, implementing a common set of policies governing national judicial systems and penal law, and developing a complementary and reinforcing set of external policies directed at limiting the terrorist threat.[14]

Domestic political violence in Europe preceded the end of the Cold War and represented a chronic internal security concern for the major European states. In Spain, France, Germany, Italy and the United Kingdom terrorist groups had national memberships with limited access to external financing and proffered an explicit political or ideological agenda demanding either a reformulation of the social contract (Red Brigade in Italy and Baader–Meinhoff in Germany) or secession (ETA in Spain, the provisional IRA in the United Kingdom, and the FLNC Reconstitué in France).[15] There was also very little agreement within Europe on which groups were 'terrorist' and which were engaged in 'legitimate' armed conflict. Member states resisted into the 1990s the expansion of EU competencies in combating terrorism; terrorism was viewed as a national responsibility.[16] Although the Amsterdam Treaty provided a constitutional basis for an enhanced EU role in combating terrorism, that role was restricted to supporting 'efforts of the international community to prevent and stabilise regional conflicts'.[17]

The 11 March 2004 Madrid bombings accelerated the transformation of terrorism from a national to a common problem. The historical Other perpetrating the new terrorism – extremist Muslims – produced the momentum for a more active and prominent EU role in shaping, coordinating, and executing counter and anti-terrorism policies. It provided a definable external threat devoid of the political ambiguity surrounding the IRA or ETA that had previously impeded member-state cooperation. The characteristics of Muslim terrorism in the new millennium established the indivisibility of the terrorist threat and the need for joint action: Muslim terrorist groups generally conduct 'off-shore' operations based from sovereign-free territory, failing states or states sympathetic to their agenda, have access to an effective global network of financial intermediaries, and possess a religious-ideological agenda that present targeted countries with an unacceptable set of non-negotiable demands. Muslim terrorism (like organised crime) reaffirmed the meaninglessness of the distinction between internal and external security; it revealed the lack of protection afforded by national borders to geographically removed political grievances or civil decay.

The 7 July 2005 London underground bombings belied the notion that the threat posed by radical Muslim terrorists was external to Europe. Al-Qaeda and its loosely allied sympathisers not only operated out of and targeted European societies, but recruited successfully from Europe's disaffected Muslim citizens – a recruitment strategy replicated in the foiled terrorist plot to down civilian aircraft departing from Heathrow airport in August 2006.[18] A number of factors facilitated this internalisation of the threat: Europe's relatively lenient immigration and asylum rules, the unrestricted movement of individuals within the Schengen area, liberal political and legal systems guaranteeing civil liberties, and the culturally enforced segregation of Muslims domiciled in Europe. These factors, which constitute formidable barriers to the effective national policing of terrorist operations, also punctuated the need for approximating penal law and judicial process as well as facilitating police and judicial cooperation – a coordination task ideally delegated to Brussels.

Border control Illegal immigration and the spectre of terrorism transformed the problem of border control into an acute national security issue.[19] The Schengen *acquis*, the adoption of which is an inescapable condition for EU membership, entails a fresh set of policy challenges for the EU: disparate asylum procedures create opportunities for forum shopping by asylum seekers (producing a form of 'asylum dumping') and lax border controls present permeable transit points for illegal immigrants.[20] Asylum seekers and legal migration do not present an acute problem of internal security, even for societies that lack a tradition or willingness to integrate or absorb immigrants. While uncontrolled or illegal immigration may pose a vexing social problem, it only presents a security challenge to the extent that either aids the operation or consolidation of criminal organisations with an international rather than national character, when bordering states provide legal sanctuary or present a low probability of prosecuting organised crime, or when it brings EU member states into an intractable conflict with transit countries less likely or able to police their own borders.

Money laundering and financial crime   The drug trade forged the chief nexus between money laundering and organised crime in the early 1990s. Money laundering had attracted the attention of national law enforcement agencies as an adjunct to combating organised crime in the 1990s but, in the new millennium, money laundering in support of terrorism eclipsed those pre-existing concerns.[21] The expansion of EU policy competencies reflects four substantive concerns beyond the worrisome interpenetration of organised crime and terrorist groups. First, money laundering poses an intrinsic and corrosive threat to the integrity of the national, EU, and global financial and banking systems. Second, money laundering has the potential to destabilise and criminalise the fragile democracies and emerging market economies along Europe's periphery. Third, money laundering, as the primary mechanism for transforming illicit gains into licit ones, provides the financial wherewithal for corrupting legal systems, avoiding criminal prosecution, and creating legal sanctuaries from which transnational criminal activities can be directed or safely harboured. Finally, money laundering is increasingly linked to the financing of terrorism, particularly by extremist Muslims. The relatively parochial law enforcement concerns prior to the 1990s failed to provide a convincing rationale for enlarging the EU role. A compelling rationale only emerged in response to the growing potential for the criminalisation of economies along Europe's periphery and then to terrorism after 2001.

Computer and information network security   The vulnerability of computer and information networks to criminal or politically motivated disruptions slowly emerged as a common security threat. Information system security had not figured prominently as an EU security concern, owing largely to the initial difficulty of arriving at common definitions of cybercrime (or cyberterrorism) and of approximating penal law. The digital world, which prizes the frictionless interoperability of information systems and networks, has contributed to the loss of sovereign control over vital channels of commerce and finance.[22] This cyber threat departed from the 'classical' approach to security; it defies the 'strict organisational, geographic and structural compartmentalisation of information according to sensitivity and category'.[23] Consequently, cooperation at the EU level was deemed an essential component of any successful security strategy, since computer and information-related technologies are beyond effective national control and serve as a means whereby criminal or terrorist organisations can operate beyond the physical or jurisdictional reach of national law enforcement (Shelley 2003: 309).

The initial interest in crafting EU policies protecting network security reflected the narrow concern with protecting the private sector from disruptions to the communications infrastructure or thwarting the predations of organised crime.[24] The vulnerability of member-state information infrastructure – and the potential for criminal or terrorist disruptions of it – served as the primary rationale for joint EU action in this field.[25] The 2005 Council Framework Decision on Combating Terrorism classified information networks as a 'critical' infrastructure likely to be a terrorist target, formally designated such an attack as a security threat requiring an EU-level response.[26]

Health security Prior to 2001, a few tentative steps had been taken towards implementing EU-wide epidemiological surveillance or control of communicable diseases. The anthrax attack in the United States represented the key event galvanising the EU in this policy area.[27] Although the Amsterdam Treaty gave the EU an explicit competency in the area of public health, the individual member states retained responsibility for controlling the spread of infectious diseases. In September 1998, the Commission, in urging the member states to adopt a joint public health policy, cited the need for a 'transfrontier network' to limit the outbreak of communicable diseases across national frontiers.[28] This call followed the logic of unrestricted internal borders and the attending ease of contagion. A 2002 joint action emphasised the need for an expanded EU role in the area of 'health security': just as the unrestricted movement of persons made the transfrontier transmission of communicable diseases more likely, the ability of the member states to manage those outbreaks alone had declined proportionately to that growing mobility.[29]

The October 2001 Ghent European Council mandated a programme to '*improve cooperation in the European Union for preventing and limiting the consequences of chemical, biological or nuclear terrorist threats*' (italics in original).[30] The rationale for an expanded EU competency was declaratory rather than reasoned. But between 2002 and the publication of the ESS, the terrorist use of CBRN devices and the proliferation of nuclear weapons or materials expanded significantly the health security threat-complex; viz., it was no longer restricted to solving the relatively narrow public health problem of containing naturally occurring infectious diseases.[31] Bioterrorism was singled out as a central security threat in 2003, owing to the psychological damage and economic costs attending a chemical or biological attack, even in cases where 'the number of cases remains relatively small'.[32] Once again, the openness of member-state borders provided the rationale for an EU role since the outbreak of a communicable disease in one country or the terrorist use of CBRN devices could 'become an international public health threat if national control measures are ineffective'.[33]

Principles of action

Solidarity and sovereignty are the two central principles shaping the EU role in internal security affairs. The solidarity principle acknowledges an underlying collective responsibility for jointly fulfilling internal security tasks. The solidarity principle, lent constitutional status in the forestalled European Constitution (Chapter VIII, Article III-329),[34] survives in the 2004 Declaration on Solidarity against Terrorism. Solidarity entails the positive obligation to lend assistance to another member state in the event of a terrorist attack and requires member states to 'mobilise all instruments at their disposal, including military resources, to assist a Member State or an acceding State in its territory'.[35] Yet, a continued deference to national prerogatives remained: the nature and quantity of assistance provided to member states would be strictly voluntary. The 'principle of mutual responsibility' complemented solidarity: states accepted that their national security policies should not be confined 'to maintaining their own security, but . . . focus also on the security of the Union as a whole'.[36] This principle, which established the imperative that member states consider the EU-wide security ramifications of national policy decisions, contributed to a collective definition of the content and form of internal security threats.

The sovereignty principle significantly qualified the solidarity principle in the Vienna Action Plan; member states retained sovereign prerogatives consistent with the provisions of the Amsterdam Treaty and foreswore any effort 'to create a European security area in the sense of a common territory'.[37] The Tampere Milestones subsequently qualified the sovereignty principle: member states accepted that an area of freedom, security and justice required a *common* migration policy as well as the approximation (if not convergence) of penal law and mutual recognition of national judicial processes.[38] Despite member-state vulnerability to organised crime and terrorism, the sovereignty principle has remained largely intact and continues to exert a strong hold on the collective political imaginations of the elected and electorate throughout Europe. Divergent penal laws, judicial processes, and legal cultures – and the unwillingness to alter them – present significant barriers to the emergence of the EU as a security actor. Even in the aftermath of Madrid, the member states clung to the position that 'terrorism is first and foremost an internal security matter' and that the rules governing the exchange of information on terrorist groups should be subject to intergovernmental bargaining under the aegis of Pillar III.[39]

The subsidiarity and procedural principles also shaped the content and form of EU policies in JHA. The subsidiarity principle has effectively delegated primary responsibility for internal security to member states. Initially, the EU role was limited to the design of institutional frameworks facilitating police and judicial cooperation across the Union and brokering the approximation of national penal law and judicial processes. Even that limited role was qualified by the recognition that common or convergent EU policies must take account of 'national interests and common approaches as well as differences'.[40]

The procedural principle, which guided the policy recommendations contained in the Vienna Action Plan, the Tampere Milestones, the Millennium Strategy and the Hague Programme, governed the rationalisation of the EU decision-making process, particularly the avoidance or accommodation of overlapping policy competencies between Pillars I and III, the clear definition of member state and Union competencies, and the provision of the necessary flexibility to cope with new or urgent problems. Terrorism, in particular, required the coordination of interdependent and mutually reinforcing policies falling under all three pillars (the European Communities, the CFSP, and JHA). The cross-pillarisation of EU terrorism policy included Pillar II and partially militarised terrorism policy. This development reflected the preference for a comprehensive anti-terrorism strategy that addressed the proximate sources of the terrorist threat as well as its underlying sources.

The principle of prevention recognises that the key to ameliorating terrorism is the eradication of its underlying material causes. The principle reflects the EU 'culture of security, based on conflict prevention, political management of crises and taking account of the economic and social root causes of violent action of all kinds'.[41] Consequently, the Europeans adopted a two-fold strategy: they would attack the root causes giving rise to terrorism *in conjunction with* combating terrorism with enhanced police powers and the projection of military force.[42] A corollary of prevention is the principle of 'differentiation', which initially reflected the European decision to distinguish between governments supporting terrorists and the societies those governments represent, and then later distinguished between Islam and individual Muslim terrorists.[43] The policy implications of prevention and differentiation place a considerable emphasis on the employment of the civilian instruments of statecraft and create a policy chasm between the Europe and America on how to best manage terrorism.

Multilateralism is a final general principle animating EU internal security policy. The EU embraced multilateralism as the mechanism for building global partnerships and coalitions, particularly with those countries most likely to harbour or produce terrorists as well as those countries most likely to be targeted by them. The member-state preference that the EU be a partner to global coalitions was subject to meeting three criteria: the EU possesses a common internal policy, an EU role adds value to individual national efforts, and the EU has some prospect of achieving the stated goals.[44] The EU has also faced a set of external constraints limiting its effectiveness as a security actor: it has proved difficult to find common ground with the other major actors (China, Russia and the United States); some of the EU's putative partners (and member states) have been unreceptive to a strategy that favours the nuanced instruments of 'soft' power and prefer instead a reliance upon the blunter instruments of military force and occupation.[45]

These five principles governing the balance between member state and Union prerogatives in the area of JHA are not uniformly applied across the key security issues areas in Pillar III. Instead, there is a wide variation in the balance between solidarity and sovereignty, between multilateral and national responses, and between the member states and the Union.

Border control   The control of national borders is a key element of national sovereignty; the Schengen *acquis* has eliminated that element of sovereignty within the EU although the control of the EU border remains of sovereign interest to all of its member states. The principle of subsidiarity provides the rationale for harmonising border control procedures along the EU border as well as the establishment of a central data system available to the individual member states and law enforcement agencies. Despite the mutual concern with controlling the EU's borders and the inflow of illegal migrants or terrorists, the policing of the EU border remains a national responsibility. While the principle of open internal borders is accepted within the Union and central to the smooth functioning and deeper integration of the internal market, the Union still lacks a clear set of principles for creating a common and secure border. Where the problem of border control and terrorism or organised crime overlap, however, a number of principles governing member-state and Union policies have emerged, particularly the principles of availability, mutual exchange, and equivalent access to information. Yet those principles are qualified by the sovereign right of refusal to share information, albeit under a set of narrowly construed circumstances.[46]

Money laundering and financial crime   The 2005 draft directive on money laundering qualified the sovereignty principle. First, the directive established as a principle that all member states would prohibit 'money laundering and terrorist financing'.[47] The directive also applied the principle of due diligence to individuals and financial intermediaries. Due diligence squarely placed the burden of conforming with EU law on financial intermediaries as well as those seeking to launder illicit gains or finance terrorist activities. Customer due diligence required the vetting of a transaction in one of three cases: the transaction was greater than €15,000, there was simply the *suspicion* of either terrorist financing or money laundering, or there was a cross-frontier correspondent banking relationship.[48] The potential circumvention of national or EU law by offshore financial intermediaries also gave rise to a final principle: the quasi-extraterritorial application of national or EU law in cases where third country legislation 'does not permit application of such equivalent measures'.[49]

Computer and information network security   The principles governing the initial EU intervention in this policy area reflected a continuing persistence of the sovereignty norm insofar as certain categories of monitoring were placed off limits from EU jurisdiction: public security, defence, and criminal law. Where computer and information network policies impinged upon the operation of the single market, however, sovereign prerogatives retreated in favour of a Community-wide setting of standards. Yet, the border between the operation of the single market and those reserved sovereign prerogatives remains ill defined. As the Commission noted, information networks were critical components of a well functioning internal market (e.g., financial markets), yet the economic security of states depended upon the security of those information systems from intentional and malign disruptions. Sovereignty was also challenged by the countervailing principle of private property: the EU (and the member states) recognised that electronic networks are largely privately owned and are integral to commerce and the functioning of the European market economy.[50]

Health security   The sovereignty principle significantly narrowed the scope for a Union-wide system of epidemiological surveillance. Community action was limited to cases where the surveillance efforts of individual member states were inadequate, but even then, it did not 'affect the right of the Member States to maintain or introduce other arrangements, procedures and measures for their national systems'.[51] The deadly threat posed by chemical or biological terrorism did not modify the desire to retain sovereign prerogatives, even though the member states recognised that they individually lacked the capabilities to meet either.[52] The fear that terrorists would acquire and use nuclear or radiological materials generated a set of principles that created a greater EU identity than is found in the more prosaic task of epidemiological surveillance.

The 2004 EU Solidarity Programme contained thirteen general guidelines defining a common policy towards the proliferation of radiological and nuclear materials or weapons. Four principles shaped those policy guidelines: non-proliferation (preventing the acquisition of nuclear or radiological materials); multilateralism (developing a common global threat assessment, relying upon multilateral fora and third country cooperation, developing an effective verification regime, and forging a common approach with the United States and the Russian Federation); prevention (eliminating geostrategic conflicts giving rise to proliferation); and mutual responsibility (collectively contributing to non-proliferation). These four principles, which generally supported a cooperative and pooled response to the threat, were nonetheless qualified by the sovereignty principle: member states retained primary competence and responsibility for protecting their citizens, property, and the environment. The December 2003 strategy against WMD proliferation elaborated on those principles, particularly the importance of strengthening international law and of creating viable and effective surveillance and monitoring regimes.[53]

Goals

Critical substantive and legal lacunae in the fight against organised crime and terrorism impeded joint EU action: some member states had failed to ratify the pre-existing six EU conventions and protocols on criminal and judicial cooperation; some lacked criminal legislation outlawing money laundering; and national law on criminal proceedings and procedures were divergent and incompatible. These shortcomings were in many cases attributed to overly broad Commission recommendations, member-state inertia, the emergence of new issues on the policy agenda, and divergent legal traditions resisting penal or procedural convergence.[54] As importantly, terrorism and organised crime were treated as national policing problems rather than as an additional EU policy competence. Finally, divergent instrumental preferences complicated matters further given the transnational character of terrorist and criminal organisations.

The Vienna Action Plan – and subsequent documents on organised crime and terrorism – proposed common action 'in the dissociable fields of police cooperation and judicial cooperation in criminal matters' even though the member states were explicitly unwilling to surrender national policing prerogatives.[55] The Schengen *acquis*, the porousness of the EU's external boundary, and incompatible criminal justice systems recommended that the existing EU system of 'soft law' (nonbinding resolutions or recommendations) be replaced with binding 'hard law' – a goal that remains as elusive today as in the late 1990s.

Enhanced judicial and police cooperation and the approximation of national penal laws and judicial procedures constituted the two substantive objectives in JHA. In the immediate aftermath of 11 September, the EU member states agreed to enhance cooperation between national intelligence services, suppress terrorist financing, improve transport and border security, and intensify external cooperation. Towards those ends, the EU developed an ambitious legislative agenda, including the establishment of Eurojust as a formal network of national prosecutors, magistrates and police for easing the prosecution of transborder crime, enhanced cooperation within Europol, and the creation of additional institutional mechanisms facilitating operational cooperation between national police and intelligence services.[56] In addition, the Council identified a number of specific policy objectives: a European arrest warrant, a common penal definition of terrorist offences, a legal framework legitimising the freezing of assets anywhere in the Union, the entry into force of two extradition conventions, and the ratification of the Mutual Assistance Convention and the protocol on money laundering and financial crime.[57]

In the fight against organised crime, the member states did not commit to a particularly high or low level of procedural guarantees in reconciling penal laws or judicial process. Instead, EU policies harboured the more modest ambition of preventing any single member states from functioning as the preferred base of operation owing to differences in the rules of evidence, low criminal penalties, or high procedural barriers to conviction. Those aspects of the criminal justice systems in most need of alignment included rules governing search and seizure and the confiscation of the proceeds from crime, and minimum/maximum penalties for crimes arising from organised crime and terrorism. The member states also set the task of determining which categories of crime could be best addressed by national efforts alone or required a solution crafted at the level of the EU.[58]

The EU lacked (and still lacks) a standardised method for collecting and distributing crime statistics within the EU. Neither was there an equivalency in the definition of crimes. These lacunae seriously impeded transborder cooperation and the adoption of an 'intelligence-led' approach to the fight against organised crime and terrorism. Even though the Millennium Strategy addressed these shortcomings, very little progress was made – an outcome highlighted in the 2004 Dublin Declaration on Organised Crime.[59] The goal of standardising penal codes served the larger objectives of symbolically transforming the EU into a single legal area, ensuring that criminal conduct in the EU would be treated similarly regardless of where the offence took place, preventing criminal organisations from forum shopping when committing crimes or devising strategies to escape prosecution, and moving towards the mutual recognition of judicial decisions.[60] These relatively limited ambitions reflected the continuing difficulty of achieving a common area of justice and security and underscored the continuing importance of sovereign prerogatives in a policy area as central to national political life as the criminal justice system.

The Hague Programme equated judicial convergence with the 'progressive development of a European judicial culture based on diversity of the legal systems . . . and unity through European law'.[61] These two goals – respecting diversity and seeking unity – presented a policy paradox requiring the reconciliation of opposites. Much like the goals of deepening and enlarging the EU itself, The Hague Programme respected the continued force and necessity of sovereign prerogatives, but sought to reconcile divergent national judicial systems that blocked deeper cooperation in the fights against organised crime and terrorism. The programme recommended that the member states agree upon a standardised set of minimum procedural rights in criminal proceedings, and adopt the 2004 Framework Decision on the European Evidence Warrant.[62]

The 2004 Declaration on Terrorism clearly defined the EU's strategic goals for combating terrorism: enhancing and deepening international cooperation with third countries; ameliorating the economic and social conditions that contributed to the radicalisation of individuals, particularly in the Middle East and North Africa; and externalising EU preferences in order to moderate third country behaviour.[63] The EU was charged with creating and implementing policies that would support failing states, restore civil order and governance in failed states, mitigate regional conflicts with humanitarian aid or intervention, and support third states in their fight against terrorism.

This EU strategy – developed within the context of CSFP – integrated the principle of preventive engagement into JHA; it had a strong legal component complementing the emphasis on multilateralism, particularly the universal adoption and implementation of the existing UN Conventions on terrorism as well as concluding the additional convention on the suppression of nuclear terrorism.[64] The multilateral component of the strategy emphasised working within the UN framework (UN conventions on terrorism, for example, served as the legal and legitimising basis for EU policy), participating in the G8 programmes against terrorism and nuclear proliferation and enhancing bilateral cooperation with the United States and Russia, in particular.[65]

The EU also endeavoured to externalise its normative preferences in the fight against terrorism, particularly along its eastern and southern perimeter. The EU, in an effort to make counter-terrorism 'an integral element of our relations with third countries' integrated a counter-terrorism clause into formal agreements reached with third countries. This process 'mainstreamed' the EU's counter-terrorism objectives into assistance programmes as well as trade and cooperation agreements. It also provided a legal basis for providing EU technical assistance to their partners that nurtured a policing orientation in combating terrorism.[66] In this way, the EU developed a comprehensive anti-terrorist strategy relying upon civilian instruments and crisis management operations in conformity with Title V of the Maastricht Treaty.

Border control The January 1998 EU Action Plan on Migration established the broad goals of EU policy that reappeared in the Vienna Action Plan, the Tampere Milestones, and The Hague Programme. In each case, the Council enumerated a similar set of policy objectives, including a 'coherent EU policy on readmission and return', common policies combating illegal immigration, and the common treatment of non-EU nationals with respect to visa requirements.[67] The Tampere Milestones added to these general goals measures targeting human trafficking, the exploitation of children, and the criminal networks profiting from either. The 2002 Comprehensive Proposal for the Control of Illegal Immigration treated unwanted migratory flows as a core task of the CFSP and put forward a 'supply-chain' approach to the problem of migration; viz., the joint EU policy would be oriented towards preventing migrants from crossing either the territorial or maritime boundary of the EU and alleviating the conditions leading individuals to flee their homelands in the first place.[68]

In 2004, the Commission proposed a set of ambitious and far-reaching policy recommendations augmenting national immigration and asylum policies. These recommendations included the development of pre-frontier measures discouraging or preventing migration at the point of origin, improved border management policies (a common high standard governing national border control and a common EU training rubric), a robust readmission and return policy (an EU visa system, holding third states to obligations under international law with respect to the return of illegal immigrants, and closer cooperation with countries serving as transit points), and broadened Europol prerogatives in the policing of Europe's borders.[69]

The Hague Programme provisions on border control were shaped by two major developments. First, the uncontrolled migratory influx from southern and eastern Europe complicated the social task of integration and expanded the reach of ethnic organised criminal enterprises in the EU.[70] Second, the 11 March Madrid bombings made more acute the interdependence between effective border control and the operation of Muslim terrorists in Europe.[71] Although the member states agreed to 'the swift abolition of internal border controls', the burden for policing the EU's external border fell on those states in central and eastern Europe least capable of executing that task. The countervailing logics of national responsibility for policing third country borders and the Union-wide abolition of internal borders required a common external frontier with common entry and exit procedures. The Hague Programme, rather than settling for the convergence of national border control procedures, adopted the more ambitious goal of a common EU procedure.

Money laundering and financial crime   The EU adopted a number of initiatives in the late 1990s on money laundering, which were in turn based on the 40 recommendations adopted by the G8 Financial Action Task Force on Money Laundering (FATF) in 1996. The EU initially set itself two overarching goals to combat money laundering. First, the EU committed itself to adopt best practices and common training of law enforcement to facilitate intra-EU and international cooperation. Somewhat surprisingly, some EU member states did not treat money laundering as a serious crime and national laws governing offshore financial transactions were inconsistent or incompatible. Thus, the member states had to first agree on the need for the EU-wide criminalisation of money laundering and then design common legal instruments for policing offshore financial centres. Both the Tampere Milestones and Millennium Strategy set additional legislative goals, the most important of which were the approximation of national penal law for specific categories of financial crime, the elaboration of a legal framework enabling national authorities to trace, freeze, seize and confiscate proceeds derived from criminal activity, and the development of institutional mechanisms for fostering cooperation between national financial intelligence units.[72] The member states also agreed in a joint action that member states would provide national legislation enabling courts to deprive criminal organisations of their licit or illicit assets; and also established the principle that member state law enforcement requests would receive the same treatment as domestic requests for information on asset seizure or identification.[73]

After 11 September, the international community – and the EU – concentrated efforts on breaking the connection between terrorist financing and money laundering.[74] The first three articles of the December

2001 common position on terrorism, for example, addressed the need for the EU-wide criminalisation of terrorist financing. The common position recommended that the Union foster a legal environment proscribing the laundering or transferring of terrorist funds and ensuring that member states adopt relevant Community legislation, particularly the June 2001 Framework Decision on the execution of orders freezing assets or evidence.[75] The 2004 Third Directive on Money Laundering provided an initial framework for approximating legislation on criminal penalties, a step that would prevent an individual EU member state from emerging as an internal safe haven for terrorist groups owing to lax banking or financial regulations.[76]

Computer and Information network security   The EU's legislative ambitions in the area of computer and information network security were muted at best until 2005, when the Council identified two fundamental and preliminary tasks for common action. First, an effective EU-wide sanctioning of attacks against information systems required a common set of symmetrical and dissuasive penalties. Second, it also required institutional linkages facilitating judicial cooperation, a requirement made essential given the transborder nature of the cyber threat and the inability of any individual member state to secure or police information networks independently.[77]

Health security   Health security measures after 2001 went well beyond earlier efforts to establish a rudimentary community public health system for the surveillance of communicable diseases. First, the policy orientation shifted from the surveillance of naturally occurring infectious diseases to a concern with the purposeful weaponisation of biological and viral agents or toxins; second, health security included policies to prevent and cope with chemical attacks; and finally, the Union seized for itself a broader mandate and more intrusive role in protecting the health of the member states' citizens.[78] EU health security initiatives have consistently featured four broad goals: strengthening coordination mechanisms for 'information exchange, consultation and coordination' between national authorities; developing the capability to detect and identify biological, viral and chemical agents; establishing an EU-wide database for stockpiled vaccines, antibiotics and anti-toxins as well as a standby capability for manufacturing those medicines; and finally, enhancing cooperation with third countries (Gouvras, 2002: 1; Dekker-Bellamy, 2004: 4; and Lindstrom, 2004: 45–6). The external dimension of the EU health security strategy included the targeting of non-state actors, primarily owing to the likelihood that terrorist groups (or even criminal organisations) posed the most probable chemical, biological, radiological or nuclear threat.

The EU's December 2003 Strategy against WMD Proliferation placed emphasis on the centrality of multilateralism and global partnerships. The overriding substantive policy objective was the universal ratification of existing multilateral non-proliferation agreements, notably the Non-Proliferation Treaty, IAEA additional protocols, the Chemical Weapons Convention, the Biological and Toxin Weapons Convention, and The Hague Code of Conduct against Ballistic Missile Proliferation.[79] The EU strategy was predicated upon the successful creation of effective enforcement mechanisms that would ensure compliance with those treaties and conventions; it also sought the internal objectives of a uniform export control policy, common policies and sanctions for the trafficking of WMD-related materials, and the improved policing and control of radiological materials and chemical precursors.[80] The 2004 revised CBRN programme reaffirmed this clutch of strategic objectives, but acknowledged the limited progress towards meeting those goals, attributable in large part to the unwillingness of states to forgo sovereignty in this critical area.[81]

The acquisition of nuclear or radiological materials by non-state actors posed a fundamentally different type of policy logic and response. The EU focused on the need to control better the export of nuclear and radiological materials and technologies, including intangible technology transfers. The first step towards meeting that objective required agreement on a common set of criminal sanctions across the EU, which if achieved would abolish legal safe havens for those brokering or smuggling materials or technologies. Specific intra-EU policy initiatives included measures controlling sealed radioactive sources, physically protecting nuclear materials and facilities, and strengthening EU and national legislation monitoring and controlling the sale and use of pathogens and toxins.[82]

Institutional innovations and the networks fostering cooperation in the area of internal security

A fundamental barrier to the creation of an area of freedom, justice and security has been not only divergent judicial and legal cultures, but the absence of trust between those national authorities, particularly with respect to the exchange of information and intelligence. The EU has sponsored a series of institutional innovations that have created general networks between law enforcement and judicial authorities as well as networks specific to certain categories of crime or security threat (see Table 4.1).

Table 4.1 Major institutional innovations and networks

	Institutions and networks
Police	Europol EU Police chief's task force CEPOL Joint investigation teams
Judiciary	Eurojust European judicial network (in criminal matters) European judicial training network
Intelligence and counter-terrorism	Joint situation centre Counter-terrorism task force (Europol) ARGUS
Border control	FRONTEX
Money laundering and financial crime	Europol financial crime unit (SC4) FIU and FIU.NET
Network and information security	ENISA CERT CIWIN
Health security	ECDC BICHAT RAS–BICHAT

The Tampere Milestones targeted strengthened police cooperation within Europol in order to expedite the rapid and free exchange of information on criminal and terrorist activities. While the Vienna Action Plan designated Europol as the institutional locus for cross-border law enforcement cooperation, Tampere expanded the Europol remit to cover money laundering without regard to the source of funds.[83] Europol, the operational ambit of which was initially restricted to the drug trade when created in 1993, is now empowered to investigate most categories of serious crime and terrorism.[84] Although counter-terrorism was designated as a special area of Europol responsibility in May 1998, the security threat posed by Muslim terrorists after 11 September led to the reactivation of the Europol counter-terrorism task force. The task force, which consists of counter-terrorism experts within Europol and became operational in November 2001, was charged with the objectives of collecting information and intelligence, analysis of that intelligence, and the production of a threat assessment document for distribution to national law enforcement authorities. The unit within Europol has been aided in its efforts by the pre-existing network of national liaison officers and national Europol units which serve as contact points for cross-border investigations.

Europol produces three major reports on an annual basis: an annual report describing the activities and performance of Europol in each of its areas of responsibility, annual organised crime reports (recently replaced by an annual organised crime threat assessment), and an annual terrorism situation and trend report. In addition, Europol maintains, *inter alia*, an open source digest on Muslim terrorists, bomb database, and a Europol virtual private network for national police forces and other law enforcement authorities.[85] An additional number of operational measures have been undertaken since 2001, the most important of which include assigning Multidisciplinary Group on Organised Crime responsibility for monitoring the nexus between terrorism and organised crime and engendering closer cooperation between Europol and the Police Chiefs' Task Force towards improving the flow of terrorist-related intelligence. In 2003, a Council decision required national police forces to create counter-terrorism units tasked with the collection of intelligence on terrorists and terrorist groups that would be shared with Europol. This requirement is likely to be expanded: a proposed Council decision obliges national security and intelligence agencies to transmit information relating to terrorist offences to their national Europol contact officer.[86] The Commission has also proposed that the Europol convention be replaced with a legal instrumental ensuring that 'political decisions taken to improve its functioning can be implemented without undue delay'.[87] In other words, the Commission seeks the power to initiate infringement proceedings against member states that fail to transpose regulations and directives governing Europol. Europol's importance in cross-border investigations of serious crime is evident from the rising budget allotted to Europol, the steadily rising number of cases referred to Europol, and the steady rise in the number of operational messages exchanged between national law enforcement authorities and Europol (see Table 4.2). The absence of comparable crime statistics makes it virtually impossible, however, to determine the direct impact of Europol activities on the level of serious crime or the success of criminal investigations, but it would be safe to assume that if Europol did not add value, the budget and reliance upon Europol as an interlocutor would remain flat at best.

The EU introduced two additional institutional innovations strengthening police cooperation: a Police Chiefs operational task force complementing and supporting Europol; and a European Police College (CEPOL) providing common training and exchange of best practices for senior law enforcement officers. The Police Chiefs' Task Force (PCTF) was created in October 2000; CEPOL was established in December 2000 and is located in Copenhagen. The PCTF undertook three goals: improving operational cooperation between the EU and third countries;

coordinating terrorist-related policy measures between the member states; and determining which policing tasks should be delegated to the Europol counter-terrorism unit. To date, PCTF has crafted a Comprehensive Operation Strategic Planning for Police document and produced a common manual for improving counter-terrorism training at the local level throughout the Union.[88] As important, the task force has emerged as an advocate for strengthened cross-border cooperation in the fight against organised crime and terrorism: in 2001, the police chiefs recommended that national anti-terrorist units find mechanisms for enhancing cooperation; the 2004 Dublin PCTF meeting produced a recommendation that there be a greater sharing of high-quality intelligence with Europol, particularly to aid in the common fight against terrorism – a recommendation that the Commission put into effect in 2005.

The creation of CEPOL satisfied the immediate goal of developing a network amongst senior law enforcement officials and providing a forum for their common training. The Council defined the long-term goal of CEPOL as the creation of 'a European approach to the main problems . . . in the fight against crime, crime prevention and the maintenance of law and order and public security'.[89] The common training courses offered by CEPOL enhance the mutual understanding of differences and similarities in national policing methods and procedures, focus on serious crimes and law enforcement problems of common concern, and facilitate operational cooperation with Europol and Eurojust in the investigation and prosecution of serious crime.[90] Aside from seminars on topics ranging from terrorism to criminal intelligence and risk assessment to high-tech and internet crime, CEPOL also manages the European Police Learning Net (EPLN). The EPLN provides additional training opportunities, including the development of e-learning modules, a common information base on police practices, and a secure method of communication.[91]

Table 4.2 Europol budget and activities, 2000–2005

	2000	2001	2002	2003	2004	2005
Budget (million euros)	27.45	33.2	48.1	57.8	61.12	65.8
Number of cases referred	1,922	2,429	3,413	4,700	6,345	6,705
Number of operational messages exchanged	9,409	45,211	69,822	94,723	151,150	180,920

The potentially most important innovation in the area of law enforcement and investigation has been the introduction of joint investigation teams (JIT). The JIT were set down as an objective for the Union with the Tampere Milestones in 1999 for the limited tasks of combating terrorism and the trafficking in drugs or humans. After 11 September, the member states concluded that the task of policing serious crime and terrorism within the EU required a 'specific legal binding instrument' to facilitate cross-border cooperation even though a basis for joint investigation teams was already present in the 2000 Convention on Mutual Assistance on Criminal Matters.[92] The JIT legislation envisioned bilateral arrangements whereby individuals seconded to operate on the territory of another member state would enjoy the same investigatory prerogatives as national law enforcement. Participation in investigations required the seconded officers to adhere to national law; a requirement that was not only necessary for the purposes of ensuring that evidence collected would be admissible in national courts but also created a mutual understanding between law enforcement authorities responsible for serious crime and terrorism. While bilateral investigations have already taken place within the framework of Europol, the JIT decision was intended as a mechanism facilitating bilateral cooperation; a subsequent protocol to the Europol convention provided for Europol participation in JIT if invited. The potential role that the JIT could play in enhancing police cooperation has been frustrated by the inability or unwillingness of the member states to transpose the provisions of the framework decision into national law. Only Spain has fully complied with the framework decision, and even then the January 2003 deadline for national implementation was missed. The other member states have been judged delinquent in varying degrees in implementation, although many member states insist that existing legislation accommodated the framework decision.[93] The principle of JIT has been accepted within the Union and the framework decision has provided an EU-sanctioned platform for deeper law enforcement cooperation and the integration of Europol into cross-border investigations. Nonetheless, the operation of criminal organisations in a borderless EU has not yet been complemented with borderless law enforcement; the member states and national law enforcement remain unwilling to accept significant encroachments on their policing prerogatives.

Tampere also targeted greater judicial cooperation via a set of ambitious policy recommendations. In addition to the mutual recognition of judicial decisions, the member states also agreed on the need for enhanced judicial cooperation, an objective facilitated with the creation of a European Judicial Cooperation Unit (Eurojust) in 2002. The 2001

Treaty of Nice provided the constitutional basis for enhancing judicial cooperation; in the framework decision creating Eurojust, the Council of Ministers initially expected that Eurojust would deepen coordination and cooperation between national authorities responsible for the prosecution of serious crimes with a cross-border component. A provisional unit was established in 2001, known as Pro-Eurojust, and was replaced by a permanent one in 2002. Eurojust consists of a college comprised of prosecutors, judges or police officials from each member state. Although Eurojust became operational in 2002, it took until June 2004 for each member state to second a permanent representative to the college.[94] The operational role of Eurojust was described 'a case coordination centre or a clearinghouse for coordination and facilitation of cooperation between competent authorities concerned with investigations and prosecutions into serious or organised crime'.[95] The Eurojust mission was to encourage cross-border cooperation within the Union, particularly in cases involving transnational criminal organisations.

The first annual report, however, identified twenty-two barriers to mutual legal assistance which included the lack of domestic legal authority to request or accede to a request for information, disparate procedural requirements to establish the admissibility of evidence, barriers to the extradition of nationals, unwillingness to share intelligence, and the absence of uniform extradition procedures.[96]

Eurojust assumed an important operational role within the Union, primarily as a mechanism for exchanging information and linking cases in different jurisdictions towards meeting the threat posed by organised crime. One mechanism developed to implement those goals is the coordination meeting which bring together senior magistrates, prosecutors and police of different member states. Although the number of coordination meetings has risen steadily since 2002, the nature of the cases involving Eurojust has remained stubbornly bilateral; in fact, multilateral cases as a share of total cases referred to Eurojust declined sharply after 2001 and have hovered between 25 and 30 per cent (see Tables 4.3 and 4.4).

Table 4.3 Eurojust coordination meetings, 2002–2005

	2001[a]	2002	2003	2004	2005
Number of meetings	15	20	26	52	73

Note:
a Pro-Eurojust.

Source: Pro-Eurojust 2002; Eurojust 2003, 2004, 2005, 2006.

Table 4.4 Categories of cases referred to Eurojust, 2001–2005

	2001[a]	2002	2003	2004	2005
Bilateral	116	144	222	272	na
Multilateral (3 states)	26	27	47	44	na
Multilateral (4 or more states)	43	31	31	65	na
Total number of cases	185	202	300	381	588

Note:
a Pro-Eurojust.

Eurojust made a singular contribution to judicial cooperation with the guidelines developed to settle where a suspect should be tried if two national legal systems have a legitimate jurisdictional claim. The guidelines reflect practical considerations to expedite trials and maximise the likelihood that the prosecution will be successful. Other guidelines reflected concerns that justice also be rendered in any proceeding: a legal proceeding could not be held in one jurisdiction rather than another owing to less restrictive rules of evidence or harsher criminal penalties.[97] What is remarkable, however, is that the Commission and Council have created a more permissive context for cooperation with successive framework decisions seeking to align penal law and judicial process; there has been progress towards removing the incentive to forum shop by either prosecutors or the indicted.

While great emphasis has been placed on assuring a capability to foster cooperation in the investigation and prosecution of terrorist offences, the case work of Eurojust remains concentrated on 'traditional' crimes favoured by criminal organisations, particularly drug trafficking and fraud. While cases dealing with terrorism only exceed cases of VAT fraud, the total number of cases referred to Eurojust rose from 277 cases in 2002 to 707 cases in 2005, a 255 per cent increase (see Table 4.5). This progress towards deeper judicial cooperation across the EU was established with the European Judicial Network (EJN) which now is a part of Eurojust.

The EJN (in criminal matters) was established in 1998. Its purpose was to improve judicial cooperation in the prosecution of serious crime, particularly organised crime, corruption, trafficking of drugs and terrorism. The EJN consists of contact points in each member state, which were responsible for helping judiciaries prepare effective requests for judicial cooperation or coordinated action in cases with a cross-border aspect. The joint action designated as contact points the judicial authorities responsible for international judicial cooperation.[98] The operational aspects of EJN cooperation and assistance take the form of *fiches belges* (which contain information about national criminal procedural rules in each member state), a judicial atlas (which identifies the appropriate local judicial authority when making a request for judicial assistance), and the Solon (which is a dictionary of legal equivalences). One by-product of the EJN is the emergence of the European Judicial Training Network (EJTN), established in 2000. This network is comprised of the national institutions responsible for judicial training. The network serves the larger purpose of bringing a 'genuine European dimension' to the training of judges on a systematic basis and developing common programmes facilitating judicial cooperation in criminal proceedings.[99] More specifically, the EJTN ambition was to facilitate the comparison and exchange of judicial practice, enhance mutual understanding of national judicial systems; increase awareness of those Community instruments available to facilitate cooperation; support the training of judiciaries in accession and candidate countries; and create a European judicial culture.[100] The network membership targets those institutions responsible for training judges and prosecutors as well as institutions that provide judicial training at the Community level (e.g., the Academy of European Law, Trier).[101]

Table 4.5 Categories of offenses referred to Eurojust, 2002–2005

	2002	2003	2004	2005
Drug trafficking	132	71	95	135
Fraud	61	69	94	120
Property crime	–	–	–	92
Money laundering	4	25	34	48
Personal crime	–	–	–	45
Homicide	14	14	34	43
Tax fraud	–	–	–	42
Criminal organisations	–	–	27	35
Trafficking in humans	–	–	–	33
Forgery	–	13	–	26
Terrorism	18	18	33	25
VAT fraud	–	–	–	24
Other	48	93	148	39
Total	277	303	465	707

Source: Pro-Eurojust 2002; Eurojust 2003, 2004, 2005, 2006.

The desire to create an autonomous capacity to gather and disseminate intelligence between national law and security authorities was furthered with the establishment of the Joint Situation Centre, the reactivation of the counter-terrorist unit within Europol (see above), and the ARGUS network. The EU Joint Situation Centre (SitCen) was established on the initiative of the Secretary General/High Commissioner Javier Solana. As an intelligence gathering agency, it remains relatively underdeveloped: it remains dependent upon intelligence analysts seconded from national intelligence agencies and has a very small dedicated staff. As Björn Müller-Wille (2004: 30–1) notes, SitCen does not yet possess (or does the EU) the capability to collect or analyse intelligence; it also remains handicapped by a limited staff and a dependence upon national sources of intelligence and intelligence analysts. The need for an autonomous intelligence capability has become recognised as critical to any EU response to terrorism; at the end of 2004 the European Council assigned SitCen the task of providing a 'strategic analysis' of the terrorist threat facing Europe. This additional task did not produce a commitment to an autonomous intelligence capability for the Commission. Rather, SitCen intelligence reports relied upon intelligence flows from the member-state intelligence and national security agencies.[102]

A final addition to the intelligence capability of the Union has taken the form of ARGUS, a secure general rapid alert system created in early 2006 and managed by the Commission Crisis Centre (CCC). The Commission, in establishing ARGUS and the CCC, responded to the 2004 Brussels European Council request that it establish 'within its existing structures . . . [an] integrated and coordinated EU crisis-management arrangements for crises with cross border effects'.[103] ARGUS is intended to increase the flow of information and intelligence within the Community and to provide a mechanism for consolidating pre-existing alert systems. This task is viewed as particularly important in mounting an effective crisis-management operation in the event of a terrorist attack with cross-border and multi-sector characteristics. ARGUS, the CCC and SitCen jointly present the prospect of an integrated and potentially autonomous EU capability to gather, assess and distribute intelligence and information in response to terrorist attacks or any other kind of civil crisis, natural or man-made.

Border control Despite the significant progress made towards the harmonisation of the EU's visa, asylum and immigration procedures and regulations, the problem of controlling the common external border after enlargement was aggravated by the heightened threat of terrorism and the growing sophistication of organised crime. The Council, in an effort to meet those challenges, issued a regulation in October 2004 that established the European Agency for the Management of Operational Cooperation at the External Borders (FRONTEX). This agency, the first significant step towards the common policing of the external frontier, became operational in May 2005. The agency was assigned two major tasks: coordinating member state operations in the management of external borders; making progress towards the 'integrated management of operational cooperation' along the common external border.[104] The specific operational tasks assigned the agency included the establishment of common training standards for border guards, the support of R&D for the control and surveillance of external borders, and the provision of aid to member states in need of enhanced technical and operational assistance.[105]

Money laundering and financial crime   Money laundering and financial crimes are coordinated largely outside the EU framework. The Moneyval Committee, for example, coordinates European policies and law enforcement strategies for the Council of Europe member states. The Financial Action Task Force (FATF), created by the G8 in 1989, is comprised of representatives from 33 nations, the Gulf Cooperation Council, and the EU Commission. The FATF is the locus for generating, *inter alia*, international standards governing financial crime, particularly the nexus between money laundering and terrorism after 2001, and ensuring compliance with the 40 FATF recommendations. Those FATF recommendations have set the standards governing member state legislation as well as actions taken at the EU level. In addition to the FATF framework, the EU and other G8 states designated the Counter-Terrorist Action Group as the nexus for cooperation, while the G7 Finance Ministers developed an Action Plan in 2001 presenting a common set of policies for freezing terrorist assets and limiting the access of terrorists to their financial systems.[106] By June 2004, the US and EU reached a bilateral accord that committed both parties to liaise with the UN Counter-Terrorism Committee, support UN Security Council Resolutions 1267 and 1373, and continue cooperation within the FATF framework on thwarting money laundering and other financial crimes by terrorist organisations. Finally, both parties undertook to exchange information on terrorist activities and strengthen cooperation between Europol and the appropriate Federal law enforcement agencies.

Within the EU, the agency with primary responsibility for monitoring and enforcing laws against money laundering and financial crimes is the Europol Financial Crimes Unit (SC4). SC4, which produces an annual analysis working file (AWF) on money laundering, provides member-state law enforcement agencies with a common source of information. This unit also has a liaison officer at SitCen, another mechanism for monitoring more effectively the nexus between money laundering and terrorism.[107] Policy cooperation has also benefited from the creation of financial intelligence units (FIU) that provided each member state with a national contact point responsible for the exchange of financial information in cases of suspected money laundering. The FIU were reinforced with the establishment of the FIU.NET (the financial information unit network); FIU.NET provides a cyberlink for coordinating money laundering policies and investigations within the Union. This network, fully operational in November 2005, has gained greater importance owing to the provisions of the Third Money Laundering Directive, which focuses on identifying linkages between money laundering and suspected terrorist financing.[108] Eurojust also plays an important role in combating money laundering; it has successfully assisted the coordination of criminal investigations between national authorities within the EU, particularly where transnational criminal organisations are involved.[109]

Computer and information network security   The European Network Information and Security Agency (ENISA), established in October 2004 and funded from the common budget, represents an important institutional development. Agency tasks include responsibility for identifying and defending against threats to the information infrastructure, which have been elevated to national security threats with the advent of Muslim terrorism.[110] Perhaps the most innovative aspect of the regulation was not so much the creation of the ENISA, but the member-state recognition that the problem of network and information security cannot be achieved solely by states or the EU given the innumerable private actors that have a vested interest in the security of their own networks, the difficulty of balancing the state's responsibility to protect that infrastructure without compromising the proprietary interests of the private sector or the privacy of citizens, and the necessity of protecting the information and computer networks enabling the state to execute its social welfare as well as security tasks.

The member states, in establishing ENISA, acknowledged that the smooth functioning of the common internal market required safety protocols at the EU level replacing the patchwork of national regulations. Despite the need for action at the EU level, the effective protection of network and information systems requires global cooperation given the relative unimportance of national jurisdictional boundaries to cyberspace. The EU viewed ENISA as an institutional address for global cooperation in this important policy area; it was also considered the institutional basis for creating the 'culture of security' identified as a policy goal in the 'eEurope 2005' action plan. [111] Despite the recognition that ENISA had a role to play in protecting information systems critical to national defence, Article 3 of the regulation provides that the tasks and objectives of ENISA would be 'without prejudice to the competencies of the Member States' in the areas of public security, defence, state security and criminal law.[112] In establishing ENISA, the Union hoped to create a clearing house for intra-EU cooperation in a specific policy area, provide a common and standardised source of information about best practices, serve as a source of expertise for the Commission and member states, and establish a security nexus for private and public actors to help resolve the knotty collective action problem attending the challenge of network and information security.

ENISA's accomplishments have been as modest as the Work Programme for 2006 attests. In 2005, ENISA established a network of national liaison officers responsible for information and technology security, created an ad hoc working group addressing the problem of risk assessment and risk management, created an EU-wide network of Computer Emergency Response Teams (CERT), and sponsored training programmes designed to harmonise the level of CERT competencies across the Union. This network found parallel expression in the establishment in 2005 of a Critical Infrastructure Warning Information System (CIWIN). While CIWIN is designed as a rapid alert system covering the entire spectrum of critical infrastructure, its competencies overlapped with those of ENISA and CERT. [113] This duplication is purposeful, however: any critical infrastructure disruption will inevitably affect Europe's electronic infrastructure and CWIN provides a network linking the competencies of ENISA and CERT with those infrastructures heavily dependent upon secure electronic networks.

ENISA has also established a Permanent Stakeholders' Group comprised of representatives from the leading technology and information systems firms operating in Europe as well as liaison relationships with industry representatives (e.g., the European Telecommunication's Network Operators association, the European Information & Communications Technology Industry Association, and the Business Software Alliance) and with national information security officers from Japan, the United States, Russia and Australia. Finally, and in keeping with its mandate to create a 'culture of network and information security' within the EU, the ENISA produces a quarterly bulletin providing a singular source of information on the security technology activities and practices of its member states. Despite these limited steps, ENISA makes a not unimportant contribution to EU security. The retention of sovereign prerogatives across a broad spectrum of government and private networks and categories of information pose a formidable barrier to organising security on an EU-wide basis in this policy domain.

Health security In 1999, the Commission established a Health Surveillance System for Communicable Diseases within the European Public Health Information Network (EUPHIN-HSSCD). This surveillance system had three designated tasks: creating an integrated early warning and response system, providing a mechanism for the exchange of information between the responsible member state authorities, and establishing exchange networks for diverse categories of infectious and communicable diseases. This system, in turn, spawned the BICHAT (Taskforce on Biological and Chemical Agent Attacks) programme. BICHAT identified 25 specific actions towards meeting the health challenge posed by the malign use of toxins and biological, viral or chemical agents against civilian populations. The bioterrorism challenge generated a subsequent initiative, RAS–BICHAT (Rapid Alert System), which functions as a mechanism for the exchange of information and coordination of national responses between member state public health agencies in the event of a terrorist attack (Deckker-Bellamy, 2004; Lindstrom, 2004). A number of other networks are in place monitoring developments in the health field, the most notable of which are the Community Emergency Communications and Information System (CESIS), the Monitoring and Information Centre (MIC), the Early Warning and Response System in the field of communicable diseases (EWRS), the EC Urgent Radiological Information Exchange (ECURIE), and the Medical Intelligence System (MedISys). These various communications networks present the EU with a number of mechanisms for tracking and treating communicable diseases or responding to radiological or biological terrorist attacks.[114]

The regulation establishing the European Centre for Disease Control (ECDC) identified the missions and tasks of the centre as well as the responsibilities of the member states towards it. The primary purpose of the centre was 'to identify, assess and communicate current and emerging threats to human health from communicable diseases. In the case of other outbreaks of illness of unknown origin which may spread within or to the Community, the Centre shall act on its own initiative until the source of the outbreak is known'.[115] The power of the centre was circumscribed, however, insofar as it was given no regulatory powers, and in the event of a bioterrorist attack, national authorities retained responsibility for determining the appropriate public health response. Arguably, the most important tasks assigned to the ECDC are the collection and dissemination of information about infectious diseases and the fostering of an effective public health network capable of responding to potential pandemics or bioterrorist attacks. Specific tasks included the development of an early warning and response system, the provision of technical assistance to member states in need, the identification of emerging health threats, and finally, the collection and analysis of data, including vaccination strategies – an area where member states have firmly rejected a common or pooled EU policy.[116]

EU policies of protection: how well has the EU performed?

The Tampere Milestones and Hague Programme, buttressed by the successive strategies and action plans for combating terrorism and organised crime, described the Union's ambitions in defining and implementing an area of freedom, security and justice. There are two general yardsticks for measuring the performance of the EU in meeting the challenge of internal security: the first would measure the rates of change in (trans)national criminal or terrorist acts within each member state and then determine the impact that EU policies have had on that rate of change; the second would measure the progress that the EU has made towards defining the content of internal security and the extent to which national governments transposed EU legislation into national law. The first approach presents a problem of causality: it is difficult to determine whether the increase or decrease in serious crime or police cooperation, for example, should be attributed to EU-sponsored initiatives, national policies and practices, or simply demographic change – a problem aggravated by the lack of comparable crime statistics. The programmes, policies and supporting institutional developments in this security arena are in their infancy; it is doubtful whether a five-year period is sufficient to judge whether EU policies have changed the rate of crime, have eased the prosecution of cross-border crime, or effectively harmonised or aligned the criminal justice practices and priorities of the individual member states. What can be determined, however, is the progress that the EU and the member states have made towards meeting the political and policy goals identified in the major framework programmes governing internal security and the transposition of those initiatives into national law. While various Europol and Eurojust reports present selective cases studies of the joint investigation or prosecution of crimes as well as measures providing a rough measure of cross-border police and judicial cooperation, those statistics obscure the more critical and substantive concern: the security consequences of the balance struck between sovereignty and solidarity in the policies of protection.

Freedom, justice and security

The EU failed to achieve fully the two central goals of the Tampere Programme: harmonising judicial practices and penal law and fostering greater police and judicial cooperation, particularly in the fight against transnational crime. Yet the progress made towards those goals between 1999 and 2004 cannot be underestimated. Perhaps the most important first step towards achieving the overall goal of a single area of justice was the mutual recognition of judicial decisions. This step, introduced by the Commission in a July 2000 communication, established as a general principle that a judicial decision in a criminal proceeding in one member state would be enforced throughout the entire Union. This principle generated three important framework decisions on the European Arrest Warrant and uniform surrender procedures,[117] the mutual recognition of freezing of assets and evidence in criminal cases,[118] and the EU-wide application of financial penalties and confiscation orders.[119] Mutual recognition also spurred the Commission to initiate efforts to guarantee minimum procedural rights that would govern criminal prosecutions; the recognition of final decisions in criminal matters;[120] and a European evidence warrant, which if adopted will establish a procedural floor for the collection and admissibility of evidence collected anywhere in the Union. Other important steps eventually taken towards harmonising national judicial processes found expression in two Commission Green Papers: the first set out the necessary conditions for the approximation, mutual recognition, and enforcement of criminal sanctions across the EU; and the second addressed the knotty problem of resolving conflicting jurisdictional claims and avoiding double jeopardy.[121] These framework decisions and green papers collectively moved the Union towards realising the Tampere Milestones. The principle of mutual recognition is now integral to any initiative taken in Pillar III. The rules governing jurisdiction and applicable law are under development. Yet the opportunity for cross-border jurisdictional conflicts has been significantly reduced and where conflicts do arise, they are more likely to be resolved according to a mutually accepted set of rules and procedure.

The 2004 Green Paper on mutual recognition of criminal sanctions proposed guidelines for harmonising penal sanctions for a range of serious crimes, but did not seek (and lacks the power) to establish minimum custodial sentences, including the enforcement of custodial sentences anywhere in the Union, either on the territory where the crime was committed or in the country of national origin.[122] Successive framework decisions have set the minimum level of maximum penalties for a wide range of crimes as well as agreed upon definition of those crimes, including counterfeiting, certain categories of fraud, terrorist offences (differentiating between mere membership and a leadership role), corruption, and illicit drug trafficking. While the Commission averred that it did not propose the 'standardisation of all criminal penalties', the goal was to establish a degree of harmonisation that would create a 'European law-enforcement area'.[123] Two of the legislative goals identified in the Green Paper – similar penalties for similar crimes and non-conflicting rules governing judicial process – have neither produced a significant approximation of criminal law within the Union nor narrowed significant differences in the definition of crimes.[124] A single European law enforcement area remains bedevilled by wide variations in national penal systems with regard to mandatory vs. discretionary sentencing, the definition of participation in a crime, whether the legal penalty of an attempted crime differs from a completed crime, and the relevance of mitigating or aggravating factors in sentencing guidelines. These differences are widespread within the Union and create a legal context lowering the risk of basing a criminal organisation in one jurisdiction as opposed to another.

Progress has been made towards aligning judicial processes, however. One of the most important developments has been the agreement in principle that there should be a standardisation of procedural rights in criminal proceedings within the EU. The 2004 Framework Decision defined those procedural guarantees narrowly and was limited to rights integral to Anglo-Saxon jurisprudence: free and competent legal counsel, the right to free translation of the proceedings in cases where the defendant does not understand the language used in court, and the right to communicate with family members or consular authorities.[125] These basic procedural guarantees have been augmented by the right to the presumption of innocence and the *neb is in idem* principle (no double jeopardy).[126] A final procedural development is the European Arrest Warrant, which has replaced extradition procedures between the EU member states. The surrender of individuals is now a matter of direct contacts between national judiciaries rather than ministries of justice. However, the European Arrest Warrant has not been applied evenly across the Union: some member states breached the substantive scope of the Framework Decision with regard to the minimum threshold of sentences requiring obligatory surrender or excluded categories of offence. Moreover, differences emerge in how states interpret or have transposed the admitted grounds for non-execution of the warrant.[127]

The free exchange of information between national prosecutors and investigators is an essential component of a single European law enforcement area. The two major steps towards that goal have been the Council

Decision on the exchange of information extracted from the criminal record and the Framework Decision on the exchange of information governed by the 'principle of availability'. The Council Decision had a very narrow frame of reference: it mandated a Union-wide database for exchanges of information on criminal convictions 'for the purpose of criminal proceedings'. Moreover, it specified that the transmittal of information was mandatory for those convicted of a range of crimes, including terrorism, participation in a criminal organisation, trafficking in narcotics or weapons, money laundering, and computer-related crime.[128] More important, however, was the Framework Decision invoking availability as the general principle governing the exchange of information in criminal and judicial matters within the Union. [129]

Efforts to create a single European judicial culture have been furthered with the EJN, funding devoted to projects nurturing a common judicial culture, sharing best practices, and improving mutual understanding of Europe's diverse legal and judicial systems. These three objectives serve the larger goal of facilitating the effective prosecution of crimes anywhere in the Union. The three major programmes established to create this outcome are Grotius II – Criminal (2001), AGIS (2002) and the Exchange Programme for Judicial authorities (2004). Grotius II projects fund common training, exchanges, research, and meetings; over the period 1996–2001, the Commission supported projects that had a cumulative budget of €21.2 million that financed 227 projects. AGIS superseded and consolidated Grotius II and other Title VI programmes. AGIS, which runs from 2003 to 2007, has a budget of €65 million dedicated to increasing cooperation between law enforcement and judicial authorities. The projects so far funded have targeted the creation or strengthening of judicial (and police) networks, the exchange and dissemination of best practices, and judicial (and police) training.[130]

Another programme dedicated to facilitating exchanges between judicial authorities was established as a two-year pilot programme beginning in 2004. Similar to AGIS, the Union has devoted funds to projects improving the mutual understanding of national legal systems, providing language training to facilitate direct communication between individual judges and prosecutors, and creating the basis for practical cooperation in the prosecution of serious crime. The 2005 programme, which targeted judges and public prosecutors, had a €3 million budget which funded, *inter alia*, the exchange of approximately 1,000 judges. The demonstrated interest in continuing judicial exchanges extended the programme into 2006 and has found a place in the framework programme on fundamental rights and justice covering the period 2007–2013.[131]

While the achievements of the Union in the area of judicial cooperation have fallen far short of meeting all the goals set by the Tampere Milestones, the Millennium Strategy on Organised Crime or The Hague Programme, there has been much progress. Moreover, prosecutors and judges can rely upon a European arrest warrant rather than lengthy extradition proceedings and may eventually be able to avail themselves of a European evidence warrant as well (see Table 4.6). The establishment of minimum procedural rules has enabled national magistrates and prosecutors to increase cross-border cooperation and successfully prosecute non-nationals for serious crimes.

Table 4.6 Major EU initiatives strengthening judicial cooperation

	Measures furthering the Tampere Milestones, the Hague Programme and the Millennium Strategy on Organised Crime, 1999–2006
Cooperation in judicial matters	*Framework decisions* On the European Arrest Warrant and surrender procedures (June 2002) On the European Evidence Warrant (not yet on force) *Council decisions* Convention on the adoption of mutual assistance in criminal matters (May 2000) On judicial training in the EU and exchange of magistrates (2005)
Judicial process	*Framework decisions* On certain procedural rights in criminal proceedings (April 2004) *Commission communication* Mutual Recognition of Final Decisions in Criminal Matters (November 2000) Green Paper on the approximation, mutual recognition, and enforcement of criminal sanctions (April 2004) Green Paper on conflicts of jurisdiction and double jeopardy (*neb is in idem*) (December 2005) Green Paper on presumption of innocence (April 2006)
Information sharing	*Framework decisions* On the exchange of information under the principle of availability (December 2005) *Conventions* On the adoption of mutual assistance in criminal matters
Mutual recognition	*Commission communication* Mutual Recognition of Final Decisions in Criminal Matters (November 2000) On mutual recognition of decisions in criminal matters (May 2005)
Programmes	AGIS (2002) Grotius II (June 2001) Exchange Programme for Judicial Authorities (2004–2013)

The incomplete fulfilment of The Hague Programme reflects a persistent unwillingness by national authorities to subordinate national goals to the goals of the programme; it also underscores that these initiatives touch 'policies which remain at the core of national sovereignty'.[132] A second, connected limitation reflects the Commission's inability to enforce compliance with Framework Decisions taken in Pillar III.[133] These twin barriers reflect the unresolved conflict between the imperatives of sovereignty and solidarity that militates against the sacrifice of national prerogatives.

A number of important measures have been taken to improve cooperation between police (see Table 4.7). The general effort has been aimed at improving the flow of information between law enforcement authorities, in addition to the cross-border cooperation via JIT, Europol and Eurojust. The legal foundation for creating a European-wide law enforcement system in criminal matters was laid with the protocol to the 2000 Convention on Mutual Assistance in Criminal Matters.[134] The protocol identified ways in which law enforcement could enhance cooperation in the areas of organised crime, money laundering, and other financial crimes. Articles 2–8 proscribed banking secrecy laws as a rationale for not complying with a request, prohibited a member state from rejecting a request for assistance on the grounds that it would merely aid in the prosecution of a political offence, and finally provided an appeals process that allowed states to forward a denied request to the Council for its assessment.

This effort to ease the flow of information between police and judicial authorities received a fillip with the 2005 proposal to establish availability as the principle governing police cooperation at the operational level.[135] The principle of availability overcame a series of obstacles to police cooperation, particularly the patchwork of bilateral and multilateral agreements between the member states, the absence of a positive obligation to provide certain categories of information, the inability of police authorities to contact each other directly rather than through an intermediary, and a lack of uniformity in standards of data protection, the conditions of access and use of information, and the type of data available for exchange.[136] This framework decision expanded and deepened police networks insofar as it requires that governments designate national contact points for the collection and exchange of the various categories of information, creates a method for establishing the equivalency between competent authorities in the member states, and specifies the conditions governing the exchange of information as well as the reasons for non-compliance with a request. Annex II of the protocol identified the kinds of information subject to the decision: DNA profiles,

Table 4.7 Major EU initiatives facilitating police cooperation

	Measures furthering the Tampere Milestones, the Hague Programme and the Millennium Strategy on Organised Crime, 1999–2006
Cooperation	*Framework decisions* On the European Arrest Warrant and surrender procedures (June 2002) On joint investigative teams (June 2002) On the European Evidence Warrant (not yet in force) *Council decisions* On the exchange of information extracted from the criminal record (October 2004) On the transmission of information emerging from the activities of security and intelligence services (December 2005)
Enforcement and prevention	*Council decision* Expansion of Europol mandate to deal with international crime (June 2001) *Commission proposal* On developing a strategy on tackling organised crime (June 2005) On developing a strategic concept on tackling organised crime (June 2006)
Information sharing	*Framework decisions* On the exchange of information under the principle of availability (December 2005) On simplifying the exchange of information and intelligence between law enforcement authorities of the member states (April 2004) *Council decisions* On the transmission of information emerging from the activities of security and intelligence services (December 2005) *Commission communication* On the interoperability of European databases (November 2005) *Conventions* Protocol to the Convention on the adoption of mutual assistance in criminal matters (November 2001)
Programmes	Falcone Programme (March 1998) OISIN II (June 2001) AGIS Programme (July 2002) Hippokrates Programme (June 2001) Grotius II (June 2001) Argus (December 2005)

fingerprints, ballistics, vehicle registration information, and a limited range of communications data. While the provisions of the annex would, along with the requirement that the information be available to competent authorities online, create an accessible EU-wide criminal information database, Article 2 (2) of the protocol specifically excludes a positive obligation 'to collect and store information either with or without coercive measures for the sole purpose of making it available . . .'.[137] Thus, different sensibilities to privacy across the Union could potentially limit the effectiveness of the protocol as well as the more ambitious goal of fostering closer cooperation between member state police forces.

Two other major measures have been taken to enhance the flow of information between law enforcement authorities. First, a 2004 JHA Council framework decision expanded the applicability of the availability principle: it mandated an EU-wide system for the exchange of information that would benefit a criminal investigation or criminal intelligence operation. Moreover, it identified 5 categories of information to be made available upon request over 37 separate categories of serious crime, including terrorist offences.[138] Second, the decision contained a positive obligation to share information without a formal request if 'there are factual reasons to believe that the information and intelligence could assist' in a criminal investigation or prosecution. A final measure facilitating the free exchange of information between national law enforcement agencies is the 2005 Commission communication on ensuring the interoperability of databases within the Union.[139] While the emphasis was placed on integrating the Schengen Information System (SIS) II, Visa Information System (VIS) and the European Union-wide Electronic System for the Identification of Asylum Seekers (EURODAC) systems to monitor and control EU borders more effectively, the communication also proposed the development of a European criminal Automated Fingerprints Identification System (AFIS) that would consolidate EU fingerprint data files and serve as a model for other biometric measures as well as a ready criminal information data base. The proposal, however, could have the practical effect of moving from interoperable to interconnected national databases, a development that would ease the exchange of information, but also make it more difficult for national authorities to retain control over it.[140]

The major initiatives in the area of policing, particularly when it comes to serious crime, have been the broadening Europol competencies, the creation of JIT, and efforts to generate threat assessments of organised crime towards facilitating common policies within the EU.[141] These developments have been buttressed by a large number of EU-sponsored

Table 4.8 EU programmes targeting police and judicial cooperation
(millon euros)

	Cooperation of law enforcement authorities	Cooperation of judicial authorities	Fight against terrorism	Fight against specific forms of crime
AGIS	1,268	4,760	3,620	11,360
OISIN II	4,270	220	780	5,020
Falcone	951	394	1,052	1,603
Hippocrates	618	0	303	1,742
Total:	7,107	5,374	5,755	19,725

Source: Ramboll Management 2005: annex A, table 0–5.

programmes targeting methods for encouraging cooperation between national law enforcement agencies. The most important programmes are: Falcone (1998–2002), OISIN and OISIN II (1996–2001), and AGIS (2002–2007).[142] The Falcone programme provided Community funds to facilitate greater police cooperation in the investigation and prosecution of organised crime; OISIN and OISIN II funded the exchange, common training and cooperation between law enforcement and customs officials; and AGIS funds the entire spectrum of police, customs, and judicial cooperation and exchange. The projects most relevant to securing Europe internally – enhancing police and judicial cooperation, and aiding in the fights against terrorism and specific forms of crime (e.g., drugs and money laundering) – received an aggregate €37.96 million between 1996 and 2005. Just over 50 per cent of this amount was devoted to fighting or preventing specific categories of crime, while substantially less – even after 11 March – was spent on fighting terrorism. Moreover, the Commission has shifted its priorities: AGIS has favoured programmes enhancing judicial cooperation, while the preceding programmes overwhelmingly funded closer cooperation between law enforcement (see Table 4.8).

Slightly more than 54 per cent of the projects funded by AGIS programme have been directed towards mitigating organised crime and specific forms of criminal activity, while approximately 23 per cent of the projects have been devoted to judicial cooperation and 6 per cent dedicated to police cooperation. Moreover, national, regional and local authorities have accounted for approximately 61 per cent of the projects funded, while NGOs, universities, and non-profit organisations received 38 per cent. [143] As interesting, however, is the preponderance of six states as lead project countries (number of projects in closed parentheses): Italy

(152), Germany (135), UK (117), (France 64), the Netherlands (61), and Spain (55).[144] An independent assessment of the AGIS programme concluded that it largely served to meet the external challenges facing the EU (particularly cross-border cooperation against terrorism, organised crime, and economic crime) *and* continued to support the structural objectives of implementing EU legislation, particularly the development of a single European law enforcement area (Ramboll Management, 2005: Tables 3–4).

On combating terrorism

The Union agreed to a common definition of terrorism and a terrorist act in December 2001. The common position on combating terrorism identified three general categories of terrorist acts: the serious intimidation of the population; the effort to persuade or dissuade a government to undertake a specific course of action; and acts 'seriously destabilising or destroying the fundamental political, constitutional, economic, or social structures of a country'.[145] An initial common legal definition of a terrorist group was put forward in the December 2001 common position. The June 2002 Framework Decision on Terrorism narrowed the definition of a terrorist group to include only structured rather than random groups of individuals. The framework decision also rendered a common definition of terrorist acts, aligned national criminal penalties for terrorist organisations, terrorists and certain categories of terrorist acts; it also established guidelines determining national jurisdiction in cases where terrorist acts had a transborder component.[146]

The partial militarisation (and cross-pillarisation) of the EU's approach to terrorism occurred with the 2002 Seville European Council, where the decision was taken to adapt Pillar II to the task of internal security (albeit in addressing its external origin). The incorporation of Pillar II into the fight against terrorism had two direct consequences: first, it required the Europeans to reconsider the types of military capabilities it wished to acquire; second, it expanded the range of military contingencies for which Europe had to prepare.[147] The expanded remit of the CFSP and ESDP required additional arrangements for intelligence sharing, the capability to develop a common threat assessment mechanism, the acquisition of appropriate capabilities for protecting EU forces engaged in counter-terrorism operations, and the integration of military assets into civil crisis management operations in the event of a terrorist attack.[148] The specific policy measures attending these policy ambitions included the pledge to develop EU military capabilities appropriate to the fight against terrorism (yet consistent with the Petersberg tasks), to improve capabilities for the protection of critical infrastructures from terrorist threats, and to inventory EU civil defence capabilities, including those relevant to terrorist CBRN attacks.[149]

The EU has made significant progress in crafting a joint policy in the fight against terrorism, particularly with respect to three major policy objectives found in the Revised Action Plan on Terrorism: cutting of terrorist access to financial resources; improving the ability of the member states to detect, investigate and prosecute terrorism and terrorist offences on a pan-EU basis; and improving border control measures to prevent (potential) terrorists from crossing undetected the EU common external border (see Table 4.9).[150] The task of eradicating terrorist access to financial resources does not differ fundamentally from the parallel efforts to eliminate the opportunity for criminal organisations to launder illicit gains. Yet, the attacks on Manhattan, the Pentagon, Madrid and London between 2001 and 2006 underscored the centrality of finance for the successful execution of major terrorist attacks and redoubled efforts to improve the ability to monitor, control and identify the sources of terrorist finance. Although a large number of instruments were adopted in the immediate aftermath of 11 September, the more wide-reaching efforts of the Union only occurred after 2004, particularly with the Third Money Directive.

The Third Money Directive and Directive 2005/60/EC on money laundering and terrorist financing are perhaps the most important pieces of EU-level legislation on terrorist financing. The Third Money Directive introduced due diligence and reporting requirements even if terrorism is only suspected; Directive 2005/60/EC defined money laundering, established the categories of serious crime, required the application of customer due diligence, and holds member states responsible for implementing 'effective, proportionate and dissuasive' criminal penalties for terrorist-related money laundering.[151] The member states also authorised the SitCen to develop an intelligence capacity tailored to terrorist financing thereby creating an autonomous source of intelligence that each member state would have equal access.[152]

Efforts to improve cross-border detection, investigation and prosecution of terrorist offences are important to realising the larger effort to create a single area of freedom, justice and security. But because the various framework document provisions that enhance police or judicial cooperation are generic in nature, they apply to any form of cross-border criminal activity as well as terrorism. Europol, Eurojust and the PCTF have also been drawn into the fight against terrorism, including the second protocol to the Europol Convention that expands Europol's competency to participate in terrorist investigations and JIT, and forges closer links between Europol and Eurojust in the investigation and

Table 4.9 Major EU initiatives in combating terrorism

	Measures furthering the goals of the Declaration on Terrorism, Framework decision on combating terrorism, and the Third Money Directive, 1999–2006
Police and judicial cooperation	*Council decision* On the implementation of specific measures for police and judicial cooperation to combat terrorism (January 2003).
Police enforcement and prevention	*Council directive* On the prevention of the use of the financial system for the purpose of money laundering and terrorist financing (November 2005) *Council regulation* On specific measures directed against certain persons and entities with a view to combating terrorism (December 2001) *Council positions* On combating terrorism (December 2001) *Commission communcation* On the prevention of and fight against terrorist financing (October 2004) On greater security of explosives and bomb-making materials (July 2005)
Judicial process	*Framework decisions* On combating terrorism (June 2002). *Council regulation* On specific measures directed against certain persons and entities with a view to combating terrorism (December 2001) On the prevention of and fight against terrorist financing (October 2004) On greater security of explosives and bomb-making materials (July 2005) *Council positions* On combating terrorism (December 2001)
Information sharing	*Framework decisions* On the exchange of information under the principle of availability (December 2005) *Council decisions* On the implementation of specific measures for police and judicial cooperation to combat terrorism (December 2002) On the transmission of information emerging from the activities of security and intelligence services (December 2005) On the exchange of information and cooperation concerning terrorist offenses (September 2005) Prüm Convention (July 2005) *Council recommendations* Introduction of a standard form for exchanging information on terrorists (April 2002)

prosecution of terrorist offences. The fight against terrorism has also been aided by provisions facilitating the exchange of information and intelligence between Europol and SitCen.[153] Moreover, three key initiatives for controlling the common external border and tracking asylum seekers and immigrants – SIS II, VIS and EURODAC – have been drafted into the fight against terrorism, even though their original purpose predated the current Muslim terrorist threat to internal security.

Border control   The EU has not fully achieved its ambitious goals in the area of border control, illegal immigration, or a common asylum and immigration policy, but significant progress has been made towards erasing national frontiers within the Union while improving the joint policing of the common external frontier. The control of national borders remains a national responsibility, yet the problem of securing the external border of the Union falls under the competency of the Union as a part of the Schengen *acquis*. The High-Level Working Group on Asylum and Migration, formed in December 1998, translated the Vienna Action Plan goals into concrete policy proposals. It initially developed programmes designed to staunch the flow of unwanted migrants from five countries considered critical sources of migratory instability; viz., Afghanistan, Albania, Iraq, Somalia, and Sri Lanka. The Working Group attributed that instability to non or poor governance of territory under the nominal control of central authorities in Afghanistan, Iraq and Somalia. Moreover, the absence of an internationally recognised government in each of those states made policy implementation difficult, since the EU lacked a partner state with which it could negotiate. The EU employed strategies of prevention – particularly development and economic assistance – but also made efforts to mainstream human rights, the support of democratisation and rule of law, and other efforts to dissuade individuals from migrating to Europe.[154]

The Union has also relied on a series of programmes to improve the policing capabilities of those member states directly responsible for the common external frontier. The first long-term programme – Odysseus – provided €12 million between 1998 and 2002 and targeted the joint training and exchanges of officials, particularly those engaged in the areas of asylum and immigration. ARGO, which replaced Odysseus, provided €25 million between 2002 and 2007 and supported programmes strengthening the policing of the common external frontier. Asylum and immigration also remain eligible for ARGO funds, but the Council Decision clearly placed improved control of the common external border at the top of the agenda – of the ten projects financed in the first year, all but two were devoted to that goal.[155]

The Schengen Information System (SIS) II is the most important step towards realising the joint management of the common external border. SIS II was designed for the express purpose of processing and exchanging data amongst national authorities to strengthen police and judicial cooperation in the investigation and prosecution of serious crime.[156] Moreover, SIS II, unlike its predecessor, is a part of the Schengen *acquis* and lends the Commission the power to bring infringement proceedings against member states violating SIS II provisions. Once completed, SIS II will link the member states to a computerised information system that has three components: a central database (the Central Schengen Information System), no more than two contact points (the SIRENE authorities) in each member state responsible for making and processing SIS alerts or requesting additional information in connection with an alert, and a communication infrastructure between the central database and the national contact points. National judicial and police authorities can issue alerts over the SIS II network to identify individuals wanted for arrest, extradition or trial, to initiate surveillance on an individual entering the EU when 'clear evidence' exists that the individual may or will commit a serious criminal offence, or to issue a request for the seizure of evidence in the furtherance of a criminal proceeding. [157] In addition to creating a mechanism for enforcing existing criminal investigations or tracking an individual under investigation, the SIS II guarantees that national police authorities and judiciaries will keep and transmit standardised data. This obligation is not unqualified: states retain the privilege to flag SIS II alerts if the member state 'considers that an alert . . . is incompatible with its national law, international obligations or essential national interests'.[158] States are expected to avail themselves of this article sparingly, but this proviso strongly suggests that the SIS II provisions will be difficult to enforce in practice. This network has also insinuated two Union institutions – Eurojust and Europol – into the task of policing the common external border. Neither Eurojust nor Europol has a presumptive right to use information found on the SIS II network in the course of an investigation; the use of that information remains contingent upon the consent of the state initiating the alert and the use of the information is subject to very detailed restrictions. [159]

The Council also introduced a proposal for a decision that would establish a set of 'general rules to promote strategic and operation cooperation' for controlling and policing the common external border. The content of that cooperation ranged from investigating crime, easing the exchange of information, protecting border security, and providing cross-border cooperation in the investigation and prosecution of crime. The proposal identified 13 specific types of information that police had a presumptive obligation to provide on request. It also identified a number of areas where police cooperation could be improved, particularly the ability to conduct cross-border operations that included joint surveillance, searches and seizures. The Council proposed that more legislative energy be devoted to ensuring the interoperability of equipment, creating joint training schemes, conducting joint patrols, establishing joint investigative teams in the border regions, and exchanging police personnel. Moreover, the decision provided police the opportunity to continue surveillance or engage in the hot pursuit of criminals across an internal border without the prior authorisation of the member state.[160]

Money laundering and financial crime   A Council Framework Decision of June 2001 identified money laundering as central to the persistence of organised crime and established sentencing guidelines for a variety of financial crimes.[161] Compliance with aspects of that decision was largely completed by 2006: all the member states had amended their penal law to conform with Article 2 (minimum maximum custodial sentence of 4 years when connected to organised crime) and Article 3 (which provides an EU-wide legal basis for the confiscation of illicit assets). However, the critical provision in Article 4 – mutual assistance in the prosecution of financial crime (including the freezing, seizure, or confiscation of assets) – had not yet been transposed uniformly into national law.[162] Moreover, the investigation of financial crimes has played a comparatively minor role in the case work of Eurojust and Europol. Despite the acknowledged nexus between money laundering and terrorism, only 7 per cent of the Eurojust case load was accounted for by this category of crime. Europol has not been much more successful in creating a borderless policing of financial crime; it has acknowledged that 'despite all efforts' cooperation within Europol had not reached the anticipated or desired 'level of intensity'.[163]

The Third Money Laundering Directive (October 2005) explicitly linked money laundering to the fight against terrorism. The directive made a number of changes in the legal framework governing money laundering and terrorist financing. In addition to the creation of the Committee on the Prevention of Money Laundering and Terrorist Financing (charged with responsibility for aiding the Commission) and national FIU, this Third Directive provided a common legal definition of money laundering in aid of terrorist offences, defined those offences as serious crimes and specified minimum maximum custodial sentences, and established due diligence requirements for the banking and financial sector. The directive required states to sanction legally financial institutions and intermediaries that knowingly carry out a transaction that *may* be illegal, directed financial intermediaries to contact the national FIU when money laundering is suspected, and enabled member state governments to direct those financial intermediaries to refrain from executing a transaction.[164]

Information and computer network security   In 2003, the JHA Council provided a common definition of attacks against information systems, committed member states to enact specific penal legislation criminalising those categories of action, and established minimum maximum custodial sentences when such attacks are carried out by criminal organisations. As important, the EU member states agreed upon a predetermined formula for deciding which national legal system had jurisdiction when the crime had a cross-border component. [165] In 2005, the Union made additional progress towards a single legal framework for the prosecution of and protection against attacks on information systems and networks. The framework decision provided common definitions of activities that constituted illegal access to and illegal interference with information systems or electronic data, established an EU-wide custodial sentence of between two and five years for individuals committing cybercrimes on behalf of criminal organisations, and delineated jurisdiction for the prosecution of such criminal acts.[166] This framework decision not only filled lacunae in the legal framework protecting the smooth functioning of the internal market, but ensured that the issue of cybercrime had prominent place on national security agenda.

Health security   The progress towards meeting the goals of the BICHAT programme have been mixed. The most revealing aspect of the programme's limitations is the reluctance of member states to engage in the common stockpiling of vaccines or medicines. In July 2002, the EU Health and Security Committee agreed that there was not a demonstrable need for an EU stockpile, which formally recognised that member states were unwilling to cede their right to provide vaccines and medicines on a national rather than community basis, even in the face of bioterrorism. The member states were also disinterested in diverting resources to Brussels in order to create an EU sponsored procurement programme for vaccines, particularly in the case of smallpox. The member states confined the Commission's role to monitoring national stockpiles, promoting the development of immunoglobins, anthrax vaccine and anti-toxins, and supporting the development of safer third generation smallpox vaccines.

The Union has slowly constructed a public health surveillance system tailored to the needs of responding to a biological or chemical terrorist attack. The EU made significant progress in four areas meeting the challenge of health security. First, those communicable diseases most likely to be weaponised were added to the list of diseases falling under the purview of the EU-wide epidemiological surveillance mechanism; in July 2003, the Commission added smallpox, tetanus, anthrax, botulism, diphtheria, Q-fever and tularaemia, and the annex of the decision provided for the surveillance of 'any other as yet unclassified serious epidemic disease, including diseases that are caused by agents specifically engineered for the purpose of maximising morbidity and/or mortality upon deliberate release'.[167]

Second, the Union actively participated in the Australia Group, which enforces export controls on dual-use chemical and biological agents. To reinforce international cooperation, the EU established an internal export control system laying down a list of 'biological and chemical agents for which strict provisions linked to international non-proliferation regimes and export control arrangements (exist)'.[168] The EU also participated in the G8-sponsored Global Health Security Action Group. This initiative led to the development of an 'incident scale' for developing common or coordinated response strategies and a Global Outbreak Alert and Response Network located in the World Health Organisation.

Third, the EU created a network between the safety level 4 laboratory facilities in the EU to provide 24/7 diagnostic services in the event of a suspected outbreak of viral haemorrhagic fever or smallpox. Correspondingly, EU-wide protocols were established for the ten diseases most likely to be weaponised (anthrax, smallpox, botulism, plague, tularaemia, haemorrhagic fever viruses, brucella, Q fever, encephalitis viruses and glanders). And finally, the EU built upon the 1982 Seveso Directive which provided the foundation for member-state cooperation in the identification of chemical toxins and the development of protocols for coping with chemical accidents. In the post-11 September environment, these 'civilian' concerns were augmented with a typology of terrorist chemical threats that required a precautionary public health and medical response.[169]

The chief failure of the 2003 EU programme is found in the absence of a uniform vaccine and medicine stockpiling policy and member state unwillingness to share unconditionally those stockpiles of vaccines and medicines in the event of a terrorist attack. Significant barriers prevent the development of a Community programme targeting the stockpiling and distribution of only smallpox vaccines. Even though a smallpox outbreak would present one of the most deadly (and likely) forms of bioterrorism, states are unwilling to dedicate the necessary resources to fund such a programme and are under no pressure to do so: most

Europeans assign a low probability to the occurrence of a bioterrorism attack. More important, the member states were simply unwilling to establish a Community stockpile of smallpox vaccine and were unwilling to enter into any formal arrangement for the sharing of vaccines in times of emergency.

This refusal only underscores the continuing role of the state as the guarantor of societal and individual protection against external attack; it demonstrates the continuing expectation that national governments rather than the Community should be responsible for security in this area. National governments did agree to cooperate, however, in the joint development of vaccines and anti-toxins to protect their own citizens from bioterrorism. But that willingness to cooperate did not reflect the principle of solidarity, but instead the utilitarian calculation that the development costs of such vaccines were beyond the financial resources of any individual European state.

The bioterrorism threat was complemented by a parallel concern with the threat of nuclear or radiological materials or devices falling into the hands of terrorists. This concern was aggravated with the collapse of authority in the Russian Federation and the emergence of the Muslim terrorist threat. The Russian Federation has proven incapable of monitoring or controlling its nuclear storage facilities or preventing the exodus of nuclear scientists and technicians in the moribund defence sector seeking employment. The concern with the Russian Federation manifested itself as a preoccupation with the safety of civilian nuclear reactor facilities and the security of the Soviet nuclear arsenal. The Europeans were initially concerned with the viability of Soviet-designed nuclear reactors in Russia and the successor republics of the Soviet Union – a rational policy preoccupation given the potential consequences of another Chernobyl-class reactor failure. The Americans, while also concerned with reactor safety, were more preoccupied with the storage and security of weapons grade uranium and plutonium, not to mention missiles and warheads.

The Cooperative Threat Reduction (CTR) programme initiated by the American Congress – the so-called Nunn–Lugar initiative – dispersed $1.92 billion between 1992 and 2000 (US Department of State 2000; Congressional Budget Office 2003). In contrast to the American financial support for securing or destroying Russian nuclear materials and weapons, the EU programmes targeting those same goals only began in 1999 and at a much lower level of financial and technical support. [170] The financial support for various projects, particularly the chemical weapons destruction plants in Gorny and Kambarka was relatively modest as compared to the efforts of major member states, particularly Germany.

Whereas the estimated cost of constructing and operating the Kambarka chemical weapons destruction facility is $700 million, the EU has only contributed approximately €4.05 million to the project while Germany has pledged €200 million. Similarly, the United Kingdom, France and Germany devoted €17 million to programmes targeting the disposal of plutonium and the Shchuch'ye site for destroying nerve gas, while the EU contribution was limited to €3.6 million.[171] Between 1999 and 2005, the EU devoted approximately €92 million to nuclear and chemical weapons disposal or to the physical protection of nuclear materials, far less than the German contribution to the Kambarka chemical destruction facility.[172] While the EU financial contribution to the destruction or protection of nuclear and chemical weapons materials are likely to remain relatively meagre, the EU has successfully engaged in preventive diplomacy with Russia: Europe has extracted a Russian commitment to exchange sensitive information about its weapons programmes more freely, to thwart the smuggling of weapons grade material with better border policing, and to track and prosecute organised criminal networks operating in Russia and the EU.[173]

Conclusion: assessing the EU as a security actor in the policies of protection

The expansion of the EU policy remit into the policy areas of terrorism and organised crime were spurred initially by the growing porousness of the boundaries within the EU and between the EU and its neighbours. The diplomatic and psychological consequences of 11 September, which were beyond the control of any individual European government, let alone the EU, as well as the internal political consequences of the Madrid and London terrorist attacks, forced the member states to contemplate further encroachments upon national prerogatives (Den Boer and Monar 2002: 26). The focus on terrorism and organised crime also generated pressures for the integration of a broad spectrum of Pillar III competencies into the internal security calculus, especially matters impinging on border control, money laundering, computer and information networks, and public health. This expansion of the security agenda contributed to the progressive erasure of the distinction between internal and external security and revealed deep fissures between the political and legal cultures that persist between the member states.[174]

The EU has successfully securitised these policy domains, particularly the protection of critical infrastructure, bacteriological or viral contagions and financial crimes linked to organised crime or terrorism. The internalisation of security has created an understanding amongst the member states that heretofore components of national sovereignty have become the legitimate targets of EU legislation (Monar 2004: 127). Yet, the transposition of framework documents into national law remains dependent upon the good faith of the member governments; neither the Commission nor European Court of Justice has the legal standing to sanction infringements. Non-compliance remains problematic; the 'weakest link' technology of publicness characterising this dimension of security policy places limits on the EU as an autonomous actor. Member states remain unwilling to countenance the use the bridging clauses of Article 42 TEU and 67(2) TEC and thereby empower the Commission to initiate infringement proceedings as a way to enforce the transposition of The Hague Programme-derived legislation into national law.

The EU has achieved some autonomy from the member states with the creation of Community-embedded networks intermediating relationships between national judicial or police authorities or eliminating the strict jurisdictional boundaries formed by national frontiers. The EU has also asserted a kind of autonomy with the progressive harmonisation of judicial process and penal law within the Union and the creation of legal instruments valid throughout Europe, particularly the European arrest warrant, the anticipated European evidence warrant, and guaranteed mutual access to a standardised criminal data base. The growing reliance upon these legal instruments and the cooperation engendered by Europol, Eurojust and the Police Chiefs' Task Force will inevitably compel the application of the Community method to JHA, at least in those areas touching upon serious crime and terrorism. This pressure, already evident in the provisions of the constitutional treaty which would have introduced the Community method to JHA, is unlikely to ease. Arguably, the external requirement of more effective cooperation with its allies, particularly the United States, in the fight against terrorism and the manifest multi-jurisdictional character of Muslim terrorists operating within Europe will require a harmonised criminal justice system within the EU.

The securitisation of JHA has created an internal logic that is more likely to produce a 'mere integrated law enforcement zone' (Den Boer and Monar 2002: 27) rather than the area of freedom, security and justice as envisioned by the Treaty of Amsterdam. Yet the evolution and character of the EU's role in JHA suggests that this logic will, in the end, not only contribute to a secure Union, but one that fosters freedom and justice as well. While the concrete achievements may appear limited in terms of results that are subject to measurement (the number of joint investigations or prosecutions, changing levels or incidences of serious crime and terrorism, or the rate at which framework decisions, regulations or directives are transposed into national law), the member states have acknowledged that the EU has an important role to play in crafting these policies and a critical role in coordinating them.

The policies of protection are most troubled by the underlying security policy conundrum confronting the EU and its member states: the necessity of joint action to meet internal security threats is unquestioned by the governing elites, yet governments are unable to cede sovereignty in this policy domain because national electorates remain attached to national political and legal cultures. The development of an internal security strategy harmonising national security policies, particularly with respect to terrorism and organised crime, constitutes one of the most important security challenges facing the EU and its member states. While the technology of publicness in this domain would counsel the introduction of the Community method into Pillar III as the surest mechanism for achieving the objectives of The Hague Programme, the publics and governments of the member states are still unwilling to abnegate such an important aspect of sovereignty.

Notes

1 These concepts, along with 'asecuritisation', are developed in Wæver (1995 and 1998).

2 The term 'extremist Muslim' is employed instead of 'radical Islam' or 'radical Islamists' for two reasons: first, there is considerable debate about whether terrorists of the Muslim faith can be meaningfully classified as 'radical'; second, it is individual Muslims rather than Islam that perpetuate terrorist acts.

3 This connection was first made at the 2002 Seville summit. See also European Commission (2004), 'Conceptual framework on the ESDP dimension . . .': para. 1; and Luxembourg Presidency (2005) 'Working document . . .'.

4 Justice and Home Affairs Council (1998), 'Action Plan . . . on an area of freedom, security and justice', [hereafter 'Vienna Action Plan'].

5 Council of the European Union (1999), 'Towards a Union . . . the Tampere Milestones' [hereafter 'Tampere Milestones'].

6 While this is an admittedly nebulous and fluid geographical designation, it refers generally to the western republics of the former Soviet Union, southeastern Europe and Asia Minor, and the littoral states of the Mediterranean.

7 The five-year Tampere Programme (1999–2004) serves as the basis for the assessment of the EU's progress in this area. See Council of the European Union (2004), 'Presidency Conclusions, Annex I' (hereafter Hague Programme).

8 European Council (1997), 'Action Plan to combat organised crime': 1; and European Commission (2000), 'The prevention and control of organised crime . . .' [hereafter 'Millennium Strategy']. A third document of importance, the Dublin Declaration on organised crime, simply reaffirmed

the goals of the Millennium Strategy and identified additional innovations furthering the goals of police and judicial cooperation. See Justice and Home Affairs Ministers (2004), 'Action against organised crime: the Dublin Declaration'.

9 Council of the European Union (2002), 'Council Framework Decision of 13 June 2002 . . .'; European Council, 'Declaration on combating terrorism', and Council of the European Union, 'The European Union counter-terrorism strategy'.

10 Vienna Action Plan, sections 28 and 5; Tampere Programme, para. 3; and Hague Programme: 33.

11 European Commission (2000), 'The Prevention and Control of Organised Crime . . .' (hereafter 'Millennium Strategy'): 3.

12 European Council (2003), 'A secure Europe in a better world . . .' (hereafter ESS): 2. The sources of threats identified in the ESS are not dissimilar to the Istanbul Declaration of 1999. See OSCE, 'Istanbul Document. Charter for European Security': para. 4.

13 The fear of possible nuclear or radiological terrorist attacks are not unfounded. The International Atomic Energy Agency (IAEA) trafficking data base identified 540 confirmed incidents of trafficking nuclear or radiological materials between 1993 and 2003. IAEA (nd), 'IAEA Illicit Trafficking Database (ITDB)'.

In the post-Cold War period, the Europeans were preoccupied with nuclear power plant safety, while the United States focused primarily on the problem of securing the Russian stocks of weapons grade uranium and plutonium. This divergent orientation persists: the IAEA nuclear security fund, designed to hinder trafficking in nuclear materials and to meet the nuclear terrorist threat, has a pledged budget of $22.9 billion, of which the United States contributed $15.4 billion (and Canada an additional $3.01). Of the European states, the UK pledged $1.2 billion, the Netherlands $510 million, and France $459 million. Germany made no pledge at all. See IAEA (2003), 'Nuclear Security . . .': attachment 2; and IAEA (2002) 'Nuclear security . . .': attachment 2.

14 Hague Programme, pp. 28–33.

15 The ETA (Euskadi Ta Askatasuna); the provisional IRA (Irish Republican Army), and the FLNC Reconstitué (Reconstituted Corsican National Liberation Front) represent the secessionist ambitions of Basque separatists, Irish Catholics in Ulster, and Corsicans in France, respectively.

16 The member states purposely circumscribed the EU role, including Europol. Europol was only given legal authority to deal with terrorist-related crimes in 1999. See Council of the European Union (1999), 'Council Recommendation of 9 December 1999 . . .'.

17 The La Gomera Declaration (1995) is an earlier EU statement on terrorism. Although the member states affirmed that 'terrorism constitutes a threat to democracy, to the free exercise of human rights and to economic and social development', very little concrete emerged from it (Rutten, 2002: 152; Haine, 2003: 272).

18 The larger point about internal recruitment is made in European Commission (2004) 'Conceptual Framework', para. 1; and Luxembourg Presidency (2005), 'Working Document . . .': para. 6.

19 This rationale for a common policy towards illegal immigration is presented in European Commission (2004), 'Reference document for financial and technical assistance . . . AENEAS Programme 2004–2006'. This programme provided €120 million in support of programmes reducing the flow of illegal immigrants into the EU.

20 European Commission (2002), 'Proposal for a comprehensive plan . . .': paras 60 and 61. This potential problem was felt most acutely in Germany and France, particularly the flood of asylum seekers from south-eastern Europe in the 1990s.

21 On the importance of terrorist financing, see Council of the European Union (2005), 'Draft Directive . . .'.

22 See 'Regulation (EC) no. 460/2004 establishing the European Network and Information Security Agency', Article 1(3).

23 European Commission (2000), 'Communication . . . creating a safer information society . . .': 6.

24 Council of the European Union (2005), 'Council Framework Decision 2005/222/JHA'; see also Ranck and Schmitt (2005).

25 See European Commission (2004), 'Communication . . . critical infrastructure protection in the fight against terrorism': 3–5 and 8. Critical infrastructure protection was designated as a national responsibility, although the Commission seized responsibility for critical infrastructure with a transboundary effect. See Council of the European Union (2004), 'EU Solidarity Programme . . .': 12.

26 The decision also differentiated between cybercrimes committed by individuals and those committed on behalf of criminal organisations. See European Commission (2002), 'Proposal . . . on attacks against information systems': 17 and 18–19.

27 Those attacks led to the creation of a bioterrorism task force in May 2002 (Tegnell, *et al.* 2003: 1330).

28 European Parliament and European Council (1998), 'Decision no. 2119/98/EC . . .'.

29 The action identified a list of communicable diseases best addressed at the EU level, did not contain the viruses or bacteria that state and non-state actors were most likely to weaponise even though they were cited as a key rationale for EU action at Ghent. *Ibid.* See also European Commission (2003), 'Communication . . . on preparedness and response to biological and chemical agent attacks . . .': 8; and Gouvras (2002: 1).

30 Council of the European Union (2002), 'Adoption of the programme . . . for preventing and limiting of chemical, biological, radiological or nuclear terrorist threats': 2.

31 The prospect of an avian flu pandemic has eclipsed concerns about weaponised pathogens and toxins.

32 European Commission (2003) 'Proposal . . . establishing a European centre [for disease prevention and control]': 2–3.

33 *Ibid.*, p. 3.

34 Conference of the Representatives of the Governments of the Member States (2004) 'Treaty establishing a Constitution for Europe': 176.

35 The solidarity principle figures prominently in Council of the European Union (2004) 'EU Solidarity Programme . . .': 5. The mutual assistance guarantee falls far short of the obligation found in Article V of the Western European Union, but is stronger than the Article 5 obligation of the North Atlantic Treaty. See also, European Council (2004) 'Declaration on Combating Terrorism': section 2; and European Commission (2004) 'Conceptual Framework . . .': sections 3–6. Intra-EU cooperation in the policing and prosecution of terrorist offences remained hostage to compatibility with member state constitutional and legal frameworks. See European Commission (2004) 'Interim Report . . .': section 2.2, and the Hague Programme: 13.

36 The Hague Programme emphasised that common policies and the national convergence of national law and procedure were central to meeting the collective threat posed by terrorism. It also introduced the principle of availability, which also qualified the sovereignty principle. Member states now had an (admittedly qualified) obligation to exchange information between national law enforcement agencies in order to ensure the more efficient investigation and prosecution of crime within the EU. However limited that principle is in practice, it nonetheless established an obligation for an unimpeded exchange of information. See the Hague Programme: sections I, II (1), III (1.7.1), III (2.1 and 2.2) and III (4); Permanent Representatives Council (2004) 'Adoption of Council conclusions . . .': 4–6.

37 Vienna Action Plan. The principle of proportionality also sustains the sovereign prerogatives since it leaves the operational aspects of implementing EU policies to the discretion of the states.

38 Tampere Programme: sections 5, 22, 38, 48, 62.

39 European Commission (2001) 'European Commission action paper . . .': 6. Even in an issue area as uncontroversial as limiting terrorist finance – a policy objective established in the UN International Convention for the Suppression of the Financing of Terrorism – a 1999 Council recommendation on money laundering noted that 'no member state should feel obliged to take part in these measures'. Council of the European Union (1999) 'Council Recommendation of 9 December 1999 . . .': para. 5; Council of the European Union (2001) 'Common position on combating terrorism': 192.

40 Vienna Action Plan: paras 23 and 24.

41 Council of the European Union (2003) 'Council common position 2003/805/CFSP': para. 3. This approach was the centrepiece of the EU response to the post-reconstruction tasks necessary to stabilise Afghanistan and policies towards those areas determined to be the most likely sources of terrorism – Pakistan, Iran, India, and the states of Central Asia. See

European Council (2001) 'Declaration . . . follow-up to the September 11 attacks and the fight against terrorism': points 3a–3d, 4 and 5.

42 Council of the European Union (2002) 'Council Framework Decision of 13 June 2002 . . .': para. 2.

43 This principle was extended in practice by the four-fold differentiation between separatist, Muslim extremist, anarchist, and eco-terrorisms. The various separatist movements in Europe accounted for the most prevalent category of terrorist acts, but Muslim terrorism has propelled and sustained the desired alignment between member-state penal, judicial and policing systems. See Article 36 Committee (2002) 'Terrorist activity . . .'.

44 Hague programme: 42. These principles of action were first outlined at the 2000 European Council meeting in Feira and were adapted to fit the counter-terrorism goals of the Union.

45 Council of the European Union (2003) 'Council common position 2003/805/CFSP': article 12.

46 See European Commission (2002) 'Proposal for a comprehensive plan . . .': 30; Council of the European Union (2005), 'Prüm Convention': Article 1; European Commission, 'Proposal for a Framework Decision on the exchange of information . . .': 2, 7 and 20; Council of the European Union (2005), 'Proposal for . . . second generation Schengen information system (SIS II)': 5.

47 Council of the European Union (2005), 'Draft Directive . . .': article 1.

48 *Ibid.*: articles 4, 6, 7 (1) and 11 (1b). Article 21 prescribes that member states 'shall require the institutions and persons covered in this Directive from carrying out transactions which they know or suspect to be related to money laundering or terrorist financing'. The directive also developed four other principles of action: states would guarantee high levels of transparency and consultation with financial intermediaries; EU rules would not pose unnecessary barriers to national compliance; EU legislation would be consistent with preexisting EU legislation; and the legislative agenda would protect EU citizens from the consequences of money laundering and terrorist financing.

49 *Ibid.*: article 27 (1).

50 See Council of the European Union (2005), 'Council Framework Decision 2005/222/JHA . . .'; Council of the European Union (2004), 'Regulation (EC) no. 460/2004 . . .'; and European Commission (2001), 'Communication . . . proposal for a European policy approach'.

51 *Ibid.*, article 12.

52 Council of the European Union (2002), 'Adoption of the programme . . .'. The 2002 CBRN programme, which underscored the importance of facilitating closer police and judicial cooperation, was designated a 'political and not a legal instrument'. European Commission (2003), 'Communication . . . on preparedness and response to biological and chemical agent attacks (health security)'.

53 On this last point, the Council declared that 'all the states of the Union and the EU institutions have a collective responsibility for preventing these risks

by actively contributing to the fight against proliferation'. See Council of the European Union (2004), 'EU Solidarity Programme': 8. The first three principles were prominent in European Council (2003), 'EU strategy against proliferation . . .': 313–15.

54 See Article 36 Committee (1999) 'Finalisation and evaluation . . .': 6–9.
55 Vienna Action Plan: paras 10 and 11.
56 Hague programme: section II (2.2).
57 European Council (2002), 'Presidency conclusions . . . Annex V'.
58 Vienna Action Plan: paras 32–7, 42–7, and 50–1; Tampere Milestones: paras 19 and 5. The Millennium Strategy (124/12) also cited as a key goal the adoption of 'minimum standards of the constituent elements of offences and penalties related to organised crime . . .'.
59 The Millennium strategy made 39 recommendations and rank-ordered each recommendation as a primary, secondary or tertiary priority. The 2004 Dublin Declaration on Organised Crime was much less ambitious: it made only 9 recommendations, 4 of which revisited the need for standardising the definition, collection, and distribution of crime statistics within the EU. This goal became all the more urgent as Muslim terrorism climbed to the top of the EU security agenda. Justice and Home Affairs Ministers, 2004, 'Action against organised crime . . .'.
60 European Commission (2004) 'Green Paper . . .' 9–10.
61 Hague Programme: section II (3.2).
62 Council of the European Union (2002), 'Council Framework Decision 2002/584/JHA . . .'.
63 European Council (2004) 'Declaration on combating terrorism': section 8. The Declaration also reaffirmed the ESS emphasis on strategically deploying the civilian and military instruments available to the Union in order to eradicate the sources of terrorism as well as specific terrorist groups.
64 European Council (2004) 'Declaration on combating terrorism': Annex I, objectives 1 and 7; and European Commission (2004) 'Conceptual Framework . . .': paras 10 and 11.
65 Hague programme: section II (2.3) and (2.4). In June 2005, the European Council enumerated nine priority objectives in the area of freedom, justice and security. Of those nine, seven dealt with various aspects of terrorism. See also Council of the European Union (2005) 'Brussels European Council': para. 19. Council of the European Union (2001) 'Council Common Position of 27 December 2001 . . .'; European Council (2004) 'Declaration on combating terrorism'. The external strategy of multilateral cooperation complemented the policies of prevention along Europe's periphery (see Chapter 2 for a full discussion).
66 European Commission (2004) 'The fight against terrorism: Note . . .': point 4.
67 Vienna Action Plan; Council of the European Union (1999) 'Progress report . . .'. See also, European Commission (2002), 'Proposal for a comprehensive plan . . .': para. 13; and European Commission (2004), 'Proposal . . .

establishing a European neighbourhood and partnership instrument': article 2 (2a–y); Tampere Programme.
68 European Commission (2002), 'Proposal for a comprehensive plan . . .': paras 53 and 54; and Council of the European Union (2003) 'Programme . . . maritime borders of the member states of the European Union': para. 23.
69 It also recommended the harmonisation of penalties for several categories of crime associated with the trafficking of human beings and the employment of illegal migrants. European Commission (2002) 'Proposal for a comprehensive plan . . .': annex.
70 Hague programme: section II (1.6.3). This external dimension is treated fully in Chapter 3.
71 Council of the European Union (2004) 'Brussels European Council: paras 14 and 16; European Commission (2004) 'Reference document . . . AENEAS Programme, 2004–2006': section 7.3.1.
72 Millennium Strategy: 124/20.
73 Council of the European Union (1999) 'Joint action of 3 December 1998 . . .'; and Council of the European Union (2001) 'Council Framework Decision of 26 June 2001 . . .'. The UN International Convention for the Suppression of the Financing of Terrorism (1999) served to provide many of the procedural goals of the EU in this issue area, particularly Articles 2, 3 and 18. Yet, the member states underscored that 'the standardisation of all criminal penalties in the European Union . . . would be neither desirable nor legally feasible'. See European Commission (2004) 'Green Paper . . .': 8.
74 The FATF, for example, declared that 'combating money laundering and terrorist financing . . . is the *raison d'etre* and the core of the FATF's long term mission'. Financial Action Task Force on Money Laundering 2004: 4.
75 Council of the European Union (2003), 'Council common position 2003/805/CFSP'.
76 Council of the European Union (2005) 'Draft Directive . . .': article 4. See also, European Council (2004) 'Declaration on Combating Terrorism': 4, 10–11; and Annex I, Objective 2: 'To reduce the access of terrorists to financial and other economic resources'.
77 Council of the European Union (2005) 'Council Framework Decision 2005/222/JHA . . .'.
78 The Commission was delegated responsibility for coordinating member state public health policies when the public health challenge reached the 'activation level 3'; viz., the stage where a member state had a positive obligation to inform the others of the infectious disease and measures taken to address it. See European Commission (2001) 'Programme of Cooperation . . .': x.
79 'Council of the European Union (2003) 'Council common position 2003/805/CFSP': Articles 1–8.

80   Council of the European Union (2003) 'Action Plan . . .': 110–17. There
     was also a provision for strengthening national legislation towards
     improving the oversight of pathogenic micro-organisms and toxins in both
     EU member and accession states.

81   The member states also agreed that this threat required common policies
     that would reduce the vulnerability of the European economy, population,
     food-chain, and the environment. Council of the European Union (2002)
     'Adoption of the programme . . .': Annex 1, 7–15. These strategic objectives
     were affirmed in Council of the European Union (2004) 'EU Solidarity
     Programme . . .': section 14.

82   External policy measures focused on strengthening the Nuclear Suppliers
     Group, creating effective international interdiction polices, and supporting
     cooperative threat reduction programmes to afford better protection for
     nuclear materials and facilities. Council of the European Union (2004) 'EU
     strategy against . . .': 313–14 and 319–20.

83   Tampere Programme: para. 56.

84   The Europol department for serious crime (SC) is divided into seven
     directorates: organised crime groups (SC 1), drugs (SC 2), crimes against
     persons (SC 3), financial and property crime (SC 4), terrorism (SC 5),
     forgery of money (SC6), and analysis (SC 7). The extension of Europol's
     mandate to include most categories of serious crime began in June 2001
     and then terrorist offenses after 11 September. See Europol 2005: 23.

85   See European Council (1999), 'Counter-terrorism: Report from Europol':
     2–3; Council of the European Union (2002), 'Europol Annual Report 2001':
     7–16; Council of the European Union (2003), 'Europol Work Programme
     2004'.

86   Council of the European Union, 'Council Decision 2003/48/JHA . . .': article
     2.; European Commission (2005), 'Proposal . . . on the transmission of
     information . . .': article 3.

87   European Commission (2006), 'Communication . . . implementing the
     Hague Programme: The way forward': 6.

88   Council of the European Union (2005), 'Implementation of the Action Plan
     to combat terrorism': 8.

89   Council of the European Union (2004), 'CEPOL . . .': 5; Council of the
     European Union (2005), 'Council Decision 2005/681/JHA . . .': article 1(2).

90   *Ibid.*, article 6(2a, b).

91   European Commission (2006), 'Communication . . . evaluation of EU
     policies on freedom, security and justice': 84.

92   Council of the European Union (2000), 'Explanatory report . . .': article 13;
     and *idem.* (2002), 'Council Framework Decision of 13 June 2002 . . .':
     article 1.

93   Britain, Germany, Malta, Lithuania and the Netherlands have made such
     arguments, although those arguments have been rejected by the Commis-
     sion. European Commission (2005), 'Commission Staff Working Paper.

Annex . . . on Joint Investigation Teams': 28; Justice and Home Affairs Council (2006), 'First Report on the Hague Programme'.

94 Jimeno-Bulnes 2003: 620–1; Council of the European Union (2005), 'Revised Action Plan on terrorism . . .': 17; and European Commission (2004), 'Communication . . . area of freedom, security and justice . . .': 12.

95 Pro-Eurojust 2002: 5.

96 *Ibid.*: 10–14. This list of obstacles shrunk to eight general categories in the 2002 report, but the new list underscored the divergence in judicial and prosecutorial cultures within the EU. See Eurojust 2003: 16.

97 Eurojust 2004: annex.

98 Council of the European Union (1998), 'Joint Action of 29 June 1998 . . .': articles 2 and 4.

99 European Commission (2006), 'Communication . . . on judicial training in the European Union': 4–5.

100 European Judicial Training Network 2002: article 4(2).

101 *Ibid.*, article 5 and annex.

102 Council of the European Union (2004), 'Brussels European Council': 29. In late 2005, a cooperation agreement between Europol and the General Secretariat of the Council provided for the exchange of information between SitCen and Europol.

103 European Commission (2005), 'Communication . . . Commission provisions on "ARGUS" general rapid alert system': 2.

104 European Council (2004), 'Council Regulation (EC) no. 2007/2004 . . .'.

105 *Ibid.*, Chapter II, article 2.

106 'EU–US declaration on combating terrorism' (2004); G8 (2002).

107 FATF 2004: 3–7; Europol 2005: 15.

108 Council of the European Union (2000), 'Council Decision of 17 October 2000'. Council of the European Union (2005), 'Fight against terrorism: six monthly report': annex 5.

109 Eurojust 2006: 46–7; Europol is considering the establishment of a Money Laundering Financial Investigation Unit Network in support of the AWF.

110 The budget for 2005 was €4.25 million, of which €1.098 million was unspent. At the end of 2005, the ENISA employed 52 individuals. As is clear from the General Report, the agency's primary functions are the dissemination of information and the creation of an EU-wide network information security system that coordinates and eventually harmonises national efforts; and serves as a contact point for national security information officers of other countries and international institutions. See ENISA, 2005.

111 Council of the European Union (2004) 'Regulation (EC) no. 460/2004 . . .': 2.

112 *Ibid.*: article 3(3).

113 European Commission (2005), 'Green Paper on a European . . .': 14.

114 Council of the European Union (2004), 'Press release . . .': 22–3.

115 Council of the European Union (2004), 'Regulation (EC) no. 851/2004 . . .': article 3.

116 *Ibid.*, articles 8–11; and European centre for Disease Prevention and Control (2005): 7–11. One of the first decisions undertaken by the Centre was the publication of an annual epidemiological report, beginning in 2006, and measures to ensure the integration of the new member states into the various public health networks coordinated by the centre. The resistance to the ceding of public health sovereignty is not restricted to EU member states. Interpol, for example, only established a dedicated unit for bio-terrorism at the Paris headquarters *after* receiving a grant from the Alfred P. Sloan Foundation.

117 Council of the European Union (2002), 'Council Framework Decision (2002/584/JHA) . . .'.

118 Council of the European Union (2003)'Council Framework Decision (2003/577/JHA) . . .'.

119 Council of the European Union (2005) 'Council Framework Decision (2005/214/JHA) . . .'.

120 European Commission (2005), 'Communication on the mutual recognition of judicial decisions . . .'.

121 European Commission (2004), 'Green Paper on the approximation . . .'; and *idem.* (2005), 'Green Paper on conflicts of jurisdiction'. For an assessment of progress towards these goals, see European Commission (2004), 'Commission Staff Working Paper: The area of freedom, security and justice . . .': 20–3; and Justice and Home Affairs Council (2006), 'First Report on the Hague Programme'.

122 European Commission (2005), 'Communication . . . on the mutual recognition of judicial decisions . . .': 5. A 1998 joint decision defined and criminalised membership in a criminal organisation, which was made a binding requirement for the accession countries. See Council of the European Union (1999) 'Joint Position of 29 March 1999 . . .'

123 European Commission (2004), 'Green Paper on . . . criminal sanctions in the European Union': 8.

124 *Ibid.*: 22.

125 European Commission (2004), 'Proposal . . . on certain procedural rights in criminal proceedings . . .': 12–16.

126 European Commission (2005), 'Green Paper on conflicts of jurisdiction'.

127 European Commission (2005), 'Report from the Commission . . .': 4. Eurojust reported that in 2005 there were over 50 breaches of the time limit set for states to comply with a warrant. Britian accounted for approximately three-fifths of the delinquencies. See Eurojust 2006: 33.

128 European Commission (2004), 'Proposal . . . on the exchange of information extracted from the criminal record': article 5 and form B.

129 European Commission (2005), 'Proposal . . . on the exchange of information under the principle of availability'.

130 Council of the European Union (2001), 'Council Decision of 28 June 2001 . . .'; *idem* (2002), 'Council Decision of 22 July 2002 . . .'. Forty per cent

of total expenditures were devoted to enhancing judicial cooperation in criminal matters. The cumulative expenditure on Grotius programmes is found in European Commission, 'Commission Staff Working Paper. Fifth report . . .': 6. The initial budget for AGIS was €65 million, which was raised to €77 million to in May 2004 in order to accommodate enlargement. See European Commission (2005), 'Commission Staff Working Document. Second annual report . . .': 3.

131 European Community (2006), 'Communication . . . on judicial training in the European Union': 5.

132 European Commission (2004), 'Communication . . . area of freedom, security and justice . . .': 4.

133 *Ibid.*: 5.

134 Council of the European Union (2001), 'Annex. Protocol established by the Council . . .'

135 European Commission (2005), 'Proposal . . . on the exchange of information under the principle of availability'.

136 *Ibid.*: 3. The legal authority for the Framework Decision is Article 29 TEU and the political rationale was the inability of any national authority to police effectively either terrorism or organised crime.

137 *Ibid.*: Annex II.

138 Council of the European Union (2004), 'Draft Framework Decision on simplifying the exchange of information and intelligence . . .': article 2(d).

139 Commission of the European Communities (2005), 'Communication . . . on improved effectiveness, enhanced interoperability and synergies among European databases . . .'.

140 *Ibid.*, 5.3.1 and European Data Protection Supervisor (2005), 'Comments on the Communication . . .': 4–5. The Prüm Convention, which was signed between seven member states (Austria, Belgium, France, Germany, Luxembourg, the Netherlands and Spain), commits each signatory to keep DNA, fingerprint, and automobile registration databases and to permit access to those data bases *automatically* in the course of a criminal investigation. Council of the European Union (2005), 'Prüm Convention': articles 2–4 and 8–9

141 Europol now publishes an annual *Organised Crime Threat Assessment* that identifies the major organised crime groups operating within the EU and the categories of crime that those groups are most likely to be involved in. This publication replaces the annual *European Union Organised Crime Report*, which was first published in 1994. The public versions of those reports, like the annual Europol reports, do not provide comparable crime statistics or make any assessment of the precise value added by Europol in investigating serious crime.

142 Two other programmes, STOP II and Hippocrates, were crime prevention programmes. STOP II financed programmes targeting the trafficking of human beings and the exploitation of children, while Hippocrates encouraged greater cooperation between law enforcement and the private

sector. The budgetary cost of these two programmes was €4.95 and €3.92 million, respectively.

143 European Commission (2005), 'Commission Staff Working Document: Second annual report . . .': 7.

144 The same countries were similarly over represented in the former Title VI programmes (number of projects in closed parentheses): UK (130), Italy (116), Germany (96), France (86), the Netherlands (68) and Spain (63). Data drawn from Ramboll Management (2005), annex, table 0–4. Authors' own calculations.

145 'Council Common Position 2001/931/CFSP' See also 'Council Framework Decision of 13 June 2002 on combating terrorism', article 1.

146 Council of the European Union (2002) 'Council Framework decision of 13 June 2002 . . .': para. 9 and articles 1 and 2–4 (definition of terrorist acts), 2 (definition of a terrorist group), 5–6 (penalties) and 9 (jurisidiction).

147 European Council (2002), 'Presidency Conlusions. Annex . . .': para. 6. This development also carried the secondary intent of leveraging European military capabilities towards influencing American policy in those unstable areas of the world most critical to Europe. Also see, European Commission (2004) 'Interim Report . . .': para. 3.2.1.

148 *Ibid.*: para.7.

149 *Ibid.*: para. 18 (e and f). The Commission presented an inventory of critical infrastructure sectors in late 2005. See European Commission (2005), 'Green Paper on a European programme . . .': annex 2.

150 Council of the European Union (2005), 'Commission Staff Working Document. Revised Action Plan . . .'. Other goals connected with terrorism include policies to address those factors accounting for terrorism outside Europe (see Chapter 2), the consequences of terrorism (emergency management), and external cooperation (which consisted primarily of ensuring that the EU members were signatories to the various UN conventions on terrorism and ratified those conventions once signed.

151 Council of the European Community (2005), 'Directive 2005/60/EC . . .'

152 European Commission (2004), 'Commission Communication on . . . terrorist financing'; see also, European Commission (2004), 'Joint strategy paper . . .'.

153 In a final report issued by the EU Counter-Terrorism Coordinator in cooperation with the Presidency, 16 recommendations were issued to aid in the investigation and detection of terrorist threats to the member states. The recommendations focused primarily on improving within state coordination and cooperation between various law enforcement and intelligence agencies, creating national legal frameworks facilitating the collection and secure sharing of information and intelligence, and enhanced civil protection measures in the event of a terrorist attack. The EU role was limited to the coordination of the member state efforts via existing institutions, particularly Europol, Eurojust, and SitCen; it also recommended that CEPOL develop anti-terrorism training courses and the Police Chiefs'

Task Force initiate exchanges between anti-terrorism personnel. See Council of the European Union (2005)'Final report on the evaluation . . .'.

154 While the action plans for Iraq, Somalia and Afghanistan were directed towards preventing the illegal migration from those countries to the EU, the concern with Moroccan and Sri Lankan immigrants was tied to drug trafficking and immigration racketeering, respectively. Of some significance, however, is the decision to negotiate a transit agreement with Turkey (the conduit for Iraqi migrants to the EU) allowing the forcible repatriation of Kurds to north-eastern Iraq. Chapter 2 provides a full accounting of these action plans between 2000 and 2006. See also, Council of the European Union (2000), 'Adoption of Action Plan for Albania . . .': 5–31; and Council of the European Union (2000), 'High-level working group on asylum and migration . . .': 5 and 16. The action plans targeting these five countries were endorsed at Nice. See Chapter 2 for a full accounting of these action plans between 2000 and 2006.

155 Council of the European Union (2002), 'Council Decision of 13 June 2002 . . .': particularly article 4. European Commission (2004), 'Commission Staff Working Paper. First annual Report . . .': 4. Even though the ARGO budget doubled that for Odysseus, it was dwarfed by the €250 million budgeted for the AENEAS Programme, 2004–2008. The distribution of resources reflects the double calculation that it would be better to stop migration at its source ('preventive engagement') and many of those countries supplying migrants and asylum seekers either lack the incentive or capabilities to aid the EU alone. See European Commission (2004), 'Reference document . . .'.

156 European Commission (2005), 'Proposal . . . second generation Schengen information system (SIS II)': 1.

157 *Ibid.*, articles 3, 4 7, 17–18, 23 and 35.

158 *Ibid.*, article 45.

159 *Ibid.*, articles 57 and 58 (1, 6 and 8). In the case of Eurojust, the data accessed from the SIS II network cannot be shared with Eurojust staff, transferred to any other computer system within Eurojust, downloaded or copied.

160 Council of the European Union (2005), 'Proposal for a Council Decision on the improvement of police cooperation': articles 1, 3, 4 and 5.

161 Council of the European Union (2001) 'Council Framework Decision 2001/500/JHA': 1. The UN *International Convention for the Suppression of the Financing of Terrorism* (1999) served to provide many of the procedural goals of the EU in this issue area, particularly Articles 2, 3 and 18, at www.un.org/law/cod/finterr.htm.

162 While the implementation of the framework decision was largely successful, the member states did not meet the December 2002 implementation deadline. European Commission (2006), 'Report from the Commission'.

163 Eurojust (various years), *Annual Report*; and Europol (2004), *Annual Report 2003*.

164 Council of the European Union (2005), 'Directive 2005/60/EC . . .': articles
     1–3, 6–10 and 20–4. The member states are required to transpose the
     directive into national law by December 2007; it is consequently very
     difficult to assess its ultimate impact on retarding either money laundering
     or terrorist financing.
165 Council of the European Union (2003), ' Report on . . . European Union
     strategy for the beginning of the new millennium on prevention and control
     of organised crime'; and *idem.* (2005), 'Council Framework Decision
     2005/222/JHA . . .'.
166 *Ibid.:* articles 2–4, 7 and 10. For a detailed discussion of the EU legal
     framework in this policy area, see Mitrakas (2006): 33–53.
167 European Commission (2003), 'Commission Decision of 17 July 2003
     amending Decision no. 2119/98/EC . . .': annexes 1, 2 and 3.
168 Some progress was also made in the area of increasing international
     cooperation. See European Commission (2003), 'Communication . . .
     (Health Security)': 10.
169 *Ibid.*, p. 12.
170 Council of the European Union (1999) 'Council Joint Action of 17
     December 1999 . . .'.
171 Council of the European Union (2001) 'Council Decision 2001/493/CFSP
     . . .': articles 1 and 2; annexes I–V. The United States, however, had already
     committed $229 million to the Shchuch'ye site.
172 Council of the European Union (2003), 'Council Decision 2003/874/CFSP
     . . .': articles 1 and 2, annexes I and II. An additional €60 million was made
     available for projects managing spent nuclear fuel, radioactive waste
     management, and the decommissioning of naval nuclear reactors in
     connection with the Northern Dimension Environmental Partnership.
     European Commission (2003), 'Signature of the MNEPR . . .'.
173 'Joint Statement on the fight against terrorism', EU–Russia Summit, 11
     November 2002, in Haine (2003): 278–80.
174 Wyn Rees and Richard J. Aldrich (2005: 918) identified a number of
     specific, culturally derived divergences in the European and American
     approaches to counterterrorism. While the divergence between Europe and
     America has become more pronounced with a Bush administration seeking
     to rewrite unilaterally the rules of war, there also exist deep divergences
     within Europe that explain the *necessity* of accepting intergovernmentalism
     in JHA.

Policies of compellence: projecting force into an uncertain world

In the immediate post-war period, Western European security was contingent upon the successful recovery of the European economy and institutionalised political cooperation to meet the common Soviet threat. In response to American prodding and national calculations of self-interest, the continental Western Europeans undertook the first step toward guaranteeing economic prosperity – and the requisite political stability – with the creation of the European Coal and Steel Community (ECSC). The successful pooling of sovereignty attending the ECSC led the Europeans to consider a similar institutional solution to the problem of territorial defence and security as a complement to NATO and in accordance with the American desire for an able European partner that could share the costs of deterring a Soviet invasion of Western Europe. France proposed, and then rejected, the proposed European Defence Community (EDC) that would have provided the foundation for the parallel integration of Western Europe's national economies and polities. The failure of the EDC occasioned a political trauma that put any serious discussion of defence integration out of bounds in the negotiations leading to the European Economic Community (EEC). Defence integration remained out of bounds until the 1992 Maastricht Treaty when the immediacy of the Soviet threat had passed into history and defence cooperation was largely symbolic rather than substantive. Comprehensive defence integration was moot in the immediate aftermath of the dissolution of the Soviet Union and the absence of a credible threat to territorial integrity. Moreover, defence integration was pushed off the policy agenda by the electorates' expectation of a 'peace dividend', the more pressing task of complementing the single market with a single currency, and the difficult task of fostering competitive multi-party democracies and market economies in central and eastern Europe.

Despite the broadening of the security agenda in combination with the absence of a military opponent capable of threatening the security or territorial integrity of any EU member, the EU has retained the aspiration of creating an EU defence identity. The gradual emergence of a European Security and Defence Policy (ESDP) reflected two sets of concerns, one internal and the other external. The external concerns pushing the EU towards greater defence and security cooperation, conventionally understood, stemmed primarily from the American pressure on the Europeans to shoulder a greater responsibility for systemic stability, to achieve economies of scale allowing the European militaries to reconfigure their force structure, and to achieve greater interoperability with US forces but also to undertake missions 'out of area' that required the projection of force. The inability to act militarily during the serial civil conflicts in the Balkans, despite the human suffering and genocide they occasioned, and the necessity of American military leadership also acted as a spur to substantive defence integration. The British and French were able to agree in the late 1990s that Europe required a defence capability endowing the EU with an ability to act independently of the United States when Europe's interests were at stake. The internal pressures for deepening defence and security integration grew from the very success of European monetary union and the successive EU treaties ratified after 1989 – Maastricht (1992), Amsterdam (1997) and Nice (2001) – that strengthened the EU's prerogatives in defence and foreign policy, provided the legal basis for integration across the entire range of sovereign responsibilities, and evinced an optimism that security and defence policy integration was the last meaningful barrier to political union. Europe's self-definition as an entity with an autonomous identity, global interests and global responsibilities reinforced the underlying post-war logic of European integration. Moreover, the European states did have an interest in acquiring a military capability that would enable Europe to engage in peace-making operations along its historic perimeter and even further afield. That interest required the Europeans to reconsider the taboo on defence integration and to redress the deficiencies in their capabilities which posed a significant barrier to joint military operations.

The change in the security agenda and the change in the European state have altered the security challenges facing the EU and its member states. Of equal importance, these two changes have diminished the relative importance of the military instrument as the best means for forestalling the likely threats to Europe's stability and security. Correspondingly, the policy instruments associated with the policies of assurance, prevention and protection not only address the underlying causes of the threats to Europe's security, but their manifestations as well. Yet, any accounting of the EU as a security actor, present and future, must fully consider the policies of compellence, despite its sparing exercise of military power since 1989.

Rationale, goals and principles governing the policies of compellence

Creating an EU that can function as an autonomous actor with a global military presence remains the most vexing security policy challenge facing its member states. The EU is caught between the member states' unwillingness to sacrifice significant sovereign prerogatives necessary to create a single defence policy akin to monetary union; to reconcile the different preferences of the member states with respect to the appropriate instruments of statecraft as well as a normative barrier to relying upon military force in almost any circumstance other than territorial defence; and to mitigate the unresolved tension between the construction of an EU military capability and the preservation of the NATO alliance given American suspicions surrounding the underlying purpose of greater European autonomy in defence matters.[1] The continuing failure of the United States to achieve its post-war goals in Iraq underscores the limitations of a militarised foreign policy and the importance of the civilian instruments of statecraft to achieve the strategic goals of internal and regional stability. Unlike the United States, the EU and the majority of its member states fully accept that effective crisis management requires a broad range of civilian instruments for post-conflict reconstruction and relies upon preventive engagement as the guiding security policy principle. Yet there is also a recognition that the EU and its member states do require a military capability in certain circumstances: viz., when pre-emptive engagement fails and regional instability threatens Europe's direct or indirect interest in maintaining order along its perimeter. One question that arises, however, is whether the EU should seek a capability allowing it to engage in high intensity warfare or be merely satisfied with possessing the capability to execute the less demanding Petersberg Tasks.

Defence policy differs from conflict prevention measures in one fundamental respect: whereas conflict prevention requires the 'hidden' expenditure of material resources, policies of compellence – peace-enforcement, peace-keeping and peace-making – carry a high political cost owing to the potential loss of life. For this reason alone, the EU has engaged in policies of compellence sparingly, limited to a relatively small number of peace-enforcement and peace-keeping missions. In addition to the transparent costs of these policies and the attending domestic political costs of failure, two historical circumstances condition the EU's inability to move towards greater defence integration. The first is embedded in the early post-war experience when the desire for internal security and regional amity motivated the original six member states to join territorial security within NATO and economic security within the confines of the Treaties of Paris and Rome (see Hanrieder, 1989; Eilstrup-Sangiovanni *et al.* 2005; and Laffan *et al.* 2000: 38–9). This broad approach to security animated the successive EU enlargements, particularly the central and eastern European accessions after 1989. The historical burden and legal restraints on the exercise of German power in the post-war period in conjunction with a diffuse northern European predisposition towards addressing the sources rather than symptoms of conflict created a 'civilian security culture'. This 'civilian security culture' had two effects: it minimised the pressure for greater defence cooperation since it was not seen as particularly relevant to the security tasks facing the EU; and it reinforced the European willingness to rely on NATO (and the United States) to supply the military requirements of security.

Nonetheless, the EU has made progress since the 1990s towards creating effective formal and informal authority structures facilitating security cooperation and has championed the idea of a European defence policy while tolerating bilateral and multilateral arrangements between overlapping sets of member states (Rosenau, 2000; Smith, 2003). The progress towards greater defence cooperation and its institutionalisation can be attributed to the emergence of a common European interest that itself is abetted by the development of a common identity, perhaps in opposition to the United States (Wendt, 1994; Nuttal, 1992; Jepperson *et al.* 1996).[2] The fall-out from 11 September, the Madrid and London terrorist bombings, and the invasion and botched occupation of Iraq have together eroded the emerging consensus on military cooperation and integration. The EU member states have made different assessments with respect to the relative utility of the military and civilian instruments of statecraft, the necessity of closer cooperation with or greater autonomy from the United States, and alternative assessments of where the threats to European security originate. The 2003 ESS presented a consensus view on the need for the EU to take greater responsibility for regional and global security, but the military component did not play a particularly prominent role. The strategy, which reaffirmed the importance of the Petersberg Tasks, did not commit the member states to redress the broad spectrum of capabilities shortfalls that hindered joint peace-enforcement or peace-keeping operations in regions acknowledged as critical to European stability and security (the Balkans, the Caucasus, and Mediterranean Basin).

A gap exists between the EU ambition to deepen integration in defence policy and the efforts of the member states to acquiesce to the necessary abnegation of sovereign prerogatives. At the same time, the member states have gone beyond the simple defence cooperation or coordination found in NATO, particularly the European efforts to create a multinational force under a European command and to rationalise the European defence industrial base. The gap between EU rhetoric and member state policies, in conjunction with the manifest need for greater defence cooperation if the EU is to wield global influence commensurate with its resources, begs the following questions: is the resistance to a single or common defence policy rooted in the unwillingness of national political elites to sacrifice sovereign prerogatives in the area of defence prior to some form of political union, the absence of a compelling strategic rationale for defence integration, or the strongly held expectation of domestic electorates that defence policy will remain national? Is defence integration necessary to meet the Petersberg Tasks? Would a fatal weakening of NATO attend EU defence integration and autonomy?

Rationale

The threats posed to the contemporary European state system cannot be reduced to a state-centric security calculus where the application of military force is at issue. This changed security environment raises questions about *how* states should meet these new kinds of threats. One question naturally arising is whether states can seek security unilaterally or whether security must be sought multilaterally. Europeans recognise the optimality of multilateral as opposed to unilateral security strategies, but have at the same time been caught between NATO and the EU. Five separate rationales exist for greater military integration within the EU: it would optimise resources dedicated to defence; it would match the EU's military capabilities with its global responsibilities and aspirations; it would resolve the leadership problem within Europe on security and defence issues; it would create the military capability to act independently of the United States when Europe's interests are at stake and America's are not; it would enable the EU to act as an equal partner with the United States thereby lending it leverage over American diplomacy that Europe presently lacks.

Javier Solana's comment about Europe's role and responsibility for global security captures the essential rationale for enhancing European defence cooperation and the eventual development of a European military capability:

> As the EU grows to encompass 25 countries with some 450 million inhabitants producing one-quarter of the world's GDP, we have a duty to assume our responsibilities on the world stage. As a global actor the Union must now face up to its responsibility for global security. (Solana, 2003b)

But Solana's treatment of the EU as a unitary actor in international politics is belied by national defence statements and the persistence of intergovernmentalism. Such a treatment creates the false expectation that Europe can and ought to act globally, owing to an aggregation of resources that remain intractably disaggregated.[3] Thus treating the EU or Europe *as if* it were a unitary actor of a size not dissimilar to that of the United States places an unrealistic burden on the Europeans and creates unrealistic expectations about the potential EU role in defence. The EU debate on defence cooperation was not fully and systematically engaged until the Anglo-French Saint Malo Declaration in December 1998. At St Malo, the British accepted that the EU 'must have the capacity for autonomous action, backed up by credible military forces, the means to decide to use them, and a readiness to do so in order to respond to international crises'. In what proved to be an important policy departure, France and the UK agreed that Europe required guaranteed access to the appropriate military capabilities 'pre-designated within NATO's European pillar or national or multinational European means outside the NATO framework' (St Malo Declaration, paras 2 and 3).

The Cologne European Council Declaration (June 1999) lent its imprimatur to the St Malo Declaration. The Council also agreed that once the EU absorbed the Western European Union (WEU) functions necessary to 'fulfil its new responsibilities in the area of the Petersberg Tasks . . . the WEU as an organisation would have completed its purpose'. Notably, the Council restricted the defence ambitions of the EU to the Petersberg Tasks and also added the caveat that any EU decision would be taken 'without prejudice to actions by NATO'. The Declaration stated that the ability of the EU to play 'its full role on the international stage' required a CFSP 'backed up by credible operational capabilities'. Those operational capabilities, in turn, took the form of either EU-led operations using NATO assets and capabilities or to EU-led operations without recourse to NATO assets or capabilities.[4] A second Anglo-French declaration in November 1999 elaborated upon the St Malo and Cologne declarations. The British and French governments agreed that the EU required an 'autonomous capacity to take decisions and, where NATO as a whole is not engaged, to launch and then to conduct EU-led military operations'. Moreover, both agreed that the EU should be able to deploy between 50,000 and 60,000 personnel for crisis management tasks. Both Anglo-French recommendations were accepted verbatim by the Helsinki European Council in December 1999.[5]

While Europe needs to develop a 'véritable culture européenne de sécurité et de défense' (Rutten, 2002: 20, s. 2; 16) (the need for which acknowledged its absence), no major member state is yet willing to forgo the responsibility and right to determine what is and is not in its national security interest. Security cultures not only generate a set of norms about how a state should go about achieving its goals, but generate a set of budgetary priorities consistent with those norms. National security cultures within Europe are sufficiently divergent to create tensions over not only what ought to be done militarily, but how states should go about doing it.[6]

No single state can reasonably be expected to exercise a leadership role on security affairs within Europe.[7] Of the European powers, only France and the UK have retained a 'global' perspective with respect to military tasks and responsibilities, while the other European states, owing either to limited means or size or to historical legacy, have been content to adopt a regional definition of security within the boundaries of Europe marked by the littoral states of the Mediterranean to the south and perhaps the Ural mountains to the east. Only three countries – Britain, France and, possibly, Germany – could make a plausible claim to defence leadership; any such claim is still weak and contested. Germany is not yet interested in such a role and most Europeans are not psychologically prepared to accept it. Britain and France, by virtue of their power pro-jection capabilities, relative and absolute defence expenditures, defence industrial and technological base and outward-looking foreign policy orientation, would be best placed to assume a leadership role. But their respective leadership ambitions and not always congruent interests prohibit either or both from setting the defence and security agenda for the Union. While Britain and France have exercised a sporadic duopoly after the St Malo Declaration, it remains unstable owing to the different roles ascribed to the United States in European security governance, their mutual desire to retain national prerogatives in the area of defence, competing geopolitical loyalties, and competing world views, particularly with respect to the global military role to which Europe should aspire.

The greatest external stimulant to enhanced European security cooperation resulted from the fall-out from the intra-EU and transatlantic disagreements over Iraq in the spring of 2003 and the unwelcome direction of American foreign policy captured by the Bush doctrine of pre-emptive attack. The ESS identifies the external factors contributing to the evolution of a common security and defence policy: the end of the Cold War, the emergence of new security threats, such as ethnic conflicts and the disintegration of state authority, particularly in south-eastern Europe, and the EU's inability to act independently of the United States to ameliorate those security pathologies. The ESS presents a collective rather than national definition of interest that spans the European (or at least EU) political space. The strategy discounts the probability of 'large scale aggression' against EU member states, but identifies a specific range of threats that do not necessarily call for large-scale investments in power projection capabilities or the need to acquire them (ESS: 2–5). In fact, the Europeans expressed the belief that 'none of these new threats is purely military; nor can any be tackled by purely military means' and that these threats were best addressed with policies of assurance and prevention, both of which rely almost exclusively on the civilian instruments of statecraft (ESS: 6–7).

The ESS designated three strategic objectives for the EU: regional security in the European neighbourhood, conflict and threat prevention, and a rule-based international order based on multilateralism. While these three strategic objectives do not explicitly require a common defence policy, the ESS nonetheless accepted that the capability to project force requires the transformation of Europe's militaries as well as the sharing and pooling of assets. The acknowledged need for a European military capability should not overshadow, however, the subordinate role envisioned for military force in a broader capabilities package that includes the use of civilian resources for crisis and post-crisis interventions, a stronger diplomatic presence, and the reconciliation of national threat assessments.

Despite a growing awareness that the EU member states share similar security interests, there is still a lack of trust among the major EU states when it comes to security and defence or intelligence sharing. Indeed, the rival historical and political interests of European states prevent the very definition of a common European security identity, and induce European governments to regard the Union's security organisations as primarily instruments for achieving their own foreign policy goals (Hampton and Sperling, 2002). In other words, 'national' rather than 'collective' interests continue to dominate EU members' calculations in assessing the risks posed by, and the responses to, ostensibly common security threats (Kirchner and Sperling, 2002). Moreover, disagreements manifest themselves most starkly in the definition of the relationship between Europe and America. The response to the American demonisation of the 'axis of evil' and a diplomacy that excluded anything other than war in Iraq exposed the intra-European schism. Germany and France led a coalition within the EU that refused to sanction US policy towards Iraq while ten other countries signed the so-called Vilnius letter expressing support for the United States. This division within the EU was exacerbated by Secretary of Defense Donald Rumsfeld's characterisation of France and Germany as 'old' Europe, which implied that both were irrelevant to the American security calculus, and his position that the mission would determine the coalition, a formulation that clearly downgraded the importance of the NATO alliance.

The expanding security remit of the ESS in combination with American pressure to modernise European armed forces to guarantee alliance interoperability provided the rationale for creating a European defence equipment market that would not only create globally competitive defence firms, but ensure the existence of an autonomous defence industrial base enabling the EU to act independently of the United States if necessary.[8] There is a general consensus that European defence expenditure, which ranges between 50 and 60 per cent of American defence expenditure, only purchases somewhere between 10 and 20 per cent of the same capabilities. The expanding military role foreseen for the EU in combination with limited defence budgets spent inefficiently have provided another rationale for deeper defence cooperation, including joint decisions on research, development and procurement.

The need for consolidating the EU defence market also reflects a commercial and technological calculation: the creation of a single European defence equipment market would forestall the evolution of European firms from prime contractors to European national governments to sub-contractors for American firms.[9] The rationale for managing the rationalisation and consolidation of the European defence equipment market reflected any number of calculations: the uncoordinated defence procurement strategies of the individual EU member states duplicated research and development costs, produced a plethora of redundant weapons systems that multiplied the difficulty of achieving interoperability between the EU member state armed forces, and yielded small orders that prevent European defence contractors and national defence budgets from reaping the economies of scale enjoyed by the United States.[10]

Principles

The principles guiding joint action under CFSP and ESDP emanate from the Title V Provisions of the Treaty on European Union (TEU). Article 17(1) stipulates that the 'Common Foreign and Security Policy shall include all questions relating to the security of the Union, including the progressive framing of a common defence policy'. According to Article 23(1), the voting rules for any action undertaken are subject to the principle and voting rule of unanimity in the Council of Ministers. Therefore, the CSFP and ESDP and, for that matter, the ESS, remain intergovernmental and make internal conflict and disagreement within the Council more likely where national interests diverge. Moreover, the intergovernmental nature of Pillar II dictates that burden-sharing arrangements, particularly the arrangements for financing the peace-enforcement or peace-keeping operations, tend to lie where they fall. According to Articles 28 and 27(3) TEC, the Community budget finances the 'administrative expenditure' and certain 'operational expenditures' of Pillar II and its policies, but it is not charged for 'operations having military or defence implications'. Common costs were defined in a 2004 Council Decision that established the funding mechanism for meeting those costs – Athena. Common funding for the common costs of EU missions (e.g., operation headquarters) is shared between the participating states according to each state's gross national income (GNI) as a per centage of the contributing states' aggregate GNI.[11]

A third important principle governing EU policies in the area of defence and foreign policy is constructive abstention. This principle grew out of the notion of 'enhanced cooperation' and was given constitutional status with the 2001 Treaty of Nice; it allows states to opt out of individual decisions without inhibiting or blocking the desire of the other members to move forward. In other words, it pushes decision-making forward by providing a feasible alternative to the unit veto still available in Pillar II without institutionalising qualified majority voting in an area where every state wishes to retain the right of non-participation in military action. In matters relating to the CFSP, Article 23(1) of the TEU enables member states to 'opt out' of any decision and relieves any member state from an obligation to implement the policy, while accepting that the decision nonetheless commits the Union. Unsurprisingly, unanimity, qualified by constructive abstention, remains the predominant practice in the field of security and defence; there is a lack of continuity in EU decisions on security matters, and decisions are made on a case-by-case basis involving different constellations of member states.

The ESS put forward the fourth principle of 'preventive engagement' as the preferred means for achieving EU security goals – a principle developed in response to the Bush administration's doctrine of pre-emptive war. Preventive engagement targets the sources of instability in societies and the causes of failed or failing states; it calls for a 'civilian' rather than militarised response; it points to a demilitarised conception of security. This demilitarised security strategy also reflects the tenacity of the sovereignty principle in defence affairs; states remain unwilling to pool their resources or authority over the use of military force to achieve common foreign policy objectives. The principle of solidarity, developed largely in response to the Muslim terrorist threat that emerged after 11 September, should be transferable to the task of territorial defence, yet the EU has refrained from incorporating Article V of the WEU into the Community treaty system. The principle of solidarity exerts a relatively weak force on EU member state defence policies even though many member states are bound by the WEU and NATO to come to the other's defence in the event of aggression.

Defence procurement collaboration and the rationalisation of defence expenditures are limited by the principles of sovereignty and *juste retour*. A major barrier to defence collaboration, however, is the sovereignty principle animating Article 296 TEC: 'any member state may take such measures as it considers necessary for the protection of essential interests of its security which are connected with the production of or trade in arms, munitions and war material'.[12] The principle of *juste retour* has also hindered the development of joint arms projects within the EU; this principle requires participation in a collaborative weapons programme to yield industrial benefits commensurate with national investment and procurement. The principle of *juste retour* has been replaced, at least among the members of the Joint Organisation for Armaments Cooperation (OCCAR), with the principle of ensuring an 'overall' *juste retour*, which retains the notion that each state should receive benefits commensurate with national contributions to the collaborative projects, but that outcome would be diffused over a number of weapons systems over a period of years.[13]

Goals

Two policy goals define the military requirements of an autonomous EU capability: assuming global responsibility for stability and order consistent with the EU's material capabilities and interests; acquiring the necessary capabilities to discharge the Petersberg Tasks, which encompass 'humanitarian and rescue tasks, peacekeeping tasks; [and] tasks of combat forces in crisis management, including peacemaking'.[14] Both the EU's global aspiration and the functionally defined Petersberg Tasks are contingent upon the member states' ability to acquire the range and mix of necessary military capabilities to execute a broad range of military missions, and the implementation of a coordination mechanism endowing the EU with the political ability to plan and execute military missions outside Europe.

The focus on acquiring an EU capability was introduced with the British–Italian joint statement on defence capabilities in July 1999, largely in response to the European inability to respond to the Kosovo crisis without American leadership (UK Parliament Select Committee on Defence, 1999). Even though the British and Italians called on the EU states to enhance Europe's military capabilities, there was no suggestion that national requirements should be subordinated to or shaped by the EU. The 1999 WEU audit of European capabilities, which followed the 1998 St Malo Declaration, set the capabilities agenda at the December 1999 Helsinki Summit (WEU Council of Ministers, 1999). At that time, the EU declared that it would meet what became known as the Helsinki Headline Goal (HHG) – the fielding of an EU force of 50,000 to 60,000 soldiers by 2003 capable of executing the entire range of Petersberg Tasks. At the beginning of 2000, the EU member states of NATO were obliged to meet both the goals of the HHG and the NATO Defence Capabilities Initiative (DCI).[15] These dual obligations produced an imperfectly overlapping set of EU capabilities targets complicated by evolving national preferences and technological change.

The capabilities shortfalls plaguing the EU included the absence of deployable headquarters and communications, strategic immobility, inadequate search and rescue capabilities, underdeveloped C^3 capabilities, and an insufficient number of attack and support helicopters. The tension between the capability shortfalls within NATO and EU heightened the difficulty of reaching an intra-EU consensus on what types of capabilities were required and the purpose to which those capabilities would be put. The goal of defence autonomy, central to the development and rationale of the ESDP, requires the interoperability of EU forces, a task logically preceding interoperability within NATO (see Solana, 2004). Moreover, since NATO interoperability can only be understood as Europe adjusting to an American standard, placing NATO requirements before those of Europe would only deepen the asymmetry within Europe, hamstring progress towards an effective ESDP, and deny the non-NATO EU member states access to critical equipment and technology.

These military capabilities shortfalls reflect, in turn, the underlying political debate about the kind of military force the European states wish to acquire, the contingencies where they wield that instrument, and how they want to wield it. This political debate has two components: the degree of EU autonomy from the United States and NATO (NATO/US-led coalition, EU-led with NATO/US support, or an autonomous EU operation); and the kinds of conflicts for which the EU should prepare (low-intensity humanitarian intervention, medium-intensity peacekeeping or peace-making intervention, or high intensity warfare) (US–CREST, 2002). Despite a consensus within the EU that it should not seek a high-intensity warfighting capability, the major EU states remain far apart on what the EU *ought* to do militarily outside of Europe and its periphery and assign different probabilities to the likelihood that the EU will find itself acting alone outside of Europe in a major conflict. The precise assessment of the EU capabilities gap, therefore, is highly dependent upon a set of political and strategic assessments that reflect not only the concurrence of US and European interests outside Europe, but also the extent to which those interests diverge.

The weapons acquisition aspect of the capabilities gap posed a three-fold challenge to the EU: first, the member states required agreement on which categories of weapons systems were essential for acquiring the capability to execute the Petersberg tasks and to meet the requirements of the Battlegroup initiative; second, budgetary constraints limited weapons acquisitions to those capabilities shortfalls that provided the greatest barrier to an autonomous EU military capability; third, the EU would have to develop a defence industrial policy facilitating greater economies of scale, enhancing the interoperability of European armed forces, encouraging the consolidation of the fragmented European defence industrial sector, and creating a competitive environment for EU defence contractors enjoying equal access to national procurement processes. Since the 1999 Helsinki Summit, the Commission has identified a set of general principles framing the collective effort to meet the strategic goal of redressing the EU's military capabilities shortfalls: greater cooperation and government support in the area of research and development; R&D expenditures should rise as a share of defence budgets; a larger share of European R&D expenditures should be spent collaboratively to avoid duplication and encourage the joint development of weapons systems. Specific goals include: the harmonisation of the European approach to defence standardisation; the simplification of intra-EU licensing agreements; the limited application of Article 296 TEC in the defence sector; the progressive application of competition rules to the defence sector; and the harmonisation of national procurement legislation within the EU towards optimising defence acquisition at the national and EU level and removing administrative barriers to non-national procurement.[16]

The institutional evolution of the EU as a military actor

The EU's ability to act independently in defence and security policy was limited into the late 1990s. The EU not only lacked a military planning capability, but NATO membership and the American fear that an militarily autonomous EU would undermine the alliance created a significant barrier to developing an autonomous political and planning capability. In response to the flaring of civil conflicts along the European perimeter and the American insistence that Europe develop a military capability in line with its material resources and human capital, the EU constructed the necessary organisational framework for autonomous action. It established between 1999 and 2003 a number of committees and policy units that constituted the ESDP decision-making process, notably the High Representative for CFSP, the Policy Unit, the Joint Situation Centre, the Political and Security Committee (PSC), the European Union Military Committee (EUMC) and the European Union Military Staff (EUMS).

The creation of the EUMS is of particular importance since it represents an embryonic European general staff. The EUMS was assigned two categories of tasks: first, to engage in early warning, situation assessment and mission planning; second, to identify the European national and multinational forces prepared to carry out EU missions and to operationalise the policies and decisions mandated by the EUMC. The latter task was particularly important because it located in the EUMS responsibility for assessing and reviewing the EU's capabilities goals and programmes and to coordinate EU military planning with NATO. During the execution of EU military missions, the EUMS is also responsible for supporting or supplementing the national headquarters designated to manage an autonomous operation.[17]

New methods of decision-making, such as 'enhanced cooperation' or 'constructive abstention' have also been introduced to provide flexibility in decision-making and to remove unanimity – in practice – as a barrier to EU military action. The EU still lacks a Council of Defence Ministers and decision-making remains essentially intergovernmental. If unanimity persists as the principle governing decision-making in security and defence, intergovernmental negotiations leading to the exercise of the military option will become more protracted within the enlarged EU. Moreover, the Council of Ministers and the European Commission remain competitive rather than collaborative: each competes with the other in the issuing of mandates and the carving out of competencies (Rusi, 2001; and Youngs, 2004).

The EU must not only acquire the physical capabilities allowing it to project force, but the political will essential to the development of an autonomous planning capability.[18] Just as the middle ground provided by the Berlin-plus arrangements left the United States with a potential veto over the use of certain categories of NATO assets, the hostile American reaction to the 'Gang-of-Four' proposal to establish an independent EU planning cell and headquarters at Tervuren in 2004 suggests that the concern with duplication is as much about power as it is inefficiency.[19] As NATO member states, it is unnecessarily redundant and wasteful for the Europeans to seek an autonomous planning capability; as EU member states, the acquisition of an autonomous planning capability may be essential to undertake military missions independently of the United States and to satisfy the operational requirements attending the Petersberg Tasks.

The Berlin-plus agreements relaxed the tension between maintaining the integrity of NATO (from the American perspective) and enabling the EU to progress towards a common security and defence policy. The ESS noted that this agreement would enhance 'the operational capability of the EU and provide the framework of the strategic partnership between the two organisations in crisis management' (ESS: 12). The Berlin-plus arrangement has three key institutional components: it assured the EU access to NATO planning capabilities for preparing and executing EU-led crisis management operations; it made NATO assets and capabilities available to the EU; and it created EU–NATO consultation arrangements facilitating the use of NATO assets and capabilities. Berlin-plus fore-stalled the development of an autonomous EU military planning capability, but has enabled the EU to undertake autonomous missions with a ready-made operational infrastructure. The Berlin-plus arrange-ments, however, required modification after the experience of Operation Concordia, where the command structure was unclear and some EU member states criticised the Allied Forces Southern Europe (AFSOUTH) in Naples for assuming a key role proscribed under Berlin-plus (Monaco, 2004). This deficiency has been addressed and resolved in the case of EUFOR where the command structure is clear: the Supreme Headquarters Allied Powers in Europe (SHAPE) is formally at the top of the chain of command; the EU's PSC provides the political guidelines and the operational plan to EUFOR's commander (COMEUFOR), which are then copied and forwarded to SHAPE. This demarcation of respons-ibility and command reinforces the political capacity of the EU to act independently of NATO without running the risk of disengagement or disaffection.

The European Defence Agency (EDA) was created as the first step towards a common EU acquisitions policy. It largely replicated the objectives of pre-existing armaments cooperation organisations, notably the Western European Armaments Group (WEAG), the Western Euro-pean Armaments Organisation (WEAO) and OCCAR. While the EDA left OCCAR and the Letter of Intent (LOI) signed between the major producers of defence equipment untouched, by 2006 it assumed the responsibilities of both the WEAO and WEAG – an outcome consistent with the EU pronouncement that the WEU had outlived its usefulness in every respect save the Article V collective defence obligation.[20] The EDA was assigned a number of ambitious tasks which complemented the undertakings assigned the EUMS: to determine the military capabilities necessary to perform crisis management tasks; to implement the European Capabilities Action Plan (ECAP); to promote and coordinate the harmonisation of military requirements and procurement; to promote

European armaments cooperation; to manage weapons programmes at the behest of OCCAR member states; to consolidate and create an internationally competitive European Defence Equipment Market; and to enhance the effectiveness of European research and technology investments in the defence sector.

Despite the introduction of these innovative institutional mechanisms for coordinating defence expenditure, planning and purpose, they do not yet constitute a coherent or comprehensive security and defence planning system. These deficits will not be overcome despite the ECAP process owing to institutional and legal barriers to a consolidation of the European defence industry (particularly Article 296 TEC) (Hartley, 2006: 476) and the intergovernmentalism that will probably continue to demarcate the limits of defence integration.

The EU as a military actor: promise and performance

The relative successes and failures of the EU in creating the foundations for executing the policies of compellence can be divided into three categories of assessment: the progress towards meeting the capabilities shortfalls hindering effective joint action; the nature and purposes of EU-led missions; and the balance between maintaining member state self-sufficiency and accepting a division of labour that would diminish it.

Capabilities

The capabilities gap between the United States and its European allies has received wide attention, both within policy circles and the broader academic community. A considerable part of these deficiencies relates either to under-spending or uncoordinated military spending. While the persistence of national defence budgetary processes virtually guarantees uncoordinated spending, the under-spending of the EU reflects two conditions: first, the European electorates expected, and their governments delivered, the post-Cold War peace dividend; second, the initial euphoria of the immediate post-Cold War environment, the absence of an acute military threat to the European states, and the parochial foreign policies of the EU member states almost guaranteed declining defence budgets. The 25 EU member states spent around $186 billion on defence in 2004 as compared to the American expenditure of $460 billion. The absolute gap between EU and American defence expenditures has widened owing to the American 'war on terror' and the ongoing low-intensity warfare in Iraq and Afghanistan. What is of some interest, however, is that the American and aggregate EU defence expenditures have both increased by approximately 40 per cent between 2001 and 2004.[21]

While the gap in defence expenditures could foreshadow the end of NATO as an operational military alliance, there exists an important a gap within the EU which illustrates the limits of anything other than an intergovernmental approach in crafting policies of compellence. The three major military powers in Europe – Britain, France and Germany – face different capabilities challenges, which in turn reflect not only differences in threat perception, but different ambitions for the EU and attitudes towards NATO. For Britain, Kosovo starkly demonstrated Europe's inability to act militarily without the US – the same lesson drawn in the aftermath of the Suez Crisis some forty years earlier. Britain's Strategic Defence Review (1998) identified capability shortfalls needed to field joint rapid reaction forces allowing the UK to project power globally in partnership with the US. The follow-on New Chapter, written in the aftermath of 11 September, was both a response to the requirements of asymmetrical warfare against international terrorism and the British embrace of net centric warfare, both of which will align British capabilities more closely with those of the United States (see Ministry of Defence, 1998; 2002: 14–18; and 2003: 2).

Similarly, France drew the same lesson from Kosovo that it drew after Suez: Europe could not expect an equal military or political partnership with the US until Europe had an autonomous operational capability. France has not made the same level of effort to reconcile French and American force postures, but has placed emphasis on the acquisition of autonomous capabilities, including the effort to break the American global positioning system (GPS) monopoly and to develop an autonomous friend or foe identification (FFI) technology that could serve as the ESDP standard. Yet the self-identified French capabilities shortfalls are consistent with the task of force projection and the Petersberg Tasks. In many respects, the French and British concerns complement rather than compete with one another, despite their different levels of 'trust' and preference for autonomy vis-à-vis the United States.

German military planning is presently hostage to its structural budget deficit and the more pressing political concern with reducing unemployment and implementing economic reforms facilitating that goal. Unlike France and Britain, German armed forces face a double transformation: first, the transition from territorial defence against a known enemy to rapidly deployable expeditionary forces capable of operating in diverse geographical and geopolitical environments; second, the transition from a state with limited sovereignty comfortable with the exercise of civilian power to a fully sovereign state ready and able to deploy military forces with its allies. Unlike France or Britain, German defence planning guidelines have generally refrained from identifying discrete weapons systems shortfalls, an oversight no doubt explained by a procurement budget largely mortgaged to the purchase of Eurofighters and the A 400M transport aircraft.

The differences between Britain, France and Germany should not obscure the underlying common understanding that the Europeans do not need to acquire high-intensity warfare capabilities and that European armed forces do need to become more mobile and rapidly deployable. Even the British, while accepting the need for a broad range of capabilities, discount the need to plan for autonomous large-scale, high intensity operations (Ministry of Defence, 2003: 4–5, 8). These self-imposed limits on the exercise of British power are not as evident in French statements, but it is clear that French defence policy and strategic goals are conditioned by participation in the European rapid reaction force (ERRF) and interests in Africa, the 'priority for France's actions abroad' (Embassy of France in the United States, 2002; 2005).[22]

The capabilities shortfalls within Europe have many sources. The input–output gap has two dimensions: the absolute level of defence expenditures; and the defence capabilities purchased with those expenditures.[23] The estimates of what Europeans purchase with their defence euros fall within a fairly narrow range: Europeans have only been able to purchase between 10 and 20 per cent of American capabilities even though Europeans have consistently spent around 40 per cent as much on defence as the Americans since 2001 (Howorth, 2003: 231). This asymmetrical outcome is related to several factors. First, procurement decisions are made on a national basis. Second, European defence expenditures are overwhelmingly devoted to personnel costs. Third, the unit costs of major weapons systems are higher for Europeans owing to the relatively large number of small-scale defence firms, fragmented markets, and the continuing desire to protect the *national* rather than European defence industrial base (Heisbourg *et al.*, 2003: 15). And where cooperative European programmes are in place (e.g., *Meteor* air-to-air missile, Eurofighter, A 400M transport aircraft), the anticipated economies of scale have not materialised: common projects have faced reductions in the original number ordered (Germany reduced their order for A 400M aircraft from 73 to 60 and *Meteor*s from 1,480 to 600) and outright cancellations (Italy's withdrawal from the A 400M). These decisions, which largely reflect budgetary exigencies attending European monetary union, have increased the unit cost of each weapons system, further squeezing procurement budgets of the other participants at a time when defence budgets as a share of GDP have remained flat or increased marginally (Missiroli, 2003b: 7; and IISS, 2003: 243–4).

The input aspect of the input–output gap has received the most sustained attention over the course of the post-war period. In the 1950s and 1960s, the United States complained about European defence budgets.[24] In the 1990s, the 'peace dividend' reduced the defence budget as a share of GDP for the major EU states as well as the United States.[25] Between 2001 and 2004, however, the American defence budget as a share of GDP rose from 3 per cent to 3.7 per cent, while the European defence budget as a share of GDP rose marginally.[26] But the gap between US and European defence spending, however measured, is substantial and likely to grow owing to American military presence in Central Asia and the Persian Gulf region.

European R&D expenditures have declined significantly since the early 1960s, when British and French R&D expenditures (measured as a share of the defence budget) were on a par with those of the United States (van Ypersele de Strihou, 1967: 532, table 6). Today, American R&D expenditures dwarf those of Europe, although some Europeans outspent the United States by this measure: the UK and Sweden spent 39.6 and 52 per cent, respectively, on procurement and R&D in 1999, compared to 32.7 per cent for the United States.[27] The R&D gap will widen between 2002 and 2008. American expenditures will rise from $48.718 billion to $66.952 billion, yielding a cumulative expenditure of $430.366 billion. By comparison, the R&T expenditures of France, Germany, Italy, the Netherlands and the UK (comparable data for Spain unavailable) rose collectively from €2.064 billion in 2005 to €2.141 billion in 2006. The R&T expenditures of those five countries also account for approximately 86 per cent of total EU R&T expenditures.[28] The R&D budgets of the EU states have remained unchanged, with the notable exceptions of France and the UK (see Rohde and Frenzel, 2003: 64; for US figures, see IISS, 2003: 237, table 7). This transatlantic gap will remain unbridged and is probably unbridgeable. To reverse the decline in defence expenditures, increase R&D expenditures, and mitigate the uncoordinated procurement decisions of the major military powers within the EU, the Council established the EDA in July 2004. Some progress has been made in closing the gap: the Council established a new benchmark for R&D collaboration within the EU, raising the level of collaborative research from 5 to 20 per cent of total European R&D expenditures in the hope of encouraging the joint production and procurement of weapons systems as well as increasing the return on each R&D euro spent. Progress has been made towards that 20 per cent goal: in 2006 between 9 and 11 per cent of R&D expenditures were intra-EU collaborative.[29]

The procurement gap within the EU constitutes a significant barrier to joint military action. Between 1997 and 2005, the four major European states collectively spent $243.5 billion on procurement, although French and British procurement budgets amounted to $172.6 billion, or 71 per cent of total procurement outlays (Stålenheim, 2003: 360–2; SIPRI, 2006). Personnel expenditures partially explain the relatively small procurement budgets within the EU: personnel costs, which consume between 60 and 70 per cent of the average European defence budget, cap procurement budgets and limit the opportunities for rapid modernisation or progress towards greater interoperability.[30] Moreover, the procurement gap within Europe ranges from 41: 1 (procurement as a share of GDP) to 8.4: 1 (procurement as a share of defence spending). Clearly, those intra-European gaps place a significant barrier to moving beyond limited force integration as well as a meaningful ESDP or CSFP that requires a military component.[31]

Procurement is also suppressed owing to the high cost of developing and purchasing weapons systems designed and manufactured in Europe.[32] The European defence industrial base is too fragmented to achieve the economies of scale found in the US; the domestic political pressure on European governments to protect national defence contractors prevents the rationalisation of the European defence industry; the divergent military traditions, military requirements and geopolitical ambitions of the individual states make it strategically undesirable to consolidate the European defence industrial base. The EDA lacks the ability to enforce the rationalisation of the European defence industry or to choose the most efficient or technologically advanced weapons systems for common procurement.

Compared to the United States, the European defence sector remains highly fragmented despite the presence of three major transnational defence contractors, EADS, BAE and Thales. Just as security of supply concerns have kept the American defence market relatively closed to European defence contractors, European governments have been unwilling to allow an unfettered, apolitical rationalisation of their individual national defence industrial base. The option of niche specialisation within the EU runs up against the logic of sustaining national defence autonomy, particularly for the major states. As problematically, reliance upon intra-European specialisation would create multiple veto points and collide with the sovereignty principle that still governs the EU on defence. The EU's sovereignty gap severely delimits the boundaries of European defence cooperation and the prospects for overcoming the transatlantic capabilities shortfalls. Finally, the British strategic interest in leaving the American connection intact and the ambition harboured by British military contractors to acquire the coveted status of prime contractor to the US Defense Department place additional limitations on the ability and willingness of the UK to deepen the integration of the European defence industrial base.[33]

The 2005 Hampton Court Summit revisited the problem of military capabilities and defence R&D within the EU. Prior to that meeting, the Defence Ministers had agreed upon a Code of Conduct on Defence Procurement and a Code of Best Practice in the Supply Chain. Both codes are intended to contribute to the development of a single European armaments market, an aspiration remedying market inefficiencies and ensuring the autonomous security of supply for critical weapons systems. These codes have been designed to increase the level of cross-border competition in procurement between prime contractors and strengthen the position of small and medium-sized firms as sub-contractors, respectively. However, these codes remain voluntary rather than compulsory; Article 296 of the TEC remains untouched. While those codes are an important step towards the creation of a European defence equipment market – a goal of the EDA – the voluntary subscription to those codes does not guarantee such an outcome.

At the Hampton Court Summit, the Council of Ministers noted the implementation of five 'flagship' EU-wide defence projects in the areas of C^3, the development of a unmanned air vehicles (UAV) capability, air-to-air refuelling (AAR), strategic lift, and armoured fighting vehicles.[34] Yet, the ambitious goals of the ECAP, if consummated, would redress the shortfalls identified in the NATO DCI as well as the self-identified ECAP shortfalls. The progress towards meeting those goals, however, has been limited. Between 2002 and 2006, only 7 of 42 categories of capabilities and catalogue shortfalls were judged to be 'solved' (NBC battalions, combined air operations centre, tactical air support for maritime operations and aircraft, patrol vessels, ground based air defence, medical treatment facilities, and forward tactical helicopter evacuation); only 5 of 42 were judged to have improved over that time frame (deployable laboratories, seaport of disembarkation units, operation headquarters, strategic airlift, and mechanised infantry battalions); and the remaining 30 categories showed no marked improvement.[35]

The European allies have generally accepted the American critique of NATO's condition; on the capabilities question the Europeans have allowed themselves to adopt policies they cannot afford and seek capabilities that do not meet their foremost security concerns. The Americans have set the terms of the debate, have assumed a *droit de regard* with respect to what is and is not the duplicative acquisition of capability, and have defined 'modernisation'. The creation of Allied Command Transformation in 2003 committed the Europeans – at least at the level of rhetoric – to a Rumsfeld-inspired reorganisation of their militaries.[36] Such a transformation, if it is to take place, will of necessity require the dilution of European defence sovereignty: budgetary constraints will force the Europeans to engage in cooperative arms programmes and perhaps adopt intra-European specialisation out of necessity rather than choice. The American pressure for the modernisation of European forces could have the paradoxical outcome of lessening the taboo on an integrated EU defence policy and the dilution of sovereignty.

The existing capabilities shortfalls relevant to the lower end of the spectrum will be filled over time owing to French and British procurement strategies that will improve, *inter alia*, strategic mobility and logistics.[37] This bridging of the capabilities shortfalls, however, reflects national exertions that have been loosely coordinated at the EU level and in response to national ambitions as well as NATO obligations. None-theless, the ECAP improvements and the meeting of the HHG force requirements in 2003 have given the Europeans the capability to meet the full range of Petersberg tasks. A remaining management challenge is overcoming the compartmentalisation of national contingents and creating an effective unitary force, a prospect helped along with the Battlegroup Initiative. Europe will be incapable of significantly improving the input–output gap, so long as the EU remains something other than a state. Redundancies in expenditures and capabilities will remain a fixed feature, particularly amongst the major European states, because the dominant calculus for defence planning remains national.

The September 2003 Joint Declaration on EU–UN Cooperation in Crisis Management committed the EU to deploy military force in support of UN operations under Chapter VII. Subsequent to this agreement, Britain, France and Germany announced in spring 2004 the establishment of battlegroups comprised of 1,500 combat soldiers that could be deployed within 15 days, be sustainable for 30 days, and would operate under a UN Chapter VII mandate. The Battlegroup initiative has become a key feature of the 2010 Headline Goal. The EU Military Capabilities Commitments Conference, held in November 2004, yielded an aggregate commitment of 13 battlegroups and 4 niche supporting capability groups drawn from 22 EU countries and Norway.[38] Of those 13 battlegroups, 4 are entirely national in composition (contributed by France, Italy, Spain and the UK), 2 are bilateral (Belgium and France, the Netherlands and the UK), 3 are multilateral with three national components, and 5 are multilateral with 4 or more national components. These battlegroups in combination with the ERRF force lend the EU an autonomous military capability that has been put to use in the recent past.

Missions

There have been four EU-led military interventions since 2001. The first intervention occurred in 2001 when the EU, working in tandem with NATO, intervened in the Macedonian conflict. The NATO intervention began on 26 August 2001 with Operation Essential Harvest. While Essential Harvest was a NATO-led mission, almost half of the 4,500 troops were British and the operation was commanded by a Danish general. Essential Harvest created the context enabling ethnic Albanians to surrender a part of their arsenal, to agree to a cease-fire with the regular Macedonian army, and to sign the Ohrid Agreement, which protected the rights of the Albanian minority and provided the political framework document permitting the political normalisation of the country. The NATO presence in Macedonia was scheduled to end on 26 September 2001. The EU member states, however, feared the outbreak of a renewed civil war once NATO troops withdrew and pressed NATO to continue its presence. The EU envoy to Macedonia, François Léotard, proposed that a 1,500 strong EU-led force replace NATO troops. His proposal was rejected: the EU Defence Ministers declared that the EU was not yet ready to conduct an autonomous operation. NATO subsequently launched a follow-on mission on 25 September, Amber Fox, which fielded a much reduced force of 700 soldiers, only 10 of which were American with the balance consisting exclusively of Europeans. Although NATO declared that its mission in Macedonia would end on 15 December 2002, the Macedonian government invited NATO to remain. NATO accepted the invitation and undertook a third mission, Allied Harmony, which only fielded 400 soldiers. After the North Atlantic Council declared the mission at an end in March 2003, the EU, on the basis of UN Security Council (UNSC) Resolution 1371, launched Operation Concordia. Operation Concordia was an EU-led operation of a six-month duration, but was extended to end on 15 December 2003. The mission relied upon NATO assets and capabilities; the EU Operational Headquarters were located at SHAPE.[39] In this instance, the EU played a long-term and significant role in restoring peace and preventing the continuation of armed conflict in Macedonia (Brenner, 2002: 55).[40]

The second mission – Operation Artemis (2003) – was an autonomous, EU-led military intervention in the Democratic Republic of the Congo. In response to a UN request and consistent with UNSC Resolution 1484, the EU agreed to send 1,400 French-led troops to the Congo within a five-day timeframe with less than two weeks planning.[41] This mission improved the Congolese security situation, facilitated the return of refugees, revived economic activity, and worked closely with a number of humanitarian agencies and NGOs (Faria, 2004: 2004). Artemis lasted for three months and established a new role for the EU in global governance; viz., the EU assumed a 'bridging function' that provides a window for the UN either to mount a new peace-keeping operation or to reorganise an existing one. Subsequent to Artemis, the European Council launched a third military mission, Operation EUFOR RD Congo, which supported the UN Organisation Mission in the Democratic Republic of the Congo (MONUC) in accordance with UNSC Resolution 1761 (April 2006).[42] Operation EUFOR RD Congo, which had the limited mandate of protecting the Election Observation Mission in Kinshasa, consisted of approximately 1,100 troops stationed there with a readily deployable battalion-sized force on standby stationed outside the Congo. The Congolese presidential election was held successfully on 30 July 2006 without any widespread violence or intimidation, an outcome for which the EU can claim some credit.[43]

The fourth EU-led military intervention was Operation EUFOR–Althea in Bosnia–Herzegovina. EUFOR–Althea was the culmination of EU member state participation as peace-keepers in Bosnia as members of UNPROFOR until 1996, when the UN mission was assumed by the NATO in Operation Endeavor (60,000 troops). This IFOR mission was replaced by Operation Joint Guard in 1996 (40,000 troops) and subsequently by Operation Joint Forge (7,000 troops by the end of the NATO presence). The EU committed 7,000 troops to assume the responsibilities of SFOR detailed in the Dayton Peace Agreement and to conduct military operations in Bosnia and Herzegovina as a UN mandated Chapter VII mission. UNSC Resolution 1575 (2004) authorised the EU to lead a multinational stabilisation force that would be the legal successor to the NATO SFOR. The operation began on 2 December 2004 and has continued into 2006.

The operation is EU-led, and relied upon NATO assets under the Berlin-plus agreement.[44] Twenty-two member states committed troops to Operation EUFOR, although the largest troop contingents were supplied by Germany (1,100), the UK (950), France (500), Italy and the Netherlands (530 each), Spain and Turkey (380 each), Finland (200), Sweden (70) and Ireland (56).[45] The UK initially assumed operational command of Althea and Italy assumed command in December 2005. The EU budgeted €71.1 million for common costs and the remaining costs were shared under the Athena mechanism. Althea was conceived as fulfilling a peace stabilisation role, although the specific objectives of the EU force were to sustain the existing level of political stability, to prevent the outbreak of intercommunal violence, and to contribute to the necessary political conditions qualifying Bosnia and Herzegovina for eventual EU membership. Operation Althea has achieved the overall objective of peace stabilisation, was reviewed in June 2006, and will continue into the foreseeable future at its current strength. EUFOR has undertaken operations targeting the seizure of small arms and explosives, munitions destruction, border control, and the support of police in the fight against organised crime and internal reform. EUFOR has been reduced to a secondary role in the latter tasks by the EU Police Mission in Bosnia and Herzegovina, which is tasked to aid the reform of local police operations, make more effective local law enforcement, and reduce corruption towards building a stable civil society.[46]

These EU military interventions indicate that much progress has been made towards the goal of an autonomous operational capability in low to medium intensity conflict interventions, albeit the EU remains heavily dependent upon NATO assets within the Berlin-plus framework. The peace-enforcement missions demonstrate not only that joint EU–NATO operations as in Macedonia (2001) can be successful, but that the EU can carry out autonomous missions as in the Congo. With regard to peace-keeping, there has also been a positive trajectory: the Macedonian operation was of relatively limited duration and only committed 300 combat troops, while the follow-on EUFOR intervention in Bosnia is of a much longer duration and placed 7,000 troops on the ground. Yet, the EU still suffers from too much rhetoric and too little action when it comes to dealing with international crisis situations, such as those in Bosnia and Kosovo. Its performance has steadily improved, however, with the recent interventions in Macedonia, the DR Congo and Bosnia–Herzegovina. As compared with the 2001 demurral to commit EU-led military forces in Macedonia, the increasing willingness and ability to undertake EU-led missions with or without NATO assets is remarkable. Nonetheless, the EU, as compared to the United States or even its major member states, possesses the comparative diplomatic advantage of implementing long-term conflict prevention or peace-building measures rather than undertaking peace-making or peace-enforcement missions. It still has some way to go before it can act effectively and independently of the United States in international crisis situations.

Autonomy

There are two significant barriers to replicating economic and monetary integration in the areas of security and defence and to achieving EU autonomy vis-à-vis the United States. The first barrier derives from the persistence of national sovereignty over decisions leading to the use of military force and defence policies generally. The second barrier derives from the tension between the desire for a militarily capable and autonomous Europe and continuing expectation of European acquiescence to

American preferences mediated within NATO. A British select committee report, for example, accepted that a division of labour within the EU in defence had the merit of rationalising the member states' collective effort, but added the caveat that were the larger European states to accept role specialisation, Britain and France 'would have to rely on allies to provide the forfeited capabilities when necessary. This requires a willingness to accept a reduced capacity to act alone in the pursuit of national foreign policy' (UK Parliament Select Committee on Defence; 2002: s. 135). Neither the British nor the French, whose participation would be essential to the development of a full-spectrum EU force capability, are presently willing to 'relinquish a capability which will affect the ability of their forces to act alone' (UK Parliament Select Committee on Defence; 2002: s. 136). The desire to retain sovereign prerogatives in the realm of defence are no less intense today than in the early 1950s; that desire inhibits an intra-European division of labour that would enable the EU to develop an effective military profile and to execute the Petersberg Tasks with greater facility or efficiency. Moreover, the coordinated procurement of weapons systems, the rationalisation of the European defence industrial base, and a coherent EU decision-making capability remain hostage to the continuing imperatives of national autonomy, sovereignty and prestige. Until those imperatives wane or outlive their usefulness, the EU member states will possess a 'suboptimal' military capability and EU military interventions will continue as *ad hoc* arrangements between an internal coalition of the willing and able.

European autonomy is also a victim of American pressures to develop military capabilities in line with the transformation of the US armed forces. Europe's continuing subordination within NATO – and willingness to live with it – reflects Europe's continuing dependence upon the United States as the ultimate guarantor of regional and global security. The pressure to develop power projection and high intensity warfare capabilities within NATO rubs against the more limited military capabilities and objectives that the EU has set for itself. The force structure and missions capabilities sought by the United States comport with the American responsibility for global order, but are inappropriate to Europe's more limited regional role. Different instrumental preferences compound the divergent geopolitical requirements of the American and European military strategies. While Robert Kagan (2003) effectively employed the metaphor of Mars and Venus to differentiate between the European and American approach to foreign affairs, he wilfully ignored the military responsibilities assumed by Britain and France over the course of the post-war period.[47] Moreover, the metaphor feminised the Europeans – it plays off the self-help book entitled *Men are from Mars and Women are from Venus* – a rhetorical gambit that appealed to the American neoconservative prejudice that Europe is comprised of decadent societies led by effete political elites. The American preference for a 'muscular' (i.e., militarised) diplomacy is not matched in Europe; generally, the Europeans have preferred a diplomacy that views the resort to military force as a last resort and a not very effective one in most circumstances.

The relatively poor showing of European forces during the Kosovo intervention drew attention to Europe's military shortcomings and caused concern over the future of NATO as a military alliance. Europe's defence capabilities shortfalls would be best met, at least in terms of economic efficiency, with a greater dependence upon intra-European role specialisation, integrated multinational forces, and the procurement of cheaper (and possibly superior) American weapons systems. Such a solution conflicts with the requirements of sovereignty and the expectation held by electorates that national defence is 'national' in name and substance. Britain and France, in particular, wish to retain 'the widest possible range of defence capabilities as insurance against worst-case contingencies' (Cottey *et al.* 2002). Yet European autonomy can only be purchased in the coin of abnegated national sovereignty, pooled or subsumed within the EU. Were the Europeans to take that step, there is no guarantee that the United States would reconcile itself to a militarily autonomous and capable Europe. The reorientation of NATO away from regional collective defence and towards a global expeditionary force under American command has generated both the European effort to meet its capabilities shortfalls and growing resistance to an increasingly militarised American foreign policy. A more capable and politically unified Europe is unlikely to subordinate its preferences to those of the United States as the price for transatlantic cooperation. Likewise, the United States will probably remain unwilling to accept co-determination as the price for a militarily capable and autonomous EU.

Conclusion: assessing the EU as a military actor

The European states, with the notable exceptions of Britain and France, have gravitated explicitly towards a 'civilianised' foreign policy culture that places an emphasis on expanding and consolidating the rule of law and adoption of European norms within its geopolitical neighbourhood. This difference shapes their publics' willingness to accept rising or high defence expenditures, changes the national understanding of security threats and the best ways of meeting those threats, and affects the connections made between political developments in geographically distant parts of the world and national security. The Europeans met the American challenge to assume greater responsibility within the European security space and explicitly delineated a new division of labour within the Atlantic Alliance. Europe claimed responsibility for executing the Petersberg tasks within Europe and has committed itself to act on behalf of the UN under a Charter VII mandate, while relying upon NATO and the United States for Article 5 obligations and the conduct of high-intensity conflicts 'out of area'.

Disparate levels of national expenditures on defence coupled with an inability to homogenise national command structures provide a barrier to the greater interoperability of intra-EU military forces and sustain the gap between the actual and potential military capacity of the EU. Since 1999, the EU has made important strides towards strengthening its military capacity through the establishment of the ERRF, thirteen battlegroups, the EDA, and a growing institutional structure enabling the EU to decide when to employ military force and the operational wherewithal to do so. In response to the internal and external pressures for a greater EU responsibility for global security and stability, the ESS legitimised the use of military force as an EU instrument for tackling security threats outside EU territory – an option the EU has availed itself of on four occasions between 2002 and 2006. However, the emphasis that the ESS placed on 'preventive engagement' signifies a preference for positive civilian rather than coercive military measures. Despite the solidarity clause in the moribund EU Constitution, Article V of the WEU has been carefully excluded from the EU treaty system and the member states have not even entertained an equivalent of NATO's much weaker Article 5 with regard to a common defence obligation. Finally, the institutional framework governing EU coordination and cooperation in the area of defence need deepening. It remains unclear whether the member states will look to the EU as the coordinating mechanism for formulating and executing policies of compellence or whether the member states will continue to accept the trade-off between the benefit of retaining national prerogatives at the considerable cost of continuing diplomatic weakness and economic inefficiency.

Notes

1 EU enlargement in conjunction with the St Malo Declaration generated such a debate in the American Congress. See Sperling (2001a).

2 The persistence of negative identities within the EU, however, continues to set limits to defence integration. See Hampton and Sperling (2002).

3 See European Convention/Working Group VIII on Defence (2002) 'Introductory note by the Secretariat . . .': s. 1; von Plate (2003: 11); and Bertram *et al.* (2002: 30).

4 European Council (1999) '. . . Strengthening the European Common Policy . . .'.

5 See 'Joint Declaration by the British and French Governments . . .': 132; and European Council (1999) '. . . Helsinki European Council . . .'.

6 For a comparative study of the European security cultures, see Kirchner and Sperling (2007: chs 2–6).

7 This point is made by Rob de Wijk (2000: 414) and Anand Menon (2003: 209–11), who attribute the problem, respectively, to the organisational weakness of the EU and to different decision-making cultures within NATO and the EU.

8 European Defence Agency (2005) 'Report by the head of the European Defence Agency': para. 2.

9 European Commission (2003) '. . . European defence: Industrial and market issues . . .': 11.

10 The Pentagon has agreed to purchase 2,900 F-35 Joint Strike Fighters, while the Europeans have ordered 150. While the purchasing power and procurement preferences of the EU governments are not likely to reach American proportions, it is the case that Europe cannot afford the luxury of producing three competing combat aircraft (Eurofighter, Rafale and Gripen) that are more costly than their American counterparts. European Commission (2003) '. . . European defence: Industrial and market issues . . .': 11; for comparisons across other categories of weapons systems, see Hartley (2006): 481, Table V.

11 Council of the European Union (2004) 'Council Decision 2004/197/CFSP'.

12 European Commission (2004) 'Green Paper . . .': 6.

13 European Commission (2004) 'Green Paper . . .': 8.

14 WEU (1992) 'Petersberg Declaration': para. 4, part II.

15 The interaction of the NATO and EU capabilities is explored in Sperling (2006).

16 European Commission (2003) '. . . European defence: Industrial and market issues . . .': 13–15; European Commission (2004) 'Green Paper . . .': 7.

17 Council of the European Union (2005) 'Council Decision 2005/395/CFSP'.

18 The duplication debate is 'a discussion on the degree of dependence from the US that is best for Europe . . . and on the sincerity and strength of the American commitment towards its European allies'. See Heisbourg *et al.* (2003): 32.

19	The group consisted of Belgium, France, Germany and Luxembourg. Council of the European Union (2003) 'European defence meeting . . .'.

20	European Council (2004) 'Council Joint Action 2004/551/CFSP . . .'; Council of the European Union (2006) 'Presidency Report on ESDP'.

21	The aggregate EU expenditure in 2001 was $133.67 billion, while US expenditures equalled $329 billion. The French, German, Italian and British defence budgets account for 80 per cent of the aggregate increase in EU defence expenditure (Schmitt, 2005). Authors' own calculations.

22	Differences also emerge with regard to the instrumental preferences. For example, France and the UK still rely heavily on their nuclear weapons arsenals as a guarantor of security against external threats. In contrast, despite significant changes in Germany's self-perception of its role in the world in recent years, the country and its government nevertheless have a strong preference for civilian means to resolve conflicts, which could hamper European military action. However, as in the case of Kosovo, Germany has increasingly demonstrated a willingness to engage in military operations: it currently has approximately 7,700 troops committed to military operations 'out of area'. *The Economist* (2006: 51).

23	The second of these aspects is most fully covered in de Wijk (2000); Missiroli (2003b); and Howorth (2003).

24	In the period 1949–1964, the defence budget as a share of GDP averaged 10.5 per cent of GNP for the US, 8.31 per cent for the United Kingdom, 8.03 per cent for France, 5.16 per cent for Germany, and 4.44 per cent for Italy. Data drawn from van Ypersele de Strihou (1967: 528, Table 1).

25	Defence budgets declined to an average of 4.0 per cent of GDP for the United States, 3.3 per cent for the United Kingdom, 3.15 per cent for France, 1.85 per cent for Germany, and 2.0 per cent for Italy. See NATO (2003a).

26	For the period 2001–2004, see Schmitt (2005): 2, Table 1. For analyses of defence expenditures during the 1990s, see Bundeswehr (2004); SIPRI (2003): 316, Table 10.7. For a detailed study of the German case in comparative perspective, see Meiers (1999).

27	Raw data on R&D spending is drawn from Béchat and Rohatyn (2003: 58).

28	See European Defence Agency (2006) 'National defence R&T data'.

29	Secretary General/High Representative (2006) 'Attachment 1 . . .': 1–2.

30	See Secretary of Defense (2003): Tables C-4, C-5, D-8, and D-9. Other data drawn from NATO (2003b).

31	Ratios found in Heisbourg, *et al.* (2003: 57–8). For a full discussion of the procurement gap, see European Convention/Working Group VIII on Defence (2003) '. . . Barnier Report . . .': 263.

32	For a full discussions, see Hartley (2006); and Mörth and Britz (2004).

33	Moreover, employment in the European defence sector is low compared to the level found in the US. Total employment in the British, French, German, Italian, Spanish and Swedish defence sectors stood at 614,554 in 2001 compared to 3 million in the American. While employment in the American defence sector remained roughly the same between 1990 and 2001, each

European country experienced a significant decline that ranged from a high of 68 per cent in Germany to a low of 34 per cent in France. Data drawn from Secretary of Defense (2003): 35–6.

34 European Defence Agency (2006) 'Report by the Head of the European Defence Agency . . .': 1–3; European Defence Agency (2006) '22 EU Member States . . .'; European Defence Agency (2005) 'The Code of Conduct on Defence Procurement . . .': 2.

35 Council of the European Union (2006) 'Capabilities Improvement Chart I/2006'.

36 The NATO defence ministers accepted that Europeans should reprioritise defence budgets, reduce force levels and shift resources to weapons modernisation, and increase the overall size of national defence budgets. See NATO (2002): s. 7.

37 According to one estimate, the EU will be capable of carrying out autonomous military operations across the combat spectrum by 2015 in virtually every category of capability and redress existing shortfalls to carry out low to medium-intensity combat operations by 2005 (NATO, 2002: 80–4).

38 Common funding for the common costs of the EU missions (e.g., headquarters) is shared between the participating member states according to the each state's gross national income as a per centage of the contributing states aggregate gross national income. Common costs were defined in 2004 Council Decision that also established a funding mechanism for meeting those costs - Athena. House of Lords/Select Committee on European Union (2005); and Council of the European Union (2004) 'Council Decision 2004/197/CFSP'.

39 Council of the European Union (2003) 'Council Joint Action 2003/92/CFSP; Council of the European Union (2004) 'Council Decision 2004/803/CSFP . . .'.

40 The EU military presence was replaced with its follow-on police mission to Macedonia, Operation Proxima.

41 The Security Council Resolution passed on 30 May 2003, a framework decision was agreed upon on 5 June 2003, and a Council decision to launch Operation Artemis was reached on 12 June. The Council requested that the SG/HR Solana study the feasibility of sending an EU military operation on 19 May 2003.

42 Council of the European Union (2006) 'EU military operation . . .'.

43 Council of the European Union (2006) 'EU military operation . . .'; Euronews (2006) 'History is made as DR Congo holds elections'.

44 Council of the European Union (2004) 'Council Decision 2004/803/CSFP . . .'; Political and Security Committee (2004) '. . . Decision BiH/4/2004 . . .'.

45 The remaining EU states contributed token forces and 11 other non-EU states (including Albania, Bulgaria, Norway and Turkey) contributed forces to the operation as well. See Political and Security Committee (2004) '. . . Decision BiH/4/2004 . . .'; von Wogau (2005).

46 Council of the European Union (2006) 'Presidency Report on ESDP':
    Annex 3.
47 The Europeans are less likely to worship at the altar of Venus than of
    Minerva, the goddess of wisdom and war. Positing a single European security
    culture is a dubious proposition in the first instance (the British are readier
    to rely on military force than the Dutch or Danes; the French have not been
    hesitant to rely upon military force when it has been in their interest to do
    so; and the Germans still are not quite sure what to do). Moreover, the choice
    between war and diplomacy is not a dichotomous one; it is a instead a choice
    between matching the appropriate instruments to the threat at hand, and
    assessing costs and benefits – conventional realist assumptions about good
    statecraft.

6

Conclusion: securing Europe in the twenty-first century

From its inception, European integration has served first and foremost the national interests of its member states. The European Coal and Steel Community and the European Economic Community emerged as important components of the six founding members' foreign and security policies. France, Germany, Italy and the others responded to the external pressure emanating from the United States to pursue economic and political integration as a mechanism for supporting the American containment of the Soviet Union. The push for deeper integration also reflected the desire to find an internal solution to the security dilemma vexing Europe since German unification in 1871. It has been difficult to speak of the European Union (EU) as having a 'foreign policy' exhibiting any effective autonomy from the particularistic interests of its member states prior to 1989; the EU fulfilled an instrumental value for its member states even though it increasingly shaped those states' definition of interest over time. The steady transition to a post-Westphalian identity has further enhanced the instrumental value of the EU for its members in the area of security, but in that process the EU has also assumed a substantive value as a foreign policy actor. The level of EU autonomy – and the level of EU autonomy necessary to achieve the member states' collective security interests – is differentiated across the categories of security threat that the EU and its member states face.

The changed European context after the dissolution of the Soviet Union in 1991 and the task of securing its central, eastern and southern perimeters provided both the opportunity and necessity for an autonomous EU foreign and security policy disengaged from the particularistic interests of its members. The immediate challenge of institution and state-building in the former Warsaw Pact states compelled the member states to combine their resources and exertions at the Community level; it subsequently lent the European Commission a greater degree of latitude in shaping the *content* of EU policy, particularly with respect to the disbursement of resources and the rank-ordering of priorities in shaping Europe's milieu. The eastern enlargement and the European Neighbourhood Policy (ENP) – two major policies of assurance – represent cases of the EU as a successful and relatively autonomous foreign policy actor. Both indicate that the EU can function as an autonomous actor with its 'own' foreign policy when a number of conditions are met in whole or part: member state policy preferences are identical rather than merely overlapping or parallel, there are high financial costs or inefficiencies attending independent national policies, and where national elites are shielded by low domestic political costs owing to policy objective opacity and the difficulty of distinguishing success from failure.

How then are we to assess the EU as a security actor? As Christopher Hill famously noted, the EU faces a 'capabilities-expectations gap': the economic wealth and diplomatic presence of its member states has not been converted into a workable and effective EU foreign policy (Hill, 1993: 305–28).[1] While the constitutional and institutional innovations introduced by the Amsterdam Treaty of 1997 promised greater foreign policy cohesion and cooperation, the absence of common security and defence policies is inevitably assessed as the major failing of the EU. Although some early sceptics have reassessed their position that the EU is an ineffective and inconsequential security actor (Hill and Smith, 2005), the empirical evidence presented in the preceding chapters strongly suggests that the EU has indeed emerged as a significant, consequential and autonomous actor. The present and future roles of the EU as a security actor remain contingent upon the member states' (in)ability to discharge individually the policies of assurance, protection, prevention and compellence as well as their willingness to subcontract those policies to the Union rather than turning to fixed internal, intergovernmental coalitions. That willingness presupposes, however, that the member states will pool more and more of their sovereignty in order to redress the vulnerabilities attending their post-Westphalian condition. A comparison of the salient dimensions of assurance, protection, prevention and compellence reveals the progress that the EU has made towards its emergence as an autonomous security actor and also points to its limitations as one. The EU possesses a much greater degree of freedom from its constituent states in the creation and execution of policies of prevention and assurance, while that freedom remains severely circumscribed or qualified when developing or implementing policies of compellence and protection. This concluding chapter seeks to explain why this is so.

Rationale, goals and principles of the EU
as a security actor

The rationale for the EU as a security actor supplementing or supplanting the member states reflects five major calculations: first, the EU can aggregate national capabilities, thereby facilitating the economies of scale currently eluding Europe, and release Europe's latent diplomatic, economic and military-strategic power in the service of European security interests; second, the EU, if it were to achieve a foreign policy and security identity, could leverage European security preferences in international negotiations, particularly vis-à-vis the United States; third, the EU provides at a minimum the institutional framework enabling the member states to coordinate and harmonise their security strategies; fourth, the post-Westphalian character of European states has made it manifestly impossible for those states to achieve many of their security objectives autonomously; and finally, the very variety of security challenges confronting the Europeans today presents a particularly acute collective action problem owing to the absence of an uncontested leader or even a stable duopoly or oligopoly that consistently exerts leadership or is unwilling to provide a collective security goods in the presence of free-riding.

The post-Westphalian hypothesis implies that since every security objective now possesses a degree of publicness, the EU member states should be then compelled to transfer increasing degrees of sovereignty to the EU in order to alleviate the leadership and capabilities inadequacies engendered by strict intergovernmentalism. Post-Westphalianism is the cause and symptom of the difficulty the Europeans face in adequately protecting themselves given the broadened security agenda, the diffuseness of threat, and the sheer number of policies required to mitigate or ameliorate those threats. As has become a commonplace observation, few security goods are purely public; most assume the character of impure public goods which have an admixture of the public and the private. These goods provide a broad range of incentives for contributing to the provision of security as well as opportunities for free-riding. The categories of threat addressed by the policies of assurance, prevention, protection and compellence are sufficiently public that all EU states have some stake in ensuring these policies are implemented, yet do not provide symmetrical incentives for contributing to the task of providing or implementing them.

The problem confronting the EU – and its member states – is that the contemporary security challenges represent a very broad range of impure public goods. Thus, as the private component *and* heterogeneity of the security goods increases within the group, so too does the hesitancy of states to act on the principle of solidarity or to invest their sovereignty in the EU. As the public component rises, there is a greater willingness to forgo sovereignty and lend the EU greater latitude in shaping and executing security policies on behalf of the member states. But the willingness to act in conformity with the principle of solidarity does not guarantee the optimal provision of the good; free-riding still remains a potential barrier to collective action. Arguably, those EU security goals directed primarily at the milieu – e.g., the stabilisation of the European perimeter, particularly in the Balkans and Mediterranean basin – represent security complexes that exhibit a high degree of publicness and few opportunities for free-riding: the member states have yielded significant sovereignty to the EU in the formulation and execution of policy, they have accepted qualified majority voting within the Council, and their behaviour generally conforms to the principle of solidarity. Security policies that have significant impacts on domestic constituencies or do so asymmetrically, in terms of the disruptive consequences that EU policies have on the domestic social contracts, the transparency of costs associated with those policies, or the domestic political costs of policy failure, enhance the collective action problem within the EU, a trait endemic to the policies of protection as well as compellence.

The heterogeneity of the security challenges facing Europe encode different technologies of publicness, which may be defined as 'the manner in which [actors'] provision or subscription levels are aggregated to yield a group provision or consumption level' of the public good (Sandler, 1992: 36). There are three basic technologies of publicness: weakest link, strongest pillar, and summation. Summation represents the simplest case: the provision of the collective good is simply dependent upon the substitutability of the actors providing the good insofar as the definition of the privileged group is not dependent upon the identity of any individual member of the collective; the amount of the good supplied is simply determined by the sum of the individual contributions of the group. Weakest link technology exists where the smallest level of the good provided by an individual actor determines the absolute level of the public good available to all.[2] Strongest pillar technology obtains where the amount of the public good provided to the collective depends upon the largest effort of an individual state (Sandler, 1992: 36–7).[3] These alternative technologies of publicness can help explain the difficulties of transforming the EU into a security actor with the attributes of the traditional state across the entire range of security policies; they provide a plausible set of reasons why the persistence of sovereign prerogatives may very well enhance rather than diminish the security of Europe's citizens. Moreover, those different technologies explain why the EU plays a variegated rather than uniform role as a security actor, and why different divisions of labour between the EU and its member states have emerged in these four policy arenas.

The key difference between the policies of protection and compellence, for example, is found in the negative consequences that one state's noncompliance with a regulation, directive or framework decision will have on the success of the EU in realising its collectively defined security objective. The weakest link technology of publicness vexes the policies of protection: the defection of one member state from a common EU policy – on rules of evidence, lenient penal law and the sharing of information or epidemiological surveillance – will hamper the ability of the others to achieve the common goal of combating organised crime, terrorism, or pandemics, natural or otherwise. The strongest pillar technology of publicness defines the policies of compellence: the unwillingness of any state or group of states to participate in a Petersberg intervention, for example, is unimportant so long as either France or the UK – the two EU states with the force projection capabilities necessary for any extra-European intervention – participate. Finally, the technology of summation is relevant to understanding the EU's relative success in executing the policies of assurance and prevention: individual member state contributions to those policies are compulsory and subject to the gross national income scale that predetermines each member's contribution to a Pillar I undertaking. Not only is defection not an option, but there are mechanisms in place ensuring an optimal supply of the good once the member states and the Union jointly define its content.

The EU plays a differentiated role as a security actor owing to the technologies of publicness attending the four categories of security policy. The milieu policies of prevention and assurance possess a high degree of publicness; the rationale for the EU as a security actor is compelling; and the Community method prevents free-riding. The policies of protection and compellence, on the other hand, remain largely intergovernmental, the content of those policies remains contested and heterogeneous, participation in joint EU initiatives or interventions is not compulsory, and free-riding remains an attractive, non-sanctioned option. Moreover, the political costs attending policies of compellence and protection are transparent to the electorate and the benefits are diffuse and asymmetrical. Consequently, the principle of solidarity loses its force as does the rationale for delegating responsibility to the EU, despite the merit of a joint solution from a narrow cost–benefit calculation. Where policies are directed towards milieu goals and where delegating sovereignty to the EU is relatively cost free for the electorate or political elites, however, the rationale for retaining national control over policies wanes and the logic for acting collectively waxes. Where policies require the expenditure of blood as well as treasure, where security policy initiatives transparently alter the domestic social contract (e.g., notions of privacy), it is more likely that electorates will insist that political elites retain sovereign prerogatives and the collective action problem remains.

Deeper integration within those four policy domains is propelled by overlapping security calculi that have, in turn, raised the profile of the EU as a security actor. In each case, there is broad agreement among the member states that joint action mediated by the EU is superior to mere intergovernmentalism. Yet the specific challenges facing the EU and the differentiated objectives of its member states create different opportunities and barriers to the harmonisation of national policies and the eventual adoption and execution of security policies possessing the coherence of the single market or European monetary union, either substantively or procedurally (see Table 6.1).

Table 6.1 Rationale for collective action

	Assurance	Prevention	Protection	Compellence
Rationale for collective action	Stability and security of western Balkans is intrinsically linked to the EU's stability	Obligation of EU to maintain stability and order in own neighbourhood Emergence of EU identity with external character Vulnerability of EU to disorder along its perimeter	Perforated sovereignty of post-Westphalian state Transnational criminal or terrorist organisations are not constrained by national boundaries	European identity and material resources require global presence Resource optimisation in defence spending Solving intra-EU leadership gap Autonomy from US
Technology of publicness	Summation	Summation	Weakest link (except where Schengen *acquis* applies)	Strongest pillar

Principles

The policies of protection, prevention, assurance and compellence are interdependent and pursued concurrently; it is also as clear that economic instruments and military force can be employed to achieve not dissimilar goals. There is an elective affinity between the different security governance functions facing the EU and the range of policy instruments appropriate to performing them; most EU member states have a pronounced normative preference that subordinates military force to the economic and diplomatic instruments of persuasion and dissuasion. The policies of compellence – and the auxiliary objective of pushing forward the integration (or merely interoperability) of member state military forces – retain importance not only owing to the continuing utility of force to alleviate particular categories of threat, but in recognition that defence integration is the penultimate step prior to political (con)federation. A core component of state sovereignty remains the ability to defend against external attack and protect national values and interests, by force if necessary. Consequently, the sovereignty principle still forms a residual and fundamental barrier to defence and political integration. As in the case of protection, the sovereignty norm inhibits deeper integration just as the solidarity principle propels integration forward. Moreover, it underscores the instrumental rather than substantive importance of subsidiarity as the principle guiding EU governance, particularly in the area of security.

The sovereignty principle constitutes a formidable barrier to the EU emerging as an effective security actor within the territory of the EU itself. Member states have jealously guarded their sovereign prerogatives in this sensitive area, consistent with the provisions of the Amsterdam Treaty, and they foreswore any effort 'to create a European security area in the sense of a common territory', despite the mutual recognition that the EU has a common external border. The internal logic of pooling sovereignty in each of the four categories of security policy is persuasive, but the sovereignty principle has remained largely intact and continues to exert a strong hold on the collective political imaginations of the elected and electorate throughout Europe. The countervailing principle of solidarity acknowledges an underlying collective responsibility for jointly fulfilling common security tasks. It entails a positive obligation in the event of an attack to 'mobilise all instruments at their disposal, including military resources, to assist a member state or an acceding State in its territory'. This principle of conduct nonetheless defers to national prerogatives when it comes to the assessment of a member state's interest: the nature and quantity of assistance provided to a member state experiencing an attack is non-specified and strictly voluntary. Article 42 of the now stalled European Constitution lent the solidarity principle constitutional status. Thus, solidarity and sovereignty are the two principles setting the floor and ceiling of security policy integration and collective action; it delimits the boundaries of the EU as a security actor with prerogatives superseding those of its members. The sovereignty principle outweighs the solidarity principle in the policies of protection and compellence, while the converse characterises the policies of assurance and prevention.[4]

The subsidiarity and procedural principles intermediate the contra-imperatives of sovereignty and solidarity in the formulation and execution of EU security policies. The subsidiarity and procedural principles mediate the horizontal division of labour between member states seeking to forgo as few sovereign prerogatives as possible while at the same time recognising that the exercise of sovereign prerogatives is insufficient to the security tasks at hand. The subsidiarity principle, as it has been so far applied, has effectively delegated primary responsibility for protection and compellence to member states. Initially, the EU role was limited to the design of institutional frameworks facilitating police and judicial cooperation across the Union and brokering the approximation of national penal law and judicial processes. With respect to the policies of protection, the initial ambitions of the EU focused on creating mechanisms facilitating the development of an interoperable and autonomous EU force projection capability and protecting the European defence industrial base and infrastructure

The procedural principle governs the vertical division of labour within the EU once states determine that the EU is the appropriate actor to address some collective action problem. To date, the procedural principle governs the rationalisation of the EU decision-making process, particularly the avoidance or accommodation of overlapping policies between Pillars I (assurance and prevention), II (compellence) and III (protection), the clear definition of member state and EU competencies. Despite the neat division of horizontal and vertical competencies, the security challenges facing the EU have initiated the cross-pillarisation of the various security strategies, particularly between Pillars II and III (e.g., CBRN threats) and Pillars I and III (e.g., judicial cooperation in combating terrorism). What remains an open question, however, is whether the process of cross-pillarisation will effect the gradual intrusion of the community method into Pillars II and III, or whether the community method will be diluted owing to the countervailing pull of sovereignty.

The four categories of security policy share these major principles, sometimes explicitly animating policy initiatives and sometimes implicitly as a matter of settled practise and constitutional agreement. Prevention

Table 6.2 Principles of action

	Assurance	Prevention	Protection	Compellence
Principles of action	Regionalism	Regionalism	Sovereignty	Sovereignty
	Conditionality	Effective multilateralism	Solidarity and mutual responsibility	Unanimity or constructive abstention
		Development and stability are interdependent	Subsidiarity	Solidarity
			Procedural	Preventive engagement
		Multilateralism		

and assurance policies, which are conducted within the binding legal framework of Pillar I, are less vexed by the tension inherent between sovereignty and solidarity, while that tension is unresolved in the areas of compellence and protection, located in Pillars II and III, respectively. These categories of security policy are also governed by principles specific to each (see Table 6.2). Even a cursory examination of Table 6.2 reveals that in fact the principles governing compellence and protection are preoccupied with the barriers erected by sovereignty to collective action and the emergence of the EU as a security actor, while the principles governing prevention and assurance identify relations of causation and the ways in which policies will be implemented and assessed.

Goals

Although the number and type of security challenges have multiplied over the entire course of the post-war period, the process of securitisation accelerated after the end of the Cold War. The rapid proliferation of security threats represents a fundamental change in the contemporary security environment; viz., the altered relationship between the agents and the targets of threat. The intractability of the security threats arises from non-state actors as the chief antagonists threatening European security; the need for security policies executed jointly is matched by the intractability of the security environment. Traditionally, states have had the option of using military force against a well-defined enemy, another state. War was conducted on battlefields between opposing armies; civilians (in theory, if not practice) and the economic infrastructure were only secondary theatres of war. States are no longer the sole target or agent of threat; security threats are more likely to emanate from dysfunctional societies or failing states; non-state actors are more likely to wage 'war' against civilians and societal infrastructure, rely upon terrorism to do so, and pursue a non-negotiable agenda. Nonetheless, traditional forms of conflict still persist along Europe's perimeter and beyond. The EU and its member states have not only had to develop a broad array of policies tailored to the expanding number of security pathologies targeting internal tranquility and external stability, but strike a politically sustainable balance between the sovereign prerogatives of the member states and the abnegation of those prerogatives to meet collective threats (see Table 6.3).

Two imminent threats to European security and stability arise from the persistence of intrastate conflict and disintegration along its perimeter, most particularly in southeastern Europe. The policies of assurance and prevention are intended to ameliorate the root causes of both. The strategy

Table 6.3 Policy challenges and goals

	Assurance	Prevention	Protection	Compellence
Principal policy challenges	Intra-state conflict resolution and building institutions of civil society	State and nation-building	Institution-building within EU	Interstate conflict resolution
	Humanitarian assistance and reconstruction of infrastructures in CEE (1992–1997)			
Principal policy goals	Supporting regional stability via support for democracy, rule of law, and minority rights (1997–present)	Address root causes of instability Regional integration Crisis management capability	Increased police and judicial cooperation Approximation of penal law and judicial process Border security Infrastructure security Health security	Acquire necessary capabilities (political, planning, operational, and material) to discharge Petersberg Tasks

of preventive engagement, while formulated as a security policy principle in the ESS, was manifest in the early decision to embark upon the eastern enlargement of the EU. The policies of assurance and prevention jointly expand the governing capacity of failed or failing states, provide the wherewithal for a social and political infrastructure capable of containing political conflicts between opposing societal groups, and provide the basis for economic reconstruction and development. Assurance policies generally address the immediate needs of regions recovering from civil conflict; the primary policy goal is to provide sufficient humanitarian assistance to improve the lives of individuals in war-torn societies and to facilitate the transition to self-government and the rule of law. The policies of prevention represent 'second stage' security policies – they consolidate the process of state- and nation-building – as well as a prophylaxis against social unrest or disintegration.

Creating a European area of freedom, security and justice is the core task of the policies of protection. Although the rationale for undertaking such policies to enhance European security is unambiguous, it is likewise uncontestable that the policies of protection are the most domestically intrusive security policies on the EU agenda. The EU has undertaken to harmonise the institutional and legal infrastructure of its member states. Not only do the tasks of enhancing police and judicial cooperation reach into areas that affect core elements of national identity, but the approximation of judicial process and penal law could potentially upset national social contracts that reflect a negotiated balance between the prerogatives of the state and the rights of the individual.

The bailiwick of compellence is the traditional one of mediating interstate conflicts and deterring or defending against the violation of territorial integrity. Although the traditional concern with territorial defence continues to occupy national authorities, that threat is no longer a primary, let alone immediate, preoccupation. Rather, national defence efforts are directed towards meeting the responsibilities for regional and global management assumed in the ESS. The EU seeks a force projection capability enabling it to intervene in armed conflicts where the EU and its member states have critical interests. Despite the ongoing pursuit of an effective expeditionary capability, the EU has restricted itself to the modest goals of acquiring an autonomous planning and decision-making capability that would allow 'Europe' to act independently of the United States where European interests diverged from those of the United States or where the United States simply did not share the European threat assessment.

The empirical analyses of these different security goals undertaken in the preceding chapters underscore that the EU has not been willing or able to assume exclusively the attributes of a 'civilian' or a 'normal' power in the current threat environment. Perhaps unsurprisingly, Europe's post-Westphalian states and the EU face a less tractable security environment in the post-Cold War international system; the complexity of the contemporary security environment is bewildering, although not as imminently lethal as the prospect of mutually assured destruction that regulated Soviet–American rivalry in the postwar period. The variety of security challenges and goals falling under the complete or partial jurisdiction of the EU also points to a capability-mix trap into which the EU could fall *if* too great an investment is made in the acquisition of force projection capabilities at the expense of addressing the root causes of conflict and instability outside Europe. The EU must acquire a military capability commensurate with Europe's economic wherewithal and consistent with its geopolitical interests. If the EU is to emerge as a full spectrum security actor, it must not only be capable of implementing all four categories of security policy, but be able to do so with equal aplomb.

Institutional innovations

The four categories of security policy have generated two general categories of institutional innovation: those that consolidate the leadership role of the Commission in policy implementation; those that create policy and institutional infrastructures that facilitate the development of policy networks between national authorities responsible for implementing Union initiatives. The policies of assurance and prevention conform to the first form of innovation, while protection and compellence conform to the second.

The policies of prevention and assurance, governed by the Community method, are financed through the EU common budget. The exception is the European Development Fund (EDF), which assists African, Caribbean and Pacific countries and does not come under the general Community budget; instead, it is funded by the member states, covered by unique financial rules, and managed by a specific committee. Institutional innovations in the policies of prevention have primarily assumed the character of instruments managing the preaccession process and implementing the European Neighbourhood Policy (ENP) and economic development policies (Lomé and Cotonou conventions). The main agencies responsible for implementing these policies, the European Initiative for Democracy and Human Rights (EIDHR), the European Community Humanitarian Office (ECHO), the Rapid Reaction Mechanism (RRM), and the Committee (funding) for Asia and Latin America (ALA) are located in the Commission. Similarly, the core institutional developments found in the policies of assurance are the Stabilisation and Association Process (SAP) and the Stability Pact for South Eastern Europe, both of which were initiated in response to the disintegration and civil conflicts that erupted in the former Yugoslavia, but now include all the Balkan states. Europeaid manages two policy instruments on behalf of the Community, CARDS and the European Agency for Reconstruction (EAR). The Stability Pact, a multi-actor arrangement, consists of three working tables mimicking the division of labour between the three pillars of the Union: working tables I and II (Democracy and Human Rights, and Economic Reconstruction, Development and Cooperation, respectively) fall under Pillar I competencies, while working table III (Security, and Justice and Home Affairs) falls under Pillars II and III. This institutional arrangement provides the political and bureaucratic institutional infrastructures necessary for the Balkan states to meet their obligations under their pre-accession agreements with the EU. Taken together, the institutional innovations supporting the policies of assurance and prevention function as Community instruments for implementing collective policies within the existing Community framework. These instruments and institutions do not so much expand Community competencies as reinforce the effectiveness of the Union as a foreign policy actor, particularly with regard to the shaping of the external milieu.

Institutional changes attending the policies of protection and compellence, however, have expanded the role of the Community in their formulation and execution; it has created an institutional infrastructure that provides the foundation not only for autonomous EU action externally (compellence), but the eventual transition to the Community method and common funding of single policies for both. The establishment of Eurojust and the addition of criminal law to the competencies of the European Judicial Network have contributed to two developments: increased opportunities for intra-EU cooperation and continuous progress towards harmonising penal law and judicial practices. Police cooperation with respect to the fight against terrorism and organised crime has been likewise facilitated by a set of institutions, particularly the expansion of Europol's competencies to address crimes with an international dimension and terrorism, the creation of the EU Chief of Police Task Force, and the European Union Police College (CEPOL). These networks provide a mechanism for better communication and cooperation between police and judicial authorities within the Union, two developments particularly critical to any effort to police and prosecute terrorists on an EU-wide basis. The EU has also expanded the number of Community institutions responsible for monitoring different facets of internal security policies, including epidemiological surveillance (the ECDC and RAS–BICHAT), policing external borders (FRONTEX), and infrastructure security (ENISA and CIWIN). The common polices that these institutions monitor, in turn, prepare the Union to assume sovereign responsibilities and help the member states become accustomed to that eventuality.

The EU member states have also made important progress towards creating an EU profile if not competency in the shaping and operational implementation of the policies of compellence. A clear institutional hierarchy has been established that enables the EU to execute the Petersberg tasks: the Political and Security Committee, the High Representative for the CFSP, and the Council of Ministers decide when and where the EU should intervene; the EU Military Staff and EU Military Committee are responsible for the operational command of EU forces participating in a military intervention. The EU Planning Cell at NATO Headquarters,

Table 6.4 Institutional evolution of the EU as a security actor

	Assurance	Prevention	Protection	Compellence
Major institutional innovations	Stabilisation and Association Process	IPA	Eurojust	Political and Security Committee
		ENPI	European Judicial Network	
	CARDS	Europeaid		EU Military Committee
	European Agency for Reconstruction	ECHO	Europol	EU Military Staff
		RRM	Chief of Police Task Force	EU Planning Cell at NATO HQ
	Stability Pact for South Eastern Europe	EIDHR	European Union Police College	
		EDF		European Defence Agency
		ALA	FRONTEX	
			ECDC	European Rapid Reaction Force
			RAS–BICHAT	Battlegroup initiative
			ENISA	
				Situation Centre
			CIWIN (proposed)	

in conjunction with the Berlin-plus arrangements, have increased the EU capability for making autonomous decisions and leading military operations with or without NATO assets. Two other institutional developments have increased the short-term and long-term ability to wield military force autonomously: first, the European Rapid Reaction Force and the Battlegroup Initiative created the wherewithal to deploy troops quickly and for extended periods of time where Europe's interests are threatened; second, the European Defence Agency could eventually function as the arbiter of procurement policies for the individual member states and as the instrument for protecting the European defence industrial base and enhancing the global competitiveness of European defence contractors. The EU Joint Situation Centre (SitCen) monitors and assesses events and situations worldwide on a 24-hour basis with a focus on potential crisis regions, terrorism and WMD-proliferation. The SitCen also provides support to the EU High Representative and other senior officials as well as for EU crisis management operations; its primary task is providing a common intelligence base for the member states, particularly with respect to counter-terrorism, and the handling of communications security issues.

The policies of protection are largely derived within the context of intergovernmental negotiations, while the policies of compellence are subject to Joint Action. Unanimity persists as the decision-making rule; Community institutions function as facilitators of common action, rather than as the driving force of common action; and responsibility for implementation remains with the member states and immune to the infringement process in the face of non-compliance. The Union institutions developed to implement framework decisions and security strategies do not encroach upon the sovereign prerogatives of determining the content or execution of security policies. Yet, these institutions *have* increased the ability of the member states to act jointly and enhanced the role of the EU in areas once exclusively reserved for the member states (see Table 6.4).

The EU's performance as a security actor

The goals that the Commission and the member states have set for the EU in the four security policy arenas serve as the benchmarks for measuring the EU's performance. The principle of preventive engagement governs both the policies of assurance and prevention; each is directed towards the external milieu and has the overarching goals of developing effective civilian crisis management capabilities, contributing to regional stability, mitigating ongoing civil conflicts, and promoting civil liberties, the rule of law and democratic government. Correspondingly, the counter-indicative principles of solidarity and sovereignty shape and constrain protection and compellence policies. Every EU policy initiative inevitably encroaches upon the core elements of state sovereignty in order to lend the EU greater diplomatic and military autonomy externally (compellence) and greater resiliency internally (protection).

Prevention has become the distinguishing hallmark of the EU external policies. The development of civilian crisis management capabilities and a comprehensive strategy for ensuring the stability and prosperity of Europe's neighbourhood are the twin goals that the Union set for itself in the European Security Strategy and the ENP. The ENP, which develops comprehensive Action Plans for the strategic disbursement of aid to the recipient states, is reinforced by assuring those states access to the internal market as well as other sources of EU finance. EU success in conflict prevention can also be noted in the wider international environment through the conduct of the Lomé and Cotonou conventions. These conventions have contributed to conflict prevention outside its immediate neighbourhood. As is the case with the ENP, Lomé and Cotonou promote regional stability with a view towards removing the root causes of regional and domestic instability. Moreover, the EU supports regional integrative or cooperative organisations outside Europe, particularly those possessing a clear mandate to prevent conflict such as the Economic Community of West African States (ECOWAS) and the African Union (AU). EU support of these organisations has focused since 11 September on aiding Europe in the fight against terrorism. More generally, the EU has met its civilian crisis capability objectives. It now possesses the political will and capability to undertake anticipatory civilian crisis management interventions (e.g., EUPT Kosovo and EPAT Macedonia). The EU has mediated intra-societal or interstate conflicts, created favourable contexts for the implementation of ceasefire agreements, sponsored confidence-building measures between regional antagonists, provided emergency aid in support of the electoral process when threatened by internal disruptions or lack of domestic capability, and contributed to the demobilisation of combatants in conflict-torn societies.

The Stability Pact has had the greatest success in meeting the objectives of post-conflict reconstruction, democratic institution building, and regional political stability. While the Stability Pact is not a process exclusively under the jurisdiction of the EU, the EU is the largest donor and is directly involved in its management. The bulk of Stability Pact financial resources has been devoted to developing the economic and transportation infrastructure necessary for rapid and sustained regional economic growth. The Stability Pact has also financed programmes supporting small and medium sized enterprises, particularly the creation of a viable banking sector. In addition to the underlying requirements for economic growth, which are viewed as essential to the emergence of sustainable democracies, the Stability Pact has increasingly dedicated funds to the strengthening of institutions, governance and combating corruption. CARDS, the EU programme dedicated to post-conflict reconstruction, has shifted its financing from infrastructure rehabilitation and democratic stabilisation to the improved performance and accountability of the police and judiciary. The long-term aim of the CARDS programme, like the Stability Pact, is the integration of these Balkan countries into the European economic and political system, eventually as accession candidates that meet the Copenhagen criteria. The EU's post-conflict

Table 6.5 The EU's performance as a security actor

	Assurance	Prevention	Protection	Compellence
Major policy initiatives	Stability Pact	European Neighbourhood Policy	Tampere Milestones	Helsinki Headline Goals
	CARDS			
			Hague Programme	European Capabilities Improvement Programme
	EUPM–Bosnia	European Security Strategy		
	EUPOL PROXIMA– Macedonia	Civilian Crisis Management and Headline Goals	Millennium Strategy on Organised Crime	European Battlegroup initiative
	EUPOL Kinshasa			
			Declaration on Terrorism	
	EUPOL COPPS	ECHO		Operation Artemis (DR Congo)
	EUBAM Ukraine and Moldova	Rapid Reaction Mechanism	CBRN Programme	Operation Concordia (Macedonia)
	EUBAM Rafah	EIDHR		
	EUROJUST Lex	EUSEC DR Congo		EUFOR–Althea (Bosnia and Herzegovina)
	AMM Monitoring Mission	EUPT Kosovo		
		EUPAT fYRM		EURFOR RD Congo
	EUROJUST Themis			

interventions are not limited to the supply of technical and financial assistance. Interventions include not only EU rule of law and police missions that train national judiciaries (e.g., EUJUST Themis and EUJUST Lex), police forces (e.g., EUPOL Proxima and EUPOL COPPS), security forces (e.g., EUSEC Congo) and border guards (e.g., EUBAM Rafa and EUBAM Ukraine and Moldova), but serve as a bridge between a successful military peace-keeping operation and the restoration of civil order (e.g., EUPM Bosnia).

The policies of compellence required the Union to acquire autonomous planning and operational capabilities. Those capabilities, in turn, required the member states to sacrifice, in principle, some sovereign prerogatives in order to achieve the common goal of executing the Petersberg Tasks. As recently as 2001, the European Defence Ministers refused a request to commit 1,500 peace-keeping forces under an autonomous EU command to Macedonia, citing the absence of the operational capability to do so. But by the middle of the decade, the EU had undertaken four military interventions of increasing size and complexity. NATO's Defence Cooperation Initiative, which prodded the European members of NATO to address their military capabilities shortfalls, was supplemented by EU initiatives to acquire the necessary military capabilities necessary for the execution of the Petersberg Tasks, notably the Helsinki Headline Goals, the European Capabilities Improvement Programme, and the Battlegroup initiative. These programmes have enabled the EU to carry out autonomous military missions, provided the foundation for greater defence cooperation between the major military powers, and have progressively contributed to the closer coordination of procurement and weapons development policies. The acquisition of these capabilities increased Europe's diplomatic heft, enabled the Europeans to assume greater responsibility for global and regional stability, and freed Europe from a debilitating dependence upon the United States. As important, the rising role of the EU as a military actor and the institutions put in place to facilitate that development have created yet another institutional framework allowing Germany to play an operational military role commensurate with its economic capabilities and interest in global stability (see Table 6.5).

Assessing the EU as a security actor

The EU is a quasi-autonomous actor; it remains dependent upon the acquiescence and resources of its member states in the formulation and execution of security policy. But the EU is a significant and increasingly autonomous security actor, particularly in formulating and executing the policies of prevention and assurance. The EU's importance as a security actor may be attributed to its ability to resolve the collective action problems facing the individual member states, particularly as it pertains to exercise of the civilian instruments of statecraft towards achieving the milieu goals of stability and state-building. But the nation states remain largely autonomous from Community interference in the transposition or enforcement of decisions and programmes which touch upon areas affecting the social contract or political culture (penal law and judicial process) or the expenditure of blood and treasure (military interventions to keep, enforce or make peace in civil conflicts).

Community institutions exercise considerable autonomy in formulating the policies of prevention and assurance and enjoy considerable latitude in the execution of those policies. Even though those policies are financed out of the common budget, the Commission and other Community institutions still require member-state acquiescence and cooperation to implement them effectively. The policies of protection and compellence remain, with the exception of border control for those states that have acceded to the Schengen *acquis* and Prüm Convention, firmly within the purview of member states, despite their compromised sovereignty. The logic of the post-Westphalian condition that the member states find themselves in has not overpowered the Westphalian impulse to retain policy autonomy in the areas of internal protection and defence. The Commission, in effect, possesses the prerogatives attending the *Resortprinzip* in the policies of prevention and assurance; it possesses the ability to implement policies without interference from the member states and has acquired the legal standing to ensure member state compliance once the Commission and Council agree on the content and form of policy. The Commission enjoys neither the prerogatives of the *Resortprinzip* nor the agenda setting prerogatives of the *Richtlinienkompetenz* – the right to establish the content and form of policy – in the areas of protection and compellence. The EU remains a contingent security actor, but its autonomy from the member states varies from significant (assurance and prevention) to limited (compellence) (see Table 6.6). Arguably, this state of affairs is desirable: national habits of mind, the diverse range of legal and political cultures, and the persistent expectation that national governments should be responsible for security preclude the displacement of the state as the primary supplier of security. Where these factors shape the policy calculus of national elites, the EU has been limited to reducing transaction costs of intergovernmental bargaining, establishing common institutional and legal frameworks facilitating cross-border cooperation, and minimising the consequences of persistent and divergent national interests.

Table 6.6 Assessment of the EU as a security actor

	Assurance	Prevention	Protection	Compellence
Degree of freedom from constituent parts	Mostly Community oriented (Pillar I) action complemented by CFSP/ESDP missions (e.g., rule of law, police, border assistance, etc) and member state contributions, (e.g., to the SP in SEE)	Mostly Community oriented (Pillar I) action complemented by CFSP/ESDP sanctions, missions (e.g., monitoring) and specific group efforts (e.g., the EU-3 with Iran)	Primarily intergovernmental. Article 67(2), second indent, TEC provides for co-decision in JHA and Article 68 TEC, which empower the Court of Justice to rule on infringements, does not apply in JHA	Joint Action. However, decisions to augment EU military capabilities taken outside Community Framework (e.g., St Malo Declaration)
Degree of autonomous action and/or multilateral activities	Distinct role in SEE through SAP and SAA; complemented by the SP. Supportive role to multi-lateral peace-building efforts elsewhere	Mixture of distinct and multi-lateral efforts. Highly distinct in European region (enlargement and ENP); partially distinct in development activities (Cotonou); mostly multi-lateral role in crisis management activities	The transposition of Framework Decisions is a matter of national competence. EU provides a coordination role and establishes standards that represent a common floor for police powers and judicial process	Despite the introduction of politically responsible policy organs within the Commission and the development of a nascent European general staff, the EU remains dependent upon the good-will of its member states, particularly Britain and France

| Degree of policy effectiveness | Successful (especially in the western Balkans) in contributing to:
• good governance rules
• self-government and state- and nation-building
• development of civil society
• regional stability | • Substantial success in securing stability in EU neighbourhood
• partial success in linking development and security objectives
• limited success in defusing potential crisis situations, e.g., attempts to stop Iran's uranium enrichment programme | • Successful insofar as framework documents in place that harmonise police, customs, and judicial procedures
• Community institutions have been created to coordinate national policies and facilitate the harmonisation of policies
• non-compliance remains problematic. Article 226 TEC not applicable and Commission desire to use bridging clauses of Article 42 TEU and 67(2), second indent, TEC to ensure compliance with Hague Programme and JHA not accepted

Border security is the exception to this rule. As part of the Schengen *acquis*, these policies are subject to the Community method and infringement proceedings (Pillar I) | There have been notable successes:
• Europe possess force projection capabilities
• Europe is now an autonomous military actor
• EU military interventions have been relatively successful |

Yet any assessment of the EU's success or failure as a security actor in these four security policy arenas remains heavily dependent upon the yardstick employed to do so. The most demanding yardstick would define success in terms of policy outcomes: have EU policies of assurance produced democracies and market economies? Have EU policies of prevention stopped civil conflicts before they have emerged or mitigated their savagery when they erupt? Have EU policies of protection reduced the success of criminal enterprises operating in and around Europe or thwarted terrorist attacks? Have EU policies of compellence created a Europe with force projection and high-intensity warfare capabilities commensurate with the aggregated economic, technological, and diplomatic resources of its member states?

The validity of these questions, however, rests on the political end station envisioned for the EU. If the EU remains a form of political organisation that falls far short of a (con)federal state possessing fully the sovereign prerogatives now held by its members, then a different yardstick for assessing its success or failure as a security actor is in order. But to assess the EU as *if* it were a state or *ought* to seek the full range of sovereign prerogatives attending statehood creates an unreasonable and unattainable standard. The more fruitful approach to the problem of assessment would question whether the EU adds value to the security efforts of the member states, mitigates the collective action problem intrinsic to the four categories of security policy, and has achieved its programmatic objectives governing the behaviour of the member states. On such an accounting, the EU has been a relatively successful and important actor.

The EU has had the greatest relative success in meeting those collective security challenges where the technology of publicness is summation. The policies of prevention and assurance fall into that category. One of the key milieu objectives assumed by the EU has been providing support and incentives for those states in its 'neighbourhood' to adopt desirable political and economic reforms. One strategy for achieving that goal has been the offer of membership if the targeted state meets the Copenhagen criteria. For states that are ineligible for membership, the EU has developed Action Plans tailored to the shortcomings of the target states and the member states have delegated responsibility for implementing and managing those policies to the Commission. Nonetheless, the challenge of translating financial and technical assistance, privileged access to the internal market, and political dialogue into compliance with human rights, democracy, the rule of law and good governance remains beyond the exertions of the EU or its individual members – the efforts of the United States and the panoply of aid organisations falling under the umbrella of the UN system attest to the difficulty, if not futility, of an external actor seeking to foster political or economic reform without the willing participation of the targeted state or society. The EU has contributed directly to the stabilisation of failing states or states in transition with a growing number of police missions, rule of law missions, monitoring missions, and border assistance missions. These missions demonstrate that the EU has successfully facilitated the pooling of national capabilities, including intelligence and information, and coordinated the individual and collective efforts of the member states.

The most significant policy of assurance has been the promise of accession to the EU. The EU instrumentalised accession as the final step in the stabilisation and socialisation process for states 'belonging' in Europe. Two key instruments, the SP and SAP, were relied upon to strengthen civil society and state building, promote democracy, enhance regional stability and bring the Balkan countries within the EU orbit. The successful grafting of EU values and norms onto the social and political fabric of these countries is central to the overall objective of regional stability and an instrumental goal for meeting the Copenhagen criteria. In the western Balkans, the EU-funded programmes have improved the physical, social and economic environment, and have created or improved the institutions of civil society. This assistance has supported, if not produced, democratically elected governments, which in turn have contributed to regional stability. While it would be untenable to credit success to the EU alone, it would be as negligent to underestimate the impact that the EU has had on the political development of the region. Arguably, the EU's regional policies in its own 'neighbourhood' have contributed to good governance and rule of law domestically, improved the capacity of civil institutions, and created a network of bilateral and multilateral commitments creating the foundation for the long-term stability along its eastern and southern periphery.

The policies of protection occupy the middle ground between the policies of assurance and prevention. Whenever the Schengen *acquis* is modified to strengthen the policing of the common external frontier, particularly in the fight against terrorism, the collective action problem is resolved by the Community method and enforced by the Commission's ability to institute infringement proceedings. The other categories of policy – penal law, judicial process, police and judicial cooperation, and the variety of issues falling under the rubric of protection – remain intergovernmental. The policies of protection present an acute collective action problem; the EU has only been partially successful in carving out an autonomous role for itself in shaping policy and coaxing its member states to comply with the variety of framework decisions and action plans governing a policy domain including health security, information and network security and money laundering. Even more difficult have been efforts to reconcile or harmonise penal law and judicial process, two policy domains that electorates expect to remain national in character. The EU, therefore, waivers between independence and dependence from the member states in seeking to create an area of 'justice, freedom and security'.

The EU has been successful, however, in securitising these policy domains, particularly the protection of critical infrastructure, bacteriological or viral contagions and financial crimes linked to organised crime or terrorism. The internalisation of security has created an understanding amongst the member states that heretofore components of national sovereignty have become the legitimate targets of EU legislation. Yet, the transposition of framework documents into national law remains dependent upon the good faith of the member governments; neither the Commission nor European Court of Justice has the legal standing to sanction infringements. Non-compliance remains problematic; the 'weakest link' technology of publicness characterising this dimension of security policy places limits on the EU as an autonomous actor. Article 226 TEC is not applicable in JHA and the states are not yet willing to accede to the Commission's proposal to rely upon the bridging clauses of Article 42 TEU and 67(2) TEC to lend the Commission the ability to sanction infringements of Hague Programme legislation.

One way in which the EU has been able to distance itself from the member states and exert an autonomous influence, however, is in the establishment of EU sponsored networks that intermediate relationships between national authorities, judicial or police, or eliminate the barrier posed by national borders to direct contacts formally segregated by strict jurisdictional boundaries created by national frontiers. The EU has also asserted a kind of autonomy with the progressive harmonisation of judicial and penal law within the Union and the creation of legal instruments valid throughout Europe, particularly the European arrest warrant, the European evidence warrant, and the guaranteed mutual access to a standardised criminal database. The growing reliance upon these legal instruments and the cooperation engendered by Europol, Eurojust and the Police Chiefs' Task Force will inevitably compel the application of the Community method to JHA, at least in those areas touching upon serious crime and terrorism. While the concrete achievements may appear limited in terms of results that are subject to measurement (the number of joint investigations or prosecutions, the level or incidence of serious crime and terrorism, or the failure to transpose precisely framework decisions, regulations or directives), the EU gained member state acknowledgement that it has an important role to play in crafting these policies and a critical role in coordinating member state policies.

The policies of protection are most vexed by the underlying security policy paradox confronting the EU and its member states: the necessity of joint action to meet the threats to internal security are unquestioned by the governing elites, yet the policy initiatives in this domain directly touch upon the daily lives of the national electorates in spheres impinging upon national political and legal cultures as well as prerogatives that governments still protect from EU encroachments. The policies of protection constitute the most important security domain today in view of the palpable threats posed by terrorism and organised crime. Moreover, the existing technology of publicness suggests that greater EU independence from the member states, most easily achieved with the introduction of the Community method into Pillar III, would ameliorate the collective action problem currently plaguing policy initiatives designed to enhance internal security on a Union-wide basis.

Perhaps surprisingly, the EU pursuit of common security policies falling under the rubric of the policies of compellence has been relatively successful. The success of those policies is surprising for at least two reasons: first, with the notable exceptions of Britain and France, the majority of the EU member states have gravitated towards a 'civilianised' foreign policy culture; second, the retention of sovereign prerogatives in defence has been often treated as the final barrier to the 'ever closer union' of the European peoples. The success enjoyed by the EU – witnessed by the growing number, size and variety of military interventions since 2002 – reflects not only the strongest pillar technology of publicness facilitating EU military interventions, but the recognition that Europe must play a larger regional and global role *if* it is to protect European interests and retain a close and mutually beneficial relationship with the United States.

Only the EU – with the critical support of Britain, France and now perhaps Germany – can coordinate the defence policies of its member states and thereby guarantee the long-term survival of a European defence industrial base and provide the necessary assurance that an intra-Union division of labour in force structure or weapons systems acquisition will not expose individual member states to an unacceptable level of risk. The EU provides the forum for mediating the intergovernmental negotiations and institutionalising intergovernmental bargains.

In the wake of the Anglo-French Saint Malo Declaration, the EU has enhanced Europe's military capabilities with the establishment, *inter alia*, of the Helsinki Headline Goals, thirteen battlegroups (the majority of which are multinational), the European Defence Agency, and an emerging institutional structure enabling the EU and the member states to decide jointly when to employ military force as well as the command and operational infrastructure to do so. The exercise of the military option under an EU flag nonetheless remains hedged and depends upon the good offices of the major member states. The EU member states have not pledged themselves to collective defence, the solidarity clause of the moribund EU Constitution notwithstanding. Despite the progress made towards the operational integration of the member state armed forces, the EU at present remains a coordinating mechanism for formulating and executing policies of compellence; the member states appear content to accept the trade-off between the dubious benefit of retaining national prerogatives at the considerable cost of diminished diplomatic leverage, economic inefficiency and military ineffectiveness.

The Europeans have met the American challenge to assume greater responsibility within the European security space and progressively delineated a new division of labour within the Atlantic Alliance, particularly as it pertains to the projection of force in southern Europe and Africa. Europe claimed responsibility for executing the Petersberg tasks within Europe and has committed itself to act on behalf of the UN under a Charter VII mandate, while relying upon NATO and the United States for meeting Article 5 obligations and conducting high-intensity warfare 'out of area'.

Conclusion: the European Union and the governance of Europe's security

The post-Cold War period has not provided much reassurance that the EU will consolidate its role as a foreign policy actor in Europe and the world. The national interest still takes precedence over the Community interest. One of the first major foreign policy challenges facing the EU was the ill-executed decision to recognise the dissolution of Yugoslavia. While the EU was able to hammer out a compromise that acknowledged the secession of Slovenia and Croatia from Yugoslavia, the rump Yugoslav state descended into chaos and a savage civil war. Europe's inability to manage such crises outside the EU demonstrated at that time the continued need for American leadership and NATO-led interventions in Bosnia (1995) and Kosovo (1999). In each case, American leadership and matériel rather than EU declarations cauterised the ethnic blood-lettings in the Balkans. Moreover, the EU played virtually no role in the run-up to Desert Storm despite the clear violation of international law and Kuwaiti sovereignty (which legitimised military intervention under a UN mandate) and the near certainty that the Iraqi absorption of Kuwait would inevitably disrupt international oil markets of particular concern to Europe. While the Germans were only able to write a cheque covering American expenses, France, Britain and other Europeans contributed troops under national flags rather as part of an EU contingent. The diplomacy prior to the invasion of Iraq in 2003 split the EU between those wishing to seek a diplomatic solution or were unconvinced that Iraq posed an imminent threat to European or American security (France and Germany) and those wishing to support the United States for narrow national calculations (the central and eastern European NATO states sought to curry favour with its major military ally) or from shared convictions (the Blair and Berlusconi governments in Britain and Italy, respectively). The policies of compellence have so far defined the limits of security cooperation under the aegis of the EU, while the policies of prevention and assurance identify the opportunities for security cooperation within the EU as well as the potential role the EU can play as an autonomous security actor on behalf of its member states. The policies of protection demonstrate the manifest need for the EU to emerge as an autonomous actor as well as the persistent barrier to such a role posed by distinct and divergent national political and legal cultures.

The scholarly treatments of the EU as a security actor range from those treating it as a cipher for promoting the national interest to those anticipating that the EU will emerge as an actor on the world stage autonomous from and representing its member states. These different assessments rest upon a perceived persistence of divergent strategic cultures or an emerging common European one. There are those who treat national strategic cultures as relatively fixed and incorrigibly national (Lindley-French, 2002; Rynning, 2003; and Longhurst and Zaborowski, 2005). Others, particularly Christoph Meyer (2005), Mette Eilstrup-Sangiovanni and Daniel Verdier (2005) and Janne Matlary (2006) detect instead a convergence of strategic cultures. While these two orientations are oppositional – the topic of analysis inevitably revolves around the prospects for a successful European Security and Defence Policy, it is of little practical consequence if divergent national security cultures reflect the dynamic of disparate material interests or the retarded development of ideational assimilation.[5] Both material interests and cultures can change; changes in material interests are likely to be in sudden response to an exogenous shock changing the context of action, while the process of ideational assimilation will be slow and evolutionary. It is clear that Europe has experienced a series of exogenous shocks that have changed the security calculations of its member states *and* there has been an ongoing process of ideational assimilation over the previous five decades. However, the underlying source of the disagreement between those detecting either a divergence or convergence in the European security culture is a function of the initial frame of reference: viz., a broad or narrow conceptualisation of security. Should security policy be restricted to the normative and instrumental values given to military force or should it encompass the entire range of threats to national security, ranging from territorial defence to guaranteeing the public health system after a bioterrorist event? We have chosen the latter definition of security; consequently, the convergence and divergence of national strategic cultures vary depending upon the character the threat these states face collectively and individually. The European Security Strategy reveals elements of a common EU security culture.[6] Those common elements emerge most markedly in the policies of assurance and prevention and to a lesser extent compellence. While differences remain, there is an underlying agreement on the principle of preventive engagement and a shared assessment that civilian instruments of statecraft are the preferable means to achieve the goal of regional stability, particularly along the EU's periphery. The absence of a complementary internal security strategy consolidating the plethora of programmes and action plans constituting the policies of protection is a major failing of the EU. Without such a strategy, EU and member state efforts in this policy domain will remain piecemeal and ineffective.

Regardless of the position taken on the limitations that national security cultures place on the EU as an autonomous security actor, the EU *does* remain a foreign policy objective for the majority of its members and retains an instrumental character. For the smaller European states, old and new, the EU provides a forum for shaping their own destiny and counter-balancing the material and diplomatic resources of the major powers. The major economic and military powers, however, have more compelling (yet divisive) rationales for supporting the development and consolidation of the EU's role as a security actor. Germany, despite the questionable claim it is undergoing a process of 'de-Europeanisation', still clings to its European avocation (Paterson, 2006); France views the EU as the basis for a European and French-led challenge to American capriciousness and Russian instability; and Britain still considers the EU as a channel for wielding global influence, for preventing regional mischief, and providing a potential security partner for the United States within the NATO framework. These divergences in motivation have not inhibited movement towards an autonomous European defence capability let alone the delegation of prevention and assurance policies to the EU.

The EU occupies a central and unique role in the governance of European security. The Council and the Commission have not only created a plethora of quasi-autonomous networks and institutions sapping the policy and sovereign prerogatives of the member states, but replaced the hierarchy of the Westphalian order with post-Westphalian heterarchy. This system of governance has not yet produced a clear division of labour between the EU and its member states, but it has gone beyond a system of governance where the EU and its member states simply govern the security environment concurrently and in parallel (Ekengren *et al.* 2006: 119–20). Instead, some policies remain largely reserved to the state (compellence) or have been claimed by the EU (assurance and prevention) or have an indeterminate and shifting status (protection). Thus, the EU performs as an increasingly autonomous security actor *and* functions as a clearing station for member states in their collective efforts to meet an array of security challenges. The EU has been given (or seized) responsibility for coordinating member state policies across the four security domains; the success of those coordination efforts, however, remains subject to member state acquiescence on most decisions touching upon the projection of force and the criminal justice system. The European governance system lends credence to those who argue that a state-centric analysis of contemporary security policy obscures more than it reveals. The EU member states have sanctioned the institutionalisation of principles eroding sovereign prerogatives in an effort to resolve the collection action problems attending the provision of security in the twenty-first century.

The four security policy domains constituting the empirical core of this study do demonstrate if anything the continuing force and vitality of the sovereignty principle, the persistent privileging of the state when invoking the principle of subsidiarity, and the dominance of intergovernmental bargaining in the two most important security policy arenas, compellence and protection. The empirical evidence also casts doubt on those claiming that multi-level governance has largely displaced intergovernmentalism, at least in security policy (Hooghe and Marks, 2003). The EU only acts autonomously in the formulation and implementation of civilian security policies directed towards stabilising the regional political and economic milieu. The emergence of the Commission as an autonomous actor reflects a confluence of member-state calculations: the Commission can lower the transaction costs of negotiating or implementing policies as compared to the process of intergovernmental bargaining; and the member states are less likely to expend energy and resources protecting sovereign prerogatives in those areas of security policy where the stakes are low enough that foreign policy 'failure' has no immediate or transparent domestic political repercussions. The limited autonomy of the Commission in formulating or executing the policies of protection and compellence can be largely explained as a byproduct of the EU treaty system: neither ESDP nor JHA are subject to the Community method. Consequently, the Commission – even when the Council reaches agreement on a common policy initiative – remains powerless to enforce those decisions and the decisions themselves usually contain an article providing that the grounds for non-compliance exist where compliance would jeopardise national security, no doubt an unintended irony.

What accounts for the unevenness in the jurisdictional boundaries established between the state and Union? The Europeans are vexed by a nettlesome policy paradox. The post-Westphalian character of the European state has impelled the Europeans to surrender sovereign prerogatives to the EU in order to meet the challenges of a broadened security agenda. This post-Westphalian impulse coexists with persistent Westphalian national identities, which have prevented the optimal transfer of sovereign prerogatives to the EU. Europe's societies and citizens have not made the transition to a post-national identity that would complement post-Westphalianism. The ratification of the Constitutional Treaty, particularly those articles eradicating the pillar structure of the Union and subjecting all policy areas to the Community method, would be as likely to retard as accelerate progress towards finding joint responses to common threats. Consequently, instead of lamenting the failure of the treaty, the EU and its member states should wish the treaty a good riddance and reconsider the persistent presence of national identities. National electorates, despite the inability of any individual European state to provide security alone, still expect their governments to remain directly responsible for ensuring their security from internal and external threats alike.

Notes

1   The capabilities-expectations gap also generates a capabilities-expectations paradox; viz., the more the EU achieves in the area of foreign and security policy, the more will be expected of it. It is likely that expectations will inevitably outstrip capabilities. See Sperling, 2001b: 143–4.
2   A factor aggravating the persistence of weakest link technologies in security is the inability (or unwillingness) to expel or sanction a chronic free-rider; this characteristic of the EU could debilitate efforts to achieve policy harmonisation across any number of issue areas.
3   Whereas Sandler uses the terminology 'best shot', we use 'strongest pillar'. This change in nomenclature reflects two concerns: first, 'best shot' technologies are associated with collective goods that are most likely to be provided when resources are concentrated (e.g., devoting scare resources to a major research hospital to find a cure for cancer rather than spreading

the research funds across a large number of labs). Our concern is whether some security tasks facing the EU are better assumed by a small group of states – in effect encouraging free-riding for the common good – and whether some security tasks can only be executed if the largest states participate owing to political, diplomatic or financial economies of scale (e.g., in the provision of integrated force projection capabilities). Second, strongest pillar, unlike best shot, reproduces the weight or force-bearing metaphor evoked by 'weakest link'.

4   The subsidiary 'principle of mutual responsibility' complements solidarity: states accepted that their national security policies should not be confined 'to maintaining their own security, but . . . focus also on the security of the Union as a whole'. This principle placed a positive obligation on the member states to consider the EU-wide security ramifications of national policy decisions and contributed to a collective understanding of the content and form of threats.

5   For an overview of the debate between 'realists' and 'constructivists', see Eilstrup and Verdier, 2005: 102–04.

6   This argument is fully developed in Kirchner, 2007.

Bibliography

Books and articles

Adler, E. and Barnett, M.N. (1998) 'A framework for the study of security communities', in E. Adler and M. Barnett (eds), *Security Communities* (Cambridge: Cambridge University Press).

Albrecht, U. *et al.* (2004) 'A Human Security Doctrine for Europe: The Barcelona Report of the Study Group on Europe's Security Capabilities', Barcelona, 15 September 2004, available at www.cercle.lu/article.php3?id_article=588 (accessed 13 September 2005).

Alecu de Flers, N. and Regelsberger, E. (2005) 'The EU and inter-regional cooperation', in C. Hill and M. Smith (eds), *International Relations and the European Union* (Oxford: Oxford University Press).

Aliboni, R. (2004) 'Common languages on democracy in the Euro-Mediterranean Partnership', *EuroMeSCo Paper*, 31.

Babarinde, O. and Faber, G. (2004) 'From Lomé to Cotonou: Business as usual?', *European Foreign Affairs Review*, 9:1.

Baldwin, D. (1997) 'The concept of security', *Review of International Studies*, 32:1.

Barnett, M. and Duvall, R. (eds) (2005) *Power in Global Governance* (Cambridge: Cambridge University Press).

Baumann, R., Rittberger, V. and Wagner, W. (2001) 'Neorealist foreign policy theory', in V. Rittberger (ed.), *German Foreign Policy since Unification: Theories and Case Studies* (Manchester: Manchester University Press).

Béchat, J.-P. and Rohatyn, F. G. (eds) (2003) *The Future of the Transatlantic Defense Community* (Washington, DC: CSIS).

Bertram, C., Boyer, Y., Heisbourg, F. and Schild, J. (2002) *Starting Over: For a Franco-German Initiative in European Defence* (Berlin: Stiftung Wissenschaft und Politik).

Bianchini, S., Marko, J., Craig, R., Privitera, F. and Uvalie, M. (2006) 'Concluding remarks of the Forli International Conference', Forli, 20–21 January 2006.

Bildt, C. (2005) 'Europe Must Keep Its Soft Power', *Financial Times*, 1 June 2005, available at www.christusrex.org/www1/news/ft-6-1-05b.html (accessed 12 August 2006).

Biscop, S. (2005) *The European Security Strategy: A Global Agenda for Positive Power* (Aldershot: Ashgate).

Biscop, S. (2004) 'The European Security Strategy: Implementing a distinctive approach to security', *Sécurité & Stratégie*, paper 82.

Boin, A. and Rhinard, M. (eds) (2005) 'Shocks without frontiers: Transnational breakdowns and critical accidents', *EPC Issue Paper*, 42.

Boulding, K. (1962) *Conflict and Defence* (New York: Harper and Row).

Brenner, M. (2002) 'Europe's new security vocation', *McNair Paper*, 66 (Washington, DC: Institute for National Strategic Studies and National Defense University).

Bulletin Quotidien Europe (2005a) 'European Parliament resolution on the annual report from the Council of to the European Parliament on the main aspects and basic choices of CFSP, including the financial implications for the general budget of the European Communities', Europe Documents, 22 April 2005.

Bulletin Quotidien Europe (2005b) '(EU)EU/Iran/Nuclear: Hassan Rowhani recommends EU-3 to not rule out the Iranian Proposal on limited uranium enrichment activities, in effort to keep negotiations on track', 21 April 2005.

Bulletin Quotidien Europe (2005c) '(EU)EU/Iran/Nuclear: Iranians believe new negotiations steering committee meeting should allow for progress', 29 April 2005.

Bulmer, S., Jeffery, C. and Paterson, W. E. (2000) *Germany's European Diplomacy: Shaping the Regional Milieu* (Manchester: Manchester University Press).

Bundeswehr (2004) 'Finanzplanung Einzelplan 14', available at www. bundeswehr.de/pic/forces/040623_500_finanzplan114.gif (accessed 17 November 2004).

Busek, E. (2004) 'Presentation at the Royal Institute of International Affairs, Delivered at Chatham House', London, 17 December, available at www. stabilitypact.org/pages/speeches/detail.asp?y=2004&p=16 (accessed 12 August 2006).

Buzan, B., Wæver, O. and de Wilde, J. (1998) *Security: A New Framework for Analysis* (Boulder, CO: Lynne Rienner).

Cameron, F. and Rhein, E. (2005) 'Promoting political and economic reform in the Mediterranean and Middle East', *EPC Issue Paper*, 33.

Caporaso, J. (2000) 'Changes in the Westphalian order: Territory, public authority, and sovereignty', *International Studies Review* (Special Issue: Continuity and Change in the Westphalian Order), 2:2.

Caporaso, J. (1996) 'The European Union and forms of state: Westphalian, regulatory or post-modern?', *Journal of Common Market Studies*, 34:1.

Chauvet, L. and Collier, P. (2004) *Development Effectiveness in Fragile States: Spillovers and Turnarounds* (Oxford: Oxford University Centre for the Study of African Economies).

Checkel, J. T. (1998) 'The constructivist turn in international relations theory', *World Politics*, 50:2.

Christensen, T. J. and Snyder, J. (1990) 'Chain gangs and passed bucks: Predicting alliance patterns in multipolarity', *International Organization*, 44:2.

Congressional Budget Office (2003) *Congressional Budget FY 2003: National Nuclear Security* (Washington, DC: GPO).

Cooper, R. (2003) *The Breaking of Nations: Order and Chaos in the Twenty-first Century* (London: Atlantic Books).

Cottey, A. and Averre, D. (eds) (2002) *New Security Challenges in Postcommunist Europe: Securing Europe's East* (Manchester: Manchester University Press).

Cottey, A., Edwards, T. and Forster, A. (2002) 'Beyond Prague', *NATO Review*, 50:3.

Cronin, D. (2005) 'UN fears battle groups will cut numbers of EU peacekeepers', *European Voice*, 26 May–1 June: 6.

Dannreuther, R. (ed.) (2004) *European Union Foreign and Security Policy: Towards a Neighbourhood Strategy* (London: Taylor and Francis).

Den Boer, M. and Monar, J. (2002) 'Keynote article: 11 September and the challenge of global terrorism to the EU as a security actor', *Journal of Common Market Studies*, 40: annual review.

de Wijk, R. (2000) 'Convergence criteria: Measuring input or output', *European Foreign Affairs Review*, 5:3.

Dekker-Bellamy, J. S. (2004) 'Defining a European approach to preventing bio-terrorism: Health security policy in the 21st century', *New Defence Agenda Background Report* (Bioterrorism Reporting Group).

Economist, The (2006) 'Germany's armed forces: Abroad, by inches', 29 July 2006.

Edwards, G. (1997) 'The potential and limits of the CFSP: The Yugoslav example', in E. Regelsberger, P. de Schoutheete and W. Wessels (eds), *Foreign Policy of the European Union* (Boulder, CO: Lynne Rienner).

Egmont Group (2004) *Statement of Purpose*, Guernsey, 23 June 2004.

Egmont Group (2001) *Principles for Information Exchange between Financial Intelligence Units for Money Laundering Cases*, The Hague, 13 June 2001.

Eilstrup-Sangiovanni, E. and Verdier, D. (2005) 'European integration as a solution to war', *European Journal of International Relations*, 11:1.

Ekengren, M., Matzén, N. and Svantesson, M. (2006) *The New Security Role of the European Union: Transnational Crisis Management and the Protection of Union Citizens* (Stockholm: National Defence College).

Embassy of France in the United States (2005) 'Reform of French National Defense', at www.ambafrance-us.org/atoz/ref_def.asp (accessed 16 August 2006).

Embassy of France in the United States (2002) 'French Defense Overview', available at www.ambafrance-us.org/intheus/defense/defense.asp (accessed 16 August 2006).

'EU–US Declaration on Combating Terrorism', Dromoland Castle, 26 June 2004. G8, 'G8 Counter-Terrorism Cooperation since September 11', available at http: //www.mofa.go.jp/policy/economy/summit/2002/coop_terro.html.

Everts, S (2004) 'The ultimate test case: Can Europe and America forge a joint strategy for the wider Middle East?', *International Affairs*, 80:4.

Falk, R. (2002) 'Revisiting Westphalia, discovering post-Westphalia', *Journal of Ethics*, 6:4.

Faria, F. (2004) 'Crisis management in sub-Saharan Africa: The role of the European Union', *ISS–EU Occasional Paper*, 51 (Paris: Institute for Security Studies).

Ferrero-Waldner, B. (2005) 'The role of crisis response in external relations: From needs to solutions: Enhancing civilian crisis response capacity of the European Union', speech/05/684, Brussels, 14 November 2005.

Financial Action Task Force on Money Laundering (2004) *Annual Report, 2003–2004* (Paris: OECD).

Fuller, T. (2004) 'EU Looks on Warily as Its Eastern Neighbours Move In: Under One Flag', *The International Herald Tribune*, 29 April 2004 (accessed via Lexis-Nexis Executive).

G8 (2002) 'G8 Counter-terrorism Cooperation since September 11', available at www.mofa.go.jp/policy/economy/summit/2002/coop_terro.html (accessed 15 July 2005).

Gilpin, R. (1981) *War and Change in World Politics* (Princeton: Princeton University Press).

Goertz, G. (1994) *Contexts of International Politics* (Cambridge: Cambridge University Press).

Gomez, R. and G. Christou (2004) 'Economic foreign policy: The EU and the Mediterranean', in W. Carlsnaes, H. Sjursen, and B. White (eds), *Contemporary European Foreign Policy* (London: Sage).

Gonzales, K. W. (2004) 'Good fences make good neighbours: Ukrainian border security and western assistance', *Problems of Post-Communism*, 51:1.

Gouvras, G. (2002) 'Bioterrorism: Action by the European Community', European Health Forum Gastein, 25–28 September.

Graham, K. (2004) 'Towards effective multilateralism. The EU and the UN: Partners in crisis management', *EPC Working Paper*, 13.

Green, P. (1966) *Deadly Logic: The Theory of Nuclear Deterrence* (Columbus: Ohio State University Press).

Haine, J.-Y. (ed.) (2003) 'From Laeken to Copenhagen. European Defence: Core documents, vol. III', *Chaillot Paper*, 57 (Paris: Institute for Security Studies).

Hall, R. and Fox, C. (2001/2002) 'Rethinking security', *NATO Review*, 49:4.

Hampton, M. (1998/1999) 'NATO, Germany, and the United States: Creating positive identity in trans-Atlantia', *Security Studies* (special double issue), 8:2/3.

Hampton, M. and Sperling, J. (2002) 'Positive/negative identity: Europe's future, Germany's past?', *Journal of European Integration*, 24:4.

Hänggi, H. and Tanner, F. (2005) 'Promoting security sector governance in the EU's neighborhood', *EU–ISS Chaillot Paper*, 80.

Hanrieder, W. F. (1989) *Germany, Europe, America: The Foreign Policy of the Federal Republic of Germany, 1949–1989* (New Haven: Yale University Press).

Hanrieder, W. F. (1978) 'Dissolving international politics: Reflections on the nation-state', *American Political Science Review*, 72:4.

Harnisch, S. and Linden, R. (2005) 'German foreign policy', *Dialogue*, 6:17.

Hartley, K. (2006) 'Defence industrial policy in a military alliance', *Journal of Peace Research*, 43:4.

Heisbourg, F., Daguzan, J.-F., Lundmark, M. and Masson, H. (2003) 'The European industrial base and ESDP', in F. Heisbourg *et al.* (eds), *Prospects on the European Defence Industry* (Athens: Defence Analysis Institute).

Herz, J. H. (1957) 'The rise and demise of the territorial state', *World Politics*, 9:4.

Hill, C. (2001) 'The EU's Capacity for Conflict Prevention', *European Foreign Affairs Review*, 6:3.

Hill, C. (1994) 'The capabilities-expectations gap, or conceptualizing Europe's international role', in S. Bulmer and A. Scott (eds), *Economic and Political Integration in Europe* (Oxford: Blackwell).

Hill, C. (1993) 'The capability-expectations gap, or conceptualizing Europe's international role', *Journal of Common Market Studies*, 31:3.

Hill, C. and Smith, M. (2005) 'Acting for Europe? Reassessing international relations and the EU', in C. Hill and M. Smith (eds), *International Relations and the European Union* (Oxford: Oxford University Press).

Hoffmann, S. (1998) *World Disorders: Troubled Peace in the Post-Cold War Era* (Lanham, MD: Rowman & Littlefield Publishers, Inc.).

Holsti, K. J. (1991) *Peace and War: Armed Conflicts and International Order, 1648–1989* (Cambridge: Cambridge University Press).

Hombach, B. (1999) 'The Stability Pact: Breaking new ground in the Balkans', *NATO Review*, 47:4.

Hooghe, L. and Marks, G. (2003) 'Unraveling the central state, but how? Types of multi-level governance', *American Political Science Review*, 97:2.

Hopf, Ted (1998) 'The promise of constructivism in international relations theory', *International Security*, 23:1.

House of Lords/Select Committee on European Union (2005) 'Fourth Report: EU Battlegroups', 19 February 2005, available at www.publications. parliament.uk/pa/1d200506/1dselect/1deucom/16/16100.htm (accessed 19 July 2006).

Howorth, J. (2003) 'Why ESDP is necessary and beneficial for the Alliance', in J. Howorth and J. T. S. Keeler (eds), *Defending Europe: The EU, NATO and the Quest for Autonomy* (Basingstoke: Palgrave).

IAEA (2003) 'Nuclear security: Measures to protect against nuclear terrorism', GC(47)17, 20 August 2003.

IAEA (2002) 'Nuclear security: Progress on measures to protect against nuclear terrorism', GOV/INF/2002/11-GC(46)/14, 12 August 2002.

IAEA (n.d.) 'IAEA Illicit Trafficking Database (ITDB)'.

Ideas Factory Europe (2004) 'European security: No strategy without politics', *European Policy Centre Ideas Factory Report*, 4.

IISS (2003) *The Military Balance, 2003–2004* (Oxford: Oxford University Press).

Jepperson, R., Wendt, A. and Katzenstein, P. J. (1996) 'Norms, identity, culture and national security', in P. J. Katzenstein (ed.), *The Culture of National Security: Norms and Identity in World Politics* (New York: Columbia University Press).

Jervis, Robert (2002) 'Theories of war in an era of leading power peace', *American Political Science Review*, 96:1.

Jimeno-Bulnes, M. (2003) ' European judicial cooperation in criminal matters', *European Law Journal*, 9:5.

Judah, T. (2006) 'The EU must keep its promise to the Western Balkans', Centre for European Reform essays, July 2006.

Justice and Home Affairs Council (2006) 'First report on the Hague Programme'.

Kagan, R. (2003) *Of Paradise and Power: America and Europe in the New World Order* (New York: Knopf).

Keohane, R. (2001) 'Governance in a partially globalized world', *American Political Science Review*, 95:1.

Keohane, R. (1988) 'International institutions: Two approaches', *International Studies Quarterly*, 32:4.

Kirchner, E. J. (2007) 'EU: The European Security Strategy versus national preferences', in E. J. Kirchner and J. Sperling (eds), *Global Security Governance: Competing Perceptions of Security in the 21st Century* (London: Routledge).

Kirchner, E. J. (2006) 'The challenge of European Union security governance', *Journal of Common Market Studies*, 44:5.

Kirchner, E. J. and Sperling, J. (eds) (2007) *Global Security Governance: Competing Perceptions of Security in the 21st Century* (London: Routledge).

Kirchner, E. J. and Sperling, J. (2002) 'The new security threats in Europe: Theory and evidence', *European Foreign Affairs Review*, 7:4.

Knaus G. and Cox, M. (2004) 'Bosnia and Herzegovina: Europeanisation by decree', *Chaillot Paper*, 70 (Paris: Institute for Security Studies).

Koremenos, B., Lipson, C. and Snidal, D. (2001) 'The rational design of international institutions', *International Organization*, 55:4.

Krahmann, E. (2003) 'Conceptualising security governance', *Cooperation and Conflict*, 38:1.

Krasner, S. D. (2001) 'Abiding sovereignty', *International Political Science Review*, 22:3.

Krasner, S. D. (1999) *Sovereignty: Organized Hypocrisy* (Princeton: Princeton University Press).

Krasner, S. D. (1995/1996) 'Compromising Westphalia', *International Security*, 20:3.

Krasner, S. D. and Pascual, C. (2005) 'Addressing state failure', *Foreign Affairs*, 84:4.

Krause, K. (1998) 'Theorising security, state formation and the "third world" in the post-Cold War world', *Review of International Studies*, 24:1.

Laffan, B., O'Donnell, R. and Smith, M. (2000) *Europe's Experimental Union: Rethinking Integration* (London: Routledge).

Langer, W. L. (1950) *European Alliances and Alignments* (New York: Random House, 2nd edn).

Lehne, S. (2004) 'Has the "hour of Europe" come at last? The EU's strategy for the Balkans', *Chaillot Paper*, 70 (Paris: Institute for Security Studies).

Leonard, M. and Gowan, R. (2004) 'Global Europe: Implementing the Security Strategy', *Foreign Policy Centre Articles*, available at http://fpc.org.uk/fsblob/187.pdf (accessed 7 August 2006).

Lindley-French, J. (2002) 'In the shade of Locarno: Why European defence is failing', *International Affairs*, 78:4.

Lindstrom, G. (2005) 'EU–US burdensharing: Who does what', *EU–ISS Chaillot Paper*, 82 (Paris: Institute for Security Studies).

Lindstrom, G. (2004) 'Protecting the European homeland: The CBR dimension', *EU–ISS Chaillot Paper*, 69 (Paris: Institute for Security Studies).

Liska, G. (1962) *Nations in Alliance: The Limits of Interdependence* (Baltimore: Johns Hopkins University Press).

Longhurst, K. and Zaborowski, M. (2005) *Old Europe, New Europe and the Transatlantic Security Agenda* (London: Routledge).

Lynch, D. (2003) 'The South Caucasus: A challenge for Europe', *Chaillot Paper*, 65 (Paris: Institute for Security Studies).

Macdonald, N. and Wagstyl, S. (2007) 'UN's Kosovo compromise leaves both sides frustrated', *Financial Times* 13 February 2007.

Macfarlane, N. (2004) 'The Caucasus and Central Asia: Towards a non-strategy', in R. Dannreuther (ed.), *European Union Foreign and Security Policy: Towards a Neighbourhood Strategy* (London: Routledge).

March, J. G. and Olsen, J. P. (1998) 'The institutional dynamics of international political orders', *International Organization*, 52:4.

Martenczuk, B. (2000) 'From Lomé to Cotonou: The ACP–EC Partnership Agreement in a legal perspective', *European Foreign Affairs Review*, 5:4.

Martin, L. L. and Simmons, B. A. (1998) 'Theories and empirical studies of international institutions', *International Organization*, 52:4.

Matlary, J. H. (2006) 'When soft power turns hard: Is an EU strategic culture possible?', *Security Dialogue*, 27:1.

Maull, H. W. (2005) 'Europe and the new balance of global order', *International Affairs*, 81:4.

Meiers, F.-J. (1999) 'A German defence review', in G. Wilson (ed.), *European Force Structures*, Occasional Paper, 8 (Paris: Institute for Security Studies).

Menon, A. (2003) 'Why ESDP is misguided and dangerous to the Alliance', in J. Howorth and J. T. S. Keeler (eds), *Defending Europe: The EU, NATO and the Quest for European Autonomy* (Basingstoke: Palgrave).

Merlinger, M. and Ostrauskaite, R. (2005) 'ESDP police missions: Meaning, context and operational challenges', *European Foreign Affairs Review*, 10:2.

Meyer, C. O. (2005) 'Convergence towards a European Strategic Culture? A constructivist framework for explaining changing norms', *European Journal of International Relations*, 11:4.

Ministry of Defence (2003) 'Delivering security in a changing world: Defence white paper', London, December 2003, cmnd 6041.

Ministry of Defence (2002) 'The Strategic Defence Review: A new chapter, Volume 1', London, July 2002, cmnd 5566.

Ministry of Defence (1998) 'Strategic Defence Review', July 1998, cmnd3999, available at www.mod.uk/DefenceInternet/AboutDefence/CorporatePublications/PolicyStrategyandPlanning/StrategicDefenceReview.htm (accessed 17 August 2006).

Missiroli, A. (2004) 'The EU and its changing neighbourhood: Stabilization, integration and partnership', in R. Dannreuther (ed.), *European Union Foreign and Security Policy: Towards a Neighbourhood Strategy* (London: Routledge).

Missiroli, A. (ed.) (2003a) 'From Copenhagen to Brussels. European defence: Core documents, vol. III', *Chaillot Paper*, 67 (Paris: Institute for Security Studies).

Missiroli, A. (2003b) 'Ploughshares into swords? More euros for European defence', *European Foreign Affairs Review*, 8:1.

Mitrakas, A. (2006) 'Information security and law in Europe: Risks checked?', *Information and Communications Technology Law*, 15:1.

Monaco, A. (2004) 'Bosnia: The litmus-test for the NATO–EU strategic relationship?', *ISIS Europe*, 6:2.

Monar, J. (2004) 'Justice and Home Affairs', *Journal of Common Market Studies*, 42: Annual Review.

Mörth, U. and Britz, M. (2004) 'European integration as organizing: The case of armaments', *Journal of Common Market Studies*, 52:5.

Most, B. A. and Starr, H. (1980) 'Diffusion, reinforcement, geopolitics, and the spread of war', *American Political Science Review*, 74:4.

Müller-Wille, B. (2004) 'For our eyes only? Shaping an intelligence community with the EU', *Occasional Paper*, 50 (Paris: Institute for Security Studies).

NATO (2003a) 'Table 3: Defence Expenditures as % of Gross Domestic Product', available at www.nato.int/docu/pr/2003/table3.pdf (accessed 17 November 2004).

NATO (2003b) 'Table 5. Distribution of Total Defence Expenditures by Category', available at www.nato.int/docu/pr/2003/table5.pdf (accessed 17 November 2004).

NATO (2002) 'Statement on capabilities', 6 June 2002, press release (2002)074.

North Atlantic Council (1999) 'The alliance strategic concept', Washington, DC, 23–24 April.

North Atlantic Council (1991), 'The new strategic concept', Rome, 7–8 November.

Nuttall, S. (2005) 'Coherence and consistency', in C. Hill and M. Smith (eds), *International Relations and the European Union* (Oxford: Oxford University Press).

Nuttal, S. (1992) *European Political Cooperation* (Oxford: Clarendon).

Ojanen, H. (2006) 'The EU and the UN: A shared future', *FIIA Report*, 13.

Ortega, M. (2005) 'The European Union and the United Nations: Partners in effective multilateralism', *Chaillot Paper*, 78 (Paris: Institute for Security Studies).

OSCE (1999) 'Istanbul Document: Charter for European Security', Istanbul, November 1999, available at www.osce.org/documents/mcs/1999/11/4050_en.pdf (accessed 23 June 2004).

Osgood, R. E. (1962) *NATO: The Entangling Alliance* (Chicago: University of Chicago Press).

Osiander, A. (2001) 'Sovereignty, international relations, and the Westphalian myth', *International Organization*, 55:2.

Paris, R. (2004) *At War's End: Building Peace after Civil Conflict* (Cambridge: Cambridge University Press).

Paterson, W.E. (2006) 'Germany: Does it still have a European avocation?', paper delivered at the 2006 annual meeting of the American Political Science Association, Philadelphia, PA, 30 August–3 September.

Pentland, C. (2000) 'Westphalian Europe and the EU's last enlargement', *Journal of European Integration*, 22:3.

Pippan, C. (2004) 'The rocky road to Europe: The EU's stabilisation and association process for the Western Balkans and the principle of conditionality', *European Foreign Affairs Review*, 9:2.

Plate, B. von (2003) *Die Zukunft des transatlantischen Verhältnisses: Mehr als die NATO* (Berlin: Stiftung Wissenschaft und Politik).

Posch, W. (ed.) (2005) 'Looking into Iraq', *Chaillot Paper*, 79 (Paris: Institute for Security Studies).

Powell, R. (1991) 'Absolute and relative gains in international relations theory', *American Political Science Review*, 85:4.

Quille, G. (2004) 'The European Security Strategy: A framework for EU security interest?', *International Peacekeeping*, 11:3.

Ramboll Management (2005) 'Ex post evaluation of Grotius II, Oisin II, STOP II, Falcone and Hippocrates Programmes and Interim Evaluation of the AGIS programme', study commissioned by the European Commission.

Ranck, H. and Schmitt, B. (2005) 'Threat assessment', in B. Schmitt (ed.), 'Information security: A new challenge for the EU', *Chaillot Paper*, 76 (Paris: Institute for Security Studies).

Rees, W. and Aldrich, R. J. (2005) 'Contending cultures of counterterrorism: Transatlantic divergence or convergence?', *International Affairs*, 81:5.

Risse, T. (1995) *Cooperation among Democracies. The European Influence on U.S. Foreign Policy* (Princeton: Princeton University Press).

Rohde, J. and Frenzel, M. (2003) 'Transatlantic gaps and European armaments cooperation', in *Prospects on the European Defence Industry* (Athens: Defence Analysis Institute).

Rosenau, J. N. (2000) 'Change, complexity, and governance in globalizing space', in J. Pierre (ed.), *Debating Governance: Authority, Steering and Democracy* (Oxford: Oxford University Press).

Rosenau, J. N. (1997) *Along the Domestic–Foreign Frontier: Exploring Governance in a Turbulent World* (Cambridge: Cambridge University Press).

Rosenau, J. N. (1992) 'Governance, order, and change in world politics', in J. N. Rosenau and E.-O. Czempiel (eds), *Governance without Government: Order and Change in World Politics* (Cambridge: Cambridge University Press).

Ruggie, J. G. (1986) 'Continuity and transformation in the world polity: Toward a neo-realist synthesis', in R. O. Keohane (ed.), *Neorealism and Its Critics* (New York: Columbia University Press).

Rummel, R. (2004) 'Conflict prevention: Making EU talents work', Working Paper FG 2, 2004/3, Research Unit EU External Relations, Stiftung Wissenschaft und Politik, German Institute for International and Security Studies.

Rummel, R. and Wiedemann, J. (1998) 'Identifying institutional paradoxes of CFSP', in J. Zielonka (ed.), *Paradoxes of European Foreign Policy* (The Hague: Kluwer Law International).

Rusi, A. (2001) 'Europe's changing security role', in H. Gärtner, A. Hyde-Price, and E. Reiter (eds), *Europe's New Security Challenges* (Boulder, CO: Lynne Rienner).

Rutten, M. (ed.) (2002) 'From Nice to Laeken. European defence: Core documents, vol. II', *Chaillot Paper*, 51 (Paris: Institute for Security Studies).

Rutten, M. (ed.) (2001) 'From St.-Malo to Nice. European defence: Core documents', *Chaillot Paper*, 47 (Paris: Institute for Security Studies).

Rynning, S. (2003) 'The European Union: Towards a strategic culture?', *Security Dialogue*, 34:4.

Saferworld International Alert (2005) 'Developing EU Strategy to Address Fragile States: Priorities for the UK Presidency of the EU in 2005', available at www.saferworld.org.uk/publications.php?id=18 (accessed 12 August 2006).

Sandler, T. (1992) *Collective Action: Theory and Application* (New York: Harvester Wheatsheaf).

Schmitt, B. (2005) *Defence Expenditures* (Paris: ISS).

Schweller, R. (1998) *Deadly Imbalances: Tripolarity and Hitler's Strategy of World Conquest* (New York: Columbia University Press).

Secretary of Defense (2003) 'Report on allied contributions to the common defense', Washington, DC, July 2003.

Shelley, L. I. (2003) 'Organized crime, terrorism and cybercrime', in H. Born, M. Caparini and P. Fluri (eds), *Security Sector Reform: Institutions, Society and Good Governance* (Baden-Baden: Nomos Verlag).

SIPRI (2006) 'Appendix. Table 8B: Military Expenditure, by Category', available at http://yearbook2006.sipri.org/chap8/app8b (accessed 20 August 2006).

SIPRI (2003) *SIPRI Yearbook 2003: Armaments, Disarmament and International Security* (London: Oxford University Press).

Siverson, R. M. and Starr, H. (1990) 'Opportunity, willingness, and the diffusion of war', *American Political Science Review*, 84:1.

Smith, H. (1998) 'Actually existing foreign policy – or not? The EU in Latin and Central America', in J. Peterson and H. Sjursen (eds), *A Common Foreign Policy for Europe? Competing Visions of the CFSP* (London: Routledge).

Smith, K. E. (2005) 'The outsiders: The European Neighbourhood Policy', *International Affairs*, 81:4.

Smith, K. E. (1998) 'The use of political conditionality in the EU's relations with third countries: How effective?', *European Foreign Affairs Review*, 3:2.

Smith, M. (2005) 'Implementation: Making the EU's international relations work', in C. Hill and M. Smith (eds), *International Relations and the European Union* (Oxford: Oxford University Press).

Smith, M.E. (2004) *Europe's Foreign and Security Policy: The Institutionalization of Cooperation* (Cambridge, Cambridge University Press).

Smith, M. (2003) 'The framing of European foreign and security policy: Towards a post-modern policy framework?', *Journal of European Public Policy*, 10:4.

Snyder, G. H. (1991) 'Alliances, balance, and stability', *International Organization*, 45:1.

Solana, J. (2004) ' "Remarks", at the informal meeting of defence ministers', Brussels, 5–6 April 2004, S0097/04.

Solana, J. (2003a) *A Secure Europe in Better World: European Security Strategy* (Brussels: European Union Institute for Security Studies).

Solana, J. (2003b) 'The EU security strategy: Implications for Europe's role in a changing world', EUHR Speech, Berlin, 12 November 2003, available at www.foreignpolicy.org.tr/documents/solana_121103_p.htm (accessed 14 August 2006).

Sperling, J. (2007) 'State attributes and system properties: Security multilateralism in Central Asia, Southeast Asia, the Atlantic and Europe', in D. Bourantonis, K. Ifantis and P. Tsakonas (eds), *Multilateralism and Security Institutions in an Era of Globalization* (London: Routledge).

Sperling, J. (2006) 'Capabilities gaps and traps: Symptoms or cause of a troubled Atlantic relationship?', in M. A. Smith (ed.), *Where Is NATO Going?* (London: Routledge).

Sperling, J. (2004) 'The foreign policy of the Berlin Republic: The very model of a post-modern major power?', *German Politics*, 12:3.

Sperling, J. (2003) 'Eurasian security governance: New threats, institutional adaptations', in J. Sperling, S. Kay and S. V. Papacosma (eds), *Limiting Institutions? The Challenge of Eurasian Security Governance* (Manchester: Manchester University Press).

Sperling, J. (2001a) 'The United States: Strategic vision or tactical planning?', in M. A. Smith and G. Timmins (eds), *Uncertain Europe: Building a New European Security Order?* (London: Routledge).

Sperling, J. (2001b) 'European Union foreign policy: Still an oxymoron?', in S. W. Hook (ed.), *Comparative Foreign Policy: Adaptation Strategies of the Great and Emerging Powers* (New York: Prentice Hall).

Sperling, J. and E. Kirchner (1998) 'Economic security and the problem of cooperation in post Cold War Europe', *Review of International Studies*, 24:2.

Sperling, J. and E. Kirchner (1997) *Recasting the European Order: Security Architectures and Economic Cooperation* (Manchester: Manchester University Press).

Stålenheim, P. (2003) 'Appendix.Table 10B: NATO military expenditure, by category', *SIPRI Yearbook 2003*.

Tanner, F. (2004) 'North Africa: Partnership, exceptionalism and neglect', in R. Dannreuther (ed.), *European Union Foreign and Security Policy: Towards a Neighbourhood Strategy* (London: Routledge).

Tardy, T. (2005) 'EU–UN cooperation in peacekeeping: A promising relationship in a constrained environment, *Chaillot Paper*, 78 (Paris: Institute for Security Studies).

Taylor, A. J. P. (1954) *The Struggle for Mastery of Europe, 1848–1918* (Oxford: Clarendon Press).

Tegnell, A., Bossi, P., Baka, A., Van Loock, F., Hendriks, J., Wallyn, S. and Gouvras, G. (2003) 'The European Commission's task force on bioterrorism', *Emerging Infectious Diseases*, 9:10.

Tovias, A. and Ugur, M. (2004) 'Can the EU anchor policy reform in third countries? An analysis of the Euro–Med Partnership', *European Union Politics*, 5:4.

UK Parliament Select Committee on Defence (2002) 'Seventh Report', available at www.publications.parliament.uk/pa/cm200102/cmselect/cmdfence/914/91402.htm (accessed 17 August 2006).

UK Parliament Select Committee on Defence (1999) 'Joint Declaration Launching European Defence Capabilities Initiative, UK–Italian Summit', 19–20 July 1999, available at www.publications.parliament.uk/pa/cm199900/cmselect/cmdfence/264/26422.htm (accessed 16 August 2006).

UN (1999) 'International Convention for the Suppression of the Financing of Terrorism', available at www.un.org/law/cod/finterr.htm (accessed 28 August 2006).

US Department of State (2000) 'Cumulative expenditures (FY 1992 to date) for major NIS assistance programs by country as of 9/30/00'.

USA Today (2005) 'Iran seeks talks with Europe on uranium', *USA Today*, 14 August 2005.

US–CREST (2002) 'Future military coalitions: The transatlantic challenge. Report of a French–German–UK–US Working Group' (Arlington, VA: US–CREST).

Wæver, O. (1998) 'Security, insecurity and asecurity', in E. Adler and M. N. Barnett (eds), *Security Communities* (Cambridge: Cambridge University Press).

Wæver, O. (1995) 'Securitization and desecuritization', in R. Lipschutz (ed.), *On Security* (New York: Columbia University Press).

Wallace H. and Wallace, W. (1997) *Policy-making in the European Union* (Oxford: Oxford University Press).

Wallensteen, P. and Sollenberg, M. (2001) 'Armed conflict, 1989–2000', *Journal of Peace Research*, 38:5.

Walt, S. (1987) *The Origins of Alliances* (Ithaca: Cornell University Press).

Waltz, K. (1978) *Theory of International Politics* (New York: Random House).

Webber, M. (2002) 'Security governance and the "excluded" states of Central and Eastern Europe', in A. Cottey and D. Averre (eds), *Ten Years after 1989: New Security Challenges in Central and Eastern Europe* (Manchester: Manchester University Press).

Webber, M. (2000) 'A tale of a decade: European security governance and Russia', *European Security*, 9:2.

Webber, M., Croft, S., Howorth, J., Terriff, T. and Krahmann, E. (2004) 'The governance of European security', *Review of International Studies*, 30:1.

Weiler, J. H. H. (1991) 'The Transformation of Europe', *Yale Law Journal*, 100: 2403–83.

Wendt, A. (1994) 'Collective identity formation and the international state', *American Political Science Review*, 88:2.

WEU Council of Ministers (1999) 'WEU Audit of Assets and Capabilities for European Crisis Management Operations: Recommendations for strengthening European capabilities for crisis management operations', Luxembourg, 22–3 November 1999, available at www.weu.int/documents/991122en.pdf (accessed 16 August 2006).

WEU Council of Ministers (1992) 'Petersberg Declaration', Bonn, 19 June 1992, available at www.weu.int/documents/920619peten.pdf (accessed 16 August 2006).

Wogau, K. von (ed.) (2005) 'The Path to European Defence', available at www.european-defence.co.uk/directory/althea/html (accessed 2 March 2005).

Wolfers, A. (1963) 'Integration in the west: The conflict of perspectives', *International Organisation*, 17:3, 753–70.

Wolfers, A. (ed.) (1959) *Alliance Policy in the Cold War* (Baltimore: Johns Hopkins University Press).

World Bank (2000) *2000 World Development Indicators* (Washington, DC: World Bank).

Young, O. R. (1999) *Governance in World Affairs* (Ithaca: Cornell University Press).

Youngs, R. (2004) 'Democratic institution-building and conflict resolution: Emerging EU approaches', *International Peacekeeping*, 11:3.

Youngs, R. (2003) 'European approaches to democracy assistance: Learning the right lessons?', *Third World Quarterly*, 24:1.

Youngs, R. (2001) 'Democracy promotion: The case of European Union strategy', *Centre for European Policy Studies Working Document*, 167.

Ypersele de Strihou, J. van (1967) 'Sharing the defense burden among Western allies', *Review of Economics and Statistics*, 49:4.

Zanger, S. C. (2000) 'Good governance and European aid: The impact of political conditionality', *European Union Politics*, 1:3.

Zellner, W. (2002) 'The OSCE: Uniquely qualified for a conflict-prevention role', in P. van Tongeren, H. van de Veen and J. Verhoeven (eds), *Searching For Peace in Europe and Eurasia: An Overview Of Conflict Prevention And Peacebuilding Activities* (Boulder, CO: Lynne Rienner).

EU official documents

Article 36 Committee (2002) 'Terrorist activity in the European Union: Situation and trends', 20 February 2002, 5759/1/02 REV 1 ENFOPOL 21, DG H II.

Article 36 Committee (1999) 'Finalisation and evaluation of the Action Plan on Organised Crime: Draft Report to the Helsinki European Council', 9917/3/99 Rev 3, DG H III, 12 November 1999.

Conference of the Representatives of the Governments of the Member States (2004) 'Treaty establishing a Constitution for Europe', CIG 87/2/04 REV 2, 29 October 2004.

Council of the European Union (2006) 'Brussels European Council 15/16 December 2005 Presidency conclusions', 15914/05, 30 January.

Council of the European Union (2006) 'Capabilities Improvement Chart I/2006', available at www.consilium.europa.eu/cms3_fo/showPage.asp?id=437&lang=EN&mode=g (accessed 15 August 2006).

Council of the European Union (2006) 'EU military operation in support of the MONUC during the election process in the RD Congo', 10366/06 (Presse 180), Luxembourg, 12 June.

Council of the European Union (2006) 'Presidency Report on ESDP', 10418/06, 12 June.

Council of the European Union (2005) 'Brussels European Council 16 and 17 June 2005, Presidency Conclusions', 10255/05 CONCL 2, 18 June.

Council of the European Union (2005) 'Council Decision 2005/681/JHA of 20 September 2005 establishing the European Police College (CEPOL) and repealing Decision 2000/820/JHA', *OJ L* 256/63.

Council of the European Union (2005) 'Council Decision 2005/395/CFSP of 10 May 2005 amending Decision 2001/80/CFSP on the establishment of the Military Staff of the European Union', *OJ L* 132/18.

Council of the European Union (2005) 'Council Framework Decision 2005/222/JHA of 24 February 2005 on attacks against information systems', *OJ L* 69/67, 16 March.

Council of the European Union (2005) 'Council Framework Decision 2005/214/JHA of 24 February 2005 on the application of the principle of mutual recognition to financial penalties', *OJ L* 76/16, 22 March.

Council of the European Union (2005) 'Draft Directive of the European Parliament and of the Council on the prevention of the use of the financial system for the purpose of money laundering and terrorist financing', 10245/05, 17 June.

Council of the European Union (2005) 'Directive 2005/60/EC of the European Parliament and of the Council of 26 October 2005 on the prevention of the use of the financial system for the purpose of money laundering and terrorist financing', *OJ L* 309/15, 25 November.

Council of the European Union (2005) 'Fight against terrorism: six monthly report', 1477/05 LIMITE, 21 November.

Council of the European Union (2005) 'Final report on the evaluation of national anti-terrorist arrangements: Improving national machinery and capability in the fight against terrorism', 12168/3/05, 18 November.

Council of the European Union (2005) 'Implementation of the Action Plan to combat terrorism', 14734/1/05 REV 1, 29 November.

Council of the European Union (2005) 'Joint Statement by the Council and the representatives of the governments of the member states meeting within the Council, the European Parliament and the Commission on European Union development policy: "The European consensus"', 14820/05, 22 November.

Council of the European Union (2005) 'Press Release 2660th Council meeting, General Affairs and External Relations', Brussels, 23 and 24 May 2005, Presse 8817/05.

Council of the European Union (2005) 'Press Release 2655th Council meeting, General Affairs and External Relations', Luxembourg, 25 April 2005, Presse 86 8035/05.

Council of the European Union (2005) 'Press Release 2650th Council meeting, General Affairs and External Relations', Brussels, 16 March 2005, Presse 45 6970/05.

Council of the European Union (2005) 'Prüm Convention', 10900/05, LIMITE, 7 July.

Council of the European Union (2005) 'The European Union Counter-terrorism Strategy', 14469/4/05 REV 4 LIMITE, Brussels 30 November 2005.

Council of the European Union (2004) 'Annex. Strengthening of states' capabilities for detection and response to illicit trafficking' in 'Council Joint Action 2004/495/CFSP of 17 May 2004 on support for IAEA activities under its Nuclear Security Programme and in the framework of the implementation of the EU strategy against proliferation of weapons of mass destruction', *OJ L* 182/46.

Council of the European Union (2004) 'Brussels European Council, 4/5 November 2004, Presidency Conclusions', 14292/04, CONCL 3, 5 November.

Council of the European Union (2004) 'CEPOL Annual Work Programme for 2005', 10058/04, 8 June.

Council of the European Union (2004) 'Council Decision 2004/803/CFSP of 25 November 2004 on the launching of the European Union military operation in Bosnia and Herzegovina', *OJ L* 353/21, 27 November.

Council of the European Union (2004) 'Council Decision 2004/197/CFSP of 23 February 2004', *OJ L* 63/68, 28 February.

Council of the European Union (2004) 'Council Joint Action 2004/551/CFSP of 12 July 2004 on the establishment of the European Defence Agency', *OJ L* 245/17, 17 July.

Council of the European Union (2004) 'Draft Framework Decision on simplifying the exchange of information and intelligence between law enforcement authorities of the member states of the European Union, in particular as regards serious offenses including terrorist acts', 13869/04, 11 April.

Council of the European Union (2004) 'EU Solidarity Programme on the consequences of terrorist threats and attacks (revised/widened CBRN Programme): Adoption', 15480/04, 1 December.

Council of the European Union (2004) 'EU strategy against proliferation of weapons of mass destruction: Draft Progress Report on the implementation of Chapter III of the strategy', 10448/04, 10 June.

Council of the European Union (2004) 'Presidency conclusions, Annex I (The Hague Programme: Strengthening freedom, security and justice in the European Union)', 14292/04 CONCL 3, 4–5 November.

Council of the European Union (2004) 'Press Release. 2606th Council Meeting', 12400/04 (Presse 264), 4 October.

Council of the European Union (2004) 'Regulation (EC) no. 851/2004 of the European Parliament and of the Council of 23 April 2004 establishing a European Centre for disease prevention and control', *OJ L* 142/1, 30 April.

Council of the European Union (2004) 'Regulation (EC) no. 460/2004 of the European Parliament and of the Council of 10 March 2004 establishing the European Network and Information Security Agency', *OJ L* 77/1, 13 March.

Council of the European Union (2003) 'Action Plan for the implementation of the basic principles for an EU strategy against proliferation of weapons of mass destruction', 10 June, in A. Missiroli, 'From Copenhagen to Brussels. European Defence: Core documents, vol. IV', *Chaillot Paper*, 67 (Paris: Institute for Security Studies, 2003).

Council of the European Union (2003) 'Council Decision 2003/874/CFSP of 8 December 2003 implementing Joint Action 2003/472/CFSP with a view to contributing to the European Union cooperation programme for non-proliferation and disarmament in the Russian Federation', *OJ L* 326/49, 13 December.

Council of the European Union (2003) 'Council Common Position 2003/805/CFSP of 17 November 2003 on the universalisation and reinforcement of multilateral agreements in the field of nonproliferation of weapons of mass destruction and means of delivery', *OJ L* 302/34, 20 November.

Council of the European Union (2003) 'Council Decision 2003/567/CFSP of 21 July 2003 implementing Common Position 1999/533/CFSP relating to the European Union's contribution to the promotion of the early entry into force of the Comprehensive Nuclear Test-Ban Treaty (CTBT)', *OJ L* 192/53, 31 July.

Council of the European Union (2003) 'Council Decision 2003/563/CFSP of 29 July 2003 on the extension of the European Union military operation in the Former Yugoslav Republic of Macedonia', *OJ L* 190/20, 30 July.

Council of the European Union (2003), ' Council Decision 2003/48/JHA of 19 December 2002 on the implementation of specific measures for police and judicial cooperation to combat terrorism in accordance with Article 4 of Common Position 2001/931/CFSP', *OJ L* 16/68, 22 January.

Council of the European Union (2003) 'Council Framework Decision 2003/577/JHA of 22 July 2003 on the execution of orders freezing property or evidence', *OJ L* 196/45, 2 August.

Council of the European Union (2003) 'Council Joint Action 2003/92/CFSP of 27 January 2003 on the European Union military operation in the Former Yugoslav Republic of Macedonia', *OJ L* 34/26, 11 February.

Council of the European Union (2003) 'European Defence Meeting: Conclusions', Egmont Palace, 29 April 2003, available at www.foreignpolicy. org/tr/eng/eu/egmontpalace_290403.htm (accessed 15 December 2004).

Council of the European Union (2003) 'Europol work programme 2004', 8580/03 LIMITE, 28 April.

Council of the European Union (2003) 'Programme of measures to combat illegal immigration across the maritime borders of the member states of the European Union', 15445/03, LIMITE, 28 November.

Council of the European Union (2003) 'Report on the measures and steps taken with regard to the implementation of the recommendations of the European Union strategy for the beginning of the new millennium on prevention and control of organised crime', 10925/03 LIMITE, 30 June.

Council of the European Union (2002) 'Adoption of the programme to improve cooperation in the European Union for preventing and limiting of chemical, biological, radiological or nuclear terrorist threats', 14627/02, 21 November.

Council of the European Union (2002) 'Council Decision 2002/630/JHA of 22 July 2002 establishing a framework programme on police and judicial cooperation in criminal matters (AGIS)', *OJ L* 203/5, 1 August.

Council of the European Union (2002) 'Council Decision of 13 June 2002 adopting an action programme for administratived cooperation in the fields of external borders, visas, asylum and immigration (ARGO programme)', *OJ L* 161/11, 19 June.

Council of the European Union (2002) 'Council Framework Decision of 13 June 2002 on joint investigation teams' (2002/465/JHA), *OJ L* 162/1, 13 June.

Council of the European Union (2002) 'Council Framework Decision 2002/584/JHA of 13 June 2002 on the European arrest warrant and the surrender procedures between member states', *OJ L* 190, 18 July.

Council of the European Union (2002) 'Council Framework Decision 2002/475/JHA of 13 June 2002 on combating terrorism', *OJ L* 164/3, 22 June.

Council of the European Union (2002) 'Europol Annual Report 2001', 8381/02 LIMITE, 30 April.

Council of the European Union (2001) 'Annex. Protocol established by the Council in accordance with Article 34 of the Treaty on European Union to the Convention on Mutual Assistance in Criminal Matters between the Member States of the European Union (2001/C/01)', *OJ C* 326/2, 21 November.

Council of the European Union (2001) 'Common Position on combating terrorism' (2001/93/CFSP) in M. Rutten (ed.), 'From Nice to Laeken. European Defence: core documents, Vol. II', *Chaillot Paper*, 51 (Paris: Institute for Security Studies, 2002).

Council of the European Union (2001) 'Council Common Position of 27 December 2001 on the application of specific measures to combat terrorism' (2001/931/CFSP), available at http: //europa.eu/eur-lex/pri/en/oj/dat/2001/l_344/l_34420011228en00930096.pdf (accessed 28 August 2005).

Council of the European Union (2001) 'Council Decision of 28 June 2001 establishing a second phase of the programme of incentives and exchanges, training and cooperation for legal practitioners (Grotius II–Criminal)', *OJ L* 186/1, 7 July.

Council of the European Union (2001) 'Council Decision 2001/493/CFSP of 25 June 2001 implementing Joint Action 1999/878/CFSP with a view to contributing to the European Union Cooperation Programme for Non-Proliferation and Disarmament in the Russian Federation', *OJ L* 280/2, 3 July.

Council of the European Union (2001) 'Council Framework Decision 2001/500/JHA of 26 June 2001 on money laundering, the identification, tracing, freezing, seizing and confiscation of instrumentalities and the proceeds from crime', *OJ L* 182/1, 5 July.

Council of the European Union (2001) 'Initiative of the Kingdom of Belgium, the French Republic, the Kingdom of Spain and the United Kingdom with a view to adopting a Council Framework Decision on joint investigation teams', (2001/C 295/06), *OJ C* 259/9, 20 October.

Council of the European Union (2000) 'Adoption of Action Plan for Albania and the region' and 'Implementation of the Action Plans for Afghanistan and the region, Iraq, Morocco, Somalia and Sri Lanka', 8939/00 LIMITE, 30 May.

Council of the European Union (2000) 'Council Decision of 17 October 2000 concerning arrangements for cooperation between financial intelligence units of the Member States in respect of exchanging information', *OJ L*, 27/4, 24 October.

Council of the European Union (2000) 'Explanatory report on the Convention of 29 May 2000 on Mutual Assistance in Criminal Matters between the Member States of the European Union' (2000/C 379/02), *OJ C* 379/7, 29 December.

Council of the European Union (2000) 'High Level Working Group on asylum and migration: Adoption of the report to the European Council in Nice', 13993/00 LIMITE, 29 November.

Council of the European Union (2000) 'Implementation of the action plans for Afghanistan and the region, Iraq, Morocco, Somalia and Sri Lanka', 8939/00 LIMITE, 30 May.

Council of the European Union (1999) 'Council recommendation of 9 December 1999 on cooperation in combating the financing of terrorist groups' (1999/373/01), *OJ C* 373/1, 23 December.

Council of the European Union (1999) 'Joint Action of 3 December 1998 adopted by the Council on the basis of Article K.3 of the Treaty on European Union, on money laundering, the identification, tracing, freezing, seizing and confiscation of instrumentalities and the proceeds of crime' (98/699/JHA), *OJ L* 331/1, 9 December.

Council of the European Union (1999) 'Joint position of 29 March 1999 defined by the Council on the basis of Article K.3 of the Treaty on European Union, on the proposed United Nations convention against organised crime' (1999/235/JHA), *OJ L* 87/1, 31 March.

Council of the European Union (1999) 'Progress report on the proceedings of the High Level Working Group on asylum and migration', 9197/99 LIMITE, 11 June.

Council of the European Union (1999) 'Towards a union of freedom, security and justice: The Tampere milestones', Tampere European Council, 15–16 October.

Council of the European Union (1999) 'Council Joint Action of 17 December 1999 establishing a European Union Cooperation Programme for Non-proliferation and Disarmament in the Russian Federation (1999/878/CFSP)', *OJ L*, 331/11, 23 December.

Council of the European Union (1998) 'Joint Action of 29 June 1998 adopted by the Council on the basis of Article K.3 of the Treaty on European Union, on the creation of a European judicial network', (98/428/JHA)', *OJ L* 191/4, 7 July.

Council of the European Union (1994) 'Council Decision of November 1994 appointing an ombudsman for Mostar for the duration of the European Union administration of Mostar' (94/776/EC), *OJ L* 312/34, 6 December.

ENISA (2005) *ENISA General Report 2005* (Brussels: Enisa).

EU Operations (2006) 'Factsheet, EU police mission in Bosnia and Herzegovina', available at www.consilium.europa.eu/cms3 (accessed 1 March 2006).

'EU–US Declaration on Combating Terrorism', Dromoland Castle, 26 June 2004.

Eurojust (2006) *Annual Report 2005* (The Hague: Eurojust).

Eurojust (2005) *Annual Report 2004* (The Hague: Eurojust).

Eurojust (2004) *Annual Report 2003* (The Hague: Eurojust).

Eurojust (2003) *Annual Report 2002* (The Hague: Eurojust).

Euronews (2006) 'History Is Made as DR Congo Holds Elections', available at www.euronews.net (accessed 31 July 2006).

Europe Aid Cooperation Office (2006) 'European Initiative for Democracy and Human Rights (EIDHR) Programming and Annual Work Programme for 2005 and 2006', available at http: //europa.eu.int/comm/europeaid/projects/eidhr/documents_en.htm#eidhr (accessed 14 August 2006).

European Agency for Reconstruction (2004) 'Annual Report to the European Parliament and the Council, January to December 2003', Thessaloniki, 7 June 2004, available at www.ear.eu.int/publications/main/documents/EARAnnualReport2003.pdf (accessed 12 August 2006).

European Centre for Disease Prevention and Control (2005) 'Programme of work for 2005–2006', Reference MB2/9, 4 February.

European Commission (2006) 'Communication from the Commission to the Council and the European Parliament: Evaluation of EU policies on freedom, security and justice', COM(2006) 332 final, 26 June.

European Commission (2006) 'Communication from the Commission to the Council and the European Parliament. Implementing The Hague Programme: The way forward', COM(2006) 331 final, 28 June.

European Commission (2006) 'Communication from the Commission to the European Parliament and the Council on judicial training in the European Union', COM(2006) 356 final, 29 June.

European Commission (2006) 'Report from the Commission: Second Commission report based on Article 6 of the Council Framework Decision of 26 June 2001 on money laundering, the identification, tracing, freezing, seizing and confiscation of instrumentalities and the proceeds of crime', COM (2006) 72 final, 21 February.

European Commission (2006) 'Commission simplifies external cooperation programmes', Europa–Rapid–Press Releases Reference, Brussels, 25 January, IP/06/82.

European Commission (2005) 'Commission staff working document. Revised Action Plan on terrorism: Update June 2005', SEC(2005) 841, 17 June.

European Commission (2005) 'Commission Staff Working Document: Second annual report to the European Parliament and the Council on the implementation of the AGIS programme, Year 2004', SEC(2005) 1764, 15 December.

European Commission (2005) 'Commission staff working paper *Annex* to: "European neighbourhood policy", country report Armenia', SEC(2005) 285/3, 2 March.

European Commission (2005) 'Commission staff working paper *Annex* to: "European neighbourhood policy", country report Azerbaijan', SEC(2005) 286/3, 2 March.

European Commission (2005) 'Commission staff working paper *Annex* to: "European neighbourhood policy", country report Egypt', SEC(2005) 287/3, 2 March.

European Commission (2005) 'Commission staff working paper *Annex* to: "European neighbourhood policy", country report Georgia', SEC(2005) 288/3, 2 March.

European Commission (2005) 'Commission staff working paper *Annex* to: "European neighbourhood policy", country report Lebanon', SEC(2005) 289/3, 2 March.

European Commission (2005) 'Commission staff working paper. *Annex* to: the Report from the Commission on national measures taken to comply with the Council Framework Decision of 13 June 2002 on joint investigation teams', SEC (2004) 1725, 1 July.

European Commission (2005) 'Communication from the Commission to the Council and the European Parliament: Developing a strategic concept on tackling organized crime', COM(2005) 232 final, 2 June.

European Commission (2005) 'Communication from the Commission to the Council and the European Parliament on improved effectiveness, enhanced interoperability and synergies among European databases in the area of Justice and Home Affairs', COM (2005) 597 final, 24 November.

European Commission (2005) 'Communication from the Commission to the Council and the European Parliament on the mutual recognition of judicial decisions in criminal matters and the strengthening of mutual trust between Member States', COM(2005) 195 final, 19 May.

European Commission (2005) 'Communication from the Commission to the European Parliament, the Council, the European Economic and Social Committee and the Committee of the Regions: Commission provisions on "ARGUS" general rapid alert system', COM(2005) 662 final, 23 December.

European Commission (2005) 'Communication on measures to ensure greater security of explosives, detonators, bomb-making equipment and firearms', COM(2005) 329 final, 18 July.

European Commission (2005) 'Communication on the mutual recognition of judicial decisions in criminal matters and the strengthening of mutual trust between member states', COM(2005) 195 final, 19 May.

European Commission (2005) 'Green Paper on a European programme for critical infrastructure protection', COM(2005) 576 final, 17 November.

European Commission (2005) 'Green paper on conflicts of jurisdiction and the principle of *ne bis in idem* in criminal proceedings', COM(2005) 696 final, 23 December.

European Commission (2005) 'Highlights: Annual report 2005 on the European Community's development policy and the implementation of external assistance in 2004', Luxembourg: Office for Official Publications of the European Communities.

European Commission (2005) 'Proposal for a Council Decision on the establishment, operation and use of the second generation Schengen information system (SIS II)', COM(2005) 230 final, 31 May.

European Commission (2005) 'Proposal for a Council Decision on the improvement of police cooperation between Member States of the European Union, especially at the internal borders and amending the Convention implementing the Schengen Agreement', 2005/0131 (CNS), 18 July.

European Commission (2005) 'Proposal for a Council Decision on the transmission of information resulting from the activities of security and intelligence services with respect to terrorist offences', COM(2005) 695 final,2005/0271 (CNS), 22 December.

European Commission (2005) 'Proposal for a Council Framework Decision on the exchange of information under the principle of availability', COM(2005) 490 final, 12 October.

European Commission (2005) 'Proposal for a Council Framework Decision on the exchange of information under the principle of availability', COM(2005) 490 final, 2005/0207, 30 June.

European Commission (2005) 'Report from the Commission based on Article 34 of the Council Framework Decision of 13 June 2002 on the European arrest warrant and the surrender procedures between Member States', COM(2005) 63 final, 23 February.

European Commission (2004) 'Commission communication on the prevention of and fight against terrorist financing', COM(2004) 700 final, 20 October.

European Commission (2004) 'Commission Staff Working Paper: First annual report to the Council and the European Parliament on the implementation of the ARGO programme (2002–2003)', SEC(2004) 211, 17 February.

European Commission (2004) 'Commission Staff Working Paper: The area of freedom, security and justice: Assessment of the Tampere programme and future orientations – list of the most important instruments adopted', SEC(2004) 680, 2 June.

European Commission (2004) 'Communication from the Commission: European neighbourhood policy – strategy paper', COM(20054) 0373 final, 12 May.

European Commission (2004) 'Communication from the Commission to the Council and the European Parliament. Area of freedom, security and justice: Assessment of the Tampere programme and future orientations', COM (2004) 401 final, 2 June.

European Commission (2004) 'Communication from the Commission to the Council and the European Parliament: Critical infrastructure protection in the fight against terrorism', COM (2002) 702 final, 20 October.

European Commission (2004) 'Conceptual Framework on the ESDP Dimension of the Fight against Terrorism', 22 November 2004, available at http:// ue.eu.int/uedocs/cmsUpload/14797Conceptual_Framework_ESDP.pdf (accessed 26 August 2005).

European Commission (2004) 'Green Paper: Defence procurement', COM(2004) 608 final, 23 September.

European Commission (2004) 'Green Paper on the approximation, mutual recognition and enforcement of criminal sanctions in the European Union', COM (2004)334 final, 30 April.

European Commission (2004) 'Interim Report on the Evaluation of National Anti-Terrorist Arrangements', available at www.ue.eu.int/eudocs/cmsUpload/ Interim_Report.pdf (accessed on 17 July 2005).

European Commission (2004) 'Joint strategy paper on terrorist financing of 14 October 2004', 16089/04, 14 December.

European Commission (2004) 'Proposal for a Council Framework Decision on certain procedural rights in criminal proceedings throughout the European Union', COM(2004) 328 final, 2004/0113 (CNS), 28 April.

European Commission (2004) 'Proposal for a Council Decision on the exchange of information extracted from the criminal record', COM(2004) 664 final, 2004/0238 (CNS), 13 October.

European Commission (2004) 'Proposal for a regulation of the European Parliament and of the Council laying down general provisions establishing a European neighbourhood and partnership instrument', 2004/0219 (COD), 29 September.

European Commission (2004) 'Reference Document for Financial and Technical Assistance to Third Countries in the Area of Migration and Asylum. ANEAS

Programme, 2004–2006', available at http: //eu.europa.eu/comm/europeaid/ projects/eidhr/pdf/themes-migration-annexe2_en.pdf (accessed on 15 July 2006).

European Commission (2004) 'Report from the Commission: The stabilisation and association process for south east Europe: Third annual report', COM(2004) 202/2 final, 30 March.

European Commission (2004) 'Securing Peace and Stability for Africa: The EU-funded African Peace Facility', July 2004, available at http: //ec.europa.eu/ comm/development/body/publications/docs/flyer_peace_en.pdf (accessed 8 August 2006).

European Commission (2004) 'The Fight against Terrorism: Note by the Presidency in Association with the Counter-Terrorism Co-ordinator', available at http: //www.ue.eu.int/eudocs/cmsUpload/15523.04.pdf.

European Commission (2003) 'Commission Decision of 17 July 2003 amending Decision No. 2119/98/EC of the European Parliament and of the Council and Decision 200/96/EC as regards communicable diseases listed in those decisions and amending Decision 2002/253/EC as regards the case definitions for communicable diseases', (2003/534/EC), *OJ L* 184/35.

European Commission (2003) 'Commission Staff Working Paper: Fifth report of the Commission to the European Parliament and the Council on the implementation of the Title VI programmes (GROTIUS II–Criminal, STOP II, OISIN II, HIPPOCRATES and FALCONE programmes)', SEC(2003) 316, 14 March.

European Commission (2003) 'Communication from the Commission to the Council and the European Parliament on cooperation in the European Union on preparedness and response to biological and chemical agent attacks (Health Security)', COM (2003) 320 final, 2 June.

European Commission (2003) 'Communication on wider Europe-neighbourhood: A new framework for relations with our eastern and southern neighbours', COM(2003) 104 final, 11 March.

European Commission (2003) 'Country Strategy Paper 2003–2006. Tacis National Indicative Programme 2004–2006: Georgia', 23 September.

European Commission (2003) 'European defence – industrial and market issues: Towards an EU defence equipment policy', COM(2003) 113 final, 11 March.

European Commission (2003) 'Proposal for a regulation of the European Parliament and of the Council establishing a European Centre [for Disease Prevention and Control]', COM(2003) 441 final/2, 2003/0174 (COD), 16 September.

European Commission (2003) 'Signature of the MNEPR (Multilateral Nuclear Environment Programme in the Russian Federation) 21 May 2003, in Stockholm', IP/03/724, 21 May 2003, available at http: //ec.europa.eu/comm/ external_relations/russia/intro/ip03_724.htm (accessed 28 August 2005).

European Commission (2002) 'Proposal for a comprehensive plan to combat illegal immigration and trafficking of human beings in the European Union', *OJ C* 142/23, 14 June.

European Commission (2002) 'Proposal for a Council Framework Decision on attacks against information systems', (2002/0086) (CNS), COM (2002) 173 final, 19 April.

European Commission (2002) 'Commission Communication to the Council and the EP', EC(2002) 159 final, 13 February.

European Commission (2002) 'One year on: The Commission's Conflict Prevention Policy', available at http://ec.europa.eu/comm/external_relations/cfsp/cpcm/cp/rep.htm (accessed 8 August 2005).

European Commission (2001) 'Communication from the Commission: Network and information security: Proposal for a European policy approach', COM(2001) 298, 6 June.

European Commission (2001) 'Communication from the Commission on conflict prevention', COM(2001) 211 final, 11 April.

European Commission (2001) 'Communication from the Commission to the Council and the EP: Financing of civilian crisis management operations', COM(2001) 647 final, 28 November.

European Commission (2001) 'European Commission Action Paper in Response to the Terrorist Attacks in Madrid', MEMO/04/66, 18 March 2001, available at http: //europa.eu.int/comm/external_relations/news/2004/ip04_66.htm (accessed 28 August 2005).

European Commission (2001) 'Programme of cooperation on preparedness and response to biological and chemical agent attacks', G/FS D(2001), 17 December.

European Commission (2000) 'Communication from the Commission to the Council, the European Parliament, the Economic and Social Committee and the Committee of the Regions: Creating a safer information society by improving the security of information infrastructure and combating computer-related crime (eEurope 2002)', COM(2000) 890 final, 26 January 2001.

European Commission (2000) 'The prevention and control of organised crime: A European Union strategy for the beginning of the new millennium', 2000/C 124/01, *OJ C* 124/1, 3 May.

European Commission (1999) 'The EU & south-eastern Europe: The stabilisation and association process for countries of south-eastern Europe', May 26 1999, available at http: //europa.eu.int/comm/external_relations/see/SAP/index.htm (accessed 1 March 2006).

European Commission (1996) 'The EU and the issue of conflicts in Africa: Peace-building, conflict prevention and beyond', SEC (96) 332 final, 6 March.

European Commission, DG Enlargement (2006) 'CARDS: Financial statistics', available at http: //ec.europa.eu/enlargement/financial_assistance/cards/statistics2002-2004_en.htm (accessed 14 August 2006).

European Commission/EuropeAid Cooperation Office DG (2004) 'Euromed Report: EU Strategic Partnership with the Mediterranean and the Middle East. Final report', Issue no. 78, 23 June 2004, available at http: //ec.europa.eu/comm/external_relations/euromed/publication.htm (accessed 8 August 2006).

European Commission/External Relations DG (2007) 'The European Roadmap towards a Zero Victim Target: The EC Mine Action Strategy & Multi-annual Indicative Programming 2005–2007', available at http://ec.europa.eu/comm/external_relations/mine/intro/strat05_07.htm (accessed 21 May 2007).

European Commission/External Relations DG (2005) 'Conflict Prevention & Civilian Crisis Management: Rapid Reaction Mechanism', December 2005, available at http: //europa.eu.int/comm/external_relations/cpcm/rrm/index.htm (accessed 14 August 2006).

European Commission/External Relations DG (2001) 'CARDS Assistance Programme to the Western Balkans, Regional Strategy Paper, 2002–2006', available at www.reliefweb.int/library/documents/2001/ec_balkans_22oct.pdf (accessed 12 August 2006).

European Convention/Working Group VIII on Defence (2003) 'Final Report (Barnier Report)', Brussels, 16 December 2002, in J.-Y. Haine (2003) *From Laeken to Copenhagen. European Defence: Core Documents, Vol. III, Chaillot Paper* (Paris: Institute for Security Studies).

European Convention/Working Group VIII on Defence (2002) 'Introductory note by the Secretariat on the military capabilities which could be available to the European Union', Brussels, 20 September 2002, *Working Document 1*, WG VIII–WD 1.

European Council (2004) 'Council Regulation (EC) No. 2007/2004 of 26 October 2004 establishing a European Agency for the management of operational cooperation at the external borders of the member states of the European Union', *OJ L* 349/1, 25 November.

European Council (2004) 'Declaration on combating terrorism', 7906/04, 25 March 2004.

European Council (2003) 'A Secure Europe in a Better World: European Security Strategy', Brussels, 12 December 2003, available at http://ue.eu.int/uedocs/cmsUpload/78367.pdf (accessed 8 August 2004).

European Council (2003) 'EU strategy against proliferation of weapons of mass destruction', 12 December 2003, in Antonio Missiroli, 'From Copenhagen to Brussels. European Defence: core documents, vol. IV', *Chaillot Paper*, 67 (Paris: Institute for Strategic Studies, 2003).

European Council (2002) 'Presidency conclusions. Annex V. Draft Declaration of the European Council on the contribution of CFSP, including ESDP, in the fight against terrorism', Seville European Council, 21–22 June 2002 in J.-Y. Haine (ed.), 'From Laeken to Copenhagen. European Defence: Core documents, vol. III', *Chaillot Paper*, 57 (Paris: Institute for Security Studies, 2003).

European Council (2001) 'Declaration by the heads of state or government of the European Union and the President of the Commission: Follow-up to the September 11 attacks and the fight against terrorism', Ghent European Council, 19 October 2001 in M. Rutten (ed.), 'From Nice to Laeken. European Defence: Core documents, vol. II', *Chaillot Paper*, 51 (Paris: Institute for Security Studies, 2002).

European Council (2001) 'Laeken European Council 14 and 15 December 2001 Presidency conclusions', in M. Rutten (ed.), 'From Nice to Laeken. European Defence: Core documents, vol. II', *Chaillot Paper*, 51 (Paris: Institute for Security Studies, 2002).

European Council (2000) 'Presidency conclusions, Santa Maria da Feira European Council 19 and 20 June 2000', in M. Rutten (ed.), 'From St.-Malo to Nice. European defence: Core documents', *Challiot Paper*, 47 (Paris: Institute for Security Studies, 2001).

European Council (2000) 'Presidency conclusion, Lisbon European Council, 23 and 24 March 2000', in M. Rutten (ed.), 'From St.-Malo to Nice. European defence: Core documents', *Challiot Paper*, 47 (Paris: Institute for Security Studies, 2001).

European Council (2000) 'Common Strategy of the European Council of 19 June 2000 on the Mediterranean region', (2000/458/CFSP), *OJ L* 183/5, 22 July.

European Council (1999) 'Counter-terrorism: Report from Europol', 7514/1/99 Europol 19, REV 1, 27 May.

European Council (1999) 'Presidency Conclusion: Berlin European Council, 24 and 25 March 1999', available at www.europa.eu.int/council/off/conclu/mar99_en.htm (accessed on 23 April 2005).

European Council (1999) 'Presidency conclusions: Helsinki European Council 10 and 11 December 1999', in M. Rutten (ed.), 'From St.-Malo to Nice. European defence: Core documents', *Challiot Papers,* 47 (Paris: Institute for Security Studies, 2001).

European Council (1999) 'European Council Declaration on Strengthening the European Common Policy on Security and Defence' (Cologne European Council, 3 and 4 June 1999), *Internationale Politik*, 1:1, 2000.

European Council (1997) 'Action Plan to combat organised crime', *OJ C* 251/15, 15 August.

European Council and Commission (2000) 'The European Community's development policy: Statement by the Council and the Commission on the European Community's development policy', published by the European Commission, 10 November.

European Data Protection Supervisor (2005) 'Comments on the communication of the Commission on interoperability of European databases', 3 October.

European Defence Agency (2006) '22 EU member states to take part in new European defence equipment market', Brussels, 22 May.

European Defence Agency (2006) 'National Defence R&T Data', Brussels, 25 July 2006, available at www.eda.europa.edu/facts/National%20Defence%20R&T%20Data.htm (accessed 26 July 2006).

European Defence Agency (2006) 'Report by the Head of the European Defence Agency to the Council', 15 May.

European Defence Agency (2005) 'The code of conduct on defence procurement of the EU member states participating in the European Defence Agency', Brussels, 21 November.

European Judicial Training Network (2002) 'Charter adopted in Copenhagen by the General Assembly on 6 December 2002', 9 December.

European Parliament and Council (2005) 'Directive 2005/60/EC of the European Parliament and the Council of 26 October 2005 on the prevention of the use of the financial system for the purpose of money laundering and terrorist financing', *OJ L*, 309/15, 25 November.

European Parliament and European Council (1998) 'Decision no. 2119/98/EC of the European Parliament and European Council of 24 September 1998 setting up a network for the epidemiological surveillance and control of communicable diseases in the Community', *OJ L* 268/1, 3 October.

European Police Mission in Bosnia and Herzegovina (2006) 'Fighting Major and Organised Crime in Bosnia and Herzegovina: The State Investigation and Protection Agency', available at www.eupm.org/Clanci.asp?ID=79&lang=eng (accessed 14 August 2006).

European Police Mission in Bosnia and Herzegovina (2006) 'Securing the borders of Bosnia and Herzegovia, the State Border Service (SBS)', available at www.eupm.org/Clanci.asp?ID=65&lang=eng (accessed 14 August 2006).

European Union Factsheet (2005) 'EU Support for Iraq', available at http://europa.eu/press_room/presspacks/us20050222/iraq.pdf (accessed 15 August 2006).

European Union Summaries of Legislation (2002) 'SCADPlus: The Common Foreign and Security Policy: Introduction', 13 February 2002, available at http://europa.eu.int/scadplus/leg/en/lvb/r00001.htm (accessed 8 August 2006).

Europol (2006) *Annual Report 2005* (The Hague: Europol).

Europol (2005) *Annual Report 2004* (The Hague: Europol).

Europol (2004) *Annual Report 2003* (The Hague: Europol).

Europol (2003) *Annual Report 2002* (The Hague: Europol).

Europol (2002) *Annual Report 2001* (The Hague: Europol).

Extraordinary Council Meeting (2001) (Justice, Home Affairs and Civil Protection), 'The fight against terrorism: Conclusions' 12019/01 (Presse 327-G).

'Joint Declaration by the British and French Governments on European Defence, at the Anglo-French Summit on November 25, 1999, in London', *Internationale Politik*, 1:2.

'Joint Declaration on European Defence ("St.-Malo Declaration")', St Malo, 3–4 December 1998.

'Joint Statement by the Council and the Representatives of the Governments of the Member States meeting with the Council, the European Parliament and the Commission on "The European Consensus on Development"', document no. 14820/05.

Justice and Home Affairs Council (2006) 'First Report on the Hague Programme', available at http://ec.europa.eu/justice_home/news/information_dossiers/the_hague_2006/scoreboard (accessed 19 July 2006).

Justice and Home Affairs Council (1998) 'Action Plan of the Council and the Commission on how best to implement the provisions of the Treaty of

Amsterdam on an area of freedom, security and justice', *OJ C*, 19/01, 23 January 1999.

Justice and Home Affairs Ministers (2004) 'Action against organised crime: The Dublin Declaration', Dublin, 22/23 January.

Luxembourg Presidency of the Council of the European Union (2005) 'Working Document Relating to Point 3 of the Agenda: Conceptual Framework on the ESDP Dimension to the Fight against Terrorism', 11 March 2005, available at www.eu2005.lu/en/actualites/documents_travail/2005/03/18defterr/index. html (accessed 15 July 2005).

Office for South East Europe (2006) 'How Much Money Is Being Given', available at www.seerecon.org/gen/howmuch.htm (accessed 14 August 2006).

Office of the High Representative and EU Special Representative (2003) 'Implementation of the Property Laws in Bosnia and Herzegovina Reached 90 per cent', Press Office, 12 November 2003, available at www.ohr.int/ohr-dept/presso/pressr/default.asp?content_id=31164 (accessed 14 August 2006).

Permanent Representatives Council (2004) 'Adoption of Council Conclusions on prevention, preparedness and response to terrorist attacks', 15232/04, 25 November.

Pro-Eurojust (2002) *Pro Eurojust: Report 2001* (Brussels: Pro Eurojust Secretariat).

Political and Security Committee (2004) 'Political and Security Committee Decision BiH/4/2004 of 19 October on the appointment of the head of the EU command element at Naples for the European Union military operation in Bosnia and Herzegovina', *OJ L* 357/38, 2 December.

Secretary General/High Representative (2006) 'Attachment 1: Improving our defence capabilities by increasing levels of research spending, finding opportunities for research collaboration, tackling capability gaps and collaborating as partners on training', S416/05, 14 December.

Stability Pact documents

Special Co-ordinator of the Stability Pact for South Eastern Europe (2004) 'Newsletter, 4 May 2004, Issue 21', available at www.stabilitypact.org/newsletter/nl-21.pdf (accessed 14 August 2006).

Special Co-ordinator of the Stability Pact for South Eastern Europe (1999) 'Stability Pact for South Eastern Europe' (Cologne Document), Cologne, 10 June 1999, available at www.stabilitypact.org/constituent/990610-cologne.asp (accessed 14 August 2006).

Stability Pact for South Eastern Europe (2005) 'Newsletter, 17–18 May 2005, Issue 22', available at www.stabilitypact.org/rt/RTSOFIANewsletter%2022%20-%202%20pages.pdf (accessed 14 August 2006).

Index

EU authorised representative for GPSR:
Easy Access System Europe, Mustamäe tee 50,
10621 Tallinn, Estonia
gpsr.requests@easproject.com